D1526038

HISTORICAL DICTIONARIES OF CITIES OF THE WORLD
Series Editor: Jon Woronoff

1. *Tokyo,* by Roman Cybriwsky. 1997.
2. *Stockholm,* by Dennis E. Gould. 1997.

Historical Dictionary of Stockholm

Dennis E. Gould

*Historical Dictionaries of
Cities of the World, No. 2*

The Scarecrow Press, Inc.
Lanham, Md., & London
1997

NORTH PARK UNIVERSITY
LIBRARY
3225 W. FOSTER AVE.
CHICAGO, IL 60625

SCARECROW PRESS, INC.

Published in the United States of America
by Scarecrow Press, Inc.
4720 Boston Way
Lanham, Maryland 20706

4 Pleydell Gardens, Folkestone
Kent CT20 2DN, England

Copyright © 1997 by Dennis E. Gould

All rights reserved. No part of this publication may be
reproduced, stored in a retrieval system, or transmitted
in any form or by any means, electronic, mechanical,
photocopying, recording, or otherwise, without the prior
permission of the publisher.

British Library Cataloging in Publication Information Available

Library of Congress Cataloging-in-Publication Data

Gould, D. E.
      Historical dictionary of Stockholm / Dennis E. Gould.
          p.   cm. — (Historical dictionaries of cities of the world ;
      no. 2)
      Includes bibliographical references.
      ISBN 0-8108-3238-0 (alk. paper)
      1. Stockholm (Sweden)—History—Dictionaries.   I. Title.
      II. Series.
      DL976.3.G68   1997
      948.7'3'003—dc20   96-38621
                                                                    CIP

ISBN 0-8108-3238-0 (cloth : alk. paper)

♾ ™ The paper used in this publication meets the minimum requirements of
American National Standard for Information Sciences—Permanence of
Paper for Printed Library Materials, ANSI Z39.48–1984.
Manufactured in the United States of America.

Ref.
DL
976.3
.G68
1997

Contents

Editor's Foreword

Perhaps it was more than chance that Stockholm, the gateway to Sweden, is also the port of entry to a new series of historical dictionaries of cities. Stockholm is not only the biggest but the most important city in its country in many ways. It is the site of government, the administrative, educational, cultural, and commercial center, as well as a dynamic industrial pole. Ever since Sweden was founded in the mid-13th century, events in the capital have been decisive for the country. Today, as the city expands, its role is greater than ever. Thus, it would be hard to know and understand Sweden without also becoming acquainted with Stockholm.

This relative importance and clout, however, are only part of the reason the city was among the first chosen for the new series. Another, which anyone who has visited Stockholm will gladly concede, is that it wears its years well. Many historic structures are still standing, some more resplendent than ever. Yet they merge happily enough with the modern architecture that surrounds them. Stockholm has thus remained a beautiful place, situated on the water, with impressive palaces and public buildings, lovely parks and gardens, and delightful restaurants and recreation areas that attract not only Swedes but countless foreigners. Its charm, although harder to express, can also be sensed in this historical dictionary.

Like the historical dictionaries of most of the world's countries, those of cities also focus on influential figures, including, in this case, not only mayors but kings and prime ministers. There also are entries on men and women who have contributed significantly to the social, cultural, or commercial success of Stockholm and, in some cases, the world. Many of the notable landmarks are introduced, as well as noteworthy neighborhoods and districts, to say nothing of the guts of the city—its administration, transport and communications links, amenities, and infrastructure. While the present and recent past predominate, the author has looked back on earlier centuries as well. This course is followed by an extensive chronology. Those wishing to learn more should turn to the comprehensive bibliography.

This book was written by a foreigner, but one whose attachment could hardly be stronger. Dennis Gould first visited Sweden half a century ago and has been visiting it regularly ever since, occasionally for long periods in residence. Part of his family lives there, and it is obvious that part of his heart is there as well. Much of his time has been spent in Stockholm, which Gould knows extremely well. Yet, as a foreigner, he sees it with the eyes of an outsider and describes it clearly to other foreigners. This he already has done in several travel books, more recently a book on Swedish tennis, and now this *Historical Dictionary of Stockholm.*

Jon Woronoff
Series Editor

Acknowledgments

My first thanks go to Dr. Karin Petherick and to Irene Scobbie for suggesting that I could undertake this book. It was Karin, as head of the Department of Scandinavian Languages at University College, London, who endeavored to polish my autodidactic Swedish and guide me along the necessary academic paths toward an external degree. Through Karin, I met Irene, who was in charge of the Scandinavian departments at Aberdeen and then Edinburgh. I thank them for their confidence in me and for their support.

I am much indebted to Eva Dahlin at the Stockholm Information Office for her courtesy and practical help, and perhaps even more for putting me into contact with sources of further help. In particular, she directed me to Dr. Åke Abrahamson at the City Museum of Stockholm. I am most appreciative of Åke's kind suggestions and practical help and for reading through a draft manuscript. Inga-Lisa Dahlin at the City Archives was very helpful with my attempts to search for entries appropriate for the bibliography. At the Swedish Institute, Lena Daun introduced me to the invaluable sources of *St. Eriks årsbok* and *Suecana Extranea*. Also at Sweden House, Harriet Lindh was most helpful with the provision of photographs.

At the City Hall, Sara Blücher, international secretary for the city of Stockholm, offered time to assist me. In the City Hall Library, Susann Rönnholm helped by providing materials. Per Gullström, the director of Stockholm's Research and Statistics Office, took the time to keep me up to date on all kinds of information. At Stockholms Stadsbyggnadskontor, Siegfried Nettlich went to considerable lengths to help me with suitable maps. Henrik Arnstad, at Vasa Museum, put himself out to obtain the photographs I had hoped for. AB Stockholm Globe Arena did the same. Stockholm University, Wenner-Gren Center, and Riksbanken supplied helpful information about their institutions and I am grateful to them.

My thanks go also to author Per Wästberg. Göran Sidenblad and Carl Magnus Rosell assisted me in tracking the main events in Stockholm in the late 1970s and 1980s, during which time I was away in Africa.

I should like to thank Ingrid Hedenskog and Lena Löfstrand at the

City and County Library in Uppsala for their assistance. I was particularly fortunate to have the help of Ann Marie Blom; she has been a family friend for many years, and recently retired from the Library of the Agricultural Department of Uppsala University at Ultuna. She helped me gain access to the Libra data program, and also was a great help with the research and typing.

An American journalist and publishing friend who lives in Stockholm offered to run her experienced eye over a draft manuscript. I am grateful for her guidance.

In the later stages, Birgitta Jonsson at Stockholm Information Service was very helpful and my thanks are due to her as well.

There is always the fear, when expressing appreciation, that very helpful people may have been inadvertently omitted. I hope not, and offer my apologies if they have. The sources in Stockholm to whom I turned for assistance have been exceptionally obliging and helpful, almost without exception.

Finally, I turn to the family. Bengt Hellman, my brother-in-law in Sweden, has taken a keen interest in the project and has kept me supplied with newspaper and magazine cuttings. His son, Svante, also provided useful reference material. Two of my daughters live in Sweden, and I thank them as well for their similar assistance. My daughter-in-law, Eriko Kamikubo Gould, has given invaluable help with computing advice and has been very patient with an elderly, near computer-illiterate. And last, but by no means least, I would like to thank my wife, Inga-Lisa. I refer to her as being my living dictionary. I thank her not only for reading through material and providing criticism and corrections, but also for her patience, tolerance, and support. Only other authors and authors' spouses know just what that means.

Note on Alphabetization

There are three extra characters at the end of the Swedish alphabet. They are å, ä, and ö. In this book they are treated as unmodified and are placed alphabetically as a, a, and o.

As a general rule, Swedish proper names have been used (e.g. Karl IX for Charles IX). But there are instances in which the author felt that an English translation was more appropriate. In some cases, the name is given together with a translation (e.g. *Gamla stan* [Old Town]).

In a few cases, when the English version of a name is better known, that is used (e.g. Gothenburg for Göteborg).

Abbreviations and Acronyms

AB	Aktiebolag (Limited Company)
AIK	Allmänna Idrottsklubben
AWG	Axel Wenner-Gren Center for Scientific Research
DN	Dagens Nyheter (Daily News)
EC	European Community
ECAD	European Cities Against Drugs
ECU	European Currency Unit
EDP	Electronic Data Processing
EU	European Union
FMN	Fight Against Drugs
(fp)	People's Liberal Party
FUNKIS	Functionalism
IT	Information Technology
KB	Kungliga biblioteket (Royal Library)
(kds)	Christian Democratic Party
KF	Kooperativa förbundet (Cooperative Society)
KLTK	Kungliga Lawn Tennis Klubb (Royal Lawn Tennis Club)
KVA	Kungliga vetenskapsakademien (Royal Academy of Science)
LO	Landsorganisationen (Swedish Confederation of Trade Unions
(m)	Moderate Party (Conservative)
Mkr	million kronor (crowns)
(mp)	Environmental (Green) Party
NK	Nordiska kompaniet (Nordic Company)
(s)	Social Democratic Party
SALK	Stockholms Allmänna Lawn-tennis Klubb (Stockholm's Public Tennis Club)
SAS	Scandinavian Airlines System
SEK	Swedish crowns
SF	Svensk film AB (Swedish Film Company)
SJ	Statens järnvägar (Swedish Railways)
SL	Stockholms lokaltrafik AB (Stockholm's Local Traffic Co.)
Söder	Södermalm

SR   Sveriges Radio AB (Swedish Radio Company)
T   T-bana, Tunnelbana, or Subway
TV1, TV2   Television Channel 1, Television Channel 2
UD   Utrikes departement (Foreign Office)
USK   Utrednings-och statistik-kontoret (Stockholm Office of
            Research and Statistics).
(v)   Left Party (Communist)
WGC   Wenner-Gren Center

Chronology

1252   Birger Jarl was the ruler and founder of Stockholm.

1264   *Storkyrkan* (The Cathedral) was erected. It was initially called Bykyrkan and later St. Nikolai.

1275   Magnus Ladulås became king.

1281   The earliest remaining document bearing the seal of Stockholm is dated 12 August 1281.

1289   The Dominican monks (Black Friars) were mentioned for the first time in connection with the purchase of property near *Söderbro* (South Bridge).

1290   Magnus Ladulås died. He was buried in Riddarholm Church.

        Birger Magnusson became king.

        On July 22 the young King Birger confirmed Lübeck's charter in Sweden. His advisory council was established in Stockholm.

1290   The greater part of Stockholm was destroyed by fire.

1323   The earliest reference to the city council being divided into Swedish and German halves appears in a document dated July 29.

1352   Stockholm's charter was mentioned for the first time, in June.

1388   King Albrekt of Mecklenburg, Germany confirmed Stockholm's charter.

1395   The City of Stockholm was handed over to a number of Hanseatic cities for a period of three years.

1398   Queen Margareta took over Stockholm from the Hanseatic League.

1420   Stockholm's oldest surviving land register was started.

1434   The Swedish National Council issued the Stockholm Charter, which was called "Stockholm's Magna Carta".

1436   Engelbrekt and the Swedes marched into Stockholm and laid seige to the castle.

1446   A large fire raged in Stockholm and destroyed St. Klara Convent.

1448   In June, Karl Knutsson was chosen in Stockholm to be king of Sweden.

1449   The first known royal instruction to the master of the mint was given by the king at the castle.

1458   A large part of Stockholm was destroyed by fire on August 21.

1464   In August, Karl Knutsson returned from exile in Danzig.

        In September, the national council, Stockholm's magistrates, the nobility and commoners, requested that Knutsson return to power, which he did in 1467.

1470   Karl Knutsson died on May 15 and was buried in Riddarholm Church.

1471   On October 10, victory over the Danes at Brunkeberg under the leadership of the regent, Sten Sture the elder.

1471   The Swedish National Council abolished from law the clause referring to the two nationalities, Swedish and German.

1497   On September 29, there was a battle with the Danes at Brunkeberg.

1501   On November 12, Sten Sture was proclaimed regent for the second time.

1512   On July 23, Sten Sture the younger was chosen regent in Stockholm with the support of the city's burghers.

1518   In July, there was fighting between the troops of Kristian II of Denmark and the Swedes under Sten Sture the younger. Tradition has it that Gustav Eriksson Vasa was the bearer of the main Swedish banner.

1520   On November 4, Kristian II was crowned King of Sweden in *Storkyrkan* (The Cathedral).

1520   The Stockholm "bloodbath" (q.v.) took place on November 8 and 9.

1523   On July 23, Gustav Vasa entered ceremoniously into Stockholm.

1524   Olaus Petri became the city secretary.

1525   Mass in Swedish was held in *Storkyrkan* (The Cathedral) for the first time by Olaus Petri. It had previously been in Latin.

1539   A plague hit the city during the summer.

1548   Plague ravaged the city from spring until the following year.

1552   Olaus Petri died on April 19 and was buried in *Storkyrkan* (The Cathedral).

1560   Gustav Vasa died in Stockholm.

1566   On July 4, Erik XIV and Karin Månsdotter were married with great pomp in *Storkyrkan* (The Great Church). The seventeen-year-old queen was crowned the following day.

1570   In the time of King Johan III, it is estimated that there were about 7,000 inhabitants of Stockholm.

1593   King Sigismund landed in Stockholm on September 30 to take control of the country upon the death of his father.

1614   Svea Lower Court of Appeal was established in May.

1622   The earliest surviving map of Stockholm is dated this year.

1625   On September 1, a great fire reduced a fifth of the city to ashes.

1634   Gustav II Adolf was buried in Riddarholm Church on June 22.

1650   On October 20, Queen Kristina was crowned in solemn fashion, followed by processions, tilting, animal baiting, and a banquet.

1654   Recently crowned in Uppsala Cathedral, Karl X Gustav arrived in Stockholm on Midsummer night, to be greeted by a cannon salute from Brunkeberg.

1657   *Riddarhuset* (The House of Nobility) was completed and the nobility began to use it for their meetings.

1680   On November 25, the Danish princess, Ulrika Eleonora, was crowned queen in *Storkyrkan* (The Cathedral).

1697   On December 14, Karl XII was crowned in *Storkyrkan* (The Cathedral).

1699   After the destruction by fire in 1697 of the royal stage at *Lejonkulan* (The Lion's Den), *Stora Bollhuset* (The Great Ball House) was renovated for use as a theater.

1699   The city boundaries to last until the end of the next century were established.

1700   After the outbreak of the war with Saxony-Poland, Karl XII left his capital on April 16, never to see it again.

1710   The plague ravaged Stockholm for the last time, and claimed nearly 20,000 lives.

1719   Karl XII was interred in Riddarholm Church on February 26.

1720   Fredrik I was crowned on May 3.

1721   The restaurant *Den Gyldene Freden* (The Golden Peace) was opened at its present-day site of 51 Österlånggatan, in *Gamla stan* (The Old Town).

1739   The first insurance company was established; it was mainly concerned with marine insurance.

1740   In February, Carl Michael Bellman was born.

1746   The oldest existing insurance company, Brandkontoret, now *Stockholm stads brandförsäkringkontor* (Stockholm City's Fire Insurance Office) was founded.

1751   Adolf Fredrik and Lovisa Ulrika were crowned in Stockholm on November 26.

1753   On September 20, the Stockholm Observatory, designed by C. Hårleman, was inaugurated.

1772   Gustav III was crowned in *Storkyrkan* (The Cathedral) on May 29.

1773   The Opera was opened in *Stora Bollhuset* (The Great Ball House) on January 18.

1778   The stock exchange building, designed by architect E. Palmstedt, was completed in its present form. It now houses the Swedish Academy and its Nobel Library.

1782   Gustav III's Opera House, designed by C.F. Adelkrantz, was inaugurated on September 30.

1792   On March 16, Gustav III was mortally wounded by a pistol shot during a masked ball at the Opera. He died on March 29.

1795   C.M. Bellman died in a house at Kungsholmsbrogatan in Klara District on February 11.

1795   The park, Kungsträdgården, was opened to the public on May 1.

1809   On March 13, Gustav IV Adolf was dethroned after having been imprisoned in the palace in Stockholm.

1809   On June 29, Karl XIII was crowned.

1810   On December 13, a royal decree was issued that an institute shall be founded to be responsible for the training of men who would be responsible for medical treatment. This institute was soon given the name of Karolinska Medical-Surgical Institute.

1818   On May 11, Karl XIV Johan was crowned in *Storkyrkan* (The Cathedral).

1818   Sweden's first steamship was built in Stockholm and commenced traffic on Lake Mälaren.

1831   Stage coach mail service between Stockholm and Ystad, was introduced.

1844   On September 28, Oscar I was crowned.

1849   August Strindberg was born on January 22 in Stockholm. His parents worked at the old Palace Bakery.

1850   The extensive reconstruction of *Slussen* (The Sluice Gates), under the direction of Nils Ericsson, was completed.

1859   The first street-cleaning department was started.

1860   On May 3, Karl XV and Queen Lovisa were crowned.

1860   The Southern Railyard, the city's first, was opened.

1861   All of Stockholm's elementary schools combined to form an entity.

1863   The newly established City Council met for the first time on April 20.

1866   The National Museum was inaugurated.

1868   Blasieholm Church was consecrated.

1871   Central Railway Station officially opened.

1879   A skiing competion was held in Stockholm for the first time.

1880   The explorer A.E. Nordenskiöld returned to Stockholm, aboard the steamship Vega, having navigated the North East Passage.

1884   The first *Katarinahissen* (Katarina Elevator) was erected.

1891   Opening of Skansen, the outdoor historical museum.

1898   Official opening of the new opera house.

1900   The first Nobel Prize awards ceremony was held.

1905   On January 14, parliament moved into its new building.

1906   *Utrikesdepartement* (The Foreign Office) moved into Arvfursten's Palace.

1907   On June 6, The Nordic Museum was inaugurated.

1911   *Kungsgatan* (King's Street) was reopened to traffic after having been closed since 1905 for extension through Brunkeberg Ridge. Completion occurred in the 1930s.

1912   August Strindberg was celebrated with a torchlight procession on January 22. On May 14, he died in his residence at "*Blå tornet*" (The Blue Tower) at 85 Drottninggatan. Stockholmers lined the route of his funeral procession.

1912   *Stadion* (The Stadium) was inaugurated on June 1. The Olympic Games were held there and opened on June 6.

1914   On February 26, a new system for the sale of alcohol was introduced and passbooks were issued.

1917   On May 5, increased prices inspired severe riots.

1919   Stockholm's free port was inaugurated.

1923   *Stadshuset* (The City Hall) was inaugurated.

1923   Bus service in the inner city began.

1924   On January 21, an automatic telephone system began operation.

1925   Radio broadcasting from Stockholm, by *AB Radiotjänst* (Radio Service Company), commenced on January 1.

1925   The funeral procession of Hjalmar Branting was seen by more than 100,000 people.

1926   An ecumenical conference, initiated by Archbishop Nathan Söderblom, began with a service in *Storkyrkan* (The Cathedral) on August 19.

1926   On November 4, Crown Prince Leopold of Belgium married Swedish Princess Astrid in Stockholm.

1928   By agreement between the state and the city, Ladugårdsgärdet (q.v.) was allowed to be built on.

1930 The Stockholm Exhibition was held.

1931 In March, the Social Democratic Party gained a majority in the City Council.

1934 *Västerbron* (West Bridge) officially opened.

1935 A new *Katarinahissen* (Katarina Elevator) went into operation.

1936 Airport at Bromma officially opened.

1936 Unveiling of the sculpture "Orpheus" by Carl Milles, was held in front of *Konserthuset* (The Concert House).

1945 Work commenced on *Tunnelbanan* (subway)

1953 Stockholm celebrated its 700th anniversary. Kungsträdgården was used as the center of the festivities.

1957 Joining of western and southern subway systems.

1959 Official opening of the first part of Hötorgcity. "Skyscrapers" were a new feature of the Stockholm skyline.

1960 The center of Farsta officially opened. This was a new development in town planning.

1961 A decision was made to clear *Gamla stan* (The Old Town) while preserving valuable, historical buildings.

1962 The government announced its decision for the military to abandon Järvafältet so that it could be developed for housing.

1963 The unusually heavy snowfall during January and February created difficulties for Stockholm. In January, 900 men and 520 machines were employed to clear the snow.

In February, 1,700 men and 810 machines were needed. More than 200 vehicles had been stranded in the snow and had to be towed away. By the middle of February, the costs, since November 15, totaled 14 million SEK (Swedish crowns).

In May, the 100th anniversary of the City Council and 40th anniversary of the City Hall was celebrated in the Blue Hall in the presence of King Gustaf VI Adolf, Prime Minister Tage Erlander, Princess Sibylla, and Prince Bertil.

During the summer, Hässelby Palace (q.v.), which has been restored for use as a Nordic cultural center, was officially opened in the presence of King Gustaf VI Adolf, Prime Minister Tage Erlander, and representatives of the Nordic states.

1964 On February 12, the first proposals were made to turn plots on North and South Djurgården into park areas with no construction.

On February 13, a general plan for the extension of Järvafältet, for construction purposes, was approved.

On April 1, Skandinaviska Bank celebrated its 100th anniversary.

On April 9, Arlanda Airport put into use Europe's most modern control tower, 40 meters high.

On September 3, work began on the new 8 kilometer stretch of Huvudstaleden waterway.

1965 On March 7, Queen Louise died. She was the second wife of King Gustaf VI Adolf and sister of Lord Louis Mountbatten. She was buried in *Storkyrkan* (The Cathedral).

On May 17, King Gustaf VI Adolf opened a new museum at Waldemarsudde.

On December 19, Hagalund Church was reconsecrated after extensive restorations. Constructed in 1906, it is Stockholm's most typical Jugend-style church.

1966   On January 5, King Gustaf VI Adolf relinquished future rights to Haga Palace. In the future, it is to be used for entertaining prominent guests on state visits.

In mid-February, Stockholm Harbor was closed because of severe ice conditions.

On February 27, the last edition of *Stockholm Tidningen* was printed. The newspaper had started in 1889.

On April 3, the last stage of Vällingby Center was officially opened.

1967   On May 12, Kaknäs Tower was officially opened. At 154.7 meters, it is the highest building in the Nordic countries.

Between 10 p.m. on September 2 and 3 p.m. on September 3, all drivers began using the right-hand lanes. The transition went surprisingly well.

1968   A scribble board for public use was opened at Sergelstorg.

On May 6, the traditional donning of white student caps took place for what was intended to be the last time. However, the 100-year-old custom has been revived.

On May 24, Stockholm students occupied university premises in protest against the new reforms.

On July 12, the water fountain in Sergelstorg was officially opened.

On September 8, Skärholmen's Center was officially opened by Prince Bertil. At the time, it was Scandinavia's largest suburban center.

On December 14, a new fleet of express buses started operating from Sergelstorg to Bromma Airport.

1969   An exhibition of erotic art opened at the Liljevalch Art Gallery.

On May 3, a steamboat service between Stockholm and Drottningholm was restarted.

On June 1, rail commuter traffic between Södertälje and Märsta commenced.

On November 1, Scandinavian Airlines System (SAS) moved from Bromma to Arlanda Airport.

1970   On January 1, a new law was introduced whereby all dogs must be on a leash, except in specified areas.

At the end of February, the U.S. Embassy's Cultural Department and library moved to the U.S. Information Service on Sveavägen.

On June 9, the new U.S. Ambassador, Jerome K. Holland, arrived in Stockholm. He was later recalled to the United States when diplomatic relations were severed.

On June 1, a new minimum wage for all the city's inhabitants was guaranteed.

On August 25, a debate over elm trees in Kungsträdgården began, due to a proposed site for a new subway station.

On December 16, the last meeting of Sweden's bicameral parliament at the old Parliament House premises on Helgeandsholmen was held.

1971   On January 1, Stockholm and all other Swedish towns became a *kommun* (municipality), in compliance with a new reform.

On January 10, Margit Sahlin began her work as the new vicar at Engelbrekt Church. She was the first female vicar.

On January 11, use of the temporary new parliament building at Sergelstorg began.

On February 23, the government confirmed plans to decentralize state departments to other towns.

On April 7, Yugoslavia's Ambassador Vladimir Rolovic was shot during an attack on the embassy in Strandvägen. He later died from his wounds.

In May, the protest over the elm trees in Kungsträdgården flared up again. Trees were occupied, and some protesters slept in them in hammocks.

On October 1, the so-called 50 card was introduced. This allowed an unlimited number of journeys on Stockholm's public transport for 50 Swedish crowns (SEK) a month.

1972 On January 1, Stockholm municipality took over responsibility for all trash collection and disposal in the capital.

On February 12, the first marriage ceremony took place in Stadshuset.

In February, discussions began about the possibility of jet flights from Bromma Airport.

From June 5 through 16, a UN conference on the human environment was held at the old and new parliament buildings and at Folketshus. Twelve hundred delegates from 113 countries participated.

On December 12, Princess Sibylla, mother of the present king, was buried in the Royal Palace Chapel.

On the same day, Crown Prince Carl Gustaf distributed the Nobel prizes at St. Erik's Fair in Älvsjö.

The average December temperatures were the mildest on record since the 1700s.

1973 On April 1, limits were placed on heavy traffic in the city center. No vehicle longer than 12 meters was permitted.

On April 9, 1,700 students, teachers, and principals demonstrated for the preservation of private schools and against the withdrawal of all municipal support from private schools in Stockholm except *Franskaskolan* (The French School) from 1974–75.

On June 6, the Swedish National Day (*Svenska flaggans dag*) was celebrated at Skansen for the first time.

On September 15, Gustaf VI Adolf died at Helsingborg Hospital.

On September 16, Carl XVI Gustaf arrived at Bromma by plane from Helsingborg.

On September 18, King Gustaf VI Adolf's coffin arrived in Stockholm.

On September 19, Carl XVI Gustaf, at a special meeting of the counsel, took his oath as king and announced his title and motto.

On September 25, the burial service for Gustaf VI Adolf was held at *Storkyrkan* (The Cathedral) and the burial took place at Haga Park.

On October 7, the 600th anniversary of Birgitta's death was celebrated at City Hall in the Blue Hall, attended by Carl XVI Adolf and Princess Christina.

On December 1, a glass sculpture by Edvin Öhrström was displayed at Serge-lstorg.

On December 15, Tage Erlander resigned as prime minister after 44 years in parliament.

1974 On January 11, the official opening of parliament was held at the Royal Palace for the last time. Thus, Carl XVI Gustaf held his first and last Opening of Parliament speech.

On February 27, a man died of the rare disease rabies.

On March 8, 16 masked Iranians occupied the Iranian embassy.

On April 3, the first computerized letter-sorter was introduced by the post office, at 60,000 to 75,000 letters per hour.

On September 12, the police raided manufacturers and sellers of apparatus for home stills. More than 100 stills were confiscated.

In September, Stockholm's first mosque was opened, in Bromma.

On December 10, the distribution of Nobel prizes returned to the Concert Hall. The literature prize went to Alexander Solzhenitsyn.

On December 10, the last counsel was held at the Royal Palace. In the future it would be replaced by government meetings, with the king present. They would be held in the *Kanslihuset* (the Chancery Building).

1975 On April 4, it was announced that the waters of Strömmen were now clean enough for prime fish.

On April 17, a plan to build 300 kilometers of separate public cycle tracks was introduced.

On June 24, the German embassy suffered a violent explosion and was occupied by Baader-Meinhoff terrorists. Surviving terrorists were captured and deported.

On August 7, a temperature of 36 degrees Celsius was recorded, the warmest shade temperature in Stockholm since 1811.

1976 On February 16, the troubadour Evert Taube died at age 85.

At the end of May, St. Georgios Church came into use for the Greek Ortho-dox community. The original building was erected in 1891, but was closed in the 1930s.

On June 3, 10,000 two-year-old salmon were released into Strömmen.

On June 19, the king was married to Silvia Renate Sommarlath in *Storkyrkan* (The Cathedral).

On September 19, the conservative, non-socialist parties gained a majority in the city council.

1977 During June, the Strömma Canal Company resumed service on the route Stockholm-Sigtuna-Uppsala after 33 years.

Around mid-summer, the middle copper tent in Haga Park was rebuilt and used to sell refreshments.

On July 14, Queen Silvia gave birth to a daughter, the heir apparent.

On September 27, Princess Victoria was christened in the palace chapel by Archbishop Sundby.

On October 31, Kungsträdgårdens subway station was opened, with its many artistic decorations.

1978   On March 8, parliament decided by a 196–121 vote to return to the Parliament Building on Helgeandsholmen after it has been rebuilt for an estimated 500 million SEK.

On April 19, King Carl XVI Gustaf officially opened Skansen's Aquarium.

On September 21, the first issue of the newspaper City appeared. Its aim was to describe contemporary life in Stockholm. The paper closed down after its seventh edition, on December 14th.

1979   From May 12 through September 15, traffic was banned from South Djurgården on Saturdays and Sundays. This proved to be a successful experiment and has been repeated in subsequent summers.

On December 9, Storkyrkan (The Cathedral) celebrated its 700th anniversary with a service attended by the king and queen.

1980   At the beginning of the year, the waiting list for housing was abolished. It had grown to 130,000 people and become administratively impossible. In the future, homes would be allocated according to need.

On May 10, several cyclist organizations arranged the largest gathering ever, with 5,000 participating. The number of cyclists in Stockholm was estimated to have trebled in the previous year.

During the fall, the Swedish Academy Nobel Library opened in the basement of Börshuset (The Stock Exchamge).

1981   On September 27, the first trial since World War II of the city's defenses against a possible coup d'état took place, with about 1,500 people and a number of tanks participating.

In the beginning of December, one of the capital's oldest traditions was broken, when the royal family left the Royal Palace to take up residence in Drottningholm Palace.

1982   In January, commuter rail traffic was severely hindered by the extreme cold. On January 7, 146 of a total of 196 coaches were not usable.

On March 2, a proposal was ratified to sell Stockholm's old observatory for conversion to a mosque.

During the summer, a campaign began to clean up grafitti on the city's sculptures and to treat them with wax and silicon.

In August, 58 city council employees were charged with organized theft from parking meters.

On September 23, the Swedish state became the first Nordic country to be condemned by the European High Court for crimes against human rights. It involved the Stockholm municipality and the expropriation of properties in connection with the rebuilding of the city.

1983   On May 9, Brunkeberg Tunnel was reopened. It had been closed since 1976 because of feared risk of collapse in connection with construction work overhead. This fear was judged to be ill-founded.

On October 2, internal flights were moved from Bromma Airport, where they had commenced in 1936, to Arlanda. Private planes and flying instruction remain at Bromma.

On October 4, parliament returned to the rebuilt Riksdagshus (Parliament Building) on Helgeandsholmen.

In October, a traffic count showed that 479,000 vehicles passed in and out of the city each day.

1984   During the year, Televerket introduced a number of new replicas of "pagoda" type telephone kiosks, from the turn of the century. They are more expensive but harder to vandalize.

On Ascension Day, traffic was banned from *Kungsgatan* where a 368-meter-long smörgåsbord was arranged to celebrate the 90th anniversary of the Stockholm Hotel and Restaurant Association.

During the summer, repairs commenced on the roof of City Hall. The old materials were replaced with copper tiles and the crowns were regilded with gold leaf.

On August 23 and 24, Stockholm held Sweden's first equestrian tattoo.

On October 7, the newly constructed highway, *Söderleden,* and Johanneshov Bridge were opened to the public and attracted an estimated 250,000 visitors. They opened for traffic two days later.

1985   From January 1, 17th-century street names were reintroduced to those parts of Norrmalm that had been demolished in the reconstruction of the city.

On January 21, it was decided that Stockholm should revert to the title of *stad* (town), after 14 years as a *kommun* (municipality). However, it still officially remains a *kommun.*

In the beginning of June, a group of islands in the archipelago known as *Fjäderholmarna* was opened as an excursion destination for the public. They were visited by 40,000 people during the first season.

On August 19, a subway line to Rinkeby was opened. It is expected to be the last of the century.

At the end of the year, the bankrupt restaurant *Den gyldene freden* (The Golden Peace) was closed for rebuilding due to the demands of the environmental health authorities.

1986   On February 28, Prime Minister Olof Palme was assassinated at the corner of Sveavägen and Tunnelgatan, while leaving a theater with his wife. The murderer has not been apprehended.

On May 25, Stockholm Middle Ages Museum was opened on Helgeandsholmen, at a site originally intended as a parking space for parliament. During an archeological dig, a 1530s city wall was discovered.

On June 1, a repeat of last year's record-long smörgåsbord was held in Kungsgatan, but at 729 meters was much longer.

On August 28, Lidingö Bridge, dating from 1906, was re-opened after three years of closure for repairs.

In the begining of October, the government upheld the county administration's objection to the city's regulation to ban street music in the Old Town. It is now limited to the hours of 2 p.m. to 6 p.m.

On December 5, three new heating pumps were opened. They use lake water and air as a source of energy, and thus save a vast amount of oil. Two are in Ropsten and one is in Hammarby.

1987   On January 2, the exit from the Kungsträdgården subway to Arsenalgatan was opened. It is Stockholm's most lavish subway station and has drawn international attention.

1988 On February 28, a gay center for homosexuals, was opened at Sveavägen 59. It is thought to be the first of its kind in Europe.

On March 7, the authorities decided to ban all automobile traffic in central Stockholm for one day of the year. However, when it was discovered that this would be illegal, a compromise was reached. On a voluntary basis, there was no traffic for five hours on Sunday, October 2, between Götgatan and Odenplan.

On April 18, an experimental boat route linking Tappström, on Ekerö, and Gamla Stan and Stadsbro was launched. The aim was to relieve the heavy commuter traffic on Ekerövägen. The experiment was successful, and the boat service was made permanent.

At the end of July, the renovated swimming pool, Vanadisbadet, was re-opened. For some years it had lost the city 2 million SEK a year. It is to be let to a private organization for 25 years, it has been modernized, and entrance charges have been increased.

In September, *Utrikesdepartement* (The Foreign Office) started to move into the renovated and partially rebuilt house Brunkhuvudet on Drottninggatan.

On November 25, temporary premises at Drottninggatan 18 were opened as Sweden's first museum and archive for circus art. The venture is run by the private Academy for the Preservation of Circus Art, which was founded 14 years before.

On December 6, the vessel Vasa was towed, in its pontoon, from the previous site by Liljevalch's Art Gallery to the new Vasa Museum.

1989 On January 20, the king opened the new City Terminal in the World Trade Center.

On February 19, the vast sports stadium *Globen* (The Globe) was officially opened in Johanneshov.

On May 15, the rebuilt prison, Långholmen, was opened as a youth hostel.

On May 27, *Södra station* (South Station) was inaugurated under its new *SJ* (State Railroads) name of *Stockholms södra*.

On September 6, a well-known and popular restaurant which is situated in cellars in *Gamla stan* (The Old Town), reopened. *Den gyldene freden* (The Golden Peace), had been closed since 1986 for alterations.

1990 On June 16, the new Vasa Museum on Djurgården was opened by King Carl XVI Gustav.

On July 1, Stockholm's taxi monopoly was discontinued. This meant that the much-criticized shortage of taxis immediately became almost a surfeit. The promise of reduced fares, however, did not ensue.

From July 24 to August 5, the World Equestrian Competitions took place at *Stadion* (Olympic Stadium)

On August 30, the Communist party's daily newspaper, *Ny dag* (New Day) ceased publication. It had first appeared on January 2, 1930. It has continued as a periodical.

On September 1, Stockholms stadsteater (The Town Theater) moved to newly built premises in *Kulturhuset* (The Culture House), which originally was to house a theater, but instead had become the temporary home of parliament.

In the middle of September, the largest Finish ferry went into operation. The

Silja Serenade carries 2,500 passengers. With a length of 203 meters, it was the world's longest ferry at the time.

1991 In April, an international conference on city planning was held in *Kulturhuset* to present suggestions for improving Stockholm.

From August 9 through 18, the first Water Festival took place, centered around Norrström. The event was a great success, is held annually, and has become internationally known.

At the end of the summer, the city-owned herd of sheep, which had been moved from its summer pasture on Ladugårdsgärdet to Järvafältet, was slaughtered by the city authorities, because its winter quarters at Åkeshov farm had been destroyed by fire.

On November 14, the well-known NK department store (Nordiska Kompaniet) was opened in a new form at the same site on Hamngatan.

In November, the Nobel Prizes were awarded at Globen, because of the larger number of guests celebrating the 50th anniversary of the prize. All surviving, previous winners were invited to the ceremonies.

In December, a compromise was reached on the use of LO (The Swedish Trade Union Confederation) property as a suitable memorial building to be called Olof Palme's International Center.

1992 In February, archeological diggings conducted by *Riksantikvarieämbetet* (The Office of the King's Custodian) near Norra Cemetery and Haga Palace discovered a previously inhabitated area dating back to 400 A. D.

On June 1, city authorities decided that a limited number of local flights would resume from Bromma Airfield.

On June 5, Stockholm held the first welcoming ceremony for those who had become Swedish citizens during the previous year. The ceremony took place in the renowned Blue Hall of the Stockholm City Hall.

On June 22, a private exhibition about the troubadour Carl Michael Bellman was opened to the public in Stora Henriksvik on Långholmen.

On July 18 and 19, a Northern Europe Steamboat Meeting was held, with a cortege on Strömmen and an exhibition for the public at Vasa Museum. Some 30 Swedish and Danish vessels assembled.

On September 11, the film by Anders Wahlgren, *Staden i mitt hjärta* (The Town in My Heart) was shown on a huge screen outside *Kulturhuset*. The film opposed the rebuilding of the city, and had previously been given wide exposure in theaters and on television.

On August 18, Adolf Fredriks Music School was once again opened, after renovations that cost 110 million SEK.

On October 15, Prince Bertil officially opened Sweden's National Sports Museum next to the Globe Stadium.

On October 16, a new building was opened at the Natural History Museum called Cosmonova. It houses a planetarium with associated multimedia techniques.

1993 On January 28, a wolf was run over and killed outside Jakobsberg, north of Stockholm. It was the first wild wolf that had been killed in the Stockholm region in a hundred years.

On March 15, a newly built Finnish ferry, Silja Europa, arrived in Stockholm. It was the world's largest passenger vessel.

On September 3, the classic tennis arena—*SALK-hallen: Stockholms Allmänna Lawn-tennis Klubb Hall* (SALK Hall, Stockholm's Public Tennis Stadium)—Alvik burned to the ground. The stadium had been erected in 1937 and was rebuilt ready for use in 1994.

On the night of November 8, Sweden's biggest art heist was carried out. Thieves entered through the roof of the Modern Museum and removed eight paintings valued at 500 million SEK.

On December 21, a new computer-controlled, multi-colored illumination system in the Sergels Torg glass sculpture pillar went into operation.

1994   On March 14, an archeological investigation of the area under Mynttorget was completed. It was discovered that the city wall from Norrport (q.v.) appeared to stretch further than previously believed.

At the end of April, the steamship Waxholm III returned to service in normal traffic, after restoration at a cost of 15 million SEK. It had been built in 1903 and after 58 years became a restaurant in Vaxholm.

On October 6, the History Museum opened its Gold Room, built eight meters under the ground at a cost of approximately 35 million SEK. For security reasons, only a limited amount of the museum's gold had been displayed during the last 20 years.

On December 7, Parliament resolved to change the law regarding natural resources, and the concept of a national city park was introduced. This measure will protect Stockholm's *Ekoparken*, Ulriksdal-Haga-Brunnsviken-Djurgården (qq.v.).

1995   During 1995, the population passed the 700,000 mark.

Planners suggested the need to rebuild around *Sergels torg* (q.v.). The buildings under discussion are about 25 years old.

New attempts have been made to prevent emptying of the city after 5 p.m. by increasing housing in the center.

Biofuel has become much used. Wood from the forest floor and specially grown sallow bushes are being used to provide heated water to houses. Seven power stations in Stockholm have started using this fuel.

A high-level delegation, including Stockholm's five female vice-mayors, represented the city at the UN Conference on Women in August in Beijing.

In August, it was announced that Stockholm had been selected to host a conference of current and previous female prime ministers and presidents, to be held May 5–7, 1996. Fourteen would be invited.

Also that month, two children and their young babysitter were tragically drowned in the Älvsjö swimming pool. No lifeguard was on duty due to financial cutbacks. This raised a storm of protest, and guards were reinstated.

1996   Work is underway on the new rail route to line the main north-south tracks with Arlanda Airport. It is due to open in the summer of 1999.

Ingvar Carlsson stood down as leader of the Social Democratic Party and prime minister. In March Göran Persson was elected to replace him a few days later.

In March it was decided to divide Stockholm into about 20 *stadsdelnämnder,* or areas of local government, as already exist in Paris and Oslo.

MAPS

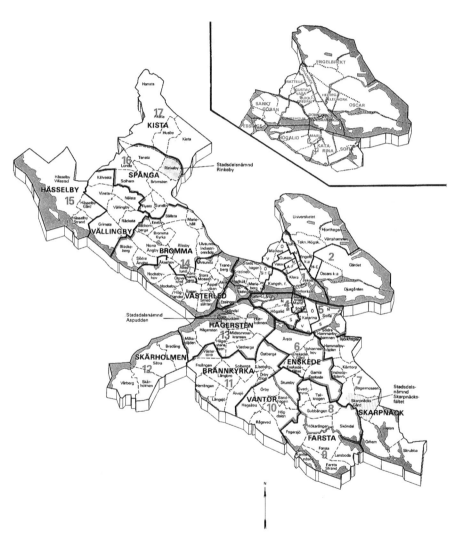

Map 1. Stockholm, inner city (above right) and outer city
(southern districts 6–13 and western districts 14–17)

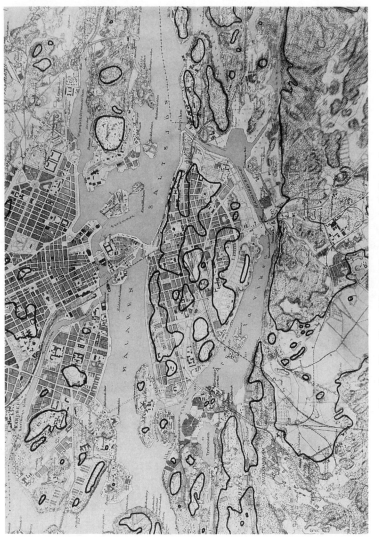

Map 2. Shoreline of Stockholm in the early Stone Age

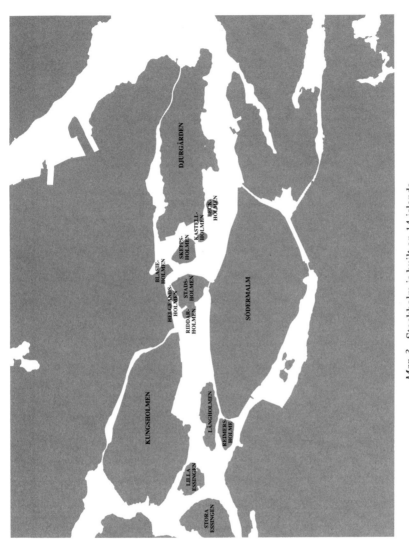

Map 3. Stockholm is built on 14 islands.

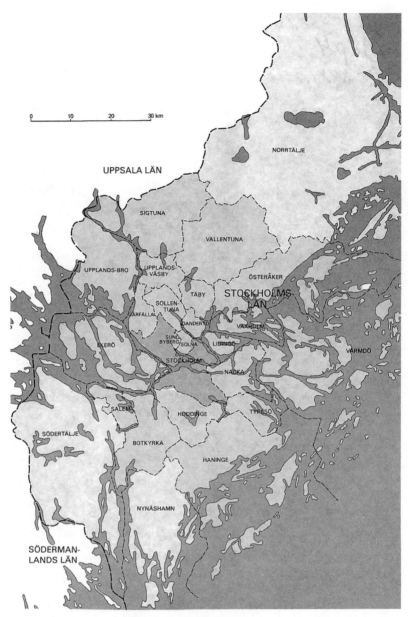

Map 4. Stockholm County

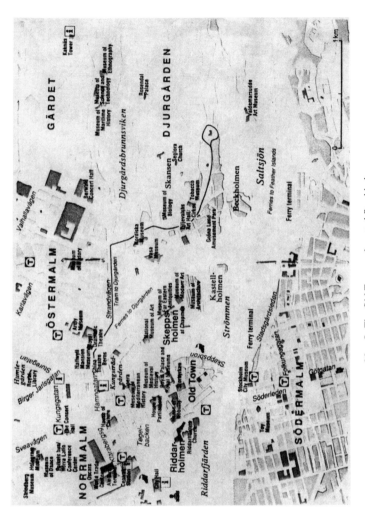

Map 5. The Old Town and central Stockholm

⊤ **Tunnelbana** *Metro*

Map 6. The Stockholm subway

Map 7. Stockholm's position in northern Europe

Introduction

Geography

STOCKHOLM is Sweden's capital city and largest town. It is the second-largest in the Nordic countries, after Copenhagen. At latitude 59° 20' north and longitude 18° 3' east, it is situated on the border between the provinces of Uppland and Södermanland and lies at the outlet of Lake Mälaren (q.v.) into the Baltic Sea. The latitude of Stockholm is almost the same as that of southern Greenland.

Stockholm is a number of inhabited islands between two great stretches of water. Altogether, there are 14 main islands. The only part of the town center on the mainland is that to the north of the city. (Map 3 shows these fourteen islands, with their present day names). Centrally situated is Stadsholmen, the site of *Gamla stan*, the Old Town. The city has 53 bridges that span the waterways between the islands. Stockholm calls itself "a city on the water," and also is known as "The Venice of the north." Nobel prize-winning author Selma Lagerlöf referred to Stockholm as "the city that floats on water."

Map 4 shows *Stockholms län*. This is a large administrative area, with a population of 1,570,320 as of January 1, 1996. This represents about 17.8 percent of the country's population. *Län* is translated as district, province, county or shire. Here, the term Stockholm county is used. As you will see, it is bordered to the north and west by Uppsala county and to the south and west by Södermanlands county.

The central area of the Map 4 is a darker shade. This area is shown in Map 5.

As the population became too large for the original Old Town, it began to spread out into *malmar* (plural of a *malm* [q.v.]). This word remains in the names of central areas of Stockholm, such as Norrmalm, Södermalm and Östermalm. But Stockholm grew far beyond these areas.

Map 5 shows the present-day inner town *(inre staden)* and outer town *(yttre staden)*. The inner town is repeated separately in the inset map in the top right-hand corner. The outer town is sometimes referred to as two neighborhoods; southern *(söderort)* and western *(västerort)*.

The inner town is divided into five social districts. They are Gamla stan-City district (the old, original Town), Vasastad, Östermalm, Kungs-holm, and Södermalm (qq.v.). The outer town has just the two main divisions—southern and western. On Map 5, the social districts of the inner town are numbered 1 through 5; those of the southern outer town 6 through 13; and western outer town 14 through 17. The term Greater Stockholm (*Stor Stockholm*) is sometimes used when referring to inner town and outer town combined. As of January 1, 1996, it had a population of 711,119. This represents 8 percent of the country's population. Stockholm county consists of 25 *kommuner* (municipalities). Greater Stockholm does not include the three *kommuner* Norrtälje, Södertälje, and Nynäshamn, which make up the rest of the county.

A word about *kommuner:* Before the 1970s, a community was a vil-lage, small country-town or market-town (*köping*), or a recognized town (*stad*). The *stad* had special privileges. Then in 1971, the arrangement changed. The term *köping* disappeared, and many communities through-out the country were regrouped into 288 districts called *kommuner*, half of which have less than 16,000 inhabitants. *Stockholms stad* became *Stockholms kommun*, the largest. However, Stockholm's council decided in 1985 to revert to calling itself *Stockholms stad.* It is still, officially, a *kommun.* The town, or city, council is still the *kommunfullmäktige.* The change of name had no legal significance or advantage. It is simply preferred.

As recently as the year 1900, there were just over 300,000 inhabitants of Stockholm. The rapid growth in population has, in part, been a result of the industrialization of what had previously been an agricultural soci-ety. At the turn of the century, more than 60 percent of Sweden's popu-lation earned its living in agriculture. Now, as the end of the century nears, only 5 percent work on the land, and the population has shifted to the centers of industry. The total area of Stockholm is 21,519 hectare, 2,808 of which is water. Including the suburbs, the area is 3,456 square kilometers.

Early History

The land on which Stockholm is situated rose gradually above sea level after the latest ice age, when central Sweden became ice-free about 10,000 years ago. The average altitude is now 44 meters above sea level. It is estimated that in prehistoric times, the island on which Stockholm now sits was rising out of the water at a rate of 50 centimeters a century.

Stone Age

At the end of the early Stone Age, about 6,000 years later, the coastline was about 30 meters above the present sea level. The Stone Age "Stockholmer" lived in a scattered, archipelagic landscape of islands and islets, rocks and skerries. Landward of these lay the sheltered creeks along which fishermen and trappers settled. Such a settlement was discovered in Vårby, and excavated by the City Museum in 1970. It lies on the shore of the long creek that stretches up into the valley where Skärholmen is now situated. Other Stone Age sites include Masmo in Huddinge and Korsnäs in Grödinge. It appears that seal-hunting was an important activity, judging from skeletal remains. Otherwise, shards of earthenware vessels are the most common discovery.

Analysis of archeological findings has provided knowledge about man's ability to use local materials. During the Stone Age, small animal heads and figures were made of clay, including moose, seals, sheep, or birds. They probably were used in hunting rituals. Tools were made of bone or, more frequently, of flint or other stone. Flint was expensive and had to be imported to the "Stockholm" area; consequently other stone, such as quartzite, often was used.

One of the farmsteads from the middle Stone Age was at Kymlinge on Järvafältet, near Kista. Man has lived there since the fourth century B.C. The Stockholm City Museum has models of the Stockholm area during this period.

Bronze Age (c.1500–400 B.C.)

Stone tools were common, even in the Bronze Age (1500 to 400 B.C.), but man learned to use metals and the bronze foundryman was highly respected for his technical ability. In some settlements, there were special places for bronze-founding, and an associated oven has been excavated at Hallunda, in the district of northern Botkyrka. Hallunda was an important Bronze Age settlement and, at nearby Slagsta, there is a petroglyph (rock carving) from the Bronze Age, discovered in 1971. Across the carving sail 13 ships. On one of them stands a man, "the first Stockholmer." All around is other evidence of religious cults. Central Spånga is another site where many Bronze Age remains have been found.

During the Bronze Age, the water level was about 15 meters higher than at present and the climate was milder. The traces of man's existence include several grave fields dating from the time soon after the birth of Christ. The largest and most remarkable is at Erstagård, in Brännkyrka district, with nearly 200 excavated graves, many containing weapons. It has been suggested that this may indicate the presence of other groups who were defending their newly acquired land against newcomers.

During the next few centuries, there was a considerable amount of migration and new settlement. Much of the new settlement is attributed to the new, fertile meadows near the shore-line, which appeared after the period of land elevation, with the accompanying increase in cattle-raising and extensive arable farming. Many homesteads from this period have been discovered.

Early Iron Age

During the early Iron Age, the climate became colder and damper, and the area around Lake Mälaren was well-populated. On Helgö, there is evidence of an Iron Age smithy. Around 800 B.C. Birka, (q.v.) came into being as something approaching a town and may be rightly considered Stockholm's oldest predecessor. Both Helgö and Birka are strategically located on Lake Mälaren, at waterway crossings that were utilized in both summer and winter by Stockholmers of the day. Although Helgö had some urban characteristics, Birka on the nearby island of Björkö was the first truly urban community in the Stockholm area. Unlike Helgö, there are written mentions of it: traces of ramparts, a fort, harbors, and "black earth" show clearly where the town flourished in the ninth and 10th centuries.

Viking Age (c.A.D. 800–1060)

The area around Lake Mälaren attracted traders from other countries early on, so that by the ninth and 10th centuries Birka, had become a sizeable trading center. Many of the Viking expeditions originated from this area. Most of the Viking-age graves found are near the site of the settlement. Surviving rune stones bear inscriptions about expeditions far into southern Russia and Constantinople. Rune stones in Spånga tell of Vikings who fell in Greece about 1000 A.D. At the same time, there were expeditions westward, with runic reference to King Canute's ransom in England.

The Viking period was the great age of runic inscriptions in Sweden, with about 1,300 having been found in the province of Uppland and about 30 in the Stockholm region. A certain amount of mystery still surrounds runic inscriptions, but they were often Christian monuments, raised to honor dead relations. The majority are still in their original position and often not easily accessible. However, some samples may be seen in Stockholm museums.

By the 11th century, Birka's importance had diminished. For a time, partly because of its ecclesiastical importance, Sigtuna became the main center of the region. However, with the growth of German colonization and the flourishing of Lübeck, trading centers sprang up around the Baltic.

12th, 13th and 14th Centuries

With its proximity to the sea, Stockholm grew and overtook Sigtuna in importance. As a consequence of land-rise at this time, Lake Mälaren now had only one point of entry, and it is recorded that even before the year 1200 there was a defense fortification there, at Stadsholmen. Excavations in 1980 indicated the presence of buildings on Helgeands-holmen that were older than those on Stadsholmen. Precise details of location and even the date are unavailable, but it is generally agreed that Birger Jarl (q.v.) was responsible for the siting and building of the town around the strong fortifications that became present-day Stockholm. Birger Jarl was the brother-in-law of the king ruling the land that approximated what is now known as Sweden. Birger Jarl had his son elected heir to the throne, thereby becoming a major power in the land. The fortifications were to protect against piracy. The first surviving record in which the name Stockholm appears is a letter of safe conduct dated 1252.

After an agreement between Birger Jarl and Lübeck, Stockholm became populated by many German burghers, who developed the town on Stadsholmen with German style and leadership. Franciscan monks founded a monastery, the church of which is now called Riddarholm Church (q.v.).

During the reign of Magnus Ladulås, 1275–90 (q.v.), the town grew rapidly, largely due to the export of copper and iron. Iron from Bergsla-gen was much sought after, and for it to reach the Baltic from Lake Mälaren it had to pass Stockholm. A protective wall was built around the town in 1300. A century later it was demolished and replaced by a larger, new one. A 15th century fortification wall was found on the small island of Helgeandsholmen, north of Stadsholmen, during the excavations in 1978.

The Hansa Period

Trade increased during the 14th century, especially with German towns that were grouped under the leadership of Lübeck in the Hansa League. This dominated trade for the next two centuries, and there was lively commerce in Stockholm as a result.

In the 14th century, Stockholm was mentioned for the first time as the capital of Sweden. The oldest surviving charter dates from 1436, earlier documents having been lost. More extensive are the 15th century source materials, which give some idea of the city's population and social structure. In 1460, there were about a thousand burghers, and by the early 1500s, about 1,200; the total population was obviously much larger. Already in the 14th century, new quarters were sprouting up outside the city walls. The General Urban Code, promulgated in the mid-14th century, remained valid, with a few amendments, until 1734. According to the code, Stockholm was ruled by a bailiff, who safeguarded the interests of the Crown, and by a council of six burgomasters and a maximum of 30 councillors, half of them Swedes and half of them Germans, in an attempt to counteract German domination.

German dominance in the town's government brought strong resistance, expressed in the Käpplinge murder (q.v.), for example, in 1389. But this dominance was not broken until the 15th century.

The Kalmar Union (1397–1521)

In 1389, through inheritance and family ties, the crowns of Denmark, Norway, and Sweden were united under the rule of the Danish Queen Margareta. In 1397, the so-called Kalmar Union was concluded under her leadership. The premise was that the three Scandinavian countries should have one and the same monarch. The whole union period, throughout the 15th and early 16th centuries, was marked by conflict between the central government, represented by the king on the one hand, and the high nobility along with the intermittently rebellious Burghers and peasants on the other.

During the later Middle Ages, Stockholm was central to several dramatic events resulting from power struggles in Sweden, and efforts to maintain national unity and the economic interests Sweden shared with the Hansa League. There was Engelbrekt Engelbrektsson's (q.v.) war of liberation, (1434 to 1436), when he led the peasantry against the ruling classes, and then the Brunkeberg Battle in 1471, when Sten Sture (q.v.) defeated the Danish King Kristian I (q.v.). Foreign influence on the council was eliminated as a result. Finally, there was "Stockholm's Bloodbath" (q.v.) in 1520, when Kristian II (q.v.) took the city and executed many of the burghers.

The Vasas (1523–1611)

After Gustav Vasa (q.v.) occupied the town and was crowned king of Sweden in 1523, Stockholm duly became the seat of centralized government. The state increased its authority over the city, curtailing the freedom and autonomy it had enjoyed, bringing changes in the composition of the residents, many of whom were now employed by the state. In 1527, the lands of the church were confiscated, and the reformation that led to the establishment of the Lutheran Church in Sweden was begun. It was decided in 1527 to demolish the churches in the suburbs and also *Klara Kloster* (The Convent of St. Clare), partly to provide building materials for the city's defenses. Gustav Vasa fortified the town, somewhat at the expense of old buildings in the surrounding island suburbs that were incorporated into the town in 1529. However, the defenses of the realm were established in many other strategic places around the country, so that Stockholm lost its position of importance for national defense. However, it retained its significance as the nation's most important port and remained long into the future. Sweden's main naval base was extended in the late 16th century and moved to what is now Blasieholmen (q.v.).

In the time of Johan III (q.v.), Klara Maria Church and Jakob Church were built to replace the monasteries and churches that Gustav Vasa had allowed to be destroyed. The old medieval fortress was rebuilt and crowned in 1544 with an iron spire bearing three crowns, which gave rise to its name of "Three Crowns."

Vädersolstavlan, a painting from 1535 that depicts Stockholm as it appeared at the end of the Middle Ages, is preserved in Storkyrkan (q.v.) and the massive Three Crowns fortress dominates the scene. Stockholm was defended from attack from sea attack by a palisade. The city wall with crenelated battlements and fortified gates with draw bridges gave protection from all directions. Also pictured are whitewashed chimneys rising high above the roofs of turf or tiles. On the heights of Söder stood a windmill, and on Stigberget the gallows can be identified.

Toward the end of the 16th century, increasing use was made of the areas outside the fortified city, Norrmalm and Södermalm, for more permanent settlements. The two suburbs were built almost entirely of wood. Norrmalm was appropriated by the crown at the reformation. By the end of the 16th century, there also was a substantial artisan and merchant population. In 1602, Norrmalm received its own municipal rights, and later became known as *Norra Förstaden* (the Northern Suburb). It remained a town in its own right for 30 years. Södermalm, on the other hand, had belonged to the city of Stockholm since the 13th century, and its citizens remained closely tied to the mother city. At the end of the 16th century, the city's population probably totaled between 8,000 and 9,000.

The Era of Great Power (1611–1718)

The 17th century brought many changes to Stockholm. During the reign of Gustav II Adolf (1611–1632) (q.v.) Stockholm became the capital city—capital of a great power. A general reorganization of urban local government already had been proposed in 1619. The state made a conscious effort to develop Stockholm. In 1634, Stockholm became administratively independent from state control centered in Uppsala. Government offices and flourishing trade resulted in the growth of the town, and island suburbs were built up. The granting of a charter in 1636 assured the city of large revenues.

Gustav II Adolf used toll gates, subsidized trading companies, and the extension of the harbor as means to strengthen Stockholm as a national port. The city wall was demolished and replaced by fence palings with toll gates. As the city grew, these fences were moved. Trade and maritime commerce increased. Sweden became an important power. The period of 1611–1711 was the Era of Great Power *(Stormakts tid)*.

This period is associated with victories on the battlefield during the Thirty Years War, a religious war fought in Germany between Catholics and Protestants from 1618 to 1648. The riches and prestige bestowed on Sweden as a result of the war left their mark on Stockholm, as palaces and fine mansions were built.

During the Era of Great Power, Stockholm's population rose above 50,000. One of the prerequisites for the city's expansion was the acquisition of land. Ladugårdslandet (now Östermalm) was incorporated into the city during Queen Kristina's time. She also donated present-day Kungsholmen (qq.v.) to the town. In 1637, a policy of city improvement was implemented. Narrow alleyways were widened and a system of residential blocks was introduced, together with a grid system for streets. The old, flammable, wooden houses were gradually replaced by stone structures, including palaces on Stadsholmen, Riddarholmen and Blasieholmen. In 1697, Tre Kronor castle was destroyed by fire.

During the expansion of the 17th century in the city itself, almost half the houses were rebuilt or given new façades. During the first stage of expansion, the dominant style was German-Dutch Renaissance, with gabled brick houses and copious sandstone ornamentation. The dominant style of the second stage was the classicism of France and Italy. Most of the noblemen's palaces were built in the 1650s and 1660s, and often designed by Jean de la Vallée or Nikodemus Tessin the elder (qq.v.). Immigrant Dutch businessmen often built their houses on Södermalm. Louis de Geer's house, on Götgatan, dates from about 1650 and shows the typical Palladian style of the Netherlands. Numerous public buildings also were erected in the 17th century, including *Riddarhuset* (House of Nobles), *Riksbankshuset* (National Bank), and *Södra stadshuset* City Museum of Stockholm (qq.v.). New churches were built in the suburbs: Katarina Church was commenced in 1656, and was soon followed by Hedvig Eleonora Church on Östermalm, and Ulrika Eleonora Church at Kungsholmen. At the end of the 17th century, however, times were hard, development stagnated, and the building boom came to a halt. Under Karl XII, the Era of Great Power collapsed. In addition, there were severe plagues and devastating fires. In 1710, plague wiped out one-third of the city's population. Stockholm became impoverished.

The head of the Swedish government of the time, Arvid Horn, is quoted as stating, "We see that not only trade but also the arts and crafts are dying and being extinguished." Starvation, dilapidated homes, drunkenness and prostitution were rife after the end of the war. The only new building of importance constructed at this time was a replacement for the destroyed royal palace, which remains to this day.

The Age of Liberty (1718–1772)

A new constitution during the reign of Queen Ulrika Eleonora limited the power of the monarchy. This period is known as the Age of Liberty. Fredrik I became king in 1720, following the abdication of Ulrika Eleonora. Both he and his queen were little more than figureheads.

Gustavian Age (1772–1809)

Conditions in Stockholm barely improved before the reign of Gustav III (q.v.). In 1772, he staged a bloodless coup and introduced a new constitution, taking more power into his own hands, amply assisted by the burghers. His reign represented their period of great power. This brought to an end the so-called Period of Liberty. Foreign trade allowed Sweden and the capital, Stockholm, to recover remarkably fast. The population grew—from 35,000 in 1720 to 75,000 by 1760. However, the population and the city soon stagnated due to a long-lasting proto-industrial crisis. Large trading houses were established. Skeppsbro Quay was enlarged to provide more space for the increase in shipping. Slussen (q.v.), the lock between Lake Mälaren and the Baltic, was rebuilt. A rich cultural life characterized the time of King Gustav III, which was accompanied by strong French influences. An opera house was opened.

19th Century

But with the loss of Finland in 1809, Stockholm no longer held a central position in the kingdom and its importance as a trading center diminished. Also, Sweden's political axis was thought to be more north-south rather than east-west.

After the abolishment of the system of guilds in 1846 and the introduction of free trade, Stockholm became an industrial town. There was not much in the way of impressive constructions but the mayor, Carl Lindhagen, was influental in bringing about a new town plan. This influence continued into the 20th century. Between 1880 and 1890, the population of Stockholm increased from 168,000 to 246,000. Steamboats and railways also accelerated Stockholm's growth from a small to a large city.

20th Century

The turn of the century saw a prosperous Stockholm, based on income from its industrial development. During the 19th century, Sweden had gradually recovered from war and debt, and a flourishing industrial and professional middle class, with liberal and reforming ideas, became a major force in the land, starting with Stockholm. The industrial revolution reached Stockholm rather late. One pioneer industrial building was the Eldkvarn (q.v.), a steam-powered mill erected in 1806, on the site of the present City Hall.

In the 1820s, Stockholm enjoyed its first steamboat service between Lake Mälaren and the Baltic coast. The expanding traffic and larger vessels necessitated yet another extension of the sluice gates at Slussen. The opening of the railroad in 1860 put an end to Stockholm's winter isolation. This was the track from the west. But the line northward took longer. The railroad which ran through the city did not begin operating until 1871. In 1861, the first water mains were laid, and in 1864 the sewers and drains were constructed.

An important year in the history of Stockholm was 1863, when the city became self-governed, and elected city councillors took over the management of the capital. Previously, the representatives of the community had dealt only with those matters allocated to them by law and statutes. Free trade was introduced in 1864. Streetcars were in use by 1877.

In 1900, the city had 300,000 inhabitants. The population continued to increase during the 20th century, and more and more of the surrounding area became incorporated into the city. By 1930 the population had reached 500,000, and in the 1960s it reached 800,000. Since then, the city's population figures have steadily declined and now Stockholm accounts for less than half of Stockholm county's inhabitants. On January 1, 1996, there were 711,119 Stockholm residents and 1,570,320 in the entire county.

The improvement in traffic and transport facilities meant that housing could be developed away from the city center, but major steps were not taken until after World War II, when the subway system was built. New housing developments, which were intended to be self-contained towns, were built first in Vällingby in the west and then in Farsta to the south. The very thorough renovation of the city's buildings, which took place between the 1950s and the 1970s, were hotly debated. The character of lower Norrmalm changed completely as the colorful, bohemian appearance of the Klara district virtually disappeared. People left the city and the innermost districts shrank to just a few hundred inhabitants. The inner city is lightly populated, compared with most other western capitals. Dwellings were replaced by offices, banks, stores, and shops. Financial difficulties and the overabundance of property resulted in the demolition of whole blocks of buildings. A shortage of housing at the time led to a marked increase in illegal occupation. However, the bulldozers were reined in somewhat, so that the city retains one of the most interesting and picturesque old towns in Europe, although the greater part of Stockholm is determinedly modern. The Old Town (*Gamla stan*) (q.v.) could easily have suffered the same fate as the Klara district, but instead was tastefully restored. It is now the "town between the bridges," an extremely lively community.

The environmental struggle of the century came about when a group of elm trees in Kungsträdgården (q.v.) were to be cut down to make way for a new subway station. Protesters occupied the trees in 1972, and gained nationwide, even international, attention.

Eventually the protesters won out over the authorities. The green oasis of the elm trees still stands, not far from the Kungsträdgården subway station. Conservationists also have been successful in limiting vehicular traffic in the city center.

Almost as important to the character of Stockholm as its waterways and islands are its parks, trees, and flowers. More than a million flowers are planted every year in Stockholm's municipal parks. Stockholm is only a quarter of the size of New York City, but has 12,500 acres of parkland, to New York's 25,000 acres. Many of the city's streets are lined with large, old trees, which do much to soften the impact of often stark, functional architecture. The opening of a unique National City Park in 1995 increased the greenness of the city.

Because Sweden remained neutral in both world wars, Stockholm did not suffer the fate of so many European cities at war. Yet, in its own way, it is said to have seen greater changes than the cities of the German Ruhr district. The enormous change in Swedish society in less than a hundred years inspired the rapid growth of Stockholm, and much of the 19th–century inner city has been replaced by the architecture of the second half of the 20th century.

There are no fewer than 30 open-air theaters in the city, where concerts, dramas, and ballets are staged in summer. Stockholm lays claim to the longest art gallery—the subway system. The ceilings and walls of most of the principal stations are a feast of paintings, mosaics, and sculptures.

Stockholm is, above all, a city that should be enjoyed.

City Management

Sweden has a long tradition of local self-government. However, it has been little more than a century since civil and church matters were separated. In 1862, the local government ordinances decreed that the parishes of the Lutheran State Church should be responsible for church matters, and that civil matters should be managed by municipal districts.

Sweden has two levels of secular local government. At the regional level, there is a county council *(landsting)*, whose territory is normally the same as the national government's administrative unit, the county *(län)*. The second level of local self-government is the municipality *(kommun)*, which is the smaller unit. The new Local Government Act of 1992 defines the roles of the two levels.

The municipalities are primarily responsible for education. They are in charge of child and elderly care, schools, social services, refugees, and asylum-seekers, physical planning and building, certain environmental tasks, and emergency services.

Medical care and public dental services are the responsibility of the county councils.

Local and regional public transportation is operated either by municipalities or county councils, often through jointly owned companies.

The Church of Sweden also has local units, called parishes *(församlingar)*.

As the largest municipality in Sweden with more than 700,000 inhabitants, Stockholm obviously requires a large organization to control the city's affairs. Each consideration is referred to a board and committee before being decided upon by the City Council. This decision-making body can be called Stockholm's parliament. The Stockholm City Council has 101 members who are elected by permanent residents over the age of 18 years. There are 49 female members.

A high-level delegation, including Stockholm's five female vice-mayors, represented the city at the August 1995 United Nations Conference on Women in Beijing. During the conference, Stockholm delegates presented the city's approach to gender issues and equality.

Non-citizens are eligible to vote in local elections. The City Council meets twice a month. Meetings are open to the public and the agenda appears in daily newspapers prior to a meeting. A local radio station carries a direct broadcast of proceedings. Municipal elections are held every three years.

At the City Council elections held in September 1944, more than 81 percent of those eligible cast their votes—a high percentage when compared internationally. Following the 1994 elections, the political organization was reorganized to function more like a parliament, in which the political majority and opposition have more clearly defined roles. The City Executive Board consists of 13 members. Each political party is represented in the same proportion as on the City Council. (See also APPENDIX NO. 7: MISCELLANEOUS STATISTICS, Municipal Council Election 1994.) The Executive Board expresses its opinion on all deliberations before the City Council comes to its decisions.

A resolution must be adopted within a year of the submission of a motion. The Executive Board is then responsible for executing the resolution. This large municipality comprises seven divisions. The chief executives of the divisions constitute the Council of Mayors. Their task is to link the activities of the Council, Executive Board, and the administration. All members of the Council of Mayors who head the various divisions are appointed by the political majority. The opposition will be allocated a number of seats on the Council of Mayors, which consists of full-time, professional political officials, unlike the other council members. Mayors also are elected every three years.

(See also DICTIONARY entry: COUNCIL OF MAYORS) The chief executive of the Finance division is the most senior and assumes the role of mayor. In addition to being responsible for the city's budget, which is presented in November each year, he or she is chairperson of the Council of Mayors. However, the Executive Board is taking over the financial responsibility held by the Finance Committee. In the future, the Finance Office will be responsible for those activities required to be carried out on the direct request of the political majority, financial management, and strategic matters.

The Administrative Office will be responsible for administrative service and policy matters of a long-term administrative nature.

The city's Administrative Office services the municipality's political bodies, and ensures that City Hall is efficiently run. The town clerk is the head of the Administrative Office of the city of Stockholm.

The Administration Department consists of the following sections:

The secretariat provides the Council with service and publishes the Stockholm Municipality Almanac. The City Hall Reception, Library and Archives, as well as the Post and Internal Services Bureau, service employees and visitors.

The finance and personnel sections of the Administration Department service the various official requirements of the Administrative Office and Finance Office, as well as those of the various divisions and political party offices at City Hall.

The city attorney and the legal department represent the city in the courts and deal with public authorities. In addition, this department, can be called upon, for a fee, to provide the city's committees and administrations with legal advice, not only on matters relating to municipal law but also on civil and tax law and general legal questions.

The personnel department deals with matters relating to municipal policy, such as salaries and wages, negotiations, recruitment of managerial staff and leadership development, personnel policy, and restructuring of and developments on the labor market. It also handles inquiries and projects on behalf of the administrations.

The Research and Statistics Administration is independent of the Administrative Office and is paid per assignment. It prepares forecasts for the city's central organization, as well as for the administrations and external clients. A special bureau has been set up primarily to provide investigatory services to opposition party councillors.

The Accounts Section is responsible for the City's central accounting, annual report, and liquid funds. It also coordinates financial administrative routines and financial systems.

The Electronic Data Processing (EDP) Section safeguards the City's EDP systems and advises the Executive Board on general and strategic EDP issues.

The Finance Office helps to implement the strategies of the political leadership. It has the overriding responsibility of preparing the budget and dealing with other major financial issues. The Finance Office also is the driving force behind efforts to restructure and reorganize the city. It monitors the implementation of major political resolutions by the administration. The activities of the Finance Office are governed by the intentions of the political majority, and are carried out within the parameters of a set financial framework. The office works in close cooperation with the city's administrations and their executive groups.

The Finance Office is organized into a number of sections, departments, and special project groups:

The Budget and Development sections monitor the budget. One of these sections also tracks current events to ensure that the city's overriding principles are implemented and supported by the administrations. Two others handle matters relating to the budget that affect schools and social welfare services, as well as issues of technology, the infrastructure, culture, and recreation.

The Treasury Department is primarily responsible for cash flow planning, and for assessing the city's loan requirements, investments, and potential risks. It operates the city's Internal Bank, which makes long and short-term external loans, and helps the city's administration and enterprises raise capital. The Treasury also manages the city's donated funds.

The Department of Greater Stockholm Affairs is responsible for managing cooperation among other municipalities, the County Council and the state. It conducts its activities on behalf of the Executive Board and divisional committees, participates in working teams, and carries out investigatory work.

The Information Department is responsible for "Information Stockholm," which keeps the residents of Stockholm abreast of the workings of local government, the democratic process, and the utilization of tax revenue. It also disseminates information regarding resolutions of political and economic importance to the city's executive officers and employees, as well as to groups directly affected by the resolutions.

The Special Projects Group is developing methods of increasing competition within the municipality's sphere of activities in order to allow colleagues the opportunity to streamline their activities. The group also is engaged in the improvement of quality standards.

Finally, the Premises Group of the Finance Office attempts to improve the effective use of the city's premises in order to reduce administration costs.

The seven mayoral divisions have jurisdiction over the various committees or boards, which have specific areas of responsibity, such as planning, recreation, schools, etc. All chairpersons with key positions are appointed by the political majority.

In 1991, a trial project was begun in which the district (borough) committees of Rinkeby, Aspudden, and Skarpnäcksfältet assumed responsibility for such activities as schools, social services, child care, and libraries in their own districts. This experiment was reviewed in 1993. Subsequently, new reforms of *Stadsdelsnämnder* (Borough Committees) are due to come into force in 1996.

Almost all political parties support the proposal that each of the 23 borough committees be responsible for their own public services. The larger portion of the city's activities is managed by majority-interest joint stock companies in which the city is the major shareholder. Stockholm Energi AB (energy), Stockholm Vatten AB (water supply), and Stockholms Stadsteater AB (theater) are examples of such enterprises.

On May 6, 1973 "Open City Hall" was organized. On this Midsummer's Day, the City Hall celebrated its 50th anniversary with an open house, offering coffee, buns, music, and fireworks. This annual event gives some 20,000 Stockholmers the opportunity to meet the city's leading politicians.

Like so many other cities throughout the world, Stockholm has serious financial problems, hindered by the severe recession in which the country finds itself. In the annual financial balance for 1993, the city's income was 7.189 billion SEK and the expenditure was 21.759 billion SEK resulting in a *negative* balance of 14.57 billion SEK. In 1995, the income was 33.683 billion SEK and the expenditure 34.995 billion SEK.

Further information may be obtained from the City Administrative Offices, 08–785 90 00.
(See also APPENDIX NO. 7: MISCELLANEOUS STATISTICS. Taxes 1994 and The Use of Local Tax in 1993.)

The Future

In spite of difficult financial times much effort and investments are being made in the city of Stockholm. Among other things, much effort is being put into the marketing of tourism and the establishment of businesses in Stockholm. It is hoped that the city will become Europe's center for Information Technology (IT) and its tele-metropolis. Also a lot is being invested in environmental matters.

Stockholm is going to host several exciting events in the near future. In 1997, an industrial exhibition, called Exposition 1997, will be held in the city. In 1998, Stockholm will celebrate its role as the Culture Capital of Europe and exhibit the rich and varied cultural pleasures it offers. In 1999, it is due to host the World Police and Fire Games.

The City Council is well aware that less money must be spent on existing services without sacrificing quality. This demands efficient municipal operations.

Greater Stockholm, which comprises 22 municipalities in Stockholm County, is Sweden's most expansive area. In recent years, concrete plans for a common jobs and housing region—the Mälar Valley—have been drawn up. Work to improve transport is under way. This region is an economic power center, with a 100–kilometer radius and 2.2 million inhabitants. Recent developments in the Mälar Valley suggest that the importance of the Stockholm region will increase with time.

But whatever the future holds, Stockholm will surely remain an exceptionally beautiful city by the waters.

The Dictionary

A

ABBA. This world famous pop group, formed in 1972, had their recording studio at St. Eriksgatan (q.v.) The group included Agnetha Fältskog, Benny Andersson, Björn Ulvaeus and Anni-Frid (Frida) Lyngstad. The name ABBA is formed from the initials of their first names. They were highly successful commercially, but after sales of their records and cassettes exceeded 200 million, the group disbanded in 1982. The ABBA studio still attracts many overseas visitors who hope to find a museum dedicated to their idols, but there is little there to kindle any ABBA memories. Those who wait long enough and have a little luck may catch a glimpse of Björn and Benny, who still use the studio from time to time. It was there that they recorded the musical "Chess."

ACADEMY OF FINE ARTS (*KONSTAKADEMIEN*). The Academy of Fine Arts was opened in 1897. See also EXPOSITION 1997 STOCKHOLM.

ACADEMY OF SCIENCE *(KUNGLIGA VETENSKAPSAKADEMIEN)* *(KVA).* Founded in 1739, it has as its aim the advancement of knowledge, particularly in the fields of natural sciences and mathematics. Among the institutions associated with KVA are the Bergian Foundation and the People's Museum (qq.v.). See BERGIAN BOTANICAL GARDENS.

ADELCRANTZ, CARL FREDRICK (1716–1796). A baron and a renowned architect in rococo and new classicism, he became a first commissioner in 1776. He was responsible for the uniquely preserved Drottningholm theater and the rococo *Kinaslott* (China Palace). On November 28, 1774, Adolf Fredrik's Church, designed by Adelkrantz, was consecrated. In 1775, Adelcrantz submitted a proposal, at the request of Gustav III, to redesign Gustav Adolf's Square (q.v.), then named Norrmalm Square, in a more stylish manner. After the rebuilding of Fredrikshov's Palace (q.v.) in 1776, under Adelcrantz's direction, the widowed Queen Lovisa Ulrika (q.v.) took up residence there. Adelcrantz also designed the present-day North Bridge (*Norrbro*) (q.v.), which was completed in 1797. The gardens at Drottningholm were designed by him, as was the English Park.

ADELCRANTZ, GÖRAN JOSUAE. Another architect in the Adelcrantz family, he was responsible for work in Hedvig Eleonora Church, together with Jean de la Vallée. The design of the new dome, which was built between 1724 and 1744 in Katarina Church, is credited to him.

ADELCRANTZ PALACE. Situated at Karduansmakaregatan 8. It was built in 1755 according to drawings by C.F. Adelcrantz (q.v.), but the oldest parts date from the 17th century.

ADOLF FREDRIK (1710–1771). Born Aldolf Fredrik av Holstein-Gottorp, the son of Karl XI (q.v.). He and Lovisa Ulrika (q.v.) were crowned king and queen of Sweden in Stockholm on November 26, 1751. As his royal motto, he chose "The Kingdom's prosperity—my prosperity". This was during the so-called Age of Liberty, when the crown had limited political influence. He sought support from the Hat Party (q.v.). The queen was the sister of Prussia's Frederick the Great and a forceful personality. Adolf Frederik was the father of Gustav III and Karl XIII (q.v.).

ADOLF FREDRIK CHURCH. Situated on Holländargatan on the west side of Sveavägen. In 1675, a chapel dedicated to St. Olof was erected on the site where Adolf Fredrik Church is now situated—a plot that has been used as a churchyard since 1640. Nearby Olovsgatan takes its name from that chapel. The present-day church was built between 1768 and 1774. The ground plan is in the shape of a cross with arms of equal length. The French philosopher Descartes, who was summoned to Stockholm by Queen Kristina (q.v.) in 1649, died on February 11, 1650, and his remains were returned to France in 1666. One of the sculptures of him, created by J.T. Sergel (q.v.) was erected in Adolf Fredrik Church in 1770. On November 28, 1774, the church, designed by C. F. Adelcrantz (q.v.), was consecrated. Sergel also was responsible for the fine altar relief, the model of which dates from 1779, but was not completed until 1885. The paintings in the dome date from 1889 to 1890. There is an epitaph in memory of the well-known Asiatic explorer Sven Hedin, created in 1959. The church underwent restoration between 1957 and 1959. The churchyard contains the graves of Sergel, 1740–1814; Hjalmar Branting, 1860–1925 (q.v.); Hedin, 1865–1952; and also, since March 15, 1986, Olof Palme (q.v.), who lies buried not far from the place where he was murdered.

ADOLF FREDRIK'S MUSIC SCHOOL. On August 18, 1889, Adolf Fredrik's Music School was once again opened, after renovations that cost 110 million SEK.

ADOLF FREDRIK'S SQUARE. See MARIATORGET.

AF CHAPMAN. A white full-rigger that defied the stormy seas until 1939, and is now one of Stockholm's distinct town symbols and a very attractive hostel. Because of its popularity, it tends to be heavily booked in advance. It is moored at Västra Brobänken, on Skeppsholmen. See also YOUTH HOSTELS.

AF CHAPMAN, FREDRIK HENRIK (1721–1808). A British sea captain who worked in Sweden as a shipbuilder of high renown. He greatly influenced the Swedish fleet. His ships played an important role in the Russian War.

AFTONBLADET. A liberal newpaper started by Lars Johan Hierta (q.v.) in 1830. Under his guidance, it became Sweden's first modern daily paper and an organ for the liberal opposition against the monarchy. In the beginning of the 20th century, mainly because of its interest in defense matters, the paper became conservative. It is published in Stockholm, but since 1964 has also been printed in Gothenburg and Malmö. It has been owned by LO (q.v.) since 1956, and is now a Social Democratic evening tabloid. The average circulation in 1993 was 342,500. It is read by 12 percent of the households in the Stockholm region.

AGE OF LIBERTY (*FRIHETSTIDEN*). The period in Swedish history between 1718 and 1772 in which there was a weak monarchy and parliament and strife between the political parties. See also CAP PARTY and HAT PARTY.

AIR POLLUTION. Although already enjoying comparatively clean air, Stockholm has decreased the amount of air pollution by approximately one-sixth since 1980. It is said this is not so much due to a reduction in the number of vehicles but more to the introduction of unleaded gasoline.

AKALLA. A suburb at the end of the subway line through Kista on the very edge of the countryside. In 1962, parts of Järvafältet (q.v.) were acquired from the state. This allowed for gradual homebuilding in the northern suburbs. At the end of the '60s and during the '70s, this resulted in the coming into being of Akalla. It is at the end of the subway line through Kista and is on the very edge of the countryside.

ÅKESHOV. A western suburb. The number of communities of home-owner properties surrounded by gardens grew during the 1910s, '20s and '30s, in Åkeshov. There also were English-styled terraced houses.

ALBERT ENGSTRÖM MUSEUMS. These include Engström's (q.v.) studio and house at Grisslehamn. The studio, which is near the sea, displays photographs and drawings; an easel, complete with an unfinished drawing, is set up by the window. The home of this popular author is complete with original furnishings and decor. Engström (q.v.) was born in 1869. Although not originally from Stockholm, he spent much of his later life in Grisslehamn, in Stockholm county. He is renowned for his descriptions of nature and the people of the Roslagen region. He died in 1940.

ALBREKT OF MECKLENBURG. (1340–1412). The young Albrekt of Mecklenburg anchored with his fleet in Stockholm's basin in 1363. The mayor and council of Stockholm paid homage to him as their rightful ruler on November 30. In 1388, he confirmed Stockholm's charter.

ALCOHOL. On February 26, 1914, a new system for the sale of alchohol was introduced. A *motbok* (passbook) was required to be shown and marked when purchasing alcohol, somewhat like a ration book. The scheme started in Stockholm, and in 1920 was adopted throughout the land. In 1955, the *motbok* was abolished; ever since alcoholic drinks can only be purchased at special state-run stores, called *Systembolaget*, or at restaurants. There are no real "pubs," although there is a trend in that direction.

Alcohol is relatively expensive, and city authorities frequently campaign to discourage the consumption of alcohol. In 1980, total sales, in liters per inhabitant, were: spirits, 9.57, strong wines, 2.64, light wines, 21.41, and strong ale, 14.59. The corresponding figures for 1993 were 4.64, 1.33, 23.39 and 16.62.

Alcoholism is a problem in Sweden, possibly more evident in a large city such as Stockholm. Swedes tend to be lone drinkers who aim to get drunk, rather than drink socially. Stockholm's subways attract drunks, particularly in the cold winter months. In 1994, 8,429 intoxicated people were "taken care of"—the euphemism now used instead of actually "being arrested." Of these, 7,707 were men. Since Sweden's entry into the European Union, there have been discussions about the future of the current system for purchasing alcohol, but it is still used.

ALMQVIST, CARL JONAS LOVE (1793–1866). Born in Stockholm, his writings covered a wide spectrum: new romanticism and realism, religious, mystical and radical social criticism. His works describe Stockholm in considerable detail. Among the better known are *Törnrosens bok* (The Dog-Rose's Book), *Drottningens juvelsmycke* (The Queen's Necklace) and *Det går an* (It May Be Done). The latter was written in defense of free love and was shocking at the time. He worked for *Aftonbladet* (q.v.), a liberal newspaper that allowed his often extreme and critical opinions. He was suspected of poisoning someone and fled to America in 1851, where he lived under various names in abject moral and economic misery. In 1865, he returned to Bremen, Germany, where he died.

ANCKARSTRÖM, JOHAN JAKOB (1762–1792). On April 27, 1792, Anckarström was executed for the assassination of King Gustav III (q.v.), after he had been severely thrashed in various public places around the capital. He was the last political criminal to be executed in Sweden. Gustav III had gained almost absolute power, and some aristocrats paid Anckarström to assassinate him. He shot the King at a masked ball at the Royal Opera House in Stockholm (q.v.) on March 16, 1792. The dying King's request that his assassin be spared was denied. The monarch died two weeks after being shot.

ÄNGBY. A western suburb, where the number of communities of homeowner properties surrounded by gardens, grew during the 1910s, '20s and '30s. There were also terraced houses, in the English style. It is a typical Stockholm suburb.

ANNUAL EVENTS. Every February, Stockholm holds the following events: *Stockholm Museum Day*, with special programs and tours at all museums; *International Guide Day*, with guided tours of Stockholm's museums; the Caravan and Camping Exhibition in Solna; *Dagens Nyheter Games*. track and field competitions with international competitors, held in Globen (q.v.); *spring salon at Liljevalch Art Gallery* (q.v.), through to the end of March.

   In March, there are the following events: *the Swedish Open Badminton Tournament* at Kungliga Tennishallen (q.v.); *the Boat Show* (Allt för sjön) at Stockholmsmässan, Älvsjö; *the Stockholm Art Fair*

Solentunamässan, Sollentuna; *Stockholm International Antique Fair* at Stockholmsmässan, Älvsjö.

In May there is: *kite flying* on Gärdet, North Djurgården (q.v.); *Svenska Dagbladet Relays*, with track and fields events; *Bukowskis Internationella*; an auction of furniture and art; *the Ladies' Cycle Race,* in which 9,000 cyclists race from Tegeluddsvägen, around Lidingö, and finish at Gärdet. Also daily performances, including opera, ballet, and concerts, are given until August at *Confidencen*, one of Sweden's oldest theaters, by Ulriksdal Castle (q.v.). *Drottningholm Palace Theater* (q.v.) presents opera and ballet performances all summer, until the beginning of September.

In June, *The Archipelago Boats' Day* features a cavalcade of steamboats across the water from Stockholm to Vaxholm (q.v.) and back to Strömkajen. *Parks Theater* offers free entertainment in the city parks during the summer. In the *Stockholm Marathon*, 15,000 competitors race twice around the city. They start at Östermalm's sports ground, at Lidingövägen, and finish at Stadion (q.v.). Athletes from some 30 countries participate; it is one of the world's five largest marathon races. *Sweden's National Day* and *Swedish Flag Day* are held on June 6, the main celebration being at Skansen (q.v.). *PostGiro Open* is the largest cycle competition in the Nordic countries. The finish is in Stockholm. Finally, in the *Midsummer Celebrations*, Skansen and Riddarholmen (qq.v.) present opportunities to experience national celebrations with regional costumes, fiddle music, dancing, and the erection of the mid-summer pole.

During the month of July, there is the *Jazz and Blues All Star Festival*. Even rock and gospel music is played at this event, provided by international musicians. It used to be held at Skeppsholmen, but is now in Skansen. During *Musik på slottet* (Palace Music), 30 concerts are given in July and August. Orchestral concerts are held in the Palace, in Rikssalen and *Slottskyrkan* (Palace Church), while chamber music is played in the Antique Museum, Karl XV's room, and the Serafimersalen. World-class soloists join the Stockholm Ensemble for many of these performances. *Gotland runt* (Around Gotland) is one of the world's largest sailing races. About 450 boats set sail from Sandhamn on the first Sunday in July to circumnavigate Gotland and return to Sandhamn a few days later. The *Stockholm Soccer Cup* is held for young people from around the world. Some 25 playing fields are used within a radius of a few kilometers, mainly at Grimsta, Spånga, and Vällingby. *Dagens Nyheters Galan* is an international track and field competition. It is held at Stadion (q.v.) and is regarded as Sweden's best arena competition and one of the world's best Grand Prix competitions. *Krönikespelet* (The Chronicle Play) and *Tornerspelet* (The Jousting) take place further afield, the former during Norrtälje's 18th Century Week at Wallinskagården and the latter in Marie-fred, near Gripsholm Castle (q.v.). The Chronicle Play is about the Russian attacks on Norrtälje in 1719, and the jousting features medie-val costumes, weapons, and equipment based on 14th century origi-nals. *Bellman Week* includes a number of programs all over Stock-holm to honor the memory of the 18th-century bard and poet, Carl Michael Bellmam (q.v.). The main show usually takes place on Bell-man Day, July 26.

In August, there is *The Stockholm Water Festival* (q.v.), the city's largest carnival with a variety of events concentrated around Gustav Adolf's Square, Norrbro, Riddarholmen (qq.v.), and the nearby quays. *Finnkampen* ("The Finnish Struggle") features track and field competitions between Sweden and Finland. It is held in Sweden dur-ing odd years and in Finland during even years. The Swedish compe-tition is held at Stockholm Stadion (q.v.). *Roslags och getingloppet* (Roslags and Geting Race) is a motorboat competition starting at Strömmen, in Stockholm, and finishing at Öregrund in Roslagen. The Geting race is off Öregrund and is part of the European Offshore Championship. *Midnattsloppet* (Midnight Race) is part of the Stock-holm Water Festival (q.v.) and one of Söder's (q.v.) big parties, as thousands of joggers run through the August night. *Riddarfjärd's Swim* is a 3,200 meter swimming race, also part of the Stockholm Water Festival (q.v.). It starts at Smeduddsbadet and finishes at City Hall *(Stadshuset)* (q.v.). In *Tjejmilen,* about 20,000 women run, jog, or walk a 10–kilometer stretch of Djurgården (q.v.). It is one of the largest competitions in the world.

In September, there is *Segelbåtens dag* (Yacht Day) with races on most stretches of water in Stockholm and surrounding areas.

October events include: *Lidingöloppet* (Lidingö Race), a cross-country race on Lidingö for elite and amateur runners. There are 30–kilometer and 15 kilometer events in what is claimed to be the largest cross-country event in the world. *Fantomen cup* (The Phantom Cup), an international youth swimming competition with 600 competitors, has taken place at Erikdalsbadet since the 1970s. *The Game and Hob-bies Exhibition* includes a wide range of exhibits on display at Solen-tunamässan, in Sollentuna.

During November, there is the *Stockholm Open*, the tennis tourna-ment that attracts the world's elite. It was held for a time in Globen (q.v.) but, commencing in 1995, after having lost a little of its status, it was returned to *Kungliga Tennishallen* (The Royal Tennis Stadium). *Gustav Adolf's Day* is celebrated on November 6 with a concert in Riddarholm Church (q.v.). *Din villa* (Your House) is an exhibition of home products and seminars for homeowners at Stockholmsmässan, Älvsjö.

December includes *Skansen's Christmas Fair, which* is held each
Sunday from 11 a.m. to 4 p.m. at Skansen (q.v.). On *Nobel dagen*
(Nobel Day), the year's Nobel Prizes (q.v.) are awarded by King Carl
XVI Gustaf at a formal ceremony in the Stockholm Concert Hall.
The ceremony is only for invited guests. It is followed by an evening
banquet in the City Hall *(Stadshuset))* (q.v.). The *Dog Show* is held
at Stockholmsmässan, Älvsjö, and includes 5,000 dogs. *Lucia* is a
festival of light. The coronation of the young lady selected to be the
Lucia of the year takes place on December 12. Lucia, clothed in white
robes, bears a crown of candles on her head. The ceremony takes
place at Skansen (q.v.), but there are also numerous Lucia celebrations in schools, offices, plazas, and hotels. *New Year's celebrations*
include fireworks all over the city. There also are celebrations at
Skansen (q.v.), with the traditional reading of "New Year Bells,"
which is broadcast on television.

ÄPPELVIKEN. A western suburb, in which the number of communities
of home-owner properties surrounded by gardens grew during the
1910s, '20s and '30s. It also has English-styled terraced houses.

AQUARIA-WATER MUSEUM. Situated at Falkenbergsgatan 2, in
Djurgården. Through new technology, visitors experience night and
day in a tropical rain forest, see a variety of fish and frogs, and listen
to the sounds of each distinct environment. Moving on, visitors arrive
at "the sea," with tanks of sharks, moray eels, and living coral.

ARCHBISHOP JÖNS BENGTSSON. Archbishop Jöns Bengtsson and
his troops marched into Stockholm on February 24, 1457. Stockholm
Palace surrendered to the archbishop on March 17.

ARCHBISHOP JAKOB ULFSSON. In August 1497, Archbishop Jakob
Ulfsson, together with three Swedish and seven Danish councillors,
sanctioned a charter for the inhabitants of Stockholm on behalf of
King Hans.

ARCHIPELAGO. Stockholm's skerries, in the Baltic Sea off Uppland
and Södermanland, form one of the world's largest archipelagos: 140
kilometer long and 80 kilometer wide, with 24,000 islands and rocky
islets. (It is interesting to note, however, that in reference books of
just a few decades ago, this figure was regularly given as only 7,000.)
They stretch from Landsort in the south to Arholma in the north.

The archipelago was formed by land rise after the Ice Age. In contrast to the archipelago on the west coast, with its bare, polished
rocks, Stockholm's archipelago has fairly luxuriant vegetation. The

inner archipelago consists of woods and meadows cut by firths, sounds, creeks, and valleys. The outer archipelago has groups of low rocky islets with sparse vegetation, often separated by wide stretches of open water. Here, only a few groups of islands are inhabited all year around, although the inner islands are evenly, though quite sparsely, inhabited.

During the 1700s and 1800s, the archipelago played an important role in supplying wood and food, especially fish, to the capital. In the middle of the 1800s, the citizens of Stockholm began to make use of the opportunities for recreation that the islands provided. The islands were made more easily accessible by the rapidly increasing steamboat traffic.

Many so-called patrician merchant villas were built at the turn of the century, the owners living in them for a few weeks each summer with family and maids. During this century, the permanent resident population has declined, even though the islands have become easier to reach by tunnels, bridges, and car ferries. In 1959, the Stockholm Archipelago Foundation was established to protect the skerries against excessive exploitation, while seeking to preserve them for recreation. During the 1970s, a return to such communities as Sandhamn and Utö commenced, where people could provide for themselves by fishing, construction work, boat-building, and tourist services.

Today, many of the century-old houses have been beautifully restored. Some 6,000 people live year-round in the Stockholm archipelago. In the summer, the number increases by several hundred thousand, to which can be added 150,000 small boats. In fact, it has been estimated that there are more than half a million privately owned boats around Stockholm Archipelago.

The largest island in the archipelago is Värmdö, which has an area of 180 square kilometers. Värmdö has road connections to the mainland and regular boat traffic to the eastern islands, including Nämdö, Runmarö, and the largest, Möja. The biggest islands in the south, off Södertörns coast, are Muskö, Ornö, and Utö, together with Gålö and Nåttarö. The latter three are Stockholm municipality's leisure area. It was on Nåttarö that Queen Maria Eleonora hid (q.v.). There used to be iron mines on Utö, which were in use from 1607 to 1879. There is usually an art exhibition in the mill, and a small museum tells the history of the mines. The southern part of the island has been used as a military firing range since 1945. Off Muskö, which can be reached by car through a tunnel from the mainland, lies the small island of Älvsnäbben, a fleet anchorage that already was used in the Middle Ages, and from which Gustav II Adolf (q.v.) sailed to Germany in 1630. Three hundred years later, a monument was raised on nearby Kapellön to commerate that event. Off Dalarö, northeast of Ornö, lies

Kymmendö, where August Strindberg (q.v.) lived and which provided the environment for his books "*Hemsöborna*" (The Inhabitants of Hemsö) and "*Skärkarlsliv*" (The Life of a Skerryman).

A large number of sizeable islands lie off the Roslagen coast. These can be reached by car ferries. There are several nature reserves in the archipelago and one national park, Ängsö, which is south of Norrtälje. Numerous authors and artists have been inspired by the archipelago, such as Elias Sekelstedt, Albert Engström (q.v.), Gustaf Hellström, Sven Barthel, Bruno Liljefors (q.v.), Axel Sjögren, and Roland Svensson.

ARCHITECTURE (CONTEMPORARY). Housing in the 19th century was very dense as a result of rapid population growth at the end of the century. Authorities and residents eventually protested such living conditions and, simultaneously, new interest bloomed in the ideal of living closer to nature. At this time various influences from other countries reached Sweden. This all led to a new pattern of city planning and new types of dwellings. Before World War I, trade and industry flourished and the public sector grew. Many schools, railroad stations, hospitals, banks, and offices were built, with new materials leading to new types of buildings. A search for new architectural styles began with the new century and most foreign influences came from Germany. Classicism gained popularity and became the principal style during the 1920s. But at the same time, a new domestic style of architecture arose in Scandinavia. It borrowed freely from Sweden's medieval heritage, and the movement came to be known as "national romanticism." Stockholm City Hall *(Stadshuset)* (q.v.), built from 1911 to 1923, is an example of this style; the building was meant to invoke a feeling of history.

Thus came a break from the eclectic style of the 19th century, and a modern movement was heralded that would emerge at the Stockholm Exhibition (q.v.) of 1930. During the early 20th century, construction was still carried out by private business, and government attempted to counter low housing standards by introducing housing policies. Generally speaking, home-building has been the most important political issue facing the construction industry in the 1900s.

In the 1920s, a sober neo-classicism came to replace national romanticism in architecture. Gunnar Asplund was one of the leading architects during the period of functionalism. He is perhaps most associated with the Stockholm City Library (q.v.), built from 1924 to 1927. Poor housing conditions after WWI led to an increased commitment by the government to housing construction, supported by state loans. The catch phrase of the period was "light, air, and greenery."

Functionalism was given a great boost by the Stockholm Exhibition (q.v.) in 1930, and made its mark on the architecture of the time.

The post-war years saw a boom in urban area building. This continued through the affluent 1960s. There was considerable suburban development with large, rather unattractive blocks of apartment buildings. The demolition of many old buildings of architectural interest in the 1970s, as part of a rebuilding program for the city center, created much opposition.

The severe climate during half of the year makes glassed-in spaces and galleries very attractive. The project Vasa Terminal in Stockholm includes blocks of offices with glassed-in courtyards. In 1962, the government introduced state loans for art in residential areas. An interesting example of art within an industrial area is that around the Tomteboda Postal Terminal in Solna. The largest public art project in Sweden is the Stockholm subway. The turn of the last century was a transition period in Swedish architecture. The situation seems similar today. Stockholm offers remarkable opportunities to view examples of past and present styles.

See also TOWN PLAN (17th CENTURY).

ARKITEKTURMUSEUM. See MUSEUM OF ARCHITECTURE.

ARLANDA AIRPORT. See STOCKHOLM ARLANDA.

ARMY MUSEUM. Located at Riddargatan 11, the building, Stora Tyghuset, is within Artillerigården, which was erected in 1760. An extra story was added in 1883. The museum provides insight into the defense of the country over the centuries, with an emphasis on the time of Karl XII (q.v.). There also is a collection of flag trophies from battles during the Era of Great Power (q.v.).

ART MUSEUMS AND GALLERIES. See APPENDIX NO. 6.

ARVFURSTEN'S MANSION. Situated in Gustav Adolf's (q.v.) Square (q.v.), it was designed by architect E. Palmstedt (q.v.) and erected between 1783 and 1794. The west gate still remains from the original building that stood on the site—the old Torstenson Mansion, owned by Princess Sofia Albertina. In 1902, the state took over Arvfursten's Mansion. In 1906, *Utrikesdepartementet* (The Swedish Foreign Office) moved into the building, which contains some magnificent Gustavian-style rooms.

ÅSÖBERGET. This region, on Söder (q.v.), is well-known for its old houses.

ASPLUND, ERIK GUNNAR (1885–1940). An architect who, in 1930, headed an exhibition at Ladugårdsgärde to promote the new style of functionalism (q.v.). His design for *Stadsbiblioteket* (q.v.) (City Library) was ahead of its time.
See STOCKHOLM'S EXHIBITION.

ASTRID, PRINCESS (1905–1935). On November 4, 1926, Princess Astrid married Crown Prince Leopold of Belgium in Stockholm. She was tragically killed in an automobile crash in Switzerland.

AUTHORS. Many authors are, or were, associated with Stockholm by residence and/or their writings. A list—which includes the anonymous creator of *Erikskrönikan* (Eriks Chronicle) of the 1330s as well as authors through the 1990s—can be found in APPENDIX NO. 5.
See also ALMQVIST, BELLMAN, BLANCHE, BREMER, ERIKSKRÖNIKAN, FOGELSTRÖM, JOHANSSON (LUCIDOR), KEY, LAGERLÖF, LINDGREN, LO-JOHANSSON, SÖDERBERG, STAGNELIUS, WÄSTBERG, and STRINDBERG.

AUTOMOBILES. Like most large cities, Stockholm has problems with the large number of cars that crowd streets, pollute the atmosphere, and create parking difficulties. But in 1919, when the speed limit was increased from 9 miles per hour to 12 miles per hour, there were only 624 automobiles registered in the city. On January 1, 1994, there were 155,214 passenger automobiles registered in Stockholm. About 7.2 percent of families have more than one automobile. The total number of private automobiles, light trucks, heavy trucks, and buses passing 23 selected positions in the city between 6 a.m. and 9 p.m. on a weekday at the end of October 1992 was 473,110, of which 430,990 were private automobiles.
On March 7, 1988, authorities decided to ban all automobile traffic in central Stockholm for one day of the year. However, when it was discovered that this would be illegal, a compromise was reached. On a voluntary basis, there was no traffic for five hours on Sunday, October 2, between Götgatan and Odenplan. Simulated traffic accidents were set up along the route.
The number of traffic offenses reported in the beginning of 1994 for the previous 12 months was 11,327. Of these, 2,127 were for driving under the influence of alcohol. The percentage of reported offenses solved was 89 percent. The figures for traffic offenses and percentage solved are almost the same as those for 1980. Alcohol offenses had fallen from 2,326.

B

BAGARMOSSEN. During and after World War II, mostly large apartment blocks were constructed. The suburb of Bagarmossen typifies this style of living.

BALLET. Classical ballet is performed at Dansens Hus, at Barnhusgatan 12–14. The stage is in *Folkets hus* (The People's Building) (q.v.), where there is also a museum of dance. Ballet also is performed at *Operan*, at Gustav Adolf's Square (q.v.), and at the Drottningholm Palace Theater (q.v.).

Tickets must be booked months in advance, although at *Norrmalmstorg* (Norrmalm's Square) there is a booth where last-minute tickets are sold, when available.

BANDHAGEN. A suburb containing many home-owner properties, mainly terrace houses, built in the 1950s.

BATTLE OF BRUNKEBERG. See BRUNKEBERG.

BECKHOLMEN. An island named for the process of heating tar to obtain pitch. Serious fire hazards required that the operation take place on such an isolated island, away from buildings. Tar and pitch were important wares for ships of the 17th century.

BELLEVUE. An area of hilly promontory in Brunnsviken. As the name implies, Bellevue offers magnificent views, which are enjoyed from its many footpaths. Nearby is Birgerjarlsgatan and, high on the cliff, is an isolation hospital.

BELLMAN, CARL MICHAEL (1740–1795). This much-loved troubadour was born in Daureska House at 29 Hornsgatan, which was demolished in 1905. A memorial plaque marks the site. He subsequently lived in various houses in Stockholm. His writings on Stockholm life in the second half of the 18th century made him one of Sweden's greatest and most cherished poets. His verses were populated by wenches and nymphs, tipplers and troublemakers. He based many of his literary figures on characters from real life: Father Movitz, Corporal Mollberg, the clock-maker Fredman and the beautiful Ulla Winblad. It was in rooms at Yrvädersgränd that he wrote *Fredmans epistlar*. The rooms are open on the first Sunday of every month. Bellman died in his house at Kungsholmsbrogatan in Klara district. A bust of Bellman, sculptured by J.N. Byström, was unveiled in Djurgården (q.v.) in 1829 before large crowds.

BELLMANHUSET *(THE HOUSE OF BELLMAN)*. The house at Yrväd-ersgränd 3 was erected in 1723 for a blacksmith, Adam Wollman, after the great fire in Katarina community earlier in the year. The house was restored from 1938 to 1941 for Pär Bricole; it typifies the simpler, 18th-century, middle-class family house. Bellman (q.v.) lived in the house from 1770 to 1774.

BENGTSSON, JÖNS. See ARCHBISHOP JÖNS BENGTSSON.

BERGIAN BOTANICAL GARDENS. Situated at Frescati, at Stockholm University, north of the city center, on the eastern shore of Brunnsviken. It includes a tropical plant house, which contains a number of remarkable cacti and exotic orchids. Nearby is Brunnsviken Park. Of particular attraction is the huge water lily named Victoria. The plant's leaves grow up to 2.5 meters in diameter, making it one of the biggest plants in the world. The gardens were originally donated to *Vetenskapsakademien* (The Swedish Royal Academy of Sciences) (q.v.) by the brothers Bengt and Jonas Bergius, former students of the renowned scientist Carl von Linné, through the Bergian Foundation. After their death, the society kept the house at Karlbergs-vägen with its garden and library to serve as a horticultural school and center for botanical research. In 1884, the establishment was sold and, simultaneously, land in Frescati was put into use as a botanical garden. The garden was taken over by the state in 1964 and has been operated by Stockholm University since 1977, in cooperation with the Bergian Foundation.

BERGMAN, INGMAR (1918–). This world-renowned film director has many connections with Östermalm. He was born and grew up in a house belonging to the hospital, Sophia Home, on Valhallavägen, then in a parish house at Östermalmstorg. His father was a minister at Hedvig Eleonora Church. Bergman now lives at Karlaplan. He saw some of his first films as a child, at *Fågel Blå* (The Blue Bird) at Skeppargatan 60. He has directed many films at the state-financed Film House studios near Gärdet, including *Fanny and Alexander*. Among his other films are *Gycklarnas afton* (The Jesters' Evening) of 1953, *Sommarnattens leende* (Smiles of a Summer Night) of 1955, *Det sjunde inseglet* (The Seventh Seal) 9 of 1957, *Smultron stället* (Wild Strawberries) of 1957, *Såsom i en spegel* (Through a Glass Darkly) of 1961, and *Tystnaden* (Silence) of 1963. From 1936 to 1966 he was the director of *Dramaten* (The Royal Theater), where he still occasionally directs plays.

BERGSHAMRA. See SOLNA.

BERNADOTTE APARTMENTS. Located in the Royal Palace (q.v.), the apartments may be viewed by the public. King Oscar II (q.v.) and Queen Sofia were the last king and queen to reside in the Bernadotte apartments. Initially, these apartments were furnished for Fredrik I (q.v.) and Queen Eleonora the younger, but the first royal couple to move in after the work was completed in 1754 was Adolf Fredrik (q.v.) and Lovisa Ulrika.

BERNADOTTE DYNASTY. The Bernadotte family comes from Pau, in southern France. It is from there that the present Swedish royal house originates. The founder of the dynasty in Sweden was Karl XIV Johan (q.v.).

BERNS' RESTAURANT (BERNS SALONGER). This popular restaurant was opened in 1863 at Näckströmsgatan 8. In the beginning of the 1850s, Berzeli Park, where the retaurant is now situated, was created and nearby Norrmalmstorg was altered. In 1854, Henrik Robert Berns opened the Swiss-style *Gröna Stugan* (The Green Cottage) and in 1863 opened Berns Salong, in the building that now faces the park. During the 1870s, Berns was a well-regarded cabaret-café. In 1895, it became a variety-hall, but suffered under the "variety restrictions" of 1896 and resumed its activities as a concert café. Not until the removal of the variety restrictions in 1955 did Berns resume its variety programs. Berns Salong became widely known through August Strindberg's (q.v.) book *Röda rummet* (The Red Room). Now it is known as Stockholm's temple of entertainment, magnificent with its cut-glass chandeliers.

On February 20, 1989, Berns' Saloon reopened after extensive repairs and renovations. To finance improvements and running costs, the restaurant and cabaret have been combined with conference rooms and a five-story hotel. The adjacent old China Theater has been converted into a conference hall.

BERTIL, PRINCE (1912–). Born the third son of King Gustav VI Adolf (q.v.), he is Duke of Halland.

BERWALD HALL. The building on the corner of Strandvägen and Gördesgatan that is the Swedish Radio Symphony Orchestra's concert hall. It was built from 1976 to 1979 under the direction of a team of architects.

BERZELIUS HOUSE. Situated at Frescati, this museum is dedicated to the memory of the chemist Jöns Jacob Berzelius (q.v.) (1779 to 1848) and his research. His technical apparatus and laboratory are on display.

BERZELIUS, JÖNS JAKOB (1799–1848). One of the best-known chemists of his time and possibly one of the best researchers of nature ever. In chemistry, he produced a classification order similar to Linné's contribution within the field of botany. His system of chemical nomenclature is still used. For the last three years of his life, Berzelius was secretary of the Academy of Science (q.v.).

BILDT, CARL (1949–). A politician who became a member of Parliament in 1979, leader of the Moderate Party in 1986, and prime minister of a four-party, non-socialist government in September 1991. He supported the idea of Sweden joining the European Community (EC) and the referendum narrowly voted in favor of so doing. Sweden thus applied for full membership in the European Community in 1991. Sweden has been a member of the European Union (EU) since January 1, 1995.

In the spring of 1995, he became the EU's representative in the negotiations attempting to bring about peace in the former-Yugoslavia. He soon became unacceptable to some antagonists, who did not consider him to be sufficiently impartial; he tended to be more outspoken than some of his predecessors.

BIRGER JARL (died in 1266). Jarl is the Swedish word for earl. Birger Magnusson is usually referred to as Birger Jarl. It is often claimed that Earl Birger was the founder of Stockholm in 1252, as incorrectly written on the base of his statue on Riddarholm (q.v.). However, he may be said to have established Stockholm during the 13th century. Earl Birger Magnusson was regent from 1248 to 1266. He was a member of the Folkunga dynasty (q.v.).

BIRGER JARL'S STATUE. On October 20, 1854, B.E. Fogelberg's statue of Birger Jarl was unveiled on Riddarholmen. Thereafter, the site was called Birger Jarl's Square.

BIRGER JARL'S TOWER. Earl Birger's Tower was not built by Birger Jarl, even if it looks as if it dates from the Middle Ages. The tower was built in 1527 by the country's father figure, Gustav Vasa (q.v.). Material taken from Klara Kloster (q.v.), which was demolished that year, were used. In the 18th century, the tower was built and topped with a copper roof in rococo style.

BIRKA. This important early settlement and harbor on Lake Mälaren (q.v.) is situated on the island of Björkö. Birka is considered to be the first Viking trading center and was Sweden's first town. From here Vikings traded with the whole of Scandinavia and spread into Russia and much of Europe. Birka was most active in the 9th and 10th centuries A.D., when it is thought that there were about 1,000 inhabitants, but later it declined in importance. Ansgar, archbishop of Hamburg, sent missionaries to Birka in 829 to 830, and again in 850, and Birka became the center for Sweden's conversion to Christianity. Around the town was a protective wall, large sections of which remain, and nearby was a stronghold and harbor.

Many archeological digs have been conducted. A necropolis with approximately 3,000 graves has been located, and more than 1,000 of them have been thoroughly examined. The findings helped to define the extent of the trading from Birka. Discoveries included Arabic coins and silver ornaments, Friesian pottery, French glass and native articles of iron, bronze, horn, and bone. The graves are either mounds or megalithic monuments of various kinds; three are pointed or with stones laid to form the outline of a ship. One recent find at Birka proved that the Vikings also used cavalry, enabling them to travel swiftly during their landings. The Norsemen were both seamen and horsemen. Ansgar's Chapel on Birka was consecrated in 1930. Its fittings include works by Carl Milles (q.v.), Olle Hjortzberg, Gunnar Torhamn, and Carl Eldh (q.v.).

BJÖRKHAGEN. During and after World War II, mostly large apartment blocks were constructed. The suburb of Björkhagen typifies this living style.

BLACK FRIARS. The large library of the Black Friars was destroyed by fire in 1407. Sten Sture the younger was buried in the Black Friars' Monastery in 1520. See also *DOMINICAN MONKS*.

BLÅKULLA. See SOLNA.

BLANCHE, AUGUST. (1811–1868). This author grew up in the Klara district of Stockholm and was the great descriptive writer about the capital, between the time of Bellman and that of Stringberg and Söderberg (qq.v.). He became one of the most popular Swedish authors. Klara and Norrmalm (qq.v.) were the main centers in his writings.

He died suddenly, after having spoken at the unveiling ceremony of the statue of Karl XII. On Karlavägen, opposite Östermalm School, is erected a memorial plaque, on the site of his town house.

BLASIEHOLMEN. Blasieholmen was originally an island called Käpplingeholmen, and nearby was the small *Kyrkoholmen* (Church Island). Thereafter, the latter was called Skeppsholmen, when the main naval base was moved there in the late 16th century. After the region between Norrström and Nybroviken was filled, Blasieholmen and Kyrkholmen became a headland. It is thought that Blasieholmen got its present name from a Scottish merchant, Blasius Dundie, who often was in that part of Stockholm in the 1590s. On June 12, 1822, Blasieholmen was swept by fire and Holm Church burned down. In the middle of the 19th century, Blasieholmen gained a reputation of refinement and several cultural institutions were situated there, including the National Museum.

BLASIEHOLM CHURCH. When this Lutheran church was built, from 1865 to 1867, it was Stockholm's largest premises for preaching.

BLOCK-MAKER'S HOUSE. Located at Stigbergsgatan 21, on Södermalm, where Andersson the block-maker made block and tackle rigs for sailing ships in the early 1900s. The house, now a museum, features a typical interior of that era. The building itself dates back to the early 18th century. It is only open for brief periods during early and late summer, so it is advisable to make inquiries before visiting. It is under the control of the City Museum of Stockholm.

"BLOODBATH". See STOCKHOLM "BLOODBATH".

BOLLHUSET (Ball building). Originally a large building for ball games. Such structures were common in large European cities in the 16th and 17th centuries. Stockholm had two, and both were situated on Slottsbacken (q.v.). Stora Bollhuset (the larger) became a theater in 1700. Lilla Bollhuset (the smaller) became the Finnish Church. The opera was opened in *Bollhuset* on January 18, 1773.

BONDE MANSION. Situated at Riddarhustorget 8, building commenced in the 1670s for the National Treasurer, Gustav Bonde, who died before it was completed. It was once one of the large private palaces owned by generals of the Era of Great Power (q.v.). The architects were Tessin the elder and Jean de la Vallée (q.v.). In 1731, the palace was rebuilt and wings were added. A story was added in 1754. From 1732 to 1915, the palace was used as Stockholm's City Hall *(Stadshuset)*. The building was restored from 1947 to 1949. It now houses the offices of the Swedish Supreme Court (q.v.). In 1810, Lord High Steward Axel von Fersen (q.v.) was murdered outside the palace by an angry mob. See also HASSELBY PALACE.

BÖRSEN. See STOCK EXCHANGE.

BÖRSHUSET. See STOCK EXCHANGE.

BRAHE'S PALACE. See LOUIS DE GEER'S PALACE.

BRAHE, EBBA (1596–1674). Ebba is probably best-known as the lover of Gustav II Adolf (q.v.), however, the widowed Queen Kristina (q.v.) was against this relationship. She subsequently married Jakob de la Gardie (q.v.).

BRAHE, ERIK. Erik Brahe and others were executed on July 23, 1756, on Riddarholmen (q.v.) in an open area between the church and the bridges, for participation in an attempted revolution.

BRÄNDA TOMTEN. At the end of Själagatan is a square named Brända Tomten, which means burned site. It was thus named because a house burned down there in 1728. It was not rebuilt, but the square was kept as a turning place for horses and carts.

BRÄNNKYRKA. On January 1, 1913, Brännkyrka was incorporated into Stockholm, thereby increasing the population by 25,216 inhabitants. Around the turn of the century, estates and parcels of land in Brännkyrka were acquired by the city for future house construction and the creation of a residential suburb.

Stockholm's annual book of statistics states that Brännkyrka has the best-attended church, with an average congregation of 186 people each Sunday.

BRANTING, HJALMAR (1860–1925). One of Sweden's most highly regarded politicians. He played an important part, even if behind the scenes, in averting a revolution in 1917. He was prime minister three times and leader of the Social Democratic Party. He was first elected to the *Riksdag* (q.v.) in 1886. The funeral procession of Hjalmar Branting was joined by more than 100,000 people.

BREMER, FREDRIKA (1801–1865). An author born in Finland who was brought to Sweden as a baby. She grew up in Stockholm and on the family estate at Årsta, just south of the capital. In her novels, she depicted her upper middle-class background, decried the lot of women, and was very much a child of the age of liberalism. Her novels included *Teckningar utur vardagslivet* (Sketches From Everyday Life) in 1828, *Grannarne* (The Neighbors), *Hemmet* (The Home), *Hemmen i Nya Världen* (The Homes in the New World), and *Hertha eller en själs historia* (Hertha or A Soul's History) in 1858. The latter is regarded as an important work on women's rights. Soon after its publication, many of the ideas that Fredrika Bremer backed were realized. She later travelled a great deal, to Switzerland, Italy, Palestine, Turkey, and Greece. Her best literary works are considered to be two travel books (regarded as the best of their kind in the Swedish language), rather than her earlier novels.

BROMMA. Around the turn of the century, estates and areas of land in Bromma were acquired by the city for future construction and the creation of a residential suburb.

This community of 6,212 inhabitants was incorporated into Stockholm on January 1, 1916. Bromma Airport was officially opened in 1936. After the opening of Arlanda Airport (q.v.), Bromma has steadily declined in importance. There have been long discussions about its closure. In 1993, there were 35,150 landings. The Stockholm Chamber of Commerce makes a strong case for retaining it, and points out that with 600,000 passengers a year it is still Sweden's sixth-largest airport. It also claims that it is quicker to reach central Stockholm from Bromma.

BROMMA CHURCH. A round, fortress-type building and Stockholm's oldest. It was erected with two stories late in the 12th century. Later, it was enlarged by the addition of a sacristy, burial chapel, tower, and spire. The church was restored in 1680. In Solna (q.v.) and Munsö, 25 kilometers northwest of Drottningholm (q.v.), there are two similar round churches, also built in the 12th century.

BRUNKEBERG, BATTLE OF. On October 10, 1471, Sten Sture the elder led the Swedes to victory over Kristian I and the Danes. However, this was far from a straightforward struggle between two nations. Many interests were involved, and Swedes fought on both sides. Among them were members of families who were later called Oxenstierna and Vasa (q.v.). German and Scottish mercenaries were also involved.

BRUNKEBERGSÅSEN (BRUNKEBERG RIDGE). An "ås" is a gravel ridge usually formed by glacial deposits. Brunkebergsåsen is in Stockholm, but it is part of a long ridge that can be traced through the whole of the Uppland province. In Stockholm, it runs from Enskede and Skanstull in the south, over Stadsholmen, Brunkeberg, and Observatoty Hill away to the north. To a considerable extent, the dry gravel of the ridge had a great influence on building and road construction and on the way in which the original site of Stockholm has evolved.

In 1636, a small wooden chapel was erected here, where Johannes'

Church (q.v.) now stands. A new beacon tower was erected in 1683 on the southern side of Brunkeberg, from which time signals and warnings of fire could be seen and heard. It was dismantled in 1769. On March 18, 1848, severe street riots broke out at Brunkeberg Square and soon spread to *Gamla stan* (the Old Town) (q.v.). Troops intervened, but were stoned. Military fire wounded and killed a number of people. In 1886, a tunnel through Brunkebergsåsen was opened. Kungsgatan (King's Street) was reopened to traffic on November 24, 1911, after the beginning of construction through the ridge in 1905. It wasn't completed until the 1930s.

BUILDINGS. Stockholm has numerous famous and interesting buildings. Many of them may be visited. Most of the surviving buildings date from the 17th century onwards but there are a few earlier ones. Among the better-known architects are: Adelkrantz, Asplund, Simon, and Jean de la Vallée, Palmstedt, Tengbom, Tessin the elder, and Tessin the younger (qq.v.).
See also APPENDIX NO. 2 for a list of nearly 200 suggested buildings to visit.

BUSES. In 1923, the first motorbus routes in the inner city were opened. Earlier routes, at the end of the 19th century, were powered by horses and steam engines.

BUTTERFLY HOUSE, HAGA PARK. This is the most northerly tropical butterfly house in the world. It is situated in beautiful Haga Park north of the city, and was opened in 1989 as the first tropical butterfly house in Scandinavia. Butterflies fly freely in the 400–square meter hothouse, so whatever the season, visitors can experience a tropical climate. In spring of 1993, Sweden's first tropical aviary was opened nearby. There are free-flying butterflies and birds in 2,000 square meters of indoor, exotic paradise. The aviary has been arranged as an oriental mountain landscape. There are some 30 tropical bird species.

BYKYRKAN. A church erected in 1264 as Bykyrkan and later named St. Nikolai, then *STORKYRKAN* (The Cathedral) (q.v.).

C

CAMPING. Camp sites in Sweden are generally of high quality and provide good facilities. Stockholm has a mobile-home camp site in the Inner City, situated at Fiskartorpsvägen on Östermalm. It provides easy access to the sights and the city center. There also are seven camp sites in Greater Stockholm. See also YOUTH HOSTELS.

CAP PARTY (*MÖSSPARTIET*). A political party given its name in 1738 by the opposition party *Hattpartiet* (The Hat Party) (q.v.). They implied that they were dozing in their night-caps. The Cap Party was in power from 1765 to 1769 and again from 1771 to 1772, during the so-called Age of Liberty, when royal power was weak and parliament dominated. There was a strong rivalry between the Hats and the Caps. The Caps advocated freedom of the press, a more liberal economic policy and social and political debate. They were led by Arvid Horn, a Swedish politician whose forebears were Finnish aristocrats. The Cap's support came largely from farmers and clergy in Finland and on the Swedish west coast, and also attracted the lower aristocracy. Their first priority was that of peace, and the party's policies generally were very cautious.

CARL XVI GUSTAV (1946–). The present king of Sweden. His father, Prince Gustav Adolf, was killed in 1947 in a plane crash. Thus, Carl XVI Gustav succeeded his grandfather, Gustav VI Adolf (q.v.), when he died in 1973. This is the world's third-oldest monarchy. His royal motto is "For Sweden Today." Carl Gustav's mother was Princess Sibylla of Saxe-Coburg-Gotha. He married Silvia Renate Sommarlath in 1976. Although his grandfather had been a popular monarch, there were strong demands for a republic in the latter years of his reign. Many thought his death would precipitate a constitutional change. However, the young king and his commoner bride soon became popular. A daughter, Victoria (q.v.), was born in 1977; a son, Carl Philip in 1979, and another daughter, Madeleine, in 1982. Because of the change made to the Act of Succession in 1980 to allow a woman to succeed to the throne, the heir to the throne is Crown Princess Victoria.

CARLSSON, INGVAR (1934–). As former leader of the Social Democratic Party, Carlsson was *statsminister* (prime minister). He first became a member of the *Riksdag* (q.v.) in 1965. As Olof Palme's (q.v.) deputy, he took over the leadership following Palme's assassination in 1986. Carlsson led a successful party in the 1988 elections; however, in 1991, the Social Democrats lost the elections, and Carlsson resigned the premiership. The Socialist Democratic government was replaced by a four-party coalition. But in 1994, the Social Democrats were once again returned to power, under the leadership of Ingvar Carlsson.

Carlsson announced in August 1995 that he would resign as party leader at the party congress to be held in March 1996, and to resign as prime minister.

In March 1996 Göran Person (q.v.) was voted as leader of the Social Democrats and he succeeded Carlsson as prime minister a few days later.

CAROLINE AUTOCRACY. A period of absolute rule by King Karl XII (q.v.) who reigned from 1682 to 1718.

CAROLINE INSTITUTE. See KAROLINSKA INSTITUTET.

CELSING, PETER (1920–1974). This architect's work of recent decades in Stockholm, will appear as representative of the City of Culture in 1998. He started out in the 1950s providing designs for the spread of subway stations in the suburbs. He designed the church in Vällingby. In the 1960s, he was busy with *Operan* (Opera House) (q.v.) and the high-class restaurant *Operakälllaren* (Opera Cellars). In addition to these Stockholm projects, he was active in other towns, as well. In the 1960s, he designed *Filmhuset* (The Film Building) on Gärdet and *Sergels torg* with *Kulturhuset* (qq.v.). His last great project was *Riksbankshuset* (National Bank Building) on Brunkebergstorg.

CENTRAL RAILROAD STATION. Officially opened in 1871, and altered several times since. Comprehensive alterations were made from 1925 to 1927. A more recent, thorough reconstruction, combined with alterations to the tracks, commenced in 1984. In addition to being the terminal for main-line connections, Central Station also is the hub for local commuter trains and the subway. Commuter trains from Södertälje, in the south, stop at Central Station then continue northward as far as Märsta.

See also *TREDJE SPÅRET* (Third Track).

CHAMBER OF COMMERCE. This non-governmental business organization provides unbiased information on the opportunities and problems faced on the Swedish market. The Stockholm Chamber of Commerce has offices in the very heart of downtown Stockholm, within walking distance of major hotels, banks, and institutions. The address is Box 16050, S–103 22 STOCKHOLM. Telephone: (46 8)-613 18 00.

CHARTER. A Stockholm Charter was first suggested in 1352. This formed an extension of the *landslag* (laws of the realm) drawn up by Magnus Eriksson (q.v.), and appeared as the *stadslag* (town laws) with a special section covering Stockholm.

It commenced with *Konungabalken* (the King's Code) which dealt with the governing of the town by mayors and councillors. It required the presence of a King's representative, especially in the courts of law. It was very similar to the general laws of the realm.

In *Ärvdabalken* (The Inheritance Code), a daughter had the same rights as a son.

The charter included the four rules for keeping the peace, established by Birger Jarl (q.v.).

Jordabalken (The Land Code) consisted of laws governing the purchase of land and buildings in the town.

Byggningabalken (The Building Code) controlled the buildings and streets, and included fire-prevention requirements.

The original charter document no longer exists, but a copy from 1420 is preserved in *Kungliga biblioteket* (The Royal Library) (q.v.).

CHOLERA. The cholera cemetery at Sture Park was used for the last time in 1834, during the epidemic that claimed 3,500 victims in the capital. During 1854–55, cholera again spread through Stockholm.

CHRISTMAS MARKET. See *STORTORGET*.

CITIZENS' BUILDING. See *MEDBORGARHUSET*.

CITY. The city district of Stockholm is an area of 128 hectare (1.28 square kilometer) with only 735 inhabitants. It is bordered to the south by Strömmen (q.v.) and extends as far as Olof Palmes gatan to the north. It stretches from Klaraberg Viaduct to the west, to Berzeli Park to the east. *Sergels torg* (Sergel's Square) is right in the middle. There are 10 embassies in the region, including the new EU delegation (q.v.). The City Terminal, Central Station, Gustav Adolf's Square, *Hötorget* (Haymarket), and Kungsträdgården (qq.v.) all lie within the City district. The area has many positive features, but also attracts drug traffickers and prostitutes.

CITY ARCHIVES. Established in 1930 by the amalgamation of the archives of municipal buildings and the existing city archives and library.

CITY CONFERENCE CENTER. On January 14, 1991, Norra Latin School was opened for the public to see the new City Conference Center within the school. The city had restored and rebuilt the school building at a cost of 72 million SEK.

CITY COUNCIL. See THE INTRODUCTION.

CITY HALL. See *STADSHUSET.*

CITY LIBRARY. See *STADSBIBLIOTEKET.*

CITY MUSEUM OF STOCKHOLM. The City Museum was founded in 1931. It is situated at Ryssgården, on Södermalmstorg near Slussen. It is housed in a town palace, built in Italian baroque style. It was erected as the town hall for Södermalm (q.v.), and was completed in 1685. The architects were Nicodemus Tessin the elder and the younger (qq.v.). The museum mainly contains exhibits of Stockholm's history, the Era of Great Power, and the 18th century, as well as various temporary exhibitions. In the Documentary Room *(Faktarummet),* the public can easily access pictures and other sources relating to Stockholm past and present. There also is a wide variety of exhibits showing the region in the Iron Age; trade and crafts in the 17th century; the Tre Kronor Fort and the Lohe Treasure; life in the industrial city of the 1890s, and topographical art in Stockholm.

CITY TERMINAL. On January 20, 1989, the king opened the new City Terminal in the World Trade Center, a building that stretches between the viaducts over the railroad tracks at Klarabergsgatan and Kungsgatan. The terminal combines the *SJ* (State Railroads) Central Station and the central subway station, with a new airport-bus and long-distance bus terminal.

COMMERCIAL COLLEGE. See *HANDELSHÖGSKOLAN.*

CONCERT HALL *(KONSERTHUSET).* Situated on the corner of Kungsgatan (q.v.) and Sveavägen, at Hötorget (q.v.), it was erected between 1923 and 1926. It is designed in new classical style, and was created by Ivar Tengbom. It is widely considered to be one of the most interesting examples of modern Swedish architecture. Many artists have contributed to the decor, including Isaac Grünewald, who decorated *Lilla salen* (The Little Room). After recent redecorating, the façade once again has the original blue coloring. The unveiling of the sculpture *"Orpheus,"* by Carl Milles (q.v.), took place in 1936 in front of *Konserthuset* (The Concert Hall). *Konserthuset* is the hub of Stockholm's flourishing music life.

COSMONOVA. On October 16, 1992, this new building was opened at the Natural History Museum, Frescativägen 40. It is an omnitheater with a modern planetarium/film theater of vast proportions. It is Sweden's only Omnimax theater and presents shows of the largest format, including virtual reality computerized simulations.

COUNCIL OF MAYORS. Because Stockholm is such a large munici-
pality, its undertakings are divided into Divisions. The eight chief
executives (vice-mayors) of these divisions make up the Council of
Mayors. There also are four oppositional vice-mayors.
As of December 1994, those holding office were:
Finance Division:
Mats Hulth, (Social Democratic Party) (s), mayor
Dag Larsson (s), deputy mayor
City Planning Division: Monica Andersson (s)
Real Estate and Traffic Division: Annika Billström (s)
Schools and Culture Division: Tjia Torpe (s)
Labour Market and Education Division: Bertil Karlberg: (s)
Social Welfare Division: Lena Nyberg (s)
Iris Birath (The Left Party) (v) 1st vice chairperson
Environment and Recreation Division: Margareta Olofsson (v)
Eco Cycle Division: Krister Skånberg, The Green Party (mp)
Carl Cederschiöld The Moderate Party (m), opposition
Agneta Rehnvall (m), opposition
Sten Nordin (m), opposition
Jan Björklund, The Peoples' Party (fp), opposition

COURT HOUSE (*RÅDHUSET*). Erected from 1909 to 1915 at Scheelegatan 7. It is said that the castle in Vadstena served as an inspiration
for its architect, C. Westman. It is in national Vasa style, while the
special interiors are in art nouveau. Sculptures and paintings are by
well-known Swedish artists. In the park outside, a sculpture called
"*Justitia*" by Gustaf Sandberg, was provided in 1917.

COURTS OF LAW. Sweden has a three-tiered hierarchy of general
courts: the district courts *(tingsrätt)*, the courts of appeal *(hovrätt)*,
and the Supreme Court *(högsta domstolen)*.
Stockholm is the largest of the approximately 100 district courts in
the country. It is served by a large number of judges, whereas the
smaller municipalities may have only one or two who are trained in
law.
Sweden has six courts of appeal, of which the oldest and largest is
the *Svea Hovrätt* (Svea Lower Court of Appeal) (q.v.).
The Supreme Court receives appeals against decisions of the courts
of appeal. On the whole, it is only cases that would serve as possible
precedents that are tried before the Supreme Court; five justices sit
on the bench.

CRIME. The total figure for crimes committed in 1993 (statistical information published in 1995) was 158,502. In 1980, it was 124,385.

Burglaries numbered 20,224, compared with 21,310 in 1980. Thefts from motor vehicles was 22,204 (23,247 in 1980). Murder and manslaughter was 37 (19 in 1980). Only one percent of cycle thefts resulted in an arrest.

See also AUTOMOBILES and DRUGS.

CROWN BAKERY. The Crown Bakery, on Sibyllegatan, began operation in 1580.

CULTURAL CAPITAL. Stockholm has been designated as the Cultural Capital of Europe in 1998 by the European Union's Council of Ministers. Stockholm already considers itself to be the cultural center of Sweden and the Baltic region. In the run-up to 1998, Stockholm promises that its cultural life will gain an even higher profile with many new developments and events. Work already has begun on major renovations in the city-center area, as have preparations for the possible staging of the Olympic Games (q.v.) in Stockholm in 2004.

Stockholm has no less than 60 museums. Work on new buildings for the Museum of Modern Art and Swedish Museum of Architecture should be completed by 1997. Stockholm has about 40 stages. The author August Strindberg (q.v.) was honored in the fall of 1995 with a special Strindberg Festival during which many of his plays were staged.

Stockholm also is a living city for art, with about 1,500 active artists. Many contemporary works of art can be found in the galleries along Hornsgatan and in the narrow alleys of the Old Town (q.v.). Some parts of Stockholm's subway have been dubbed "the world's longest art exhibition," with their many sculptures, mosaics, and paintings.

Musical life in Stockholm offers everything from sophisticated international artists to troubadours in the pubs and cafés. The Concert Hall, the Berwald Hall, the Royal Opera House, and, in the summer, the Royal Palace (q.v.) are the main venues for classical music. The Park Theater organizes its popular free performances, and concerts are held outside the National Maritime Museum.

Stockholm's film theaters play an important role in the city's cultural life. Sweden has a long tradition of excellence in film production and, apart from Swedish films, foreign films are screened with their original undubbed sound-tracks. For the past four years, Stockholm has held its own film festival, which takes place in November each year.

The city of Stockholm has established a company, called Stockholm-Cultural Capital of Europe 1998, and has set aside 100 million SEK for use during 1998.

Writer and actor Erland Josephson is chairman of the board of company. The vice-chairman is the city of Stockholm's Deputy Mayor for Schools and Culture Tjia Torpe.

See also ART MUSEUMS AND GALLERIES, FILMS, THEATER.

D

DAGENS NYHETER (The Daily News). A liberal morning newspaper founded in Stockholm in 1864 by Rudolf Wall. It was Sweden's first popular, national newspaper. Chief editors have been Otto von Zweibergh (1898–1921), Sten Dehlgren (1921–46), H. Tingsten (1946–60), and, subsequently, O. Lagercrantz and S.E. Larsson. The current chief editors are Hans Bergström and Arne Ruth. Dagens Nyheter is read in 40 percent of households in the Stockholm region. During the first half of 1995, circulation in the Stockholm region increased by 2,000 to more than 300,000. It publishes approximately 400,000 copies a day.

DALARÖ CUSTOMS MUSEUM. Located at *Tullhuset* (The Customs Building), on the idyllic island of Dalarö to the south of Stockholm's archipelago (q.v.). The customs house was built in 1788, and now is a museum with exhibits that illustrate the long history of customs organization in Sweden, how contraband and liquor were smuggled in, and how today's illegal trade in narcotics is carried out.

DALECARLIA (DALARNA). In 1743, about 4,000 farmers from Dalecarlia, accompanied by 600 soldiers from the Dalecarlia Regiment, marched to Stockholm, arriving on June 20 to protest after the unsuccessful war against Russia. The farmers were armed with a variety of weapons: guns, clubs, halberds, and axes. They were met by King Fredrik outside Norrtull (q.v.). They marched into the city and camped in and around Gustav Adolf's Square (q.v.). The men from Dalarna were defeated in battle by some 2,000 troops stationed in the capital. Many of the farmers were killed, others drowned, and 3,000 were taken prisoner, including most of the soldiers. More people lost their lives than at the infamous Stockholm Bloodbath (q.v.). This event became known as *Stora daldansen* (The Great Dalecarlian Dance). On August 17, the survivors were driven out of town and escorted in a miserable procession back to Dalarna. There is no record of burials of the dead in Stockholm.

In July 1944, new material came to light, that makes it appear as though the call to arms was not a conspiracy against the state but aimed to give the farmers their right of determination in parliament.

DALIN, OLOF von (1708–1763). In December 1732, a newspaper, *Then Swänska Argus* (The Swedish Argus), appeared in the capital.It became quite a sensation in the coming years and was of great importance in the development of the Swedish language. At the time, it was published anonymously by Olof Dalin.

DANDERYD. A municipality north of Stockholm. It now incorporates Djursholm and Stocksund.

DE GEER, LOUIS (1587–1652). A Walloon who moved to Dordrecht, in Holland, from where he conducted a flourishing trade with Sweden during the time of Gustaf Adolf (q.v.). He became a Swedish citizen at the age of 40, but did not move to Sweden for 14 more years. He settled first in Norrköping, but later in Stockholm. He was Sweden's foremost businessman of the time. In addition to developing factories around the country, he also was an arms supplier to the Swedish forces.
     See also LOUIS DE GEER'S PALACE.

DE LA GARDIE, JAKOB (1583–1652). A member of a noble family, he was a count and field marshal in the war against Russia in 1609–1617. He owned a magnificent house, known as *Makalös* (Peerless) (q.v.), and was married to Ebba Brahe (q.v.).

DE LA VALLÉE (1590–1642). Simon de la Vallée, was an architect of great repute. His son, Jean de la Vallée, was also a successful architect and lived from 1620 to 1696. Jean became mayor of Stockholm in 1671. They were both architects of major influence during the Era of Great Power. Their best-known building is *Riddarhuset* (q.v.). They were responsible for many palaces and gardens, which were built for important people.

DENNIS AGREEMENT. A comprehensive project to considerably organize traffic and build new roads in the Stockholm region, whilst bearing the environment in mind.
     It takes its name from Bengt Dennis (q.v.), who heads the project. Its aim is not only to solve today's problems, but to prevent others in the future.
     The Stockholm region's population increases by an average of 12,000 residents a year. During 1994, it rose by about 20,000. Every year, about 7,000 new workplaces are established in the area.

The volume of traffic and the length of a Stockholmer's daily commutes increases all the time. Since 1970, the population of the region's central section (Stockholm, Solna, Sundbyberg) has shrunk by 8 percent. At the same time, the population of the rest of Stockholm county has increased by 40 percent.

Motor vehicles are thought to be responsible for 85 per cent of the air pollution.

Against this background, various proposals have been made. Officials intend to reduce the amount of traffic in the inner city, from 550,000 vehicles a day to 430,000, which was the volume of traffic in 1970. This will be achieved by directing traffic out onto ring roads and by increasing the number of commuters using public and other collective means of transport.

The project includes a third rail track (*tredje spåret*) (q.v.) at Riddarholmen and two new tracks from Stockholm south to Årsta, via a new bridge over Årstaviken. New roads will include an extension to the existing Essingeleden at a cost of 13.5 billion SEK. Thirteen of the new 14 kilometers will be in tunnels. Additionally, there will be an outer ring to link the surrounding communities of the region, at an estimated cost of 8.3 billion SEK. Work already has commenced in some areas, in 1994, and is due to be completed by 2005.

To help offset the cost of these projects, toll fees may be introduced, payable at about 25 toll stations, both automatically and manually operated. It is hoped that tolls will be collected on the inner-ring road by 1999. It is anticipated that tolls will continue until at least 2025.

Other plans include renovations and repairs on the subways, new bus routes and cycle tracks, improvements for pedestrians, better streetcars, etc.

This ambitious Dennis project has caused a great debate, especially at a time of financial difficulty and increased awareness of environmental considerations. Opponents, while recognizing the traffic congestion that cries out for speedy remedies, still query the wisdom of sacrificing the beautiful water views to concrete, in the form of bridges and fly-overs. However, the Chamber of Commerce has expressed its regret that after more than four years little seems to have been realized. In February 1997, the Socialist-dominated Stockholm City Council was shaken by an agreement between the Socialist government and the Center Party, which proposes heavy cutbacks in the Dennis Agreement project, from 39.1 billion SEK to 16-18 SEK. These proposals seem almost certain to pass. It is proposed to stop the Österleden (q.v.) and Read Toll projects. The Northern Link and Västerleden projects would be postponed until the next century.

DENNIS, BENGT (1930–). A civil servant, director of Sweden's Central Bank since 1982. After working as a journalist for Stockholms-Tidningen and Sveriges Radio (qq.v.), he began working for the Finance Department in various positions over the years, including the Foreign Office. He later became chief editor of Dagens Nyheter. He currently is in charge of the Dennis Project (q.v.).

DESIDERIA, QUEEN (1777–1860). Désirée Clary, daughter of a rich French businessman, married a French general, Jean Baptiste Bernadotte, at the age of 21. In 1810, Sweden invited Bernadotte to become crown prince of Sweden; he accepted. He took the name Karl Johan (q.v.), and she became Desideria. Although she and their son Oscar joined the crown prince in the Swedish capital, Desideria was happier in France, and lived there for many years—despite having become queen of Sweden and Norway in 1818. She left behind little trace of her time in Sweden.

DJURGÅRDEN. A huge island devoted almost entirely to the enjoyment of parkland and open spaces. It stretches out eastward toward the Baltic. Originally, Djurgården was owned by royalty and was named after the animal park that Johan III had arranged for hunting. It was surrounded by a high fence to protect deer and moose against predatory animals. *Djurgården* means animal enclosure.

A few dwellings were erected in 1920 and 1930, concentrated in Djurgårdsstaden, the old wharf area, which was characterized by wooden buildings from the 18th and 19th centuries. The park has open air restaurants in the summer, dance halls, a circus and tivoli, which have been in operation since the 17th century. There are several museums, including Skansen (q.v.) and *Nordiska muséet* (The Nordic Museum) (q.v.). Djurgården represents a much larger area of Stockholm than most people realize.

The island of *Södra Djurgården* (South Djurgården), which is what most people think of as Djurgården, is little more than 4 kilometers long and 1 kilometer wide. The western part of the island is occupied by Skansen, Gröna Lund (qq.v.), restaurants, museums, most of the embassies, and the idyllic wooden houses of Djurgårdsstaden. The rest of South Djurgården is a large park.

Norra Djurgården (North Djurgården) belongs to Ladugårdsgärdet, or Gärdet, in everyday speech. It lies on the northern side of *Djurgårdsbrunnsviken* (Djurgård Creek), with the *Sjöhistoriska* (Maritime History), *Tekniska* (Technology), and *Etnografiska* (People's museums) (qq.v.). The most prominent feature on Djurgården is Kaknästornet (q.v.).

The northern part of North Djurgården is twice the size of the

southern part. North Djurgården is an area of unspoiled beauty to the
north of the inner city. It is almost wild and much money has been
spent to keep it an open-air space for man and nature to share.

South Djurgården has been described as Bellman's (q.v.) terrain.
"City of pride, now I am happy," wrote Bellman, when his character
Mowitz left the bustling city for Djurgården. In 1829, a bust of Bellman, sculptured by J.N. Byström, was unveiled in Djurgården (q.v.)
before large crowds, including King Karl XIV Johan (q.v.). Although
this was 31 years after his death, the Stockholm poet was appreciated
even more than he had been during the halcyon days and those of his
patronage by Gustav III (q.v.). Every year, on the anniversary of the
statue's unveiling on July 26, Bellman Day is celebrated with festivities that last for a whole week.

DJURGÅRD BRIDGE. Opened in 1897, the bridge is decorated with
four sculptured figures from Norse mythology. This formed part of
the special preparations for the Stockholm Exhibition of 1897. The
bridge led to the nearby, newly completed Nordic Museum.
See also STRANDVÄGEN.

DJURSHOLM. The high-class housing area of Djursholm was the first
"alternative residential district." The community was founded in
1889. It gained town status in 1915. Djursholm made use of the railroad from Stockholm Östra (East) to Rimbo, which opened in 1885
and 10 years later was extended from Östra Station to Engelbrektsplan. A sideline came into being in 1890 and more followed later.
The part of the track to Engelbrektsplan was subsequently closed.

Djursholm has become incorporated with Danderyd municipality.

DÖBELN, GEORG KARL von (1758–1820). Probably the most successful army commander during the 1808–1809 war. He is particularly associated with the Battle of Jutas, in Finland, which was the
subject of a poem by Runeberg. However, he fell from favor, was
court-martialed and sentenced to death. But he was pardoned. He is
buried in Johannes' Church graveyard.

DOMINICAN MONKS (BLACK FRIARS). An order first mentioned
in a document dated 1289. The monks built a monastery in the southern part of the city on ground donated in 1336. Its vaulted cellars
survive, although everything above-ground was demolished after the
reformation. See also BLACK FRIARS.

DROTTNINGGATAN (QUEEN STREET). This main street is named
after Queen Kristina (q.v.). It originated as a medieval country road

that wound over the high ridge, northward toward Uppsala. In the beginning of the 17th century, this part of Norrmalm was still not built on beyond the area around present-day Hötorget (q.v.), where the city gates were situated. There was no real town plan before great fires laid waste to this part of town in the first half of the 1600s. Then a main street called *Stora Kungsgatan* (Great King's Street) was built. Its name was later changed to Drottninggatan. On June 8, 1751, extensive acts of arson raged in Stockholm, severely damaging Drottninggatan. A proper sidewalk was not provided before 1849.

Popular and every day life can be found on Drottninggatan which runs in a northwesterly direction. Most of it is a pedestrian precinct.

DROTTNINGHOLM PALACE. Drottningholm Palace was first called Torvesund. It became royal property in the time of Gustav Vasa (q.v.). It was given its present name when Johan III had a stone house built on the grounds. It was named after Drottning (Queen) Katarina Jagellonica. After passing through several hands, Drottningholm was bought by the widow Queen Hedvig Leonora. It was rebuilt after a fire in 1660. Nicodemus Tessin the elder (q.v.) supervised most of the reconstruction of the main building and some wings and pavilions before his death. Tessin the elder is best-known for his building of this palace, which is on Lovön in Lake Mälaren (q.v.), between 1662 and 1686. From 1695 to 1700, Nicodemus Tessin the younger worked on the interior of the palace and the terraces and French garden, giving them a baroque style. The gardens are sometimes called "a miniature Versailles." In 1744, the palace was given to crown princess Lovisa Ulrika (q.v.). It was Gustav III's (q.v.) favorite palace, and court life at Drottningholm reached its zenith.

The English Park was the work of Adelcrantz (q.v.), who also was responsible for the uniquely preserved Drottningholm Theater (q.v.) and the rococo palace, called Kina (China), which is considered to be one of the finest Chinese-influenced buildings in Europe.

Drottningholm Palace is now the residence of King Carl XVI Gustaf (q.v.) and Queen Silvia. It was recently placed on UNESCO's "World Heritage" list.

DROTTNINGHOLM PALACE THEATER AND THEATER MUSEUM. Situated adjacent to Drottningholm Palace, it is the world's best-preserved 18th-century theater, including the original scenery, which is still in use. It was built in 1766 to replace an earlier building, erected in 1754, which had been destroyed by fire in 1762. It is said that only the lighting, the actors, and the audience have changed since the performances in the reign of King Gustav III (q.v.). The king was an enthusiastic supporter of the arts, with a keen interest in the theater. He was much encouraged in this by his mother, Queen Lovisa Ulrika (q.v.). Having fallen into disrepair after the death of Gustav III, the theater was rediscovered in 1921, and has become a living theatrical museum. An exhibition showing the development of scenery art is located in the Hertig Carls Pavilion, next to the theater.

DROTTNINGHUSET (THE QUEEN'S HOUSE). A beautiful 17th century building in Johannesgatan, standing opposite Johannes' Church. The house was built for Queen Ulrika Eleonora (q.v.) as a retreat for elderly ladies, a function it still serves.

DRUGS. Like most large cities and towns, Stockholm has its share of drugs. Sweden also is known for its liberal attitude toward many aspects of life. However, Mats Hulth and opposition leader Carl Cederschiöld have jointly addressed the prime minister to express their concern over activities to legalize drugs. In April 1944, 21 European cities signed the Stockholm Resolution and formed the European Cities Against Drugs (ECAD). It advocates restrictive drug policies and rejects all attempts to legalize narcotic substances. The cities particularly renounce any distinction between so-called hard and soft drugs.

The number of drug offenses recorded for 1993 was 4,455. In 1980, it was 3,456. The percentage of reported crimes solved was 76 percent, compared with 79 percent in 1980.

In 1995, Stockholm was awarded the biennial FMN (Fight Against Drugs) prize for its initiative in forming ECAD.

DUVBERG. See SUNDBYBERG.

E

EAST ASIAN MUSEUM. See MUSEUM OF EASTERN ANTIQUITIES.

EBBA BRAHE'S HOUSE. During the prosperous days of the Era of Great Power (q.v.), the nobility built so-called summer houses out on the islands of Stockholm, where they could retire to relax, especially during the warm, summer months. As a supplement to *Makalös* (Peerless), the grand palace on Norrström belonging to Count Jakob de la Gardie (1583–1652), a less pretentious house was built on Södermalm. This house has carried the name of Jakob's wife, Countess Ebba Brahe (1596–1674) (q.v.), as she survived him by more than 20 years. The building still exists, at Götgatan 16, but the surrounding terraces, garden, and water displays have long since disappeared, leaving only the terrace wall. In spite of much rebuilding, the house is still a fine example of the Dutch classic style.

ECONOMIC BALANCE. On December 31, 1994, Stockholm City's financial balance showed a loss of 156 million SEK, down by 99 million SEK when compared with 1993. The city's debt in overseas currencies rose to the equivalent of 1.572 million SEK, 91 percent of which is in ECU.

EDUCATION. Statistics concerning the highest level of education of individual members of the population of Stockholm between ages 16 and 74 were as follows: basic comprehensive school education, 23 percent, higher secondary education (*gymnasie*), 41 percent, and post-*gymnasie* education, 30 percent.

Information is unavailable for the remaining 5 percent.

The corresponding figures for *Stockholms län* (Stockholm County) are 26, 43, 26, and 4 percent respectively.

The above statistics are taken from the Statistical Yearbook of Stockholm 1995 and are dated December 31, 1993.

The number of students attending comprehensive schools during the fall semester of 1993 were as follows: in Stockholm community schools, 50,426, in private schools, 4,463. Private schools are uncommon in Sweden, but those there are tend to be concentrated in Stockholm.

The number of students attending *gymnasier* (upper secondary schools) during the fall semester of 1993 was 22,231, of whom 1,934 were in private schools.

The latest statistics for the number of students registered at colleges are from the fall semester of 1992. For the Stockholm region, the total was 48,751, of whom 11,302 were freshmen.

Stockholm has various types of colleges.

Those providing education for administrative, economic, and social occupations include *Handelshögskolan* (Commercial College), *Sköndalsinstitutet* (Sköndals Institute), and Stockholm University.

Those providing education for cultural and information occupations include *Danshögskolan* (College of Dance), *Dramatiska institutet* (Institute of Dramatics), *Grafiska institutet* (Institute of Graphics), *Konstfackskolan* (Technical School of Art), *Konsthögskolan* (College of Art), *Musikhögskolan* (College of Music), *Operhögskolan* (College of Opera), *Teaterhögskolan* (College of Theater), and Stockholm University.

Those providing education for technical occupations include

Högskolan för lärarutbildning (Teacher Training College), *Tekniska högskolan* (Technical College) and Stockholm University.

Those providing education for the teaching profession include *Högskolan för lärarutbildning* (Teacher Training College), *Idrottshögskolan* (College of Sport), *Konstfackskolan* (Technical School of Art), *Musikhögskolan* (College of Music),

Musikpedagogiska institut (Institute of Music Teaching), and Stockholm University.

Those providing education for medical care include *Ersta diakonissällskaps sjuksköterskehögskola* (Ersta Deaconess' Society Nurses College), *Karolinska institutet* (The Caroline Institute), *Röda korset* (Red Cross), *Sofiahemmet* (The Sophia Home), and *Vårdhögskolan* (College of Medical Care).

Those providing noncategorized education include *Tekniskahögskolan* (Technical College), Stockholm University (q.v.), and other colleges.

See also SCHOOLS.

EKOPARKEN. In May 1995, King Carl Gustav officially opened Ekoparken. Called *"Stockholm's Green Lung,"* Ekoparken actually had served as the city's national park since the beginning of the year. It is Sweden's first such park mixing nature and culture. It has three palaces, 30 museums, a pleasure park and theaters. *Ekoparken* derives its name from "ecology park." It is also known as the National City Park. It comprises Skeppsholmen-Kastellholmen, South and North Djurgården (q.v.), Fjäderholmarna, Haga-Brunnsviken, Ulriksdal (q.v.), and Sörentorp.

The area gives shelter to many different flora and fauna, some of which are quite rare. Among the mammals are foxes, badgers, martens, mink, deer, and moose. Three kinds of earthworms recently have been discovered that are not found anywhere else in the world. Hundreds of types of birds nest there—more than 250 species have been recorded. Eight of Uppland's 11 types of bats live in the park. Two-thirds of the flowers in Uppland grow in the area. In addition to gardens and cultivated parkland, there are sections in which nature has been relatively undisturbed. On South Djurgården, close to Djurgårdsbrunn Canal, there is a lake, Isbladskäret, which is the home of numerous and varied waterfowl, including heron and the rare gadwell. Lappskärrsberget and Stora Skuggan are the wildest sections of Ekoparken.

Since 1988, the area has been given a facelift. At Stora Skuggan, there are giant oaks sheltering rare insects. Huge pine trees grow near Bergshamra, where Karl XII (q.v.) used to hunt bear. Gustav III also intended the area to be a royal hunting ground and parklandscape of unique grace.

Ulriksdal, Rosendal, and Haga (qq.v.) are Ekoparken's three palaces. Lord High Constable Jacob de la Gardie shaped the estate called Jakobsdal, and by 1644 the castle, built in German-Dutch renaissance style, was completed. His son, Magnus Gabriel, extended the garden. It became a magnificent park in baroque style. Near the palace, in the little stream Igelbäcken, swim rare fish known as *grönling*. Bellevue is one of the four English parks, set out around Brunnsviken. Carl Eldh's studio (q.v.) is now a museum. This area was one of August Strindberg's favorite walks, and he presented a statue that was erected there in 1909. Occassionally, there are opportunities to tour by boat through the park. (Tel: 08–24 04 70)

Information about Ekoparken will be presented in an exhibition at the Natural History Museum (q.v.), until 1997.

EKOTEMPLET. After a yearlong restoration, work was completed on *Ekotemplet* (The Echo Temple) in Haga Park (q.v.) in the spring of 1993. The building was erected in 1790, but it was restored to the way it looked in 1846.

ELDH'S STUDIO MUSEUM. Carl Eldh was born in 1873 and he became a well-known sculptor. Eldh's studio has been a museum since 1963. In Djurgården (q.v.) stands Eldh's statue of Gunnar Wennerberg, composer of Gluntarna. Gluntarna are similar to the Bellman (q.v.) style, popular with student choirs. Also in Stockholm are Eldh's monuments to the author Strindberg (q.v.) and the politician Branting (q.v.).

ELDKVARN. In 1806, a new mill replaced the old windmill on the site where the City Hall *(Stadshuset)* (q.v.) now stands. It was an impressive building for the time, four stories tall and topped with a chimney. A fire destroyed the steam-mill on October 31, 1878. The fire had such a great impact on the people of Stockholm that it became common practice to date events as happening before or after the mill fire.

See also NORRA MÄLARSTRAND.

ELECTRICAL ENERGY PRODUCTION. By the end of 1993, Stockholm was getting 28 percent of its electrical energy from hydro-electricity, 35 percent from atomic power stations and 32 percent from heat-power sources.

EMPLOYERS. At the end of 1992, there were 17 business enterprises in Stockholm employing more than 2,000 people. By far the largest was the post office, with 13,306 employees. *Televerket* (The telephone company) employed 6,756 people; L.M. Ericsson (telephone manufacturers) 5,930 (see TELEPHONES); Skandinaviska Enskilda Bank, 4,070. The remaining companies employed between 2,000 and 3,000 people.

ENGELBREKTSSON, ENGELBREKT (died 1436). Engelbrekt arrived in Stockholm on around August 1, 1434 and led the protest from *Dalarna* (Dalecarlia) (q.v.) against King Erik of Pommerania (q.v.). Engelbrekt assembled the first Swedish *Riksdag* (q.v.) (Parliament) in 1435. The parliament included representatives of the burghers and peasants as well as the nobility and clergy, which was uncharacteristic of the time. In 1436, Engelbrekt and his Swedish followers began to lay siege to the palace. The parliament elected Engelbrekt Regent of Sweden, with the intention to disassociate Sweden from the Kalmar Union (q.v.). Under this threat, those in power conspired to bring about the end of Engelbrekt. In 1434, he was murdered. One of the most highly regarded men of medieval times, he was greatly mourned by the people, who appreciated his efforts to bring an end to the wars and time of misery. On April 27, 1932, a statue of Engelbrekt was unveiled, at the City Hall *(Stadshuset)* (q.v.).

ENGELBREKT'S CHURCH. Situated high above Karlavägen, on Rådmansgatan. The church was built between 1909 and 1914. It was consecrated on January 25, 1914. The building is richly decorated in red brick and granite. In spite of its unique form, the building belongs to the Jugend style of older Swedish brick churches. The ground plan is in the form of a cross in which the center of the cross is clearly raised. The tower is in the southwest corner. The interior has fresco paintings by Olle Hjortzberg and al secco paintings by Filip Månsson. On December 1 1929, Sweden's largest church organ was inaugurated in Engelbrekt's Church.

ENGSTRÖM, ALBERT (1869–1940). An author who is probably best-known for his writings about Småland and Roslagen and his descriptions of the lives of the inhabitants there. In 1897, he founded the humorous paper *Strix*, which he also illustrated. He lived in Stockholm at Fjällgatan 12 (q.v.), but the house was later demolished. He wrote many short stories and anecdotes before becoming a full-fledged author. He also was a professor at the Art High School and, in 1922, became a member of the Swedish Academy (q.v.).

ENSKEDE. Around the turn of the century, estates and areas of land in Enskede were acquired, for residential development. In 1913, Enskede was incorporated into the city. The number of Enskede communities of home-owner properties surrounded by gardens grew during the 1910s, '20s, and '30s. There also are English-style terraced houses.

ERA OF GREAT POWER (*STORMAKTSTIDEN*). The 17th-century period of Sweden's great expansion and domination in Northern Europe. It lasted from the accession to the throne by Gustav II Adolf in 1611, through the reigns of Queen Kristina, Karl X Gustav, and Karl XI, to the death of Karl XII in 1718.

ERICSON, NILS (1802–1870). An engineer who led the building of the Trolhätte canal. He planned and was responsible for the construction of the Slussen (q.v.) sluiceway and the main railroad system, from 1850 through 1862. He was brother of John Ericson, who traveled to America and became world-famous for his development of the ship propeller.

On June 2, 1993, the statue of Nils Ericson was moved from Klara Mälarstrand in Tegelbacken, where it had stood since 1975, to a position in front of Central Station. From 1893 to 1957 it stood in *Järnväg-sparken* (Railroad Park), south of the station building.

ERICSSON, JOHN (1803–1889). The younger brother of Nils Ericson (q.v.) (although they spelled their family name differently). He is one of Sweden's most famous inventors. At age 23, he moved to England, where he invented the steam-fire engine and the propeller. In 1839, he moved to America, where he continued to invent many more products, including the torpedo and hot-air machine. Although he lived much of his life abroad, Ericsson did not lose his love for Sweden, and requested that he be buried there. After his death, his body was carried to Sweden in an American warship, where it was received in Stockholm with great pride and honor.

ERIK VIII OF POMERANIA (1382–1459). Became king of Sweden, Norway, and Denmark in 1397, when he was crowned in Kalmar before the age of 15. He began his reign in 1397. Erik of Pomerania confirmed the Charter of the City of Stockholm (q.v.) on August 29, 1398. He was a highly ambitious, fanciful king, who spent little time in Sweden. He was unpopular with his Swedish subjects. In 1435, King Erik and the Swedes reconciled on October 14, following an uprising led by Engelbrekt Engelbrektsson (q.v.) the previous year. Erik finally was deposed in 1439. He fled to the Baltic island of Gotland. In 1446, an expeditionary force sailed from Stockholm to capture the Baltic island of Gotland from Erik of Pomerania, but it returned unsuccessful. In 1449, another unsuccessful attempt was made by a force that included one of Stockholm's mayors.

ERIK IX. Saint Erik is Sweden's patron saint. In 1150, Erik Jevardsson was elected king. His royal title was King Erik IX. He was considered a magnanimous sovereign, a just legislator, and devout Christian. After ruling for 10 years, he was executed by the Danish army, according to tradition on May 18. At the end of the 12th century, Erik was chosen by the Swedes as their patron saint. His relics are preserved in Uppsala Cathedral. Later, he was chosen to be Stockholm's own patron saint. The first record of Erik represented on the Stockholm seal is 1376; it still appears on the city's coat of arms.

ERIK XIV (1533–1577). The eldest son of Gustav Vasa (q.v.). By 1544, Gustav had become established strongly enough to be able to proclaim that the Swedish throne would inherited in the House of Vasa. On July 11, 1560, the newly crowned Erik XIV made his ceremonious entrance into the capital city, and was coronated in a lavish fashion. His royal motto was, "God gives to the one He wants."

Erik's aggressive policies led to the Nordic Seven Year War. Suffering from mental illness, Erik was directly responsible for the murder of the influential Sture brothers (q.v.), in Uppsala in 1567. He suspected them of plotting an uprising against him. On July 4, 1567, Erik XIV and Karin Månsdotter were married, in *Storkyrkan* (The Cathedral) (q.v.). The 17–year-old queen was crowned the following day. In 1568, Erik XIV was imprisoned by Duke Karl, who, together with Duke Johan, started a revolt against the king. Erik was deposed in 1569, and replaced as king by his half-brother Johan (q.v.). Erik remained incarcerated until his death, supposedly by poisoning, at the command of Johan. Legend has it that the poison was put in the king's pea soup.

ERIKSKRÖNIKAN (1330). The oldest Swedish, Middle Ages chronicle and the first-known writing on Stockholm. It was written in doggerel rhyme, so-called Hudibrastic verse. It is mainly about the time of the *Folkunga* dynasty (q.v.) (1250–1389), to which Birger Jarl (q.v.) belonged.

ERIKSSON, GUSTAV. See VASA, GUSTAV.

ERIKSSON, KNUT. King in 1187, at the time when Sigtuna (q.v.) was the most important town on Lake Mälaren. Sigtuna was sacked by Vikings from across the Baltic Sea. He ordered a defense tower to be built on the largest islet at the outlet of Lake Mälaren into the sea.

He also recognized the advantages of collecting tolls from trading vessels.

ERIKSSON, MAGNUS (1316–1374). The grandson of Magnus Ladulås (q.v.) who became king of Norway and Sweden at age three. In July 1336, Magnus Eriksson was crowned in *Storkyrkan* (The Cathedral) (q.v.) together with his consort, Blanka of Namur. King Magnus Eriksson founded the Black Friars Monastery in Stockholm. He established the *landslag* (common law of the realm) in about 1350. His struggle against the nobility resulted in his loss of the Swedish crown to Albrekt of Mecklenburg (q.v.) in 1364. Later, in 1366, Magnus Eriksson was placed under arrest and held in Stockholm's palace.

No Swedish king reigned as long as Magnus Eriksson—46 years. See also CHARTER.

ESTONIA. A Baltic ferry that plied between Stockholm and Talin, in Estonia, and which tragically sank on September 19, 1994, with approximately 870 passengers and 180 crew members on board. There were 126 survivors. The vessel was on its way to Stockholm when heavy seas poured in through the bow doors. It is Europe's worst tragedy at sea since World War II. The whole country was deeply shocked, Stockholm in particular. A national memorial service was held in *Storkyrkan* (The Cathedral) (q.v.): Archbishop Gunnar Weman, Prime Minister Ingvar Carlsson, and the conservative party leader Carl Bildt (qq.v.) attended. The king and queen attended a service in Uppsala cathedral; the city lost 26 people on the ferry. Sixty Stockholm police officers were holding a union meeting onboard. All were lost.

The possibility of raising the Estonia was debated, but the government decided against it.

ETHNOGRAPHIC MUSEUM. See PEOPLE'S MUSEUM.

EUGEN, PRINCE (1865–1947). The fourth son of King Oscar II (q.v.) was a talented painter. He also collected paintings, which he hung at Waldermarsudde on Djurgården, where he had a house set on the water, at the edge of a park. His house was built from 1903 to 1905, and was bequeathed, together with his paintings, to the nation. The art collection generally spans the years 1870 to 1940, and contains approximately 1,200 pieces by about 300 artists. There are numerous, well-preserved interiors, created during from the time of Prince Eugen and a large number of the prince's own works. One of his paintings is mounted in the Prince's Gallery at the City Hall *(Stadshuset)* (q.v.).

EUROPEAN UNION. It is too early to assess the effect on Stockholm, of Sweden's membership in the EU on January 1, 1995. Stockholm City will not qualify for direct grants, but projects within the area may qualify (e.g improvements in the Stockholm archipelago). Submissions already have been prepared.

Attorneys are examining the effect that EU regulations may have on Sweden: for example, the question of water purification. While Sweden has complied with demands for improved water, the nation falls short of requirements concerning action against transgressors. There are many rather trivial items causing concern, as well, such as the four classifications of strawberries.

Twenty, or more, Swedes already are in the European Parliament.

In December 1994, an office for representation was opened in Brussels. On May 12, 1995, Information Point on Europe was opened at Norrmalmstorg (q.v.) by the European Commission's chairman, Jacques Santer. It offers public information about EU.

Stockholm would like to be regarded as the EU's "gateway to the east." The Chamber of Commerce describes Stockholm as the "hub of the Baltic".

An industrial exhibition, Exposition 1997 (q.v.), is to be held in Stockholm. The exhibition will celebrate the 100–year anniversary of the Stockholm Exhibition held in 1897.

EXPOSITION 1997 STOCKHOLM. A competition among sculptors from all parts of the country. It is to be arranged in cooperation with *Konstakademien* (The Academy of Fine Arts) (q.v.). The winning sculpture eventually will be placed in Kungsträdgården (q.v.). The sculptures by other entrants will be erected in other areas of the capital. The science center, to be built on the grounds of the Technology Museum as well as the winning entry will remain a permanent feature of Stockholm after the exhibition. King Carl Gustaf (q.v.), honored chairman of the exhibition's foundation, attended a ceremony at the Technology Museum in May 1995 to launch the project. The exhibition will be spread over three areas, with the entrance in Kungsträdgården. The Technology Museum on Gärdet (q.v.), with its new science center, will include an exhibition by the forestry industry demonstrating the latest developments in ecology. In Gälarparken, on Djurgården (q.v.), the third area will present business structure as it appears in 1997.

EXPRESSEN. A liberal evening newspaper in Stockholm, founded in 1944, with Ivar Harrie and Carl-Adam Nycop as chief editors. With approximately 500,000 copies per edition, it has the largest Nordic daily circulation. It is read by 17 percent of the households in the Stockholm region.

F

FAGERSJÖ. During and after World War II, mainly large apartment blocks that were constructed. The suburb of Fagersjö is one of the areas built up in this fashion.

FARSTA. Another suburb exemplifying the construction during and after World War II of large apartment blocks. Farsta center, with shopping mall facilities and communal amenities was opened. See also TOWN PLANNING.

FERLIN, NILS (1898–1961). A poet who wrote ballads, often in lyrical verse. He lived around *Vasagatan,* and often frequented restaurants and bars in the neighborhood. There is a statue of Ferlin at the gates of the Klara churchyard, about which he wrote in *Kejsarens papegoja* (Caesar's Parrot).

FERRIES TO FINLAND. In 1993, the number of ferries and passenger sailings from Stockholm to Finland was 3,176. They carried 295,922 motor vehicles and 3.652 million passengers.
See also ESTONIA.

FERSEN, AXEL von, the elder (1719–1794). In the 1750s, he became a leader of the Hat Party (q.v.). He held high office in Parliament (q.v.) in 1755, 1760, and 1769, but was not a member of the council. After Gustav III's (q.v.) bloodless *coup d'état* in 1772, he was persuaded to join the council, only to leave it soon afterward and join the opposition. In 1789, together with other leading opposition figures, he was imprisoned, ending his political career. He published describing his era under the title *Historiska skrifter* (Historical Writings); subjective in nature, it testifies to the political party spirit in the 18th century.

FERSEN, AXEL von, the younger (1755–1810). A count, lord high steward, son of Axel von Fersen, the elder (leader of the Hat Party) (q.v.), and a favorite of Marie Antoinette. He organized an attempted flight by the French royal family in 1791. He was murdered by a mob in Stockholm.

FESTSPEL. See STOCKHOLM FESTIVAL.

FILM. Swedish film production is based in Stockholm. *Svensk filmindustri* (Swedish Film Industry), or SF, is the largest film company. Swedish film companies produce only a relatively small number of films viewed by avid Swedish audiences. The period from 1910 to the mid–1920s is regarded as the Golden Age of Swedish film-making. Victor Sjöström and Mauritz Stiller were the popular talents, with films such as *Ingeborg Holm*, a scathing examination of poverty, and *Gösta Berling's Saga* (which brought Greta Garbo to fame) (q.v.). This renowned film actress was originally a hairdresser in Stockholm. Today, historians acknowledge the debt that the critically acclaimed French cinema industry owed to Stockholm-based film producers. Nowadays, the majority of films come from the United States and also from many foreign sources. Ingmar Bergman (q.v.) enjoys worldwide fame as a director.

Going to theaters was most popular in the mid–1950s, before the days of television. Attendance is now only about 20 percent of what is was then. Swedish filmmakers qualify for state support, which in fiscal year 1991–1992 totaled 64 million SEK.

FILMHUSET (THE FILM BUILDING). Situated at Borgvägen 1–5, it was erected from 1967 to 1970. The building contains free-standing halls, theaters, and studios, around which are two floors of offices. Film collections of historical value are stored here.

FINANCE DEPARTMENT. The house of Axel Oxenstierna (q.v.) was erected at Storkyrkobrinken 54, in 1652, possibly according to plans drawn by Nicodemus Tessin the elder (q.v.). Subsequently, *Riksbanken* (the Swedish Central Bank) (q.v.) and the Finance Department were moved there.

FINNISH CHURCH. When the Reformation swept away the international language of Latin, the Finnish community living in Stockholm felt the need for its own premises in which to worship. In 1533, they were using the Black Friars Monastery. Moving from one place to another, they at one point shared St. Gertrude's chapel with the Germans. For more than a hundred years they held services in Riddarholm Church (q.v.) at 5 a.m.

In 1725, they moved to their present well-preserved church situated at Slottsbacken 2. It was previously called *Bollhuset* (Ball Building) (q.v.).

FISKARTORPET. Situated on Norra Djurgården (q.v.), it is well-known for a variety of reasons. There is a fisherman's cottage, lying in the shadow of a huge oak tree, that was reputedly built by Karl XI (q.v.).

Fiskartorpet is famous for its natural beauty, acclaimed by Bellman (q.v.) in *Fredman's Epistle Number 71*. Also well-known are the hundreds of oak trees growing on the slopes surrounding Fiskartorpet. Another attraction, in more recent times, its ski slope, situated on the southern shore of Laduviken.

FJÄDERHOLMARNA (FEATHER ISLANDS). A collective name for a group of four islands. They form the gateway to the archipelago. The boat trip from the city to the main island takes about 20 minutes. There is a museum and an aquarium containing a collection of typical Baltic fish on the island.

In February 1995, an old lighthouse on one of the islands was declared to be a historic monument to be preserved. It was built in 1831 and is powered by acetylene gas.

FJÄLLGATAN (FELL STREET). The fact that this street, in Söder (q.v.), remains at all is due in great part to Anna Lindhagen, who wrote a book in 1923 and started a movement to save the city's old buildings, in particular those on Fjällgatan where she lived. In the 1600s, it was known as *Galgbergsgatan* (Gallows Hill Street) after the local execution site. It is a steep cliff road of light grey Stockholm granite. From its position on the northern slopes of Erstaberget, Fjällgatan has become renowned for its views and is a popular stopping place for tourists.

FLEMING, KLAS (1592–1644). Recognized as one of Sweden's most successful admirals. His fleet was victorious against the Danes in 1644, shortly before he was killed in battle. On July 29, 1634, Klas Fleming was made governor general in Stockholm and the central administrative offices were legalized there. Thus, the town became Sweden's official capital. During his time in office, Stockholm developed richly. He was influential in planning the old city and the new *malmar* (q.v.). He also was involved in the building of sluice gates at Söderström (q.v.).

FOGELBERG, B.E. On October 20, 1854, B.E. Fogelberg's statue of Birger Jarl (q.v.) was unveiled on Riddarholmen. The site was, thereafter, called Birger Jarl's Square. The same sculptor's statue of Karl XIV Johan (q.v.) was unveiled at Skeppsbron on November 4, 1854.

FOGELSTRÖM, PER ANDERS (1917–). This author has written prolifically about Stockholm. Many of his novels are about modern Stockholm youth. Among the better-known are *Sommaren med Monika* (Summer with Monica), 1951, *Mina drömmars stad* (City of My

Dreams), 1960, *Barn av sin stad* (Child of his City), 1962 and *Minns du den stad* (Do you remember that City?), 1964.

Fogelström lives on *Fjällgatan* (Fell Street) (q.v.).

FOLKETS HUS (THE PEOPLE'S BUILDING). The official opening of this building, by Hjalmar Branting (q.v.), took place in 1901. Apart from various offices, there are several small assembly rooms and a large hall, known as Room A. It is here that workers' organizations hold their official gatherings and congresses. Since 1922, it has been used partly as a theater. Archives of workers' organizations are stored in this building. Folkets hus owns several well-known works of art, which decorate the interior.

FOLKUNGA DYNASTY. The members of the Folkunga family greatly influenced Sweden during the period 1250 to 1389.

FOREIGN OFFICE *(UTRIKESDEPARTEMENTET)* (UD). The Foreign Office moved into Arvfursten's Mansion (q.v.) in 1906. Situated at Gustav Adolf's Square (q.v.), it has a fine façade in the French classical style. Above the entrance, written in gold, is the name *"Sophia Albertina."* She was the sister of Gustav III (q.v.), and lived there toward the end of the 18th century. The princess had the façade rebuilt in order to make it as fine as the one on the nearby Opera house (q.v.).

FREDRIK I (1676–1751). Fredrik Vilhelm was born in Germany as Count von Hessen. He married Karl XII's (q.v.) sister Ulrika Eleonora (q.v.) on March 24, 1715. When King Karl died, leaving no offspring as heir to the throne, the Swedes regarded it as an opportunity to rid themselves of the absolute monarchy. Ulrika Eleonora was appointed queen in 1719, provided that she would accept a new constitution, the aim of which was to limit the power of the monarch. She abdicated in favor of Fredrik, who was crowned king on May 3, 1720. The period that followed is known as the Age of Liberty, continuing until 1772.

The king was not interested in power and the Swedish desire for reduced influence by the Crown was realized. Power lay with parliament. King Fredrik eventually stopped attending assemblies, and decisions could be made using a stamp of the royal signature. In his book "All the Kings of Sweden," Åke Ohlmark describes Fredrik I as "a ruthless bribe-monger, debauched by good living, a slothful and unworthy king who never even learned a word of Swedish. He could not even be bothered to invent his own motto, but simply stuck with his wife's."

After King Fredrik I, parliament's power became limited periodically but never again did a Swedish king reign supreme.

FREDRIKA DOROTEA VILHELMINA AV BADEN. In 1797, Princess Fredrika married King Gustav IV Adolf (q.v.), in Stockholm.

FREDRIKHOV'S PALACE. In 1776, after rebuilding Fredrikshov's Palace under C.F. Alderkrantz's (q.v.) directions, the widow-Queen Lovisa Ulrika (q.v.) took up residence there.

FREE PORT. Stockholm's free port was inaugurated in 1919. The harbor and harbor area of a free port are regarded, from the point of view of customs control, as a foreign region. Sweden has two other free ports—Gothenburg and Malmö.

FRESCATI. 1970 saw the beginning of the exodus by Stockholm University (q.v.) from the city center to Frescati, just north of the city center. The university is said to be one of the most modern in Europe. Most of the university departments in Frescati are situated in six tall buildings. Some departments remain in other parts of the city. The university has its own gymnasium, *Frescatihallen.*

FRÖDING, GUSTAF (1860–1911). He became a popular poet, in Sweden, with a masterly control of language and rhythm. He spent several years in a mental hospital. Fröding died at Gröndal, on Djurgården (q.v.).

FUNCTIONALISM (*"FUNKIS,"* in popular slang). A trend in the design of architecture, furniture, etc., in which the goal is functional purpose. It made its breakthrough in Sweden at the Stockholm Exhibition of 1930 (q.v.).
  See also ASPLUND, GUNNAR.

G

GAMLA STAN. See OLD TOWN.

GARBO, GRETA (1905–1990). One of the world's best-remembered film stars, she was born Greta Gustafsson. She worked as a hairdresser in Stockholm before becoming an actress. Her best-known films include *Anna Karenina,* 1935; *Kameliadamen* (The Camelia Lady), 1936; and *Ninotchka,* 1939. She discontinued her career in films in 1941. She made her home in Hollywood, and took United

States citizenship in 1951. In August 1995, an auction of many of her possessions was held in Rockport, Me. It included her personal diary from 1925.

GÄRDET. See *LADUGÅRDSGÄRDET*.

GÅSTORGET (Goose Square). An idyllic but little-known part of the Old Town (q.v.). It is a small piazza surrounded by older houses, with decorative wall-supporting irons.

GAS-WORKS. The first gas-works, at Klara, were constructed in 1853.

GAY CENTER. On February 28, 1988, the Gay Center, for homosexuals, was opened at Sveavägen 59. It was thought to be the first of its kind in Europe.

GENEALOGY. Readers are referred to the book *Forska Själv*.

GERMAN CHURCH. Also called St. Gertrude's Church, it is situated on Svartmangatan. As early as the 14th century, St. Gertrude's Guild, which comprised German merchants in Stockholm, owned a house that was taken over by the crown at the time of the Reformation. The cellar of that Middle Ages house still exists. Finnish and German congregations shared the house between 1576 and 1607. In 1580, building commenced to convert it into a church; the house was lengthened in a westerly direction. Buttresses and a tower were constructed between 1613 and 1618. The church was enlarged from a single nave in Renaissance style to a church with two naves in late-Gothic style between 1638 and 1642. The second nave was built to the south. The body of the church was vaulted and rested on two large pillars in the center of the church. A new tower was built after a fire in 1878 devastated the roof and tower. Its restoration was completed in 1887. The fittings are in Baroque style. The bells in the tower play the psalm *"Nu tackar Gud allt folk"* (Now Praise We All Our God). The altar, on the eastern wall, was built from 1641 to 1659. The socle on the altar decoration has as its theme "The Last Supper" and dates from 1743.

GERMANS. The earliest reference to the city council being divided into Swedish and German halves appears in a document dated July 29, 1323. In 1471, the Swedish National Council abolished from law a clause referring to the two nationalities. In April 1535, German burghers in Stockholm were instructed to leave the city. In the fall, Gus-

tav Vasa (q.v.) ordered Swedish burghers from other towns to move
to Stockholm. In 1558, Gustav Vasa granted Germans in Stockholm
the right to hold special church services. The German assembly was
granted a royal charter in 1571. In 1607, Karl IX gave the Germans
sole rights to St. Gertrude's Church, thereby excluding the Finns.

GLOBEN (THE GLOBE). On February 19, 1989, *Globen* was officially
opened in Johanneshov. Made of steel, it is used for various sporting
events and musical performances. In the beginning of the summer, in
the early nineties, Pope John Paul appeared there. It is one of the
largest spherical buildings in the world—85 meters high and 100 meters in diameter. It can accommodate 16,000 spectators. The Globe
itself is only part of Globen City, which is a vast complex with two
other sports arenas, both of which have recently been modernized.
Globen city includes a large shopping mall. It is estimated that
350,000 people visit Globen City each month, and that approximately
5,000 people work there.

GOLDEN PEACE RESTAURANT (*DEN GYLDENE FREDEN*).
Opened in 1721 at its present-day site of 51 Österlånggatan, in *Gamla
stan* (The Old Town) (q.v). It is at this restaurant in *Järntorget* (Iron
Square), in the Bellman Rooms, that *"The Eighteen"* of the Swedish
Academy (q.v.) holds its traditional Thursday suppers. The artist Anders Zorn (q.v.) bought the building in 1919 for 150,000 kronor, and
bequeathed it to the Swedish Academy. *Gyldene Freden* has been the
meeting place for Stockholm's poets since the 18th century. First,
Bellman (q.v.), then Stagnelius, and, more recently, Nils Ferlin and
Evert Taube (q.v.). Thus it is an appropriate venue for the eighteen
outstanding present-day Swedish literary personalities. The old sign-
board remains depicting a personification of peace, draped in pink,
swooping down towards earth with a palm of peace in his hand.

GÖTA CANAL. Built under the supervision of B. von Platen between
1810 and 1832, to become part of a water passage 387 kilometers in
length that links Stockholm with the large port of Gothenburg, on the
west coast. More than 6,000 soldiers took part in the introductory
stages of work on the canal. When it was completed, 60,000 men had
contributed 7 million days' work. Although the length of Göta Canal
is given as 182 kilometers, there are only 87.4 kilometers of actual
canal. The remainder makes use of large lakes, in particular Lake
Vänern. At the western end of the connection between Sweden's two
largest ports is the Trollhätte Canal and, at the eastern end, use is made
of the Södertälje Canal. The depth of Göta Canal is only 3 meters. Its
highest point above sea level is 91.5 meters. There are 58 lock gates

along its length. The canal is narrow in places, but has an average surface width of about 25 meters. The sides shelve, so that the bottom of the canal is about 12 meters narrower.

Gradually, the canal became less and less financially viable, and some 25 years ago discontinued its original role as a shipping thruway. In 1978, it was taken over by the state, but it continues to give pleasure to Swedes and overseas tourists. It was once the quickest means of transport between Gothenburg and Stockholm—the canal trip can take four to six days. Close to Riddarhustorget is a magnificent view of Lake Mälaren from the quay, to which come ships that ply the Göta Canal from Gothenburg.

GOVERNMENTS (Since 1945)

Year	Prime Minister	Party
1945–1951	P.A. Hansson/T. Erlander	S
1951–1957	T. Erlander	S/C
1957–1976	T. Erlander/O. Palme	S
1976–1978	T. Fälldin	C/M/FP
1978–1979	O. Ullsten	FP
1981–1982	T. Fälldin	C/FP
1982–1991	O. Palme/I. Carlsson	S
1991–1994	C. Bildt	M/C/FP/KDS
1994–	I. Carlsson/G. Persson	S

S = Social Democratic Party.
C = Center Party
M = Moderate (Conservative) Party
FP = People's Party (Liberal)
KDS = Christian Democratic Party

GOVERNOR. On July 29, 1634, Klas Fleming (q.v.) was made governor-general in Stockholm and the central administrative offices were legalized there. Thus, the town became Sweden's official capital. In 1773, Stockholm's Governor took over Tessin's Palace (q.v.) on Slottsbacken (q.v.), which was erected by N. Tessin the younger (q.v.) and completed by about 1703. In 1815, because of the growth of the city and the multiplicity of business, the work of the governor's office was divided into three departments.

GRÅMUNKEKLOSTRET *(GREY FRIARS' ABBEY)*.
The old abbey is said to have been founded by Magnus Ladulås (q.v.) in 1270. It was built on Gråmunkeholmen, now called Riddarholmen (q.v.). The abbey was used to care for the sick.

GRAND HOTEL. Situated at Södra Blasieholmshamnen 8. It was erected from 1872 to 1874. The hotel has been altered several times since. The hotel may look staid and dull from the outside, but the interior has been magnificently modernized; it is generally regarded as Stockholm's most exclusive hotel. Just opposite the hotel are piers for the pleasure boats, which provide tours of the Stockholm waterways.

GREYFRIARS. See GRAMUNKEKLOSTRET.

GRILLSKA HUSET *(THE GRILL BUILDING)*. A house at Storgtorget 3 (q.v.) that is preserved with high gables and contributes to the olden-times atmosphere of the square.

GRIPSHOLM CASTLE. Dates back to the Middle Ages, with a round tower similar to the one on Riddarholmen (q.v.). Its first master was Bo Jonsson Grip, one of Sweden's richest and most powerful men of the 1300s. The castle has been rebuilt and extended many times since. In the 1530s, it was used by Gustav Vasa (q.v.) as a safe shelter near Stockholm for his family and valuables. Trips to Gripsholm were popular with royalty during the end of the 18th century and beginning of the 19th century. It is 70 kilometers from Stockholm to Gripsholm, and the steamboat trip takes three hours.

In the early 1770s, Gustav III allowed some 30 portraits to be moved from Drottningholm Palace (q.v.) to Gripsholm Palace, which houses the state's portrait collection. About 4,000 portraits hang in Gripsholm Castle. Originally, it only included royal personages, then the nobility was added. Since the end of the 19th century, portraits of cultural personalities, authors, and artists can be found here.

GROENS MALMGÅRD *(GROEN'S ESTATE)*. Situated at Malmgårdsvägen 53. The estate originated in the 18th century, and has a manor house in Carolean style with vertical panels.

GRÖNA LUND *(GREEN GROVE)*. A leafy garden area, that became a restaurant during the 1700s at which Bellman (q.v.) was a regular customer. Since 1883, it has been a fun park. Handicapped initially by several, serious fires, the amusement park gained increasing popularity in the 1920s. Since 1993, circus artists have performed at the variety-show theater there. Sven-Bertil Taube, son of Evert Taube (q.v.), performs, according to custom, on the open-air stage.

On January 4, 1993, an 18th century house in Lilla Allmänna Gränd in Djurgårdsstaden was destroyed by fire. The house was situated immediately behind Gröna Lund's main stage. Among things destroyed by the fire was Gröna Lund's photographic archive.

In the beginning of 1994, the figure for the number of visitors during the previous 12 months was 1,207,000.

GUARDIAN ANGELS. In the fall of 1993, an organization known as Guardian Angels commenced in Stockholm. It is based on a model from New York City. The Guardian Angels are a non-political, voluntary organization of young people who endeavour to prevent trouble on the subway and in public places. Such "protective angels" had already operated in Malmö, in southern Sweden.

GULDRUMMET *(GOLD ROOM)*. See HISTORY MUSEUM.

GUSTAV I. See VASA, GUSTAV.

GUSTAV ERIKSSON VASA. See VASA, GUSTAV.

GUSTAV II ADOLF (1594–1632). The son of King Karl IX (q.v.) became ruler in 1611. His royal motto was "With God and conquering weapons-God with us." The king was married to Queen Maria Eleonora (q.v.). Through treaties with Denmark in 1613 and with Russia in 1617, he ended two wars that had been going on before he came to power. War with Poland continued and led to the overrunning of the Baltic state of *Livland* (Livonia). Gustav II Adolf is the only Swedish king who is famed in international war history for technical and strategic improvements that he personally discovered. He was killed at the Battle of Lützen on November 6, 1632. He was buried in Riddarholm Church (q.v.) on June 22, 1634.

The era known as *Stormaktstiden* (The Age of Great Power) (q.v.) started with Gustav II Adolf. He was known as "The Lion from the North."

In the early part of the century, there were tremendous changes in Stockholm. There was a new town plan with wide, regular streets. The devastation caused by a widespread fire on January 1, 1625, resulted in rapid clearance of the city, an opportunity that Gustav II Adolf was quick to grasp.

On November 17, 1796, P.H. l'Archeveque's statue of Gustav II Adolf was unveiled. It stands alone in what is now called Gustav Adolf's Square (q.v.). The statue cost the state 175,000 SEK, a huge price in those days.

GUSTAV ADOLF'S CHURCH Situated in Gustav Adolf's Park, it was erected in the beginning of the 1890s. It is built in new Gothic style, and has a wide sanctuary. The west façade has large rose windows of early Gothic type. The interior of the church has open roof-trusses of wood. The church originally was intended to be a place of worship for Stockholm's garrison, but it now belongs to Oscar's parish.

GUSTAV ADOLF'S SQUARE (*GUSTAV ADOLFSTORG*). The Middle Ages predecessor to this square was the *Sandbro* (Sand Bridge) which was built on reclaimed land in the waters of Strömmen. The water lay between Skeppsholmen and the Old Town (qq.v.) over which a bridge crossed to *Lilla Stockholm* (Little Stockholm), which no longer exists. Little Stockholm was linked to Helgeandsholmen and Stadsholmen. Maps from the 1620s show that roads into Stockholm from the north, east, and west converged in front of the bridge over Strömmen (q.v.). Large, solid buildings surrounded the 17th-century square. One of them was Torstensonska Palace, which still remains, with its façade facing Fredsgatan. Joined to this building is Arvfursten's Palace, which was built between 1783 and 1794 for Princess Albertina. Since 1902 the building has belonged to the state, and since 1906 has been the seat of *Utrikesdepartementet* (Foreign Office).

On the opposite side of the square is *Kungliga Teatern* (*Operan*) (The Royal Opera House) (q.v.). Farmers from Dalecarlia reached Stockholm on June 20, 1743. They marched into the city and camped in and around Gustav Adolf's Square. In 1775, architect C. F. Adelcrantz (q.v.) submitted a proposal at the request of Gustav III to redesign Gustav Adolf's Square (then Norrmalm Square) in a more stylish manner. Stage-coach traffic commenced between Stockholm and Uppsala in March 1829. The departure point was originally at Gustav Adolf's Square.

GUSTAV III (1746–1792). Crowned in *Storkyrkan* (The Cathedral) (q.v.) on May 29, 1772. He succeeded his father, King Adolf Fredrik (q.v.), who had been an ineffective monarch. The country was in a poor financial state, and there was political strife between the Hats and Caps (qq.v). Initially, he did much to restore the financial situation and he brought about many reforms. His interest in and support of the arts made him popular in some quarters. He encouraged the performance of plays at Drottningholm Palace Theater (q.v.), and the Royal Opera House (q.v.) commenced performances in 1782. In 1786, King Gustav was instrumental in creating the Swedish Academy (q.v.).

But many amongst aristocrats disapproved of him and conspired against him. On March 16, 1792, Gustav III was mortally wounded by a pistol shot during a masked ball at the opera. He died on March 29.

Opinions about Gustav III vary but, unquestionably, the reforms he introduced completely altered the Swedish community. It is from this time that political and social advances by society's lower classes began. In 1808, a statue of Gustav III by Sergel (q.v.) was unveiled. It was placed on a semicircular promontary built out into Strömmen (q.v.) below Slottsbacken.

GUSTAV III MUSEUM OF ANTIQUITIES. Situated at Stockholm's Palace, Lejonbacken. It consists of a collection of marble statues that Gustav III sent back to Sweden during a visit to Italy in 1784. The king intended to place the sculptures on the grounds of Haga Palace, which he was planning. However, his death put an end to that project. Instead, in 1794, the Royal Museum was opened in the northeast wing of Stockholm's Palace. It was the first official museum in northern Europe. In 1866, the collections were moved to the newly opened National Museum, but were returned to the palace in the 1950s. By that time, the Museum of Antiquities had been restored to its condition in 1794. The collection includes a statue of Apollo and the king's collection of antique vases. Another attraction is the statue of the mythical *"Endymion,"* which is thought to be a Greek original.

GUSTAV III's PAVILION. Situated at Haga (q.v.), it was completed in 1792.

GUSTAV IV ADOLF (1778–1837). After the 1792 assassination of his father, King Gustav III (q.v.), the 14–year-old boy became king. His royal motto was "God and the People," In 1796, he took over for his uncle, Prince Karl, who had been acting as regent. The reign of Gustav IV Adolf saw the end of the brilliant Gustavian period. Sweden lost Finland, and thereby a third of its land area and a quarter of its population. Finland had been part of Sweden for 700 years. Stockholm, which had always been securely situated in the middle of the kingdom, suddenly found itself a border town. The Russians were no longer far to the east.

The king was not held in high regard, although he did make some contributions and improvements, including giving his support to the plan to build the Göta Canal (q.v.). Princess Fredrika Dorotea Vilhelmina av Baden married King Gustav IV Adolf (q.v.) in Stockholm in 1797. In the fall of 1806, Gustav IV Adolf decided the opera should be closed. On March 16, 1807, he ordered the building to be demolished, but this was not carried out. On March 13, 1809, Gustav IV Adolf was dethroned, after having been imprisoned in Stockholm Palace. He was exiled, then divorced his wife and died in Switzerland.

GUSTAV V (1858–1950). Sweden's longest-reigning monarch since Magnus Eriksson (q.v.). He was king from 1907 to 1950. When he ascended the throne, he decided that he and future monarchs should not be crowned. His royal motto was "With the People for the Fatherland." He was politically active and influential in forming Sweden's policies during both world wars. In 1881, he married Princess Viktoria of Baden. During World War I, he tried to persuade the Swedes to empathize with the German cause. In World War II his influence on Swedish foreign policy was considerable as he sought to remain neutral. The king was an avid tennis player. He was largely responsible for the introduction of that sport to Sweden and funded the building of the *Kungliga Tennishallen* (The Royal Tennis Stadium)(q.v.) in Stockholm. He participated in tennis tournaments as "*Mr. G.*" and became popularly known by that name. He died at age 92.

GUSTAV VI ADOLF (1882–1973). The eldest son of Gustav V (q.v.). Because his father lived long, Gustav did not succeed to the throne until 1950, when he was nearly 68 years old. Gustav was an industrious person with a wide range of interests. Within the fields of classic archeology and East Asian art, he was considered to be an expert. He received honorary doctorates from home and abroad. He was married to Princess Margareta of Connaught, a granddaughter of Queen Victoria of Britain, from 1905 until 1920. He was later married to Lady Louise Mountbatten, also from Britain, between 1923 and 1965. He was a quiet, unassuming, popular monarch. Toward the end of his reign there was much talk in Sweden of changing from a monarchy to a republic, yet it was widely felt the Gustav should be the first president of Sweden. His eldest son, Gustav Adolf, was killed in an air crash in 1947. This meant that his grandson, Carl Gustav (q.v.), who was only 1 year old at the time of his father's tragic death, was next in line to the throne. Gustav helped prepare his grandson for his role of monarch. He died at age 90; the young crown prince was 26 years old by then.

GUSTAV VASA'S CHURCH. Situated on the corner of Upplandsgatan and Odengatan. It is Vasastaden's (q.v.) largest church building. Like the district itself, the church is quite young. It is built in new baroque style with a raised dome. The dome was created between 1898 and 1906. The altar arrangement dates from 1725 to 1731, and originally stood in Uppsala Cathedral. The ground plan is in the form of a cross with arms of equal length. Under the church is a columbarium with niches for about 900 burial urns. The columbarium was consecrated in 1924.

GUSTAVSBERG CENTER OF CERAMICS. Located in Gustavsberg. It is housed in renovated, former workshops, and features a variety of exhibitions: the Porcelain Museum, showing the company's products between 1825–1990; contemporary exhibitions; workshop conditions and how people lived in historical times. During the summer exhibition, from May to August, potters and ceramic decorators may be seen at work. Production of the well-known Gustafsberg porcelain, which can be found in many Swedish homes, began in the 1820s. But the ceramics factory was originally a brick factory created in the 17th century by Gustaf Gabrielsson Oxenstierna (q.v.). Oxenstierna intended to build a brick manor house on his estate Farsta on Värmdön, so he constructed a small factory in Farstaviken to provide materials for the house. Oxenstierna died at age 30, but his young widow, Maria de la Gardie completed the construction and subsequently sold the surplus bricks, in Stockholm. To perpetuate the memory of her husband, she called herself "wife of Gustafsberg," combining her husband's name with the fact that the manor house was situated on a *berg* (hill).

During the 17th and 18th centuries, the Farsta-Gustafsberg estate was owned by a succession of well-known Swedish families, and a small community grew up around the brickwork factory. In the beginning of the 19th century, the property was divided into Farsta, around the manor house, and Gustafsberg, with the factory, and so it remains today. In 1821, the estate was owned by Herman Öhman and after he entered into a partnership with Johan Wennberg, the manufacture of porcelain began at Gustafsberg. In the beginning, there were many difficulties and the future of the enterprise was in doubt. Not before the 1940s, when they abandoned the German method of production for a superior English one, did they get the wind in their sails, literally as well as figuratively. Their newfound success hinged in part on a shipping company they started so their own sailing cutters could bring home high-class raw materials, such as kaolin and clay, from Cornwall, England. In addition, they enlisted the help of skilled English craftsmen, including some from the famous Wedgwood enterprise. They began stamping their products with the now-famous anchor symbol, under the word Gustafsberg, in 1839.

In 1852, Gustafsberg was taken over by Samuel Godenius, a trader and shipowner. Under his ownership, the company not only made economic and technical progress, but also improved artistically. This resulted in a medal of honor at the Paris Exhibition of 1867, where the beautiful Pariah pieces received international admiration. In 1869, Godenius resigned in favor of his son-in-law, Wilhelm Odelberg, who brought about a strongly expansive phase in Gustavberg's history. Odelberg not only became involved in the affairs of the business enterprise but also in the community. He was personally involved in the construction of *Skurubron* (Skuru Bridge) in 1915. In 1924, his sons took over the factory. The new times demanded development and the difficult recession brought about considerable problems. By the 1930s, they were forced to seek a purchaser. In 1937, Gustavsberg was taken over by *KF* (Cooperative Association) and since then the factory has enlarged its production to include sanitary porcelain products, plastics, draining boards, etc. But porcelain and artistic wares hold a prominent place.

GYLDENE FREDEN. See GOLDEN PEACE RESTAURANT.

GYLLENSTIERNA, JOHAN (1635–1680). A count, statesman, and councilor as of 1668. He also was Karl XI's (q.v.) only advisory minister from 1676. His foreign policy was based on independence and strong links with Denmark.

GYLLENSTIERNA, KRISTINA (1494–1559). The wife of Sten Sture the younger (q.v.). After his death, she became leader of the national party. She led the defense of Stockholm Castle against Kristian II (q.v.) in 1520, but had to capitulate. She was imprisoned and exiled to Denmark. Upon her subsequent return to Sweden, she was mistrusted by Gustav Vasa (q.v.) and withdrew from the political scene.

H

HAGA. See SUNDBYBERG and SOLNA.

HAGALUND. See SOLNA.

HAGA PALACE. The stone foundation of the royal country seat, Haga Palace, was laid in 1786. The district, previously called Brahelund, was renamed Haga. Gustav III's pavilion at Haga was completed in 1792. The palace is in Haga Park one of Stockholm's most popular walks, rich in natural beauty and historic memories. It is the site of The Turkish Pavilion, Ekotemplet, *Drottningenspaviljong* (Queen's Pavilion) and the three Copper Tents.

    The main entrance to the park is through Haga's southern gates, with an elegant framework and the jolly sentry boxes that remind visitors that it was once a royal park, closed to the general public. Many Stockholmers associate Carl Michael Bellman (q.v.) with the park. For others, its traditional charm is reminiscent of the days of Gustav III (q.v.).

The park used to be much more formal and more horticulturally well-tended. By the 19th century, it took on a wilder character, and the canals, which once meandered through the park, dried up.

HAGSÄTTRA. During and after the World War II, mostly large apartment blocks were constructed. The suburb of Hagsättra exemplifies this style of living.

HALLONBERGEN. See SUNDBYBERG.

HALLWYL MUSEUM *(HALLWYLSKA MUSÉET)*. Situated at Hamngatan 4, on Östermalmstorg, in the middle of the city. This palatial home was originally owned by Count Walther von Hallwyl, and was completed in 1898. It is a mixture of Spanish and Venetian Renaissance styles. From the turn of the 20th century it has been hemmed in by a pub/restaurant and a café. The building, steeped in splendor and opulence, was donated to the nation after the death of Countess Wilhelmina von Hallwyl in 1930. Some 70 salons and rooms are furnished and decorated in the tradition of various epochs, and include 17th-century Dutch paintings, European porcelain, and Chinese ceramics. In the summer evenings, concerts are held in the central courtyard.

HAMMARBYLEDEN *(HAMMARBY OPENING)*. This new waterway was opened on November 25, 1929. It links Lake Mälaren to Saltsjön (q.v.) and the Baltic Sea. Traveling through it provides a glimpse of industrial Stockholm. Hammarbyleden enters Saltsjön through *Danvikskanalen* (Danvik Canal).

HANDELSHÖGSKOLAN *(COMMERCIAL COLLEGE)*. Inaugurated on October 1, 1909. It is now housed in an impressive building at the foot of Observatory Hill (q.v.). The building was erected between 1924 and 1926. It has a simple façade reminiscent of a Roman Renaissance palace. The North wing, with its convex, domed center section, resembles the original architecture of the observatory. The center section contains the main hall and library. The large, oval book section is surrounded by a gallery.

HANS, KING. In August 1497, Archbishop Jakob Ulfsson, together with three Swedish and seven Danish councilors, sanctioned a charter for the residents of Stockholm on behalf of King Hans. King Hans of Denmark marched in procession into Stockholm on November 11, 1497. On May 12, 1502, King Hans put in with his fleet at southern

Djurgården to fetch his queen, who had capitulated to the Swedes on May 9.

HANSEATIC LEAGUE. The Hanseatic League was formally organized in 1358 and dissolved in the 17th century. Stockholm was a member of this league and many merchants got rich on its trade. Many of these merchants were Germans, who settled in Stockholm and became influential. The harbor was full of mainly German shipping.

The Germans bought up raw materials such as iron, copper, and timber, and agricultural products such as meat and butter. They sold expensive cloth and silk, salt and spices from the East; also ale, wine, fine objects and jewelry made in the Hanseatic towns. The Germans were very jealous and protective of this rich trade and drove away any other traders who trespassed on their area of control. If any Nordic ruler attempted to impose duties and damage the Hanseatic trade, they became enemies of the Germans. Initially, Stockholm was not powerful enough to free itself of this powerful influence over trade.

See LÜBECK.

HÄSSELBY. A suburb of Stockholm, the furthest west, at the end of the subway line. It lies on the shores of Lake Mälaren (q.v.), 18 kilometers northwest of the city center. During World War II, it was mostly large apartment blocks that were constructed. Parts of the suburb of Hässelby exemplify this residential style. In 1949, parts of an area called Hässelby Villastad (Villa Town), in association with Spånga, came under city authority. Since then, it has been developed quite considerably, but previously it was well-known as a market garden and nursery district. It also had a small, popular bathing beach.

HÄSSELBY PALACE. Builders began erecting the palace in the 1640s for Privy Councilor Carl Bonde; it was completed in 1657 for his son, Chancellor Gustaf Bonde. It has a main building, two wings and a beautiful garden. The architect was Jean de la Vallée (q.v.). The palace was rebuilt in 1731 and 1860. From 1961 to 1963, it was thoroughly restored. Subsequently, Hässelby Palace has been used as a museum of Nordic culture. The old orchard was turned over to allotments in the 1950s. South of the main building is a restored baroque garden. See also BONDE MANSION.

HAT PARTY (*HATTPARTIET*). A political party founded in 1734, during the Age of Liberty, which was a period in Swedish history characterized by weak royal power, domination by parliament, and rivalry between political factions. Much depended on cooperation between the spokesman for the four estates: nobility, priests, farmers, and burghers. Sweden's first political parties, the Hats and the Caps, broke away, mainly from the first three estates. The farmers did not become terribly involved in party struggles. The Hat Party put its trust in industry and dreamed of cooperation with France to gain revenge against Russia. Their opponents, the Caps, favored agriculture and sought support from England as Sweden's biggest trading partner. The Hat Party was in power from 1738 to 1765, and again from 1769 to 1771. Supporters were from Stockholm—mainly the aristocrats and businessmen. The party's name was derived from the three-cornered hat worn by officers. It was a more aggressive party than the opposition, which they called the Cap Party, referring to *Mösspartiet* (Night Caps) (q.v.).

HÄTTEBRÖDERNA. See HOODED BROTHERS.

HÅTUNALEKEN *(THE HÅTUNA PLAY)*. The name given to an event in Swedish history when, in 1306, Dukes Erik and Waldemar attacked Birger Magnusson (q.v.) in Håtuna's royal residence, after a feast. Armed men rushed into the royal sleeping chamber. Birger and his queen were held, but his sons escaped. Birger was imprisoned and robbed of his kingdom.
    See also *NYKÖPINGS GÄSTABUD*.

"HAUNTED CASTLE" See *"SPÖKSLOTTET.*

HAYMARKET. See *HÖTORGET.*

HAZELIUS, ARTUR (1833–1901). An ethnologist who in 1880 was largely responsible for the creation of the Nordic Museum (q.v.). Skansen (q.v.) was opened as the world's first open-air museum on Sunday, October 11, 1891. Hazelius was a researcher of Nordic languages and quite a collector. On his journeys around Sweden, he saw how the old rural culture was dying out as industrial society took over. He began a large collection, partly of objects of cultural and historical value, and partly of financial funding. For 10 hectic years, buildings from different parts of Sweden were transported from the countryside and reconstructed on southern Djurgården. Since then, Skansen has been expanded to display a Sweden in miniature, with about 150 historical buildings. At certain times of the year, many traditional Swedish craft-making processes are demonstrated in these old buildings, as they would have been performed in the era depicted. All of this development took place against a backdrop of growing national pride, which was expressed in art and literature at a time of friction with Norway in the union that existed between the two

Scandinavian peoples. At Skansen, there also is a modest zoological garden. Hazelius arranged the first real Flag Festival in 1893.

HEDVIG ELEONORA CHURCH. Situated on Östermalmstorg, this church also is known as Östermalm (q.v.) Church. It is of the central church building style; the architects were Jean de la Vallée and G. J. Adelcrantz (qq.v.). On October 21, 1737, Hedvig Eleonora Church was consecrated, although construction had started in 1658. The church is named after the wife of Karl X Gustav (q.v.) and the foundations were laid during his reign. Originally, the church was intended for members of the fleet, most of whom were stationed on Ladugårdslandet (q.v.). Nowadays, Ladugårdslandet is divided into three parishes. The church has been restored several times in the 19th and 20th centuries. The dome that now graces the structure was added between 1865 and 1868. A new copper roof was installed in recent years.

HEDVIG ELEONORA, QUEEN (1636–1715). On October 24, 1654, the marriage of King Karl X Gustav (q.v.) and Hedvig Eleonora was celebrated, and the queen was crowned. During the years 1660–1672, she was regent for her young son Karl XI (q.v.). She supported the arts and architecture. Her most important building project was Drottningholm Palace (q.v.), to which Tessin the elder and Tessin the younger (qq.v.) also contributed.

HEDVIG ELISABET CHARLOTTA, PRINCESS (1759–1818). Princess Hedvig Elisabeth Charlotta, wife of Duke Karl, arrived in Stockholm in July 1774, and was received with great festivity. As the wife of Karl XIII, she became Queen Charlotta, Princess of Oldenburg. Her diary notes were published, in nine volumes.

HEIDENSTAM, VERNER von (1859–1940). An author who became a member of the Swedish Academy (q.v.) in 1912 and won the Nobel Prize (q.v.) for literature in 1916. He had to leave schooling in Stockholm because of ill-health at the age of 17. He traveled widely in southern Europe, but was well-known in the restaurants and bars of Stockholm, which he often visited. Scenes from Stockholm appear in several of his books, including *Storkyrkan* (The Cathedral) (q.v.) in *Karolinerna* (The Carolines) and *Riddarholmen* (q.v.).

HELGEANDSHOLMEN. An oblong island in Norrström, where Lake Mälaren's (q.v.) opens into the Baltic Sea. It was formed partly by the land rising and partly by in-filling. *Helgeandshuset* (House of the Holy Spirit) was founded in the 13th century—the city's first establishment for the care of the sick and the poor. It combined a hospital, apothecary, chapel, and graveyard.

As building density increased in the 16th century, the Norrström islands were full of shops supplying the Three Crowns Palace (q.v.). In Queen Kristina's (q.v.) time, the shops and fishermen's cottages were cleared away to make room for the building of palaces and fine houses. Later, a stable was built for Karl XI (q.v.), which housed 200 horses and carriages. In 1893, Helgeandsholmen was cleared again, and the Parliament building and Swedish Central Bank (qq.v.) were built here.

HIERTA, LARS JOHAN (1801–1872). A newpaper journalist and liberal politician. He started *Aftonbladet* (q.v.), which paved the way for the modern Swedish press. Hierta struggled for freedom of the press and many liberal reforms.

HISTORY MUSEUM (*STATENS HISTORISKA MUSEUM*). The museum complements the Nordic Museum (q.v.), covering the period before Gustav Vasa (q.v.), 1523, i.e. ancient Sweden and the Middle Ages. It is situated at Narvavägen 13–17, and was erected between 1935 and 1940. It contains the country's largest collection of archeological material from Sweden's Stone Age, Bronze Age, and Iron Age, up to the end of Viking times. Excavations in 1980 revealed many of the defense poles used to protect the town against enemy attack. Such poles may be seen depicted in the "Mock Sun" painting in *Storkyrkan* (The Cathedral)(q.v.). There also is a collection of church treasures in wood, stone, and precious metals. Priceless gold and silver treasures may be admired in the underground *Guldrummet* (The Gold Room).

On September 29, 1987, the History Museum opened a temporary exhibition that dealt with the effect of air pollution on buildings, sculptures, and archeological materials.

HÖGBRON *(THE HIGH BRIDGE)*. This bridge, linking the islands of *Stora* (Large) *Essingen* and *Lilla* (Small) *Essingen*, was opened in 1928.

HÖGALID CHURCH. Situated in Högalid Park on Hornsbruksgatan. It is a brick construction with a single nave and small side passages. It was built in the national romantic style from 1916 to 1923. The two eastern towers are reminiscent of Visby Cathedral.

HOODED BROTHERS *(HÄTTEBRÖDERNA)*. The name given to Germans in Stockholm who, after Albrekt of Mecklenburg (q.v.) was imprisoned in 1389, formed a group that roamed the streets at night and insulted and mistreated Swedes. In 1392, the Hooded Brothers seized power in a bloody coup, known as The Käpplinge Murder (q.v.). Their name refers to their headware, probably a conical hat.

HORN, ARVID (1664–1742). A count and president of the chancery. During his long life, he was first a daring soldier in Karl XII's (q.v.) army and later became a clever and cautious politician, in typical Age-of-Liberty (q.v.) style. His aim was to preserve peace and develop the country's prosperity.

HOT AIR BALLOONS. Hot air balloons have become an increasingly familiar sight over Stockholm. They mainly carry small groups of tourists. In August 1995, a hot air balloon that is said to be the largest in the world made its maiden flight over the capital. Its basket carries 22 passengers. Apart from the passenger fares, it earns considerable income through advertising.

HÖTORGET. A tilt-yard, intended for equestrian displays and jousting tournaments, was erected at the site of present-day *Hötorget* (Haymarket) in 1621. It was demolished in 1698. In addition to being a busy marketplace, there were times when criminals, condemned to death, were publicly tormented here before being taken to their execution. Anckarström (q.v.) was one such criminal, who suffered whipping and the pillory. In 1856, all trade in wood, timber, hay, and straw was transferred from Norrmalm Square to Hötorget. The official opening of the first part of Hötorgscity took place in 1959. Hötorget has always been associated with a market. During the 16th century, farmers bought and sold hay and straw there. Around the turn of the century *Torgmadamer* (Madames of the Square) came to sell their Christmas trees, seasonal fruit, and, at Shrovetide, birch whips, made of twigs decorated with brightly colored feathers. There is a southern atmosphere in Hötorget, and Stockholmers enjoy the spring and summer sunshine sitting on the steps of *Konserthuset* (The Concert Hall) (q.v.), where one of sculptor Carl Milles' (q.v.) masterpieces, Orpheus, may be seen. The steps and the square provide natural meeting places, as planned by the architect, Ivar Tengbom, in his 1926 design.

Terraces are situated over Hötorget's Hall and Sergel Theater by the five "skyscrapers." They were a popular meeting place, with restaurants and well kept arrangements of indoor plants. But vandals and neglect chased visitors away, and on December 15, 1987, the terraces of Hötorget were closed to the public.

A cooperative project between politicians and property owners was proposed to renovate Hötorg City. The project included a new *Films-*

tad (Film Town) over the market hall and a glassed-in market at Holländargatan, together with hotels and homes. On February 26, 1994,
the Cooperative Company's department store PUB in Hötorget was
closed. It had been founded as a clothing store in 1882 by Paul U.
Bergström and became one of Stockholm's largest. The building is
being rebuilt.

HOUSE OF NOBILITY. See RIDDARHUSET.

HOUSEHOLD WASTE. More than 300,000 tons of waste are collected
each year from households in Stockholm. This represents 438 kilograms per person. Conservation, by separating paper, bottles, and bat-
teries for recycling, is underway.

HOUSING PROBLEMS. See SUBURBS.

HUDDINGE. Around the turn of the century, estates and areas of land
in Huddinge were acquired for future residential development.

HUMLEGÅRDEN (HOP GARDEN). This place takes its name from
the hop-growing that Gustav II Adolf (q.v.) allowed here in 1619. In
Queen Kristina's (q.v.) time, it grew to become quite a large orchard
and kitchen garden and royal pleasure park. In 1855, Humlegården
became a town park with gravel pathways and a more formal character. In the years 1865 to 1878, *Kungliga biblioteket* (The Royal Library) (q.v.) was built—popularly known as *KB*—and the park was
then quite a secluded place that provided a peaceful working environment.

HUSBY. In 1962, parts of Järvafältet (q.v.) were acquired from the state.
This allowed for a gradual, continuous home-building in the northern
suburbs. At the end of the 60s and during the 70s, this resulted in the
coming into being of Husby.

I

IMMANUEL'S CHURCH. Situated at Kungstensgatan 71. It is a modern, hall-like brick structure built between 1971 and 1974. It belongs
to *Svenska Missionsförbundet* (Swedish Mission Association). The
previous Immanuel's Church built in the 1880s was demolished in
1977.

IMMIGRATION. Centuries ago there was a great deal of immigration
to Sweden, particularly to the capital. But as recently as 50 years

ago, it was fairly unusual to see foreigners, even in Stockholm. That situation has changed rapidly, starting initially with World War II and continuing mainly as a result of other wars and persecution. Many Finnish children were brought to Sweden to be spared the horrors of war. Refugees also arrived from the Baltic states and Germany, including many Jews. In 1968, many people fled from Czechoslovakia to Sweden. Some deserters from the United States armed forces in Vietnam made their way to Stockholm. Political asylum was sought by many from Chile and Colombia. More recently, they have come from Iran. Adding to the racial mix were workers who were attracted by affluence and a high living standard. They came mainly from Greece, Yugoslavia, Turkey, Portugal, and Finland. The Swedish government provided free language lessons and cultural courses in the schools. These workers did not necessarily intend to remain in Sweden permanently, but often brought their families too. Swedish couples were keen on adopting children, many of whom were brought in came from Korea, Vietnam, and Colombia.

Now, that Sweden has joined the European Union, it is part of a borderless region containing 300 million West Europeans who see opportunities for work and a life in Sweden.

The opposite happened in Sweden in the period from 1820 to 1930, when a million Swedes emigrated. In 1910, it was estimated that one Swede in five lived in the United States of America.

In the beginning of 1994, there were 70,781 aliens living in Stockholm, representing 10.2 percent of the total. In 1980, it was 8.3 percent. Immigrants are equally divided between the sexes. During 1993, there were 6,089 immigrants to Stockholm. The number of aliens who became Swedish citizens during 1993 was 4,530. In 1986, it was 2,506.

Immigrants who reside for three years in Sweden have the right to vote and run for office in local elections.

Possibly, the increased number of immigrants, coupled with unemployment rates and the financial recession, have focussed attention on the question of ethnic minorities. Stockholm has been called "a divided town," and attention has been drawn to the fact that the 20 communities in which the greatest number of immigrants live are almost entirely clustered into two groups to the northwest and southwest of the city. In these communities the percentage of immigrant residents range from 44 percent to 75 percent. On the other hand, the inner city has been called a "Swedish ghetto"—in an article in *Dagens Nyheter* (q.v.)—because of the comparatively low number of southern European and non-European immigrants living there.

INDUSTRY. Stockholm's industry is dominated by the service sector, which is responsible for 80 percent of jobs. However, employment in industry has shrunk considerably since 1945, although the district around the capital still remains Sweden's largest industrial region. A hundred years ago, Stockholm already had the country's largest collection of industries. When industrialization began in earnest in the 1800s, the number blossomed, mainly because of the growth in mechanical factories (e.g., Atlas Diesel, Separator, Bolinder and de Laval). Somewhat later, large electronic companies, such as L. M. Ericsson and Electrolux, were formed. There was a boom in the textile industry and in food manufacturing. Breweries, distilleries, and tobacco manufacturers did brisk business. Right into the 1950s, industrial employment kept pace with the growth in population, but then it began to recede. By 1985, the manufacturing industry provided no more than 14 percent of the town's total employment.

The decline in industry has, during post-war years, been counterbalanced by an increase in service and administrative functions. More and more corporate headquarters of large concerns have been established in Stockholm.

INSURANCE. See LABOR MARKET.

INTERNET. In July 1995, an Internet conference was held in Stockholm—this was only the second time this annual meeting had taken place outside the United States of America in twenty three years. Some 100,000 Swedes already use the Internet system. In 1995, Stockholm City had announced its desire to become recognized as the IT and tele metropolis of Europe. IT is the abbreviation for information technology, and is used to describe computer techniques and computer communication and their application in the community and in business.

J

JAKOB'S CHURCH. In 1643, Jakob's Church was completed. It was consecrated on November 26, after the foundations had been laid in the reign of Johan III (q.v.). The decision to build a church there was made in 1580. It replaced one of Gustav Vasa's (q.v.) demolished chapels, which had stood on the same site on the edge of Kungsträdgården (q.v.). The building has three naves and shows influences of late gothic Renaissance styles. Only the portals have remained unaltered. The church was damaged by fire in 1723 and the tower burned down. A rebuilt tower was completed in 1739. In 1968, the church was plastered in red, replacing the yellow. The interior was completely renovated in the 19th century. Its present appearance is the result of two restorations, in 1936–7 and in 1969. This church is popular for society weddings. The churchyard lies behind a high iron fence. Nobody has been buried in it since 1808. It contains the graves of several representatives of the cultural life of 18th-century Stockholm. Among them is Johan Henrik Kellgren (q.v.), who lived for many years at nearby Västra Trädgårdsgatan 9.

JÄRVAFÄLTET. The government announced in 1962 that the military would stop using Järvafältet for training purposes and as a firing range for Stockholm's garrison. It has since been reserved for residential development. On September 6, 1993, city authorities decided to set aside Hansta, on Järvafältet, as a nature reserve. This reversed the proposal in the general plan for 1983, whereby 7,500 homes were to be built. The new nature reserve will link with the existing reserves at *Östra Järvafältet* (Eastern Järvafältet) in Solentuna, *Västra Järvafältet* (Western Järvafältet), and Molnsättra, in Järfälla.
See also SUBURBS.

JEWISH MUSEUM. Situated at Hälsingegatan 2, near Odenplan. The museum depicts Jewish integration into Swedish society and the Jewish contribution to Swedish culture, industry, and trade. The exhibition begins in 1774, the year of the arrival of Aaron Isaac, the first Jew to be allowed to settle in Sweden, and ends in the present day.
See also SYNAGOGUE.

JOHAN III (1537–1592). Johan was son of Gustav Vasa (q.v.). He became king in 1568, after conflicts with his brother Erik XIV (q.v.). His royal motto was "God Our Protector." Johan III was interested in church matters, and was keen on promoting plans for building new churches. He called in painters, sculptors, and, in particular, architects from overseas in order to restore old churches and build new ones. He has been described as an introverted intellectual and religious mystic. He approved the construction of Riddarholm's Church (q.v.). Under the influence of his Roman Catholic, Polish wife, Katarina Jagellonica, he introduced a Catholic-oriented liturgy in 1577. Johan's attempts to return Sweden to Catholicism encouraged the movement toward the Lutheran Church. Johan died, leaving Sweden in economic troubles. Johan's Catholic son, Sigismund (q.v.), was deposed by Johan's Protestant brother Charles, who ruled as Charles IX.

JOHANNESKYRKA *(JOHANNES' CHURCH)*. Situated on Johannesgatan-Kammakargatan. It has three naves and was built in new gothic style between 1883 and 1890. Johannes' Church was consecrated in 1890. It has a single tower on the south side. A wooden belfry was erected close to the site of the present-day Johannes' Church in 1692. It belonged to the old, now-demolished, churchyard chapel.

JOHANSSON, LASSE. See LUCIDOR.

K

K.B. See KUNGLIGA BIBLIOTEKET.

KÅKBRINKEN. A narrow passageway between houses built over brick vaults dating from the Middle Ages. It was originally a pathway along which loads were carried from boats; a narrow roadway between the Baltic Sea and Lake Mälaren (q.v.). Kåk literally means "pillory" or "whipping post" and there actually were stocks (a timber frame in which an offender's ankles were held as he sat exposed to ridicule) at the top of the hill.

KAKNÄSTORNET *(KAKNÄS TOWER)*. The tallest building in Scandinavia—155 meters tall. It is situated on Kaknäsvägen on Norra Djurgården. The tower operates as a relay station for radio and television, and offers a spectacular view of Stockholm. On April 29, 1995, a new restaurant was opened on the 28th floor.

KALMAR UNION. This union of the three Scandinavian countries, Norway, Sweden, and Denmark, was founded under the reign of Queen Margareta in 1389. It was the largest kingdom in Europe, and, was ruled over by a woman. It stretched from Iceland in the north to the German kingdom in the south, from Karelen in the east to the Viking colony on Greenland, the remains of which still exist. Additionally, the Faroes, Shetland, and Orkney islands belonged to the Union. It lasted, with occasional breaks, until 1521, when Gustav Vasa (q.v.) led an uprising following the Stockholm Bloodbath (q.v.) of the previous year, and succeeded in driving out the Danes.

KANSLIHUSET *(THE CHANCERY)*. Located at Mynttorget 2. The building has both modern and classical style influences. The Doric temple front belonged to a royal mint, from 1790 that was built by C. F. Adelcrantz (q.v.). The present-day building was erected from 1945 to 1950. It has housed the Parliament members' workroom, since 1983. On the grounds stands a sculpture, *"Mother and Child,"* by Bror Marklund, from 1956. From *Kanslikajen* (Chancery quay), situated between the Chancery and Parliament House, observers can see the difference in the water level in Lake Mälaren and Saltsjön (qq.v.).

KÄPPLINGE MURDER. Sometime between 1389 and 1392, *Hättebröderna* (the Hooded Brothers) (q.v.) seized power in a bloody coup known as the Käpplinge Murder. It is described in an account from the beginning of the 1400s. According to that source, the German Hooded Brothers seized a number of Swedes, killed three of them, and took the remainder to Käpplingen (now Blasieholmen) (q.v.), where they killed them at night by setting fire to the house in which they were being held as prisoners. There is no independent account of the event other than this, which is biased, anti-German, and unclear on several points.

KARL VIII KNUTSSON. In June 1448, Karl Knutsson was chosen in Stockholm to become king of Sweden. He is often called *Karl Knutsson Bonde* (Karl Knutsson the Farmer). He was driven to leave Sweden by King Kristian I of Denmark; he sailed to Danzig on February 23, 1457. In 1463, Kristian I held an inquisition of the followers of Karl Knutsson. However, in October 1464, the palace surrendered to Karl Knutsson and the Swedes. On January 30, 1465, in Stockholm's palace, Karl Knutsson abdicated again. He returned yet again to Stockholm's palace on November 12, 1467, where he was proclaimed king of Sweden for the third time. Karl Knutsson died on May 11, 1470 and was buried at Riddarholm's Church (q.v.).

KARL IX (1550–1611). The youngest son of Gustav Vasa (q.v.). He became king in 1604 after many struggles against brothers and other relations. His royal motto was "God Is My Comfort." Karl fought against Catholicism, and finally gained victory at the battle of Stångebro, outside Linköping, in 1598. Sweden has remained Protestant ever since. In Stockholm, Karl IX gave the Germans sole rights to St. Gertrude's Church in 1607, thereby excluding the Finns. At the time of his death, Sweden was at war with Poland, Russia, and Denmark.

KARL X GUSTAV (1622–1660). A grandchild of Karl IX. At the age of 26, he became commander of the Swedish army in Germany. Following the abdication of Queen Kristina (q.v.) on October 24, 1654, the marriage of King Karl X Gustav and Hedvig Eleonora (q.v.) was celebrated, whereupon the new queen was crowned. Having been recently crowned in Uppsala Cathedral, Karl X Gustav arrived in Stockholm on mid-summer night, in 1654, to be greeted by a salute of cannons on Brunkeberg (q.v.). His royal motto was "In God My Destiny. He shall decide it." He died at age 38, and was buried at Riddarholm's Church (q.v.). There is a bronze, equestrian statue of the king by the steps to the Nordic Museum (q.v.).

KARL XI (1655–1697). The only son of Karl X Gustav. He became king at age 4, and was crowned when he came of age in 1672. His royal motto was "God Has Become My Protector." King Karl XI's regent, Queen Eleonora (q.v.), issued orders concerning the government of the town of Stockholm in the same year. An alliance with France led to the Swedish war against the Danes. Karl became a popular king through his personal acts of bravery in this successful war. He used his power and popularity to reclaim estates and wealth from the nobility. After the war, the young king devoted himself to internal affairs. He is particularly remembered for his organizational ability. Through indiscriminate inquisition and reduction methods, the state gained the means to establish a well-organized military and civilian tenure. King Karl was popular with the farmers and was able to increase his power.

In 1697, his body was rescued, in his coffin in a mausoleum, from an extensive fire at the palace.

KARL XII (1682–1718). The son of King Karl XI. On December 14, 1697, at the age of 15, Karl XII was crowned in Stockholm, in *Storkyrkan* (The Cathedral) (q.v.). His royal motto was "God My Protector." After the outbreak of the war against Saxony-Poland, Denmark, and Russia, Karl XII left his capital on April 16, 1700, never to see it again. He was to be the last Swedish king to rule over the Baltic empire. The war continued throughout his reign. At age 36, he was killed in battle in Norway in November 1718. His body was subsequently exhumed twice, to establish whether he was shot by the enemy or his own side. These efforts were unsuccessful. There is an interesting exhibit on this subject in the Medieval Museum of Stockholm (q.v.). On February 26, 1719, Karl XII was interred in Riddarholm Church, Stockholm (q.v.). There are varying opinions of Karl XII; to some he was a hero, to others a tyrant who lost Sweden's empire. A statue of Karl XII was raised in Karl XII's Square (q.v.), which was then so named in 1868. Surrounding the statue are four mortars; they were booty from war in 1673 and 1701.

KARL XIII (1748–1818). The second son of King Adolf Fredrik (q.v.). On June 29, 1809, Karl XIII was crowned king of Sweden. His royal motto was "The People's Well-being My Highest Principle." From 1792 to 1796, he was regent for Gustav IV Adolf (q.v.), but had passed on this responsibility to the politician Reuterholm, who became very unpopular. In 1810, as a senile old man, he retained the title of monarch, but Crown Prince Karl Johan (q.v.) took over as virtual ruler. In 1814, Karl officially became king of Norway, when that country was compelled into a union with Sweden.

KARL XIV JOHAN (1763–1844). Born Jean Baptiste Bernadotte in France. He became a general during the French Revolution. He accepted the Swedish invitation to become their crown prince in 1810, and took the name Karl Johan. On May 11, 1818, Karl XIV Johan (q.v.) was crowned king of Sweden and Norway in *Storkyrkan* (The Cathedral) (q.v.). Nicholas I of Russia visited Karl XIV in Stockholm in 1838. In 1844, Karl XIV Johan was buried in Riddarholm Church (q.v.).

B.E. Fogelberg's (q.v.) statue of Karl XIV Johan was unveiled at Skeppsbron on November 4, 1854. The king may be seen, proudly astride his horse, right beside Slussen (The Sluice Gate) (q.v.), which was named the Karl Johan Sluice. The present King Carl XVI Gustaf (q.v.) is a direct descendant of Bernadotte.

KARL JOHAN'S CHURCH. See SKEPPSHOLM CHURCH.

KARL XV (1826–1872). The son of Oskar I. He married Lovisa of the Netherlands in 1850, and became king of Norway and Sweden in 1859. His royal motto was "The Country Shall Be Built Upon the Law." He had been crown prince regent from 1857. He was a keen supporter of Scandinavianism. He was a popular monarch and renowned for being "one of the people." In 1909, an equestrian statue of Karl XV was erected near the entrance to Skansen (q.v.).

KARL XVI GUSTAV. See CARL XVI GUSTAV.

KARLAPLAN. This circular, tree-framed open area was the only one of several places exemplifying French planning influence, contained in the Lindhagen (q.v.) City Plan, that actually came into being. Karlaplan, Stockholm's largest open plaza, dates from the 1920s.

KARLBERG. See SOLNA.

KAROLINSKA INSTITUTET *(THE CAROLINE INSTITUTE)*. On December 13, 1810, a royal decree was issued for the creation of an institute responsible for the training for medical treatment. This institute was soon given the name Karolinska Medical-Surgical Institute (q.v.). The first joint doctoral presentation, given with Stockholm's University (q.v.), was held in the Blue Hall of the City Hall *(Stadshuset)* (q.v.) on May 29, 1930. The institute is responsible for nominating the winners of Nobel prizes (q.v.) for physiology and medicine. In 1995, the institute was renovated.

KÄRRTORP. During and after World War II, mostly large apartment blocks were constructed. The suburb of Kärrtorp is an example of this style of living.

KASTELLHOLM. Possibly the only place in inner Stockholm where gneiss and granite rocks, beautifully smoothed by the Ice Age and with deep grooves, may be seen. The height of the rocks contrast with the surrounding verdant growth. From the castle (*kastell*) atop the hill flies a naval flag, for this has been an outlook point since 1848, offering wide views of the waterways below. On March 28, 1990, the naval flag on Kastellholmen was lowered for what was thought to be the last time. But as that broke a 350-year-old tradition and resulted in considerable public criticism, a foundation donated 100,000 SEK to cover future expenses connected with continuation of the flag ceremonies. A few months later, the flag was raised again on June 6, Sweden's National Day, and the tradition has been resumed.

KATARINA CHURCH. Located on *Högbergsgatan* (High Hill Street) the church was erected between 1656 and 1690 to replace Sturekapellet. It was consecrated in 1671. The architect was Jean de la Vallée (q.v.). Built at the request of Johan III (q.v.), it has a baroque style, influenced by the Italian late-Renaissance period, with a dome. The church was named after the mother of Karl X Gustav (q.v.). The king had considered building a new palace on Södermalm, an ideal location with commanding views. However, he later decided to build a church to accommodate the growing population. Various parts of the city were destroyed by a vast fire on April 24, May 1, and May 14, 1723. Katarina Church was among the buildings that were badly damaged. The furnishings, roof, and dome were destroyed. The existing dome, which can be seen from considerable distances around Stockholm, was completed in 1740. The church has been renovated several times; in 1829, 1891, and the between 1952 and 1954. Particularly noteworthy is the baroque dome designed by Adelcrantz (q.v.) in 1868, with its octagonal obelisk over an octagonal lanternine. Also impressive are the 1743 altar also by Adelcrantz (q.v.), the pulpit, and the organ façade. Katarina Church is the oldest of the central-church-style buildings in Stockholm. On the night of May 17, 1990, it was damaged by fire thought to be the result of an electrical fault in wires in the wooden substructure of the dome. The dome was recently repaired and given a copper roof. In May 1995, the church was reconsecrated.

KATARINAHISSEN (*KATARINA ELEVATOR*). The first *Katarinahissen* was erected in 1884. It was steam-driven, and originally cost 5 öre to go up and 3 öre to descend. (There are 100 öre in a krona). Over one and a half million people, Stockholmers and tourists alike, paid to mount this technological masterpiece and enjoy a bird's-eye view of Stockholm. From here it is easy to appreciate the strategic location of Stockholm, between the sea and Lake Mälaren (q.v.). The old elevator was closed on May 28, 1933, and demolished. The new elevator was in operation by 1935. It was built in the then-popular functionalist style.

KELLGREN, JOHAN HENRIK (1751–1795). An author and member of the Swedish Academy (q.v.) from 1786. He was Sweden's foremost exponent during the period of Enlightenment. On October 29, 1778, the newspaper *Stockholms Posten* commenced publication. Kellgren was actively involved in the publication and during his time it was Sweden's most illustrious cultural medium.

KEY, ELLEN (1849–1926). Became one of the most influential cultural personalties among the writers of the 1890s. She lived for some time at Valhallavägen 49 (now 88–90), where she held "open house" on Sundays. Her much-read titles *Tankebilder* (Thought Pictures) and *Lifslinjer* (Lines in Life) demonstrated an unusual combination of the radicalism of the 1880s with the romantic, cultural-idealism of the 1890s. Ellen Key played an important part in the development of the women's rights movement through her book *Missbrukad kvinnokraft* (Misused Woman-Power), in which she promoted woman's individuality and her primary duty to obtain an outlet for her mother instinct in the work of the community. She spent much of her life in Stockholm where she began teaching in 1880.

KINGS. See individual names.

KING'S SHEEP. In April 1989, city authorities decided that the city's approximately 500 sheep should have as their summer pasture the fields of Järva, south of Akalla, instead of at Ladugårdsgärdet (q.v.), as had been customary since 1944. In 1939, some 20 sheep were introduced around Haga Palace (q.v.) to create a pastoral atmosphere. They have since been described as "the King's Sheep." After 1943, the sheep had their winter quarters at Åkeshov farm and, in the beginning of June every year, in the small hours, they were driven through the streets across Stockholm to Gärdet, their summer pasture. More numerous public events and killings by unleashed dogs led to the decision to change their grazing field.

KISTA. In 1962, parts of Järvafältet (q.v.) were acquired from the state for gradual residential development in the northern suburbs. At the end of the '60s and during the '70s, Kista was developed. In the fall of 1977, a town center was opened in Kista, which describes itself as the suburb where the countryside begins. In 1994, 23.5 percent of the inhabitants of Kista were immigrants.

KLARA CHURCH. Erected between 1575 and 1590 to replace a church destroyed in 1527 by Gustav Vasa that had belonged to the nuns of Klara Convent. Johan III was responsible for its construction. The original church had a single, vaulted nave, an adjoining, three-side choir, and a square tower. The tower was extended in 1627 to become the highest in Sweden. On June 8, 1751, extensive acts of arson raged in Stockholm, including the burning down of Klara Church. The pyromaniacs were arrested and punished. Rebuilding began immediately, and in 1753 Adelcrantz (q.v.) took over the work. The tower was rebuilt between 1884 and 1886. It had, for that time, a remarkable height of 106 meters. The church has many fine points, including angels on the altar, created by Tobias Sergel (q.v.) in 1790, and paintings by Olle Hjortzberg. Further restorations followed in 1963–65. The building, which has a single nave, and is made of brick and retains much of its old architectural appearance. It is surrounded by a churchyard containing buildings from the 18th century. Buried there are three well-known Swedish poets: Carl Gustaf af Leopold (1756 to 1829), Anna-Maria Lenngren (1754 to 1817), and Carl Michael Bellman (1740 to 1795) (q.v.).

KLARA KLOSTER. *(CLARE CONVENT)*. The convent of the order of St. Clare, the female branch of the Franciscans, was built in the 1280s at Norrmalm outside the city, and became a very powerful landowner.

KONSERTHUSET. See CONCERT HALL.

KÖPMANGATAN *(MERCHANT STREET)*. The oldest known street-name in Stockholm. There were shops here 700 years ago. The street is still the old regulation width of 8 ells (4.75 meters). In Köpmam Square there is a bronze copy of the St. George *(Göran)* and the Dragon statue, donated by a rich merchant; the original is in *Storkyrkan* (The Cathedral) (q.v.).

KRISTIAN I, KING. Toward the end of the time of the Kalmar Union (q.v.), Sweden was governed by Sten Sture the elder (q.v.). Before the union dissolved, Kristian I of Denmark sailed to Stockholm to occupy the palace and reclaim the kingdom of which he considered himself to be ruler. Those who were against the union resisted, and a decisive battle was fought. The Danes were defeated by the followers of Sten Sture the elder (q.v.) at the Battle of Brunkeberg (q.v.) on October 10, 1471. This was a turning point in Swedish history.

KRISTIAN II, KING (1481–1559). In Swedish, he is called Kristian the Tyrant. Kristian II led a Danish army to threaten Stockholm, but was repelled near Djurgård Bridge by Sten Sture the younger (q.v.) and the Swedes in August 1517. The following year, Kristian II camped on Södermalm and started to beseige Stockholm. In July 1518, fighting broke out between the troops of Kristian II and the Swedes under Sten Sture the younger (q.v.). Legend has it that Gustav Eriksson Vasa (q.v.) was the bearer of the main Swedish banner. Later, in 1518, negotiations began between representatives of Kristian II and Sten Sture the younger at Kaknäs, on northern Djurgård. In 1520, Kristian II, who had been attacking Stockholm since May, promised an amnesty for all that had been perpetrated against the Danish soldiers and clergy, from his camp on southern Djurgården on September 5. Two days later, Kristian II made his procession into Stockholm. On November 4, he was crowned king of Sweden in *Storkyrkan* (The Cathedral).

Stockholm's *"Bloodbath"* (q.v.) took place on November 8–9, 1520. Kristian II, the union king, contrived to have two bishops in Stockholm deposed. This became a signal for national liberation, from the union and the pope.

KRISTINA, QUEEN (1626–1689). Kristina was a remarkable and enigmatic woman. She was the daughter of Gustav II Adolf. She became queen in 1633, at age 6, shortly after her father died on the battlefield at Lützen. Axel Oxenstierna (q.v.) was regent during her years of minority. She was crowned in 1644. Huge amounts of time, money, and effort were expended in making Uppsala a suitable coronation city for the queen. At the last minute, the venue was changed to Stockholm. Her royal motto was "Wisdom is the Support of the Country." Shiploads of newly acquired booty from the war arrived to furnish the queen's palace. It included many priceless treasures, including the Goths' 1,400–year-old silver bible, which is now in Uppsala at the Carolina Rediviva Library. Her private library became one of the largest in Europe.

She thanked God for having made her a woman. Yet, at the same time, she despised women and only socialized with men. One minute she was cursing like a stevedore, and the next she was rubbing shoulders with Europe's most renowned philosophers. A brilliant, eccentric, and cultured woman, Kristina made Stockholm an international center of learning and the arts.

The medieval town of Stockholm, with its narrow, crooked streets, was rebuilt with straight roads and blocks of buildings. Norrmalm (q.v.) was laid out in a manner that lasted until the 1960s. *Regerings-gatan* (Goverment Street), named after her regency, also brought improvement, as did *Drottninggatan* (Queen Street) (q.v.), named after her highness. In *Gamla stan* (Old Town) and on *Riddarholmen* (q.v.), palaces were built that still remain. Neither before nor since have such magnificent private buildings been erected—for example, Wrangel Palace, De la Gardie's Läckö, and Oxenstierna's Tidö (qq.v.). Drawings of these buildings appear in Erik Dahlberg's book *"Svecia anti-qva et hodierna,"* which was a literary masterpiece of the time, intended to demonstrate to the rest of the world that Sweden also had remarkable buildings. In 1649, Queen Kristina allowed the Lion's Den to be erected in the palace moat for a lion that was brought home from Prague as war booty. It included cages and a gallery for spectators of animal baiting. Philosophers and musicians flocked to her court, and she shed much of the warlike, Viking nature of the monarchy during the previous half-century. French philosopher René Descartes, who had been summoned by Queen Kristina in 1649, died on February 11, 1650. One of the sculptures of him, ceated by T. Sergel (q.v.), was erected in Adolf Fredrik's Church (q.v.) in 1770. In September 1652, a large fire ravaged Norrmalm (q.v.), and Queen Kristina actively participated in extinguishing the flames. Kristina did not feel at home in the Lutheran world. In 1654, she abdicated and soon thereafter gave up the religion for which her father had fought so hard. She became a Roman Catholic, and settled in Rome. She is buried in St. Peter's Church.

KRISTOFER, KING (1418–1448). Kristofer became king of Denmark in 1440. He then marched into Stockholm in 1441 and became king of Sweden. The following year, he was crowned king of Norway. He revised the common law of the realm *(landslag)*, which Magnus Eriksson (q.v.) had established in about 1350.

KULTURHUSET. See STOCKHOLM CULTURAL CENTER.

KUNGLIGA BIBLIOTEKET *(THE ROYAL LIBRARY).* Located in Humlegården (q.v.), the building is in new Renaissance style. The Royal Library was previously housed in the northeast wing of the royal palace. The new library was built between 1865 and 1878. It is Sweden's national library. On January 2, 1928, two newly built wings were opened. The building was enlarged again in 1961. The library contains many rare books, including *Djävulsbibeln* (The Devil's Bible) and the oldest Swedish book, *Äldre Västgötalagen* (The Elder Västgöta Laws). August Strindberg (q.v.) worked here as a young man. A copy of every book printed in Sweden is deposited here for the archives. There also is a vast number of foreign books. The volumes number 2 million and date back to royal collections from the 16th century.

At the beginning of 1994, the estimated figure for the number of visitors was only 18,000, due to closure of parts of the library for repairs, but in the previous year the figure was 182,000.

A new, large underground space for extra storage, currently is under construction.

KUNGLIGA TENNISHALLEN *(ROYAL TENNIS STADIUM). KLTK, Kungliga Lawntennisklubben,* Stockholm, is one of the country's best-known tennis clubs. It was formed in 1896 as HRH Crown Prince's LTK. It received its present name in 1907. Since 1943, it has been located at Kungliga Tennishallen. Among its prominent members have been King Gustaf V, Marcus Wallenberg (qq.v.), Lennart Bergelin, Ulf Schmidt, and Jan-Erik Lundquist.

See also *GLOBEN.*

KUNGLIGA TEATERN. See OPERA HOUSE.

KUNGSGATAN *(KING'S STREET).* Kungsgatan was reopened to traffic on November 24, 1911, after having been closed for construction through Brunkeberg Ridge in 1905. Full completion took until 1935. Kungsgatan passes through three city districts—from Östermalm through Norrmalm to Kungsholmen, and is sometimes called "Stockholm's Broadway."

A well-known feature of this busy steet is *Kungstornen* (King's Towers). The northern king's tower was ready in 1923. The second was built two years later.

KUNGSHOLMEN *(THE KING'S ISLAND).* A large island west of Norrmalm. In the Middle Ages, this was grazing land for the city's animals and those of the abbey. The island received its present name toward the end of the 1600s. At that time, Karl XI was king, Sweden was a great power, and Stockholm was truly recognized as the capital. The island was named in the king's honor. Kungsholmen has changed its name a number of times. At first it was called Liderne, which comes from the old Swedish word for slope or hillside. Then it became *Munkläget* (Friars' Camp), after the Franciscan monks who owned the island before Gustav Vasa (q.v.) incorporated it at the time of the Reformation. In the 17th century, Queen Kristina (q.v.) donated the land to the city. Because of its access to the water, it became a suburb for craftsmen. Like other parts of Stockholm, in the middle of the 17th century, Kungsholmen was affected by Klas Fleming's (q.v.) new city plan. The craftsmen's workshops lined the shores, and there were tanneries along Riddarsfärden; dwellings and some large houses filled the inner part of the islet, and further out lay the farm estates. In the 18th century, Kungsholmen was home to the Royal Hospital building. In the 19th century, heavy industry spread there, but hospital and residential construction continued. At this time, Kungsholmen was a poor part of the city, where underpaid workers, such as blacksmiths, pewter pot makers, and Italian workers specializing in glass-blowing sweated at tedious industrial jobs. The best-known of such employers was Bolinders, where they made machine parts for industry and railroads, as well as for stoves, ovens, fountains, and ornaments made of cast iron, the fashionable material at that time. On October 31, 1878, there was a tremendous fire that illuminated the Stockholm skyline. A steam mill that had revolutionized the Swedish flour industry in the early 19th century was ablaze. The mill, known as *Eldkvarn* (q.v.), was located where the present-day city hall *(Stadshuset)* now stands. Kronoberg prison is on Kungsholmen. It functions as a stopover place for criminals waiting to be tried or, in the case of a conviction, to be moved to one of the country's criminal institutions. No one has yet succeeded in escaping from the newly built part of the prison. An underground tunnel leads to *Rådhuset* (The Court House) (q.v.), where judgment is passed. Civil weddings are also conducted there. The court house, built in 1909–1915, has one of the most decorated interiors of any building in the city. The exterior is reminiscent of Vadstena Castle, with its Vasa-inspired Renaissance style. The city hall *(Stadshuset)* (q.v.) is the building on Kungsholmen with the most character. There also are the two large press houses that can be seen especially well from Västerbron (q.v.). *Dagens Nyheter-Expressen* (q.v.) is the taller of the two, with 24 floors. *Svenska Dagbladet* (q.v.) has 14, although its building is much broader. St. Eriksgatan (St. Eric's Street) is named after Stockholm's patron saint, Erik, (q.v.) the king of Sweden during the 12th century. It runs from Kungsholmen, across St. Eriksbron (St. Eric's Bridge) far into Vasastaden (q.v.). Kungsholmen is divided by two main highways, Hantverkargatan and Flemingsgatan. On March 6, 1987, the newly built tax office was officially opened, at the corner of Fleminggatan and Scheelegatan. The building houses many government authorities, including the computer inspection office. Kungsholmstorg is the remains of an 1860s plan to create a traversing esplanade that never materialized.

KUNGSHOLM CHURCH. See ULRIKA ELEONORA'S CHURCH.

KUNGSHUSET. *(THE KING'S BUILDING)*. On May 7, 1697, the palace *Tre kronor*, (The Three Crowns) (q.v.) was destroyed by fire. The royal family resided for the next 57 years in the Wrangel Palace (q.v.) on Riddarsholmen (q.v.). It is now called *Kungshuset*.

KUNGSKLIPPAN *(THE KING'S CLIFF)*. Known as *Jungfruberget*, (The Maiden's Hill). Legend has it that a young girl was spirited into the hill. This is the same hill as *Kvarnberget* (Mill Hill), where the mill called "*lilla munkan*" (the little monk) once stood. The mill was demolished in 1850, when the land was needed to build homes for workers. These cottages were built of stone and timber, and surrounded by small garden plots. These homes were demolished in 1936, and replaced by modern apartment buildings.

KUNGSTRÄDGÅRDEN *(THE KING's GARDEN)*. These gardens are popularly known as "*Kungsan*". They date back to the 15th century. They were then the royal fruit and vegetables garden. Erik of Pomerania is reputed to have had a cabbage plot here. Since then, it has been both a splendid court garden and a desolate parade ground. As Karl XI's (q.v.) garden, it had a French character, modeled on Versailles (q.v.), although it did not have the water displays. The garden was then much more enclosed by walls, lines of trees, and nearby Jakob's churchyard. The gardens were permanently opened to the public on May 1, 1795. They underwent considerable improvement at that time. In his *Fredmans epistel 37*, Carl Michael Bellman (q.v.) gave a fine description of Kungsträdgården in the 1760s. When Norrbro (q.v.) was opened to pedestrian traffic in 1807, Kungsträdgården became a "snobs' parade." It remained so until the 20th century, when Birger Jarlsgatan and Strandvägen took over the role of being the most fashionable places. The garden is small, but widely used and appreciated as a park in the middle of town. In 1953, Stockholm celebrated its 700th anniversary, and Kungsträdgården was the center of the festivities for the first time. On August 26, 1987, at a ceremony in Kungsträdgården, the army handed over its last remaining horses to a foundation for their care and protection.

Standing in the gardens is a statue of Karl XII (q.v.) by J.P. Molin that was erected in 1868, and one of Karl XIII (q.v.) by E.G. Göthe. Additionally, there is a fountain by J. P. Molin (q.v.), a plaster model of which was on display at the Industrial Exhibition of 1866. Stockholmers use Kungsträdgården as a gathering place in the tradition of Bois de Boulogne in Paris.

The enterprise controlling Kungsträdgården is a daughter company of Stockholm's Chamber of Commerce. It originated as a result of the celebrations of Stockholm's 700th anniversary in 1953. Since then,

Kungsträdgården Park and Events Co., in close cooperation with the city, has developed the park and its programs. They claim that no other European capital has a comparable park in the heart of town that offers visitors so much free recreation, entertainment, and information. Activities range from outdoor chess to ice skating.

L

LABOR MARKET. Greater Stockholm is Sweden's largest common labor market, with more than 20 percent of the country's total jobs. Of Sweden's 47 company groups employing more than 5,000 people, 37 have their main office in the region.

The labor market of Greater Stockholm has changed markedly over the last 20 years. Fewer and fewer work in manufacturing, and the service sector has increased tremendously. Today, more than three-quarters of the labor force is in service-related jobs.

In the 1970s, employment increased most in the public sector, while in the 1980s the private sector expanded more strongly.

The proportion of people who work in Greater Stockholm is large, especially among women. 85 percent of the female—and 84 percent of the male—labor force (16–64-year-olds) go to work. 30 percent of the women work part-time, compared to 9 percent of the men.

Greater Stockholm has one-third of Sweden's high-tech industry. Almost half the country's computer programmers and operators—and 40 percent of the finance-sector employees—work in the region.

Banking, insurance, and company services have doubled in 25 years, and today they employ 16 percent of the region's working population. During the same period, the number of employees in manufacturing dropped by half. Manufacturing accounts for only 12 percent of the jobs today. The largest manufacturing industries are machinery and printing industry.

The public sector has contracted to some extent in recent years. Nevertheless, it employs more than a third of those working in the region.

By the turn of the century, the proportion of service jobs is expected to have grown even more. While employment will decrease within almost all basic industries, the need for labor is expected to increase in some parts of the service sector—for example, child care and care of the aged. Among company services, business services are expected to expand most rapidly.

LADUGÅRDSGÄRDET *(THE BARNYARD FIELD).* Often referred to simply as *Gärdet*. This is an area of Norra Djurgården (q.v.) that was previously used for military training and parades at the beginning of the 18th century, with its heyday during the reign of Karl XIV Johan (q.v.).

On June 7, 1831, the first horse race was held at Ladugårdsgärdet. By agreement between the state and the city, in 1928, construction on Ladugårdsgärdet was allowed.

At the end of the summer of 1991, the city-owned herd of sheep, which had been moved from its summer pasture on Ladugårdsgärdet to Järvafältet, was slaughtered because their winter quarters at Åkeshov farm had been destroyed by fire. A hundred replacement sheep were accommodated in temporary farm premises.

LADUGÅRDSLANDET. By royal decrees on February 28, 1639, and later, on March 5, 1640, Ladugårdslandet was incorporated with Stockholm. The name Ladugårdslandet officially was changed to Östermalm, in 1885. In 1890, the first May Day demonstration procession to Ladugårdsgärdet took place.

LADULÅS, MAGNUS (circa 1240–1290). The son of Birger Jarl (q.v.). He became king in 1275. He was a member of the Folkunga dynasty (q.v.), who ruled for four generations from 1250 to 1364. He introduced the system whereby those who supplied the king with horseriders were excused from paying taxes. This created a new class in society, the nobility. It also was the time of knights, an idea already introduced in France. Magnus Ladulås was buried at Riddarholm Church.

LAGERLÖF, SELMA (1858–1940). An author who won the Nobel Prize (q.v.) for literature in 1909. Her best-known work, outside Sweden at least, is probably *Nils Holgerssons underbara resa genom Sverige* (Nils Holgersson's Wonderful Journey Through Sweden). It tells of a little boy's flight on the back of a goose, the whole length and breadth of Sweden. Although Selma Lagerlöf can hardly be described as a Stockholm author, her chapter in this book on Stockholm is set in Skansen (q.v.). She described Stockholm as "the city that floats on the water."

LAKE MÄLAREN. See MÄLAREN.

LANDSORGANISATION I SVERIGE (LO). The central organization for the trade unions, it was founded in 1898. LO owns the newspapers *Stockholms Tidning* and *Aftonbladet*. In May 1991, the Norra Latin School building, which had been converted to a conference center at a cost of 72 million SEK, was sold to LO.

LÅNGHOLMEN. While awaiting the arrival of King Erik (q.v.), the Swedes assembled on Långholmen on August 10, 1435. This was the first mention of Långholmen. In 1647, Queen Kristina (q.v.) gave the island to the town of Stockholm. In 1724, the estate, Allstavik, was converted to a carding and spinning factory. It later became a detention center. In the 1820s, women prisoners were moved to Smedjegården. In 1835, what had originally been a clothing factory run by male prisoners became the Crown Prison. The central building was erected between 1874 and 1880, but is now closed. Altogether, it had been the city's island prison for 250 years, an era that came to an end in 1975, when the beaches were opened to the public for walks. Since 1989, the old local prison has been a hotel and youth hostel, with 254 beds. It also has an extensive park. Långholmen, by Riddarfjärden, is close to the middle of town. The manor house at Allstavik remains, with its cross-vaulted staircase and beamed ceiling. An old toll house, erected in 1624 by Gustav II Adolf, remains on the headland, Långholmsudde, opposite Smedsudde (Smith's headland), where lake tolls were collected.

On June 22, 1992, a private exhibition about the troubadour Carl Michael Bellman (q.v.) was opened to the public in Stora Henriksvik on Långholmen.

LANGUAGE. The "standard" language spoken in Sweden today, as encountered in the mass media, is largely based on dialects of the area around Stockholm.

See also SÖDERMALM.

LANTMÄTERIKONTOR (Land Surveyors' Office). Queen Kristina's (q.v.) summer house was situated near St. Jakob's Church. Simon de la Vallée (q.v.) was the architect. The building was used as the land surveyors' office from 1689 to 1975.

LARSSON, CARL (1853–1919). This well-known Swedish artist was born near Järntorget, in the Old Town. There is a plaque on the house at Prästgatan 78 (q.v.), a street that contains more of the Old Town's genuine history than the more frequented, parallel Västerlånggatan. The plaque reminds visitors of Larsson's early days there. He settled in Dalarna, at Sandborn. His cheerful watercolors have made him internationaly famous. He is one of the few Swedish artists who has become popular outside the country. He is best-known for his studies of everyday family scenes from rural life, but also is famous for his monumental fresco paintings in the National Museum (q.v.) and the huge oil painting of Gustav Vasa's (q.v.) procession into Stockholm on midsummer-day, 1523.

LEJONBACKEN *(LION HILL)*. The rubble from the old *Tre kronor* (Three Crowns) castle (q.v.) was piled up north of the site, to form the hill known as Lejonbacken. At the foot of this hill stand two bronze lions cast from the metal of a fountain that the enterprising and warring Swedes once stole from Kronberg Castle in Denmark.

LENNGREN, ANNA MARIA (1754–1817). An author who lived in Stockholm, at Beridarebansgatan 21, where she operated a well-known literary salon. She was born in Uppsala, but married a joint editor of the newspaper, *Stockholmsposten,* and then lived in the capital. She wrote satirical and idyllic poems and ballads. She is buried in Klara Churchyard (q.v.).

She was one of Sweden's foremost women authors and along with Bellman (q.v.), helped to have preserved a picture of 18th-century life.

LEOPOLD, CROWN PRINCE OF BELGIUM. (1901–1983). On November 4, 1926, Crown Prince Leopold of Belgium married Swedish Princess Astrid in Stockholm.

LIBRARIES. At the beginning of 1994, there were 39 *stadsbibliotek* (public libraries) in Stockholm.

See also *KUNGLIGA BIBLIOTEKET* and *STADSBIBLIOTEKET.*

LIDINGÖ. The high-class housing area of Lidingö was one of the first suburbs to be regarded as an "alternative residential district." So many of Stockholm's suburbs are uniform.

Lidingö got its own railroad in 1906.

LILJEHOLMEN. A result of the industrialization during the second half of the 19th century was the influx of workers in the suburb of Liljeholmen.

See also SUNDBYBERG.

LILJEVALCH'S ART GALLERY. Many famous Swedish artists have found fame at Liljevalch's spring salon. Every year, a jury chooses from about 3,000 contributions and 200–300 works are exhibited between February and April. Liljevalch's gallery concentrates primarily on well-known, modern artists, but art and crafts from earlier periods also are displayed. The gallery is situated between the Nordic Museum and the Gröna Lund amusement park on Djurgården. It was donated to Stockholm by C.F. Liljevalch, a rich wholesaler. The building was opened in March 1916 with an exhibition of paintings by Zorn, Liljefors, and Larsson (qq.v.)

LILJANSSKOGEN. A wood that is now part of the National City Park. See also *EKOPARKEN*.

LILJEFORS, BRUNO (1860–1939). A popular and prolific artist best remembered for his lifelike portrayals of wild animal life in Sweden, and for his vibrant landscapes.

LILLA ALBY. When the Västerås railroad line opened in 1876, it helped to bring about the development of the suburb Lilla Alby, as well as Nya Huvudsta in Solna and Solhem in Spånga.

LILLA ESSINGEN *(SMALL ESSINGEN)*. A small island in Lake Ma-laren, very close to Stockholm. Nearby is *Stora Essingen* (Large Es- singen). Although Sweden has a reputation for wide-open spaces and sparse population, in the 1940s Lilla Essingen was the most densely populated island in Europe. It came to be called "Divorce Island," because of the high divorce rate, presumably brought about by the overcrowded living conditions. Both islands came under Stockholm's control in 1916.

LIND, JENNY (Johanna Lind-Goldschmidt) (1820–1887). An opera and concert singer, a soprano. She became known as the "Swedish Nightingale." She was highly successful both in Europe and North America. Near the bridge, crossing from Strandvägen to Djurgården, on the left-hand side in a circle of silver birch trees beside the lake is a statue of Jenny Lind, clad in a flounced skirt and pantelets. Many Stockholmers associate her name with the songs of Carl Michael Bellman (q.v.).

LINDGREN, ASTRID (1907–). A prolific and highly popular writer of chidren's stories. Her books have been translated into more than a hundred languages, and many of them have been made into films. Possibly the best-known of her characters is *Pippi Långstrump* (Pippi Long Stocking). Although Astrid Lindgren is not principally associ- ated with Stockholm, she is very much at home in *Vasastan* (q.v.) and it is around this area that some of her books are set; in particular, the popular *Karlsson på taket* (Karlsson on the Roof) series.

LINDHAGEN TOWN PLAN. Carl Lindhagen (1860–1946) was mayor of Stockholm 1903 to 1930. During this time, a far-reaching city plan- ning effort reformed and improved the area. In the middle of Kar- laplan, there is a pond with a high column of water. On the north side is a statue by Carl Milles (q.v.) called *Flyggarmonument* (Monument to Aviators), in memory of Swedish fliers who died in crashes. It was unveiled in 1931.

LION'S DEN. In 1649, Queen Kristina (q.v.) allowed the Lion's Den to be erected in the palace moat for a lion that was brought home from Prague as war booty. It included cages and a gallery for spectators of animal baiting. The theater *Lejonkulan* (the Lion's Den) was inaugurated in 1667. It was the first permanent theater in Stockholm. After the destruction by fire in 1697 of the royal stage at Lejonkulan, *Stora bollhuset* (The Great Ball Building) was fitted out as a theater in 1699.

LO. See *LANDSORGANISATION I SVERIGE.*

LOCAL GOVERNMENT. Although local self-government has a long history in Sweden, the laws underlying the present system go back only about 130 years. The first such legislation is generally considered to be the local government ordinances of 1862, which separated the tasks of the Church of Sweden from civil tasks at the local level. Church tasks were assigned to the parishes of this Lutheran state church, while civil tasks were assigned to cities and rural municipal districts. At the regional level, the ordinances established a new unit of self-government known as the county council *(landsting)*, the territory of which coincides with the national government's regional administrative unit, the county *(län).*

In other words, there are two levels of secular local government in Sweden, with the municipality *(kommun)* as the smallest unit and the county council as the regional unit. Before 1971, Sweden was divided into 850 municipalities, each with an elected assembly. This number has now been reduced to 286. Greater Stockholm is the largest, but Swedish urban areas are small by international standards.

The new Local Government Act of 1992 defines the roles of each of the levels of local government. In addition, the Church of Sweden has local units, each still called a parish *(församling)*, the activities of which are regulated by the 1992 Ecclesiastic Law.

The public sector has gradually increased its share of the Swedish economy. During the past 15 or so years, overall central and local government spending—including both public-sector consumption and transfer payments to households—has exceeded 60 percent, and in some years even 70 percent, of the gross domestic product.

See also the INTRODUCTION and *STADSHUSET* (City Hall).

LOCAL TAXES. The Swedish Parliament has the power to determine both national and local taxes. However, local authorities are free to set the tax rates in their respective municipalities and county council districts.

See also APPENDIX NO. 7, **Taxes 1996** and **The Use of Local Tax in 1993,** for recent details.

LOCATION. From the Middle Ages, the Old Town was divided into four quarters, called inner, eastern, southern and western. Houses were identified by the owner's name. The naming of blocks of buildings commenced in 1702. A system of numbering all plots of land or housing blocks was published in 1729. House-numbering followed in 1810; street-numbers came later.

LO-JOHANSSON, IVAR (1901–1990). The son of a poor agricultural worker. Before an agreement reached in 1945, many workers on the land received only produce as part of their low wages. They were known as *statare*. A small group of writers became known as *"Statareskolan"* (The Statare School). Ivar Lo-Johansson was their energetic leader. His breakthrough novel was *Godnatt jord* (Good Night Earth). A more influential publication was his collection of three short stories called *Statarnoveller* (Statar Short Stories). He also wrote *Bara en mor* (Only a Mother), *Traktorn* (The Tractor), and *Geniet* (The Genius). His autobiographical series was introduced with *Analfabeten* (The Illiterate), written in 1951.

Originally from Södermanland, as of 1934, his Stockholm address was on Bastugatan. From there, he had a view of most of the city, which he described extensively, both critically and lovingly. His early years were a struggle, although later in life he was a regular customer at the exclusive restaurant Den Gyldene Freden (q.v.). Lo-Johansson unveiled a bust of Gunnar Sträng (q.v.), a former finance minister, in a playpark opposite Ivar Lo's own home on Bastuvägen. The park is named Ivar Lo's Park.

LOUIS DE GEER'S PALACE. Also known as Ebba Brahe's Palace (q.v.) or Schönborg's House. It stands on Götgatan, and is now the Dutch Embassy. The house was built from 1646 to 1651, and was bought in 1660 by Ebba Brahe (q.v.). The house was purchased in 1762 by a tobacco manufacturer named Schönborg. He arranged for the construction of the buildings which had curbed roofs. In 1964, the main building was restored, the extension buildings were removed, and De Geer's Palace returned to its original form. See also DE GEER, LOUIS.

LOVISA, ULRIKA (1720–1782). The daughter of Fredrick Wilhelm of Prussia. Frederick the Great was her brother. She married Adolf Fredrik (q.v.) in 1744; they were crowned in Stockholm on November 26, 1751. In 1753, she founded the Swedish *Vitterhetsakademien* (Academy of Learning). She dominated her husband, who died in 1771. Various intrigues increased her power. She even made an unsuccessful attempt to overthrow parliament and amend the constitution in her favor. In 1776, after rebuilding Fredrikshovs Palace (q.v.) under C.F. Alderkrantz's (q.v.) direction, the widow-Queen Lovisa Ulrika took up residence there. Gustav III (q.v.) was her son.

LÜBECK. A German city, in western Schleswig-Holstein, that was the leading member of the Hanseatic League (q.v.), which was a Middle Ages commercial and protective alliance of mainly German trading towns.

LUCIDOR (1638–1674). The poet Lasse Johansson is usually called by his pseudonym, Lucidor. His verses gave him recognition in Swedish literature. After his father's death, when Lasse was still young, he was brought up by his grandfather, who was an admiral. He traveled extensively and became fluent in many languages. These stood him in good stead when, in the 1660s, he came to Stockholm and tested the uncertain life of a poet. At first he composed verses for weddings and funerals, preferably in foreign languages. Obviously, these gave little scope for his artistic talents. It was his drinking-oriented verses for which he became best-remembered. However, his writing tended to be melancholic, while Bellman's (q.v.) contained more merriment. He has been called "the poet of intoxication and remorse". The best-known of Lucidor's poems is *"Skulle jag sörja, då vore jag tokot."* ("If I should mourn, then I would be mad."). His short life ended dramatically. He was killed by a knife wound in a tavern brawl, in the Old Town in 1674. His memorial stone stands in Maria churchyard.

LUNDINS FÅFÄNGA *(LUNDIN'S FOLLY)*. In January 1992, the summer house known as *Fåfänga* (Folly) was destroyed by arson. The building, which was situated between Tegelvik harbor and Folkungagatan, was originally erected in the middle of the 1770s by a wholesaler named Fredrick Lundin. It has since been copied and rebuilt. The building, which has an octagonal pleasure house and garden, was laid out on the bastion on which construction had commenced, high on the hill at Danvikstull. Together with a similar defense works on the other side of the mouth of the harbor, where Solliden is now situated, it was intended to protect the approach to Stockholm.

M

MAGNUSSON, BIRGER (1280–1321). He became king in 1290. On July 22 of that year, he confirmed Lübeck land-register's (q.v.) char-

ter in Sweden. His advisory council was established in Stockholm. He is best remembered in connection with Håtunaleken (The Håtuna Play) and Nyköpings gästabud (Nyköping's Banquet) (qq.v.)
See also BIRGER JARL.

MAIN SQUARE. See STORTORGET.

MAKALÖS *(PEERLESS)*. See DE LA GARDIE, JAKOB.

MÄLAREN, LAKE. Mälaren is Sweden's third-largest lake. A gateway to the sea, Lake Mälaren breathes life into Stockholm. Archeological discoveries as recently as 1956 at Helgö, on the island of Ekerö, have provided strong evidence that there were merchants and sailors around Mälaren long before the Viking period. The Svea people inhabited the Mälar valley. After Helgö, Birka, on Björkö, became the Svea's most important settlement. During the Viking period, between 800 and 1000 A.D., it is estimated that a thousand people lived on Birka. Archeologists have found about 3,000 graves, and new discoveries are made quite regularly. It was to Birka that the missionary Ansgar sailed in the middle of the 800s in his attempt to Christianize the Swedish heathens. The Mälar valley retained its importance during the whole Viking period. Nowhere in Sweden are there as many runestones (q.v.) as here. Many forts and castles were built around Mälaren during the Middle Ages, the Vasa period, and the Era of Great Power. Today, many of them are museums open to the public. The two best-known are Gripsholm Castle (q.v.), at Mariefred, and Skokloster (q.v.), representing two quite different periods and styles. In April 1780, Lake Mälaren overflowed and caused extensive damage. Sweden's first steamship was built in Stockholm, and commenced traffic on Lake Mälaren in 1818.

MALM. A *malm* is a district, a part of a town. Originally, malmar were hilly districts around the city center where executions were carried out. People were not allowed to live in the malmar, but as Stadsholmen (Old Town) (q.v.) became more and more crowded, permission was granted for homes to be built in these surrounding malmar. Workers with horses and carts were moved outside the city wall to Södermalm (q.v.). Noisy and unattractive, sometimes even evil-smelling, trades were also moved there, along with lepers and mental defectives.

MAP OF STOCKHOLM. The earliest surviving map of the city is dated 1622.
See also CITY MUSEUM OF STOCKHOLM.

MARGARETA, QUEEN (1353–1412). The queen of Norway, Sweden, and Denmark. In 1398, Queen Margareta took over Stockholm from the Hanseatic League (q.v.). She founded the Kalmar Union (q.v.), an association of the Scandinavian countries, which lasted, with interruptions, until 1521.

MARIA ELEONORA, QUEEN Maria Eleonora (1599–1655). Queen of King Gustav II Adolf (q.v.). She married him in 1620. The king's death at Lützen in 1632 filled her with grief and, in desperation, she fled the kingdom. She hid on the island of Nåttarö, in a shallow cave in a steep hill above the beach of a gentle bay. It is called Stora Sand (Great Sand), and is possibly the archipelago's best beach.

MARIAHISSEN *(MARIA ELEVATOR)*. Construction was completed in 1886. An iron bridge links the elevator to Söder Mälarstrand.

MARIA MAGDALENA'S CHURCH. Situated on the corner of Hornsgatan and Bellmansgatan. The church is built in the shape of a cross in baroque style, and succeeds a Middle Ages chapel from the 14th century named Maria Magdalena. Nearby was Helga Kors kapell, (Holy Cross), which Gustav Vasa (q.v.) ordered to be torn down in 1527. Johan III (q.v.) was instrumental in the building of a new church, which commenced in 1576. It took a hundred years to build, and has subsequently been rebuilt and added to several times. Maria Magdalena's Church was consecrated in 1634. Construction of the tower, which was not highly regarded took place in the 19th century. In the churchyard, there is a row of joined graves. Twenty six of those from the 18th century remain, and behind each black, wrought-iron railing lie several of the rich citizens from the Age of Liberty (q.v.). In a joint grave lie the poets Stagnelius (q.v.) and Nicander. The last person to be buried here, was Evert Taube (q.v.).

MARIATORGET *(MARIA SQUARE)*. The square was originally a fire-break in the form of an open space, following an extensive fire in 1759. It was named Hornstorget, but renamed Adolf Fredriks (q.v.) torg after the then-reigning king, Adolf Fredrik. The king sanctioned this change, on the condition that no executions be carried out there. Later, Gustav III (q.v.) arranged parties in the square, and in 1905 it became a marketplace. In 1958, the name was changed again, to Mariatorget. The sculptures situated there are *Tors fiske* (Thor Fishing) by A. H. Wissman, 1903; *Snöklockan* (Snow Bell) and *Tjusningen* (Enchantment), 1900; and Per Hasselberg, 1917. The oldest building around the square is the Methodist church, dated 1888.

MARIEBERG. An area dominated by two huge newspaper office build-ings. The 14–story *Svenska Dagbladet* (q.v.) was erected in 1961 to 1962. The 25–story *Dagens Nyheter* (q.v.) building was completed in 1964. Below the newspaper offices is Marieberg Park and the Smeduddsbadet, a popular bathing area for Stockholmers.

MARITIME HISTORY MUSEUM (*SJÖHISTORISKA MUSÉET*). Situ-ated at Djurgårdsbrunnvägen 24. The building was erected in the 1930s. It exhibits Swedish shipbuilding, marine defense, and com-mercial shipping from the 17th century to the present. Naval history is on the lower floor and civil shipping on the upper. More than a hundred models on the same scale portray the growth in the size of ships over more than a thousand years. A unique collection of model ships from the 17th and 18th centuries is featured. There are original ship interiors, including one from the schooner "*Hoppets skans*" Hope's Defense (1878), as well as a stern with cabin from Gustav III's (q.v.) schooner "*Amphion.*"

MÅRTEN TROTZIGS GRÄND. The narrowest passageway between the old houses of *Gamla stan* (the Old Town) (q.v.). It is as narrow as 90 centimeters wide. The whole "street", from end to end, is made up of 36 steps. Mårten Trotzig was a merchant who owned a small shop selling iron, copper, and other goods. He was killed during a trip to Kopparberget to collect supplies.
See also OLD TOWN.

MAYORS OF STOCKHOLM (*BORGMÄSTARE*)
See APPENDIX NO. 1.

MEDBORGARHUSET (*THE CITIZEN'S BUILDING*). Located at Medborgarplatsen, it was erected in 1939. The building houses a gymnastics hall; a swimming pool with the south-facing wall made almost completely of glass; a branch library; a room for study; a banquet hall; and the so-called Ljunglöfska parlor. The magnificent fittings from the 1980s were donated by the snuff manufacturer Ljung-glöf, and had previously been the family's furniture in their house on Sveavägen (q.v.).
The official opening of *Medborgarhuset* took place in 1939. Oppo-site *Medborgarhuset* is Lillienhoff's Palace, erected in the 17th cen-tury.
On December 14, 1991, Sandrew Film Company opened a new multitheater at Medborgarplatsen containing eight theaters on two floors.

MEDIEVAL MUSEUM OF STOCKHOLM. Situated on Strömparterren, on Helgeandsholmen (qq.v.). When excavations for an underground car park for Sweden's parliament (q.v.) began in the 1970s,
ruins and skulls from the Middle Ages were found. This is now one
of Stockholm's most evocative museums, with low lighting and
sounds from the 15th century town. This underground museum lies
between the Old Town (q.v.) and the modern city center.

MEDITERRANEAN MUSEUM. Situated at Fredsgatan 2, it originates
from 1640. There are three sections: the Greek-Roman, the Egyptian,
and the Islamic. The main hall contains an impressive display of architecture and sculpture from antiquity, Renaissance Italy and neo-
classicist Sweden. Included are the gods of Olympus and Greek
vases; Etruscan crafts and Roman figures in marble; archeological
finds from Cyprus; Islamic art; and Egyptian.

MILLES, CARL (1875–1955). A well known and popular sculptor renowned for his monumental works, often involving fountains. They
are memorable for their fantastical nature. The sculpture *Solsångaren*
(Sun Singer), symbolizing the poet Tegnér's "Song to the Sun," was
unveiled on October 25, 1926. Milles' sculpture *Orpheus* is in front
of *Konserthuset* (The Concert Hall) (q.v.).

MILLES MUSEUM *(MILLESGÅRDEN)*. Situated on Lidingö, at Carl
Millesväg 2. In addition to the studio of the famous sculptor Carl
Milles (q.v.), the museum has an extensive Italian-style terrace featur-
ing most of Milles' famous statues. There also is a large collection of
antiquities, including Greek and Roman art, and collections of medieval and east Asian sculptures. Milles died in 1955, but the establishment, which was his private home, had been opened to the public
since 1936.

MOBERG, VILHELM (1898–1973). After he moved to Stockholm, this
author often longed for his beloved origins, in Småland. In the 1930s,
he wrote a three-volume autobiographical account of his life called
Knut Toring. Set in *Fjällgatan* (Fell Street) (q.v.) and *Frejgatan*.
Moberg became internationally known toward the end of his life,
through the highly successful novels *Utvandrarna* and *Invandrarna*
(Emigrants and Immigrants). These told the story of mass emigration
to the United State of America and were brought to the screen, enjoying worldwide success.

MODERN ART MUSEUM. Situated on Skeppsholmen, the building
was originally a drill hall for Naval personnel erected in 1854. The

building was altered in 1958, and the National Museum's collection of 20th-century art was transferred there. It holds the best collection of modern art in Sweden, with exhibits by Matisse, Picasso, Kandinsky, Gioconetti, Dali, Rauschenberg, Warhol, and many others. There are more than 4,000 works. The museum has gained considerable international renown. In addition to the permanent exhibition, one or more thematic exhibitions are often put on. While a new, larger museum is under construction, to be opened in 1998, the Modern Museum is temporarily at Birger Jarlsgatan 57.

On the night of November 8, 1993, Sweden's largest art theft was carried out. Thieves entered through the roof of the Modern Museum and removed eight paintings by Pablo Picasso and Georges Braque, valued at 500 million SEK. Seven of the paintings were subsequently recovered by the police, but the most valuable was feared to have been taken out of the country.

MOLIN, JOHAN PETER (1814–1873). This sculptor's best-known works are both in Kungsträdgården (q.v.). In 1868, the statue of Karl XII (q.v.) was unveiled, and in 1873, Molin's fountain. This fountain was originally modeled in 1866 for the Stockholm Exhibition (q.v.), then was created in bronze in 1873. It represents the water sprite playing for the god Ägir and his daughters.

MOSEBACKE TORG *(MOSEBACKE SQUARE)*. *Södra teatern* (South Theater) was erected in Mosebacke torg in 1852. Between 1899, and 1901, alterations and additions were made, including an extra story and a new parlor. In the theater square stands *Systrarna* (The Sisters), a sculpture by Nils Sjögren, that was unveiled in 1945. The water tower was erected between 1895 and 1897, and belongs to the national romantic chevalier style of architecture. From Mosebacke torg, a foot-bridge leads across to the *Katarinahissen* (Katarina Elevator) (q.v.). Unlike most plazas in Stockholm that have been affected by traffic and new construction, Mosebacke has retained much of its peaceful, character. In the north-east corner of the square, there used to be a restaurant with a terrace. From here, August Strindberg (q.v.) saw the view of Stockholm in the 1870s that he describes in the well-known book *Röda rummet* (The Red Room).

MUSEUM OF ARCHITECTURE. See ARCHITECTURE; SWEDISH MUSEUM OF ARCHITECTURE.

MUSEUM OF BIOLOGY. Located on Djurgården, it was recently renovated. It is a small brown building next to the Hazelius (q.v.) entrance to Skansen (q.v.). It was completed in 1893 for the Stockholm Exhibition (q.v.) in 1897. Its style is pure Old Norse. The museum has a variety of stuffed animals, against a background of panoramas by the well-known Swedish painter Bruno Liljefors (q.v.). The Museum of Biology claims to be the first in the world to show animals in their natural habitat.

On November 11, 1993, the Biological Museum on Djurgården was reopened. Founded a hundred years earlier, it had been closed for a year for extensive interior and exterior renovations.

MUSEUM OF DANCE. Situated at Barnhusgatan 12–14, Folkets hus (q.v.). This museum claims to be the only one of its type in the world. The Museum of Dance tells the story of dance of all kinds, although mainly European, in a variety of settings. Stage design sketches, works of art, stage models, costumes, masks, and musical instruments can be seen. There are also major exhibitions on the Swedish and Russian ballet, modern dance, and folk dance.

MUSEUM OF EASTERN ANTIQUITIES. The museum is in a long, narrow building originally designed by N. Tessin the younger (q.v.). It once housed Karl XII's (q.v.) bodyguards and their horses. It is situated next to the Museum of Modern Art. On display are collections of fine art objects from China, Japan, Korea, and India, dating from the Stone Age to the late 19th century. It includes one of the world's most eminent collections of Chinese art outside Asia.

MUSEUM OF MEDICINE. Located at Åsögatan 146. The collections are in an 18th-century house on Söder (q.v.), and display the development of medicine. One exhibit shows a doctor's reception room at the end of the 19th century. There also is an operating theater and an X-ray unit; surgical instruments dating from 1759; and an exhibition of a ward in Seraphim Hospital in 1830.

MUSEUM OF MUSIC. The museum is housed in a 300-year-old former bakery on Sibyllegatan. Instruments, pictures, and sheet and living music illustrate the role of music during various periods and in various environments. On display is Bellman's (q.v.) zither. There are also special exhibitions; for example, about how music is formed or about how the principles of music are applied. Instruments may be played by visitors.

MUSEUM OF NATIONAL ANTIQUITIES. Situated at Narvavägen 13–17, near Karlaplan. Permanent exhibitions include gold and silver treasures from the Iron Age and the Viking era through the end of the 16th century. There also are major collections of glass, ceramics, weapons, and textiles from ancient and medieval times.

MUSEUM OF NATURAL HISTORY. See SWEDISH MUSEUM OF NATURAL HISTORY.

MUSEUM OF PHOTOGRAPHY. Opened in 1971 as a subsidiary department of the Modern Museum (q.v.). It has, among other things, a permanent exhibition on the history of 20th-century photography. Like the Modern Museum, this is also temporarily at Birger Jarlsgatan, until 1998.

MUSEUMS. Museums are popular, and began with one in the royal palace. It is the oldest museum in Sweden, dating from 1628.

Stockholm has more than 50 museums. They are listed in APPENDIX 3.

MUSIC. See CULTURAL CAPITAL.

MYNTGATAN *(MINT STREET)*. Takes its name from *Kungliga myntverket* (The Royal Mint), which stood where *Kanslihuset* (the Chancery) (q.v.) now stands. The mint was built at the end of the 17th century, and was rebuilt several times. When Gustav III (q.v.) returned from his travels in Italy in the 1780s, the building was given the appearance of a Greek temple, in Doric style. Mint Square is said to be "at the center of power," surrounded by the royal palace, the parliament building and the various ministries.

Mint Square is the site of the old *Norraport* (North Gate), which had a drawbridge that sealed off the Old Town.

N

N.K. See NORDISKA KOMPANIET.

NACKA. Nacka became a town in 1949. It consists mainly of detached houses and a nature reserve. Previously independent municipalities, Saltsjöbaden, (Saltsjö) Duvnäs, and Storängen (qq.v.) are now incorporated in Nacka.

In November 1994, it was reported that a private diver had discovered eight wrecks in Kungsviken, off Nacka. They are lying at a depth of about 10 meters. Like *Lilla Sverige* (Little Sweden), the area may have been a harbor used by Danish vessels. If so, the wrecks may be connected with the blockades of Stockholm during the final stages of the Kalmar Union (q.v.).

NATIONAL DAY *(SVENSKA FLAGGANS DAG)* (Swedish Flag Day). celebrated on June 6, the date Gustav Vasa (q.v.) was chosen as king in 1523. Karl X Gustaf (q.v.) became king during the Era of Great Power (q.v.) on June 6, 1654. Oscar II married Sophia (q.v.) on the same date in 1857. Karl XIII Johan became king on June 6, 1809. It also happens to be the birthday of tennis player Björn Borg. A. Hazelius (q.v.) was the first to organize a flag festival in Stockholm, in 1893. The first Swedish Flag Day at *Stadion* (Stockholm's Stadium) was held in 1906. The public failed to support that venue so, in the 1960s, it moved to Skansen, where Hazelius had originally organized the celebrations. It is now referred to as *Sveriges nationaldag* (Sweden's National Day).

NATIONAL SPORTS MUSEUM. See SWEDEN'S NATIONAL SPORTS MUSEUM.

NATIONAL SWEDISH MUSEUM OF FINE ARTS. Housed in a large building in the Venetian palatial style on Blasieholm (q.v.), across the water from the royal palace. This is Sweden's largest museum of art, with works from the 15th century to 1900. There are paintings by international and Swedish masters; Rembrandt and Renoir, Zorn and Larsson. Many famous Swedish paintings can be viewed here, as well as sketches, engravings, and crafts from the Renaissance to modern times. There also are sculptures. Concerts are held all year round, the most popular of which are the summer evening events in the building's grand entrance hall.

NATIONAL SWEDISH MUSEUM OF SCIENCE AND TECHNOL-OGY. Located at Musievägen 7, on Norra Djurgården, it is very much a living museum with old motorcycles, steam engines, jet turbines, and model railroads. The museum, which takes up several floors, has exhibits about mining technology, the production of iron, cars, and aircraft, technology in the home, the history of electricity and chemistry, computers, and Polhem's inventions, together with engineering technology. In the *Teknorama*, visitors can try out their own technical skills. Next to the museum is the Museum of Telecommunications, including a room devoted to L.M. Ericsson, pioneer of the Swedish telephone industry. This museum also is known as the Technology Museum (q.v.)

NATURAL HISTORY MUSEUM. See SWEDISH MUSEUM OF NATURAL HISTORY.

NEWSPAPERS AND PERIODICALS. The main, daily morning newspapers in Stockholm: *Dagens Nyheter* and *Svenska Dagbladet*.
Evening newspapers: *Aftonbladet* and *Expressen*.

Stockholm periodicals in English: *Stockholm City, Stockholm This Week, Stockholm Information Service, Globen City Magazine, Stockholm's Kommun, Stockholm Business Magazine* (The magazine for business people visiting Stockholm).

NILSSON, SVANTE (STURE). Chosen in Stockholm as regent in 1504. He was regent until 1512.

NOBEL LIBRARY. Situated above the Stock Exchange (q.v.) at Stortorget. The aim of the library is not only to judge the Nobel entries but also to aid literary researchers and the general public. The stock of books contains a lot of foreign literature. The collection of Slav languages is one of the foremost in western Europe.

NOBEL PRIZE. Funds donated by the Swedish inventor Alfred Nobel are used annually to award prizes for outstanding work in various fields. Alfred Nobel (1833–1896) was a Swedish industrialist and chemist to whom the invention of gunpowder is often attributed. He bequeathed money to be invested in annual prizes for outstanding contributions in various fields. Prizes are awarded in physics, chemistry, physiology or medicine, literature, and work for peace. While the latter is decided by the Norwegian's specially appointed Nobel Committee, the Swedish Academy of Science (q.v.) is responsible for judging the physics and chemistry category; the Karolinska Institute (q.v.) determines the winner for medicine; and the Swedish Academy (q.v.) judges for literature. The first Nobel prize-giving ceremony was held in 1900. The prizes are presented by the monarch on December 10, the anniversary of Nobel's death in 1896.

NOCKEBY. In the western suburb of Nockeby, the number of communities of home-owner properties surrounded by gardens grew during the 1910s, '20s and '30s. It also has terraced houses in the English style.

NORDENSKIÖLD, ADOLF ERIK (1832–1901). The explorer returned to Stockholm in 1880, aboard the steamship *Vega*, having completed a voyage of the North East Passage. He was greeted in Stockholm with a triumphal procession. Born in Finland, he crossed to Sweden for political reasons at the age of 25. He became a professor at the Natural History Museum.

NORDIC MUSEUM (*NORDISKA MUSÉET*). The museum, situated on Djurgårdsvägen, was officially opened on June 6, 1907. It was created by Artur Hazelius (q.v.) in 1872. The number of exhibits increased rapidly, so they were moved to the present palatial building, which was completed in 1907. It is the largest museum of cultural history in Sweden. The Nordic Museum tells the story of Swedish life and work from the 16th century to the present day, thereby complementing the History Museum, which concentrates on the earlier period. There are about 20 exhibitions on various topics, including Swedish housing, food, and drink, the Lapps, Nordic folk art, village farmwork, traditional costumes, and fashion.

A "Traditions" exhibition was featured, until April 1996 about Swedish traditions through the ages and festivities throughout the year. There are full-scale, everyday environments with films, multi-image presentations, and models.

NORDISKA KOMPANIET (*NK*) (The Nordic Company). A building situated at Hamngatan 18–20. On September 22, 1915, this large, popular shopping emporium was first opened to the public. Building had commenced three years earlier. It was altered from 1961 to 1963, and again from 1971 to 1973. It is generally regarded as Sweden's top mall. It has been likened by many to Harrods of London. It is situated on *Hamngatan* (Harbour Street), opposite Kungsträdgården. Architect Ferdinand Boberg had visited the United States and seen what he thought real stores should look like. Nowadays, NK is divided into a number of different shops.

NORRA MÄLARSTRAND. When the steam mill Eldkvarn (q.v.) finally ceased operating in 1902, construction commenced at Norra Mälarstrand, along the northern edge of Lake Mälaren. The area had been dotted with various buildings, such as textile factories, tanneries, and other industrial enterprises, including Eldkvarn, which was badly damaged by fire in 1878. After changes in the city planning were made in 1918 and 1926, the present-day buildings and parks appeared along the shoreline.

NORRAPORT *(NORTH GATE)*. The old gate in the city wall. Along with Söderport (South Gate), it was the only way into Stadsholmen (q.v.). There were inner and outer towers with a drawbridge.

NORRA BANTORGET *(NORTHERN RAILTRACK SQUARE)*. Located at the end of Vasagatan, where the previous northern railroad track had its terminus. It is surrounded by a row of buildings that house workers' organizations. These include the old and newer *LO*

(*Landsorganisationen i Sverige*) buildings and *Folkets hus* (The People's Building) (qq.v.). LO is the central organization of the workers' unions. In the square stands a monument to Branting (qq.v.), by Carl Eldh (qq.v.). The monument was erected in 1952 to celebrate the great Socialist politician Hjalmar Branting (q.v.).

During the fall of 1993, a large part of *SJ's* (Swedish Railroads) old station house at Norra Bantorget was given over to workrooms for various cultural activities under the name of *Kulturstationen* (The Culture Station).

NORRBRO *(NORTH BRIDGE)*. In 1553, Norrbro was rebuilt. It became a street for parades from the palace to Malmtorget. It was a very exclusive district in the 19th century. The present-day Norrbro, designed by C.F. Adelcrantz (q.v.), was completed in 1797.

NORRMALM. In a charter, a document of privilege, issued by Gustav Vasa (q.v.) in 1529, Norrmalm was declared to be under the town's rule. Klara Kloster (Clare Convent) (q.v.) was demolished and the bricks were used to build a round defense tower in order to reduce damage by cannon balls. In 1622, toll gates were erected. However, Karl IX (q.v.) declared Norrmalm an independent town which it remained until 1635. Norrmalm was united with the rest of Stockholm by royal decree of April 21, 1635, to be followed by a royal charter on March 10, 1636. In the spring of 1640, Norrmalm was ravaged by fire, and 247 farms were destroyed. Later the same year, a new plan was established for this part of the town. In September 1652, another large fire raged there and Queen Kristina (q.v.) is said to have actively participated in extinguishing the flames. In 1686, a large part of Norrmalm was again destroyed by fire. Brunkebergsåsen (q.v.) divided Norrmalm into two parts—the western and eastern halves of the *malm* (district). A road was built along this dividing ridge that remains today and is called Malmskilnadsgatan (District Dividing Road.) Included among the residents of Norrmalm were the nuns in Klara Convent (q.v.), which was founded in 1289. In terms of population, Norrmalm was until the beginning of the 17th century a dumping ground for the many people for whom there was no room within the town walls. In the city, there were many beggars and orphans. A home to care for them was started in 1633, situated on a street in Norrmalm called Barnhusgatan (Children's Home Street).

During the 17th century, town planning (q.v.) improved conditions. In Bellman's (q.v.) time, Norrmalm was still a rural area, although it began showing signs of urban character in the area nearest Norrbro (q.v.). The town did not change much in appearance before the town-plan, by Lindhagen (q.v.) was implemented at the end of the 19th century and the beginning of the 20th century. Then, the traversing streets Odengatan, Karlavägen, Karlaplan and Narvavägen were created, and Sveavägen was extended to Kungsgatan (q.v.). The demolition and wholesale clearance that followed the town-plan of 1953 and engulfed lower Norrmalm and Klara probably inspired one of the most thorough changes in the history of Stockholm. Norrmalm, the city center, has been almost completely reconstructed in the modern architectural idiom. Since World War II, the planning of the new Stockholm was rigorously honed and single-mindedly executed. PUB and Åhléns are two well-known, eye-catching department stores there.

NORRMALM SQUARE (*NORRMALMSTORG*). In 1776, the pillory at *Stortorget* (Main Square) (q.v.) was moved to *Packartorget* (now Norrmalstorg), where the city's implements for punishment had been set up in 1773. The name of the square, Packartorget, was changed to Norrmalmstorg, in 1853. All trade in wood, timber, hay, and straw was transferred from Norrmalmstorg in 1856 to *Hötorget* (Hay Market) (q.v.).

On May 27–28, 1995, the newly arranged Norrmalmstorg was opened. It has been supplied with trees, benches, copies of four tall, chandelier-type street lights from 1911, and a Baltic freedom statue to commemorate a demonstration that took place in the square some years earlier.

NORRSTRÖMMEN *(THE NORTH STREAM)*, An opening from Lake Mälaren (q.v.) into the Baltic Sea. It is crossed by Norrbro (North Bridge) and Vasabro (Vasa Bridge) (qq.v.).

NORRTULL. One of the city gates that determined the northern limits. In 1743, farmers from *Dalarna* (Dalecarlia) reached Stockholm, on June 20, and were met by King Fredrik I (q.v.) outside Norrtull.

NOTKE, BERNT (c1440–1509). On December 31, 1489, in commemoration of the Battle of Brunkeberg (q.v.), a statue of St. George and the Dragon, created by the German sculptor, Notke, was unveiled in *Storkyrkan* (The Cathedral) (q.v.).

NYA HUVUDSTA. When the Västerås railroad line opened in 1876, it helped to bring about the development of the suburb Nya Huvudsta, in Solna (q.v.).

NYBROPLAN. On June 16, 1994, the king unveiled environmental monuments in Nybroplan. They consist of two obelisks with wave-formed pillars in color, which supply information about the city's air and water.

NYKÖPINGS GÄSTABUD *(NYKÖPING'S BANQUET)*.
This took place at Nyköping's Castle, in 1317, where Birger Magnusson took revenge on his brothers Erik and Valdemar for their attack on him at the *Håtunaleken* (The Håtuna Play) (q.v.). They were imprisoned in the dungeons, where they starved to death.

O

OBELISQUE. The Obelisque on Slottsbacken, created by Jean Louis Desprez, was erected in 1800. Gustav III (q.v.) had ordered it as a memorial to the loyalty shown by Stockholm burghers during the Finnish War. The burghers requested to be allowed to raise a statue in honor of the king.

OBSERVATORY. On September 20, 1753, Stockholm's Observatory, designed by C. Hårleman, was inaugurated. Sited high on Brunkeberg Ridge (q.v.), this astronomical observatory is the capital's oldest institution for scientific research. In a small park nearby are four statues of solidly built women; their names are Common sense, Love, Caution, and Hope.

A better-equipped observatory has subsequently been built in Saltsjöbaden (q.v.).

OLD TOWN. The Swedish name is *Gamla stan*. The Old Town of Stockholm is not actually built on one island, but three, although this is not immediately apparent. The old nucleus of Stockholm, originally called Stadsholmen (q.v.), attracts most tourists to its narrow streets and passages. It is one of the most complete and unspoiled examples of medieval city layout in Europe. Seven hundred years ago, the water level of Stockholm was two meters higher than it is today. Then, the outermost edge of the Old Town ran just beside Västralånggatan.

In some ways, *Gamla stan* is more like a small town in itself, rather than part of a larger town. There are three libraries, five schools, five churches, seven museums, and at least 11 important official buildings in an area of 42 hectare (0.42 square kilometers). In 1994, there were 2,782 residents. It is said to be "socially open."

The fact that Stockholm has not been ravaged by modern warfare has helped to preserve the heart of the city. The period most represented in the Old Town is the Era of Great Power of the 17th century. Most of the houses date from that epoch.

During the Middle Ages (1050–1500), many of the buildings were destroyed by fire. Consequently, very little written material and artifacts survived.

During the 17th century, Stockholm evolved from a poor trading center to a large town. The population quadrupled rapidly, and fine mansions and palaces were built. Many of the old houses of the Middle Ages were rebuilt and modernized. *Den Gyldene freden* (The Golden Peace) (q.v.) was opened in 1721, at its present-day site of 51 Österlånggatan, in *Gamla Stan*. On March 18, 1848, severe street riots broke out at Brunkeberg Square (q.v.) and soon spread to *Gamla stan*. Troops intervened but were stoned. Military fire wounded and killed a number of people.

In 1961, a decision was made to clear *Gamla stan* while preserving valuable historical buildings. The hub of the Old Town is *Stortorget* (Main Square) (q.v.). The Old Town has, somehow, retained a balance between residential and commercial property; although an apartment or a pied-à-terre there is extremely expensive, there is quite a large community within the ancient city. This is reflected in the diversity of shops in Västerlånggatan, the main shopping street of the old town. It is sometimes referred to as the longest store in Stockholm. The street has no modern traffic, and so retains not only the appearance but also something of the quality of the 15th century.

Some of the houses between Västerlånggatan and Österlånggatan mark the line of the wall that enclosed the medieval city, and are almost as old as the city itself. *Svartmangatan* (Black Friars' Street) is another one of the main streets leading from Stortorget. The General Urban Code decreed a minimum width of 8 ells, about 5 meters, for the main streets. Away from the main streets, a ribbed pattern of lanes grew up over time, leading to the shore. *Mårten Trotzig Gränd* (Mårten Trotzig Lane), has the distinction of being the narrowest street in Stockholm, and probably also qualifies as one of the narrowest in Europe. It is a little less than 1 meter wide. It is more of a stairway than a lane, and stretches from *Prästgatan* (Priest Street) (q.v.) to Västerlånggatan.

Helgeandshuset (The House of the Holy Spirit) is believed to have been founded as early as the latter part of the 13th century, for the purpose of caring for the old and sick. The building was later demolished, but excavations in 1978, appear to have identified its site. In the early 1420s, the building known a *Själagården* (House of Souls) was erected. Only the cellar survives.

There is a model of the Old Town in the City Museum of Stockholm (q.v.).

OLYMPIC GAMES. Stockholm has contemplated the possibility of bidding to host the Olympic Games in 2004. King Carl XVI Gustav (q.v.) has spoken quite optimistically about the idea, but in August 1995 he was reported to have said Sweden should be more realistic, especially in view of the economic recession.
See also ECONOMIC BALANCE

OLYMPIC STADIUM. See *STADION*.

OPEN AIR MUSEUM. See *SKANSEN*.

OPERA HOUSE (*OPERAN* or *KUNGLIGA TEATERN*) (ROYAL THE-ATER). The opera opened in *Bollhuset* (The Ball Building) (q.v.) on January 18, 1773 and was founded by Gustav III (q.v.). The opera house, designed by C.F. Adelcrantz (q.v.), was inaugurated on September 30, 1782. On March 16, 1792, Gustav III (q.v.) was mortally wounded by a pistol shot during a masked ball at the opera. In the fall of 1806, Gustav IV Adolf (q.v.) decided that the opera should be closed. On March 16, 1807, he ordered that the building be demolished, but this was not carried out until nearly a hundred years later. The present building, at Gustav Adolf's Square (q.v.), dates from 1898; it opened on September 9 of that year. Its form was likened to a cigar box and caused considerable debate. The building also includes an exclusive restaurant, *Operakällaren* (The Opera Cellar). This Renaissance dining room contains fine paintings, the café has an impressive late-baroque ceiling, and the bar is in Jugend style. On December 2, 1989, the Opera House was reopened after extensive restoration to the interior and exterior, which had started in the early 1970s.

Opera performances also are given at Drottningholm Palace Theater (q.v.) and at *Confidencen*, in Ulriksdal (q.v.). *Folkoperan* (The People's Opera) presents opera in an unconvential way.
See also THEATER.

ÖRBY. The residential area of Örby was one of the first suburbs to be regarded as an "alternative residential district." It is now incorporated into the city of Stockholm.
See also SUNDBYBERG.

OSCAR I (1799–1859). Oscar was born in Paris, son of King Karl XIV Johan (q.v.). On September 28, 1844, Oscar I was crowned king of Norway and Sweden. His royal motto was "Justice and Truth." He married Josefina of Leuchtenberg in 1829. He worked hard for liberal reforms and endeavoured to improve relations within the union. In

1857 his eldest son, Karl (q.v.), took over his duties and acted as regent because of his father's mental illness.

OSCAR II (1829–1907). Oscar was son of King Oscar I. He became King of Norway and Sweden in 1872. His royal motto was "The well being of the people." He married Sofia (q.v.) of Nassau in 1857. He remained King of Sweden until his demise in 1907, but surrendered the crown of Norway when the union dissolved in 1905. He had worked hard for a peaceful solution to the conflict between Norway and Sweden. In 1905, he changed his royal motto to "The well being of Sweden." He had also tried to establish a friendly relationship with Germany. In his younger years, he served in the Swedish Navy. He also wrote poetry under the pseudonym Oscar Fredrik; he also wrote on war history. His memoirs appeared in *Mina memoarer* (My memories) in 1960.

OSCARSKYRKAN *(OSCAR'S CHURCH)*. Situated on Narvavägen. Construction commenced in 1897 and was completed in 1903. It is built in the gothic style. The building has three naves over a latin cross, and a single tower. Glass paintings in the sanctuary windows date from 1908 to 1922 and 1927 to 1928; they were created by Norwegian artist Emanuel Vigeland, and replaced earlier paintings with portraits of well-known members of the congregation. One of the church's attractions is its organ, on which many of the world's outstanding musicians have played.

OSCAR'S THEATER. Primarily intended for operettas, the theater was inaugurated on December 5, 1906. At that time it was the tenth theater in Stockholm, of which seven were under the control of Albert Ranfts.

ÖSTASIATISKA MUSÉET. See MUSEUM OF EASTERN ANTIQUITIES.

ÖSTERMALM. A district to the east of Norrmalm (q.v.) that is now an expensive residential area. It is the greenest part of the town. By royal decrees dated February 28, 1639, and March 5, 1640, Ladugårdslandet (q.v.), which is now Östermalm, was incorporated with Stockholm. The name Ladugårdslandet (q.v.) was officially changed to Östermalm in 1885. The old name, which meant "barn plot" and was known colloquially as *"Lagårslanne,"* was not posh enough for the new image. The east side of town now has a prosperous and established look. Formerly Ladugårdslandet became only a dormitory of central Stockholm, but with the introduction of horse-drawn streetcars in 1877, by the 1880s many of the gentry moved out to Östermalm, as it is now called. By forcing a way through the hill, *Tyskbagarebergen* (German Baker Hill) at Karl XV's gate, in the middle of the 1860s, it became possible to clear out the area and rebuild. Shops and market halls sprang up. Östermalm Hall is at Östermalmstorg. It is a meeting place for gourmets. All sorts of delicacies are on sale, and there are several cafés and restaurants between the stands. It has been described as Stockholm's equivalent to Les Halles in Paris. *Humlegårdsgatan* (Hop Garden Street) runs from Östermalmstorg down to Humlegården. Hops are, of course, one of the ingredients of beer. The royal court cultivated hops in the park during the 17th century. *Kungliga biblioteket* (The Royal Library) (q.v.) is not the only building in Humlegården—there are two or three others—but the library is the most distinctive. It is not a lending library. It stores essentially all books printed in Swedish since 1661.

Another Royal object in Östermalm is *Hovstallet* (the Court Stables). It is the size of a residential block, and is situated at Dramaten, with the entrance at Väpnargatan. There are horses, coaches (50 altogether) and carriages used for royal processions, among them the state coach. Also it has a collection of beautifully worked harnesses.

By the end of the 19th century, Strandväg's society came into being. In 1890, Strandgatan still carried the smell of herrings, cabbage gardens, and piles of bricks crowded together. With clearance and new construction Strandvägen appeared. *Strandvägen* (Shore Road) is now the most ostentatious street on Östermalm, and indeed in the whole of Stockholm. In reality, it is neither a street nor a road. It is an esplanade, with trees planted between the traffic lanes. The houses were built for wealthy wholesalers, company directors, and forest barons in the newly rich, industrialized Sweden of the end of the 19th century.

The crowning glory is next to Nobelparken: called *Diplomatstaden* (Diplomats' Town), it is a hub for diplomatic buildings. Seventy of the world's nations have their embassies and consulates here. Actually, it is a part of town outside the real Östermalm, that appeared between 1913 and 1924.

A new feature of Stockholm life is the museum tramcars that run from Norrmalmstorg along Strandvägen to Djurgården. Östermalm has nine museums.

At the beginning of Strandvägen, at Nybroviken, is the Orrefors Gallery, famous for its glass, and the interior decorator's shop *Svenskt tenn* (Swedish Pewter). Immediately after *Djurgårdsbron* (Djurgårds Bridge), Strandvägen curves past *Nobelparken* (Nobel Park). All of Sweden's indigenous, deciduous trees are to be found in the park, except for the mountain birch, which cannot survive so far south.

Diplomatstaden leads to Gärdet, or *Ladugårdsgärdet* (Barn Meadows), as it is really called. Nowadays, Gärdet is mainly associated with kite-flying shows in May. Yet, for a long time, the large field was a theater of war. Both Gustav III and Karl XIV Johan (qq.v.) used the meadow for training pitched battles. The famous film director, Ingmar Bergman (q.v.), has spent much time in Östermalm.

OXENSTIERNA, AXEL (1583–1654). Axel was a member of an aristocratic family that dates back to the 14th century. He became chancellor in 1612. He has been described as "Sweden's greatest statesman below the throne." He was Gustav II Adolf's (q.v.) foremost helper. The house of Axel Oxenstierna was erected in Storkyrkobrinken in 1652, possibly according to plans by Nicodemus Tessin the elder (q.v.). It now houses the Department of Education.

A statue of Axel Oxenstierna stands in the garden of Riddarhuset (q.v.).

OXENSTIERNA'S PALACE. Situated at Storkyrkobrinken 2, it was created by Jean de la Vallée (q.v.) in 1653. The façade has a Roman look.

P

PALACE MUSEUM. Alongside menus and shopping lists for the royal kitchen of Johan III, the museum features an exhibition *"From Ring-Wall to Royal Palace."* On display are ruins and fragments from the old royal fort, *Tre kronor* (Three Crowns) (q.v.), which was destroyed by fire in 1697.

PALACE, THE ROYAL. See ROYAL PALACE.

PALME, OLOF (1927–1986). An outstanding Swedish politician who was well-known outside his own country. As leader of the Social Democratic Party, he was *Statsminister* (Prime Minister) from 1969 to 1976 and again from 1982 to 1986. He was prime minister at the height of Sweden's prosperity, after many years of socialism. The welfare state was a model for other countries to follow. He helped to develop and extend the policy of equality. Highly regarded internationally, Palme was involved with the work of the United Nations, in particular in mediations for peace. He also was a strong advocate of aid for developing nations. In 1986, the whole world was shocked to hear that he had been assassinated in Stockholm, as he and his wife Lisbet were leaving a cinema show on Sveavägen (q.v.). To this day, his murderer has not been caught, in spite of repeated false alarms. The immediate, spontaneous laying of red roses at the site of his murder has subsequently been honored by a simple plaque of remembrance. As always, in politics, opinions about Palme vary widely, but, unquestionably, he was a politician of considerable international stature.

On November 12, 1989, a sculpture dedicated to the memory of Palme was unveiled at Norra Bantorget, the place slated to become a memorial grove. The sculpture is called *Mitt hjärta i världen* (My Heart in the World). The sculpture was funded by 130 associations and trade unions. After a time, it met with criticism and has been likened to a kitchen whisk.

In August 1995, Kjell Olof Feldt, a former finance minister, pressed for the third investigation committee to resume concentrated examinations and not to take for granted the loyalty and high integrity of highly ranked police officers. At the same time, he stressed that he was not making accusations.

PALMSTEDT, ERIK (1741–1803). This architect was renowned in Sweden for his classicism. The stock exchange building was designed by Palmstedt in rococo style in 1778. He also was the architect responsible for Avfurstens Palace (q.v.).

PARLIAMENT. See *RIKSDAG*.

PEOPLE'S MUSEUM (FOLKENS MUSEUM). Located at Djurgårdsbrunnvägen 34, on Djurgården. This red-painted building was inaugurated in 1980. It is next to the History of Marine Technology Museum, near Gärdet. It offers an insight into how people used to live outside Europe, and still do. The upper floor has a number of basic exhibitions on north and central Africa, India, North America, and Mongolia, as well as one about Sven Hedin, the explorer/ethnologist.

The museum holds more than 150,000 objects. The oldest were collected during the 17th and 18th centuries. The lower floor is used for special exhibitions. In the garden, a Japanese tea house is open to visitors daily in the summer. Princess Christina officially opened this tea house behind the *Folkens museum* (The People's Museum), previously known as the Ethnographical Museum. An earlier tea house from 1935 burned down in 1969.

PERIODICALS. See NEWSPAPERS AND PERIODCALS.

PERSSON, GÖRAN. A Social Democrat and finance minister who was elected as leader of the party in March 1996, upon the resignation of Ingvar Carlsson (q.v.). According to current Swedish practice, he automatically became prime minister a few days later.

Göran Persson was born on January 29, 1949 in Vingåker in Sörmland. He was a member of parliament from 1979 to 1984. In 1989 Persson was an adviser in the Education Department responsible for secondary and adult education. After the change of government in 1991 he returned to parliament, where he became chairman of the Agriculture Committee until 1992. In 1992–1993, he was a member of the Industrial Committee and the Social Democratic representative on questions of industrial politics. Persson was appointed vice-chairman of the Finance Committee in 1993, and simultaneously was the Social Democrats' speaker on economic matters.

When the government changed in the fall of 1994, Persson became minister for finance. In March 1996, he became chairman of the Social Democratic Party and prime minister.

Göran Persson has been married to Annika Persson, a political secretary in the Malmöhus County Council.

PETERSEN'S HOUSE. Epitomizes the German-Dutch baroque style of building architecture from the 1640s. The most distinctive features are the high, step-shaped gable, the decorated double entrance doors, and the grayish-white sandstone decorations against the red plastered façade. It is situated at Lilla Nygatan 2.

Herman Petersen was a wealthy Swedish merchant and one of the founders of the Swedish East India Company. His family joined the nobility as Av Petersens.

PETRI, OLAUS (1493–1557). A Swedish reformer who, in 1524, became the city's secretary. In 1525, mass was held for the first time in *Storkyrkan* (The Cathedral) (q.v.) by Petri. He was Gustav Vasa's (q.v.) chancellor from 1531 to 1533, and one of his closest supporters. After a conflict between them, however, he was condemned in 1540, but subsequently pardoned. In 1542, Petri became inspector of the city's school (now at Storkyrkobrinken 9). Petri became the vicar at *Storkyrkan* in 1543. He is Sweden's best-known religious reformer. He laid the foundations for a more modern Swedish language through his translation of the Bible. Olaus Petri is the subject of Strindberg's (q.v.) well-known work, *Mäster Olof* (Master Olof). Petri was buried in *Storkyrkan* (The Cathedral) *(q.v.)*.

PLAGUE. The plague swept Stockholm in 1539 and again in the spring of 1548, lasting until the following year. Plague was once again rampant in Stockholm in 1603 and in 1611. In the fall of 1623, the plague killed an estimated 250 people each week. In 1629, plague caused the king and several officials to consider leaving the city. It broke out again in 1654. On Stadsholmen (q.v.), the sick were confined indoors. A white cross was drawn on the doors of the houses in which they stayed. Most people believed that the plague was a punishment inflicted by God that could only be cured by prayer, pilgimages, and penitence. Some doctors wore masks like long bird beaks, stuffed with sweet-smelling herbs. They believed these would protect them. The plague ravaged Stockholm for the last time in 1710, and claimed nearly 20,000 lives. In August 1710, 155 people died on Ladugårdlandet (q.v.) alone. The plague ended in December 1710. The week before Christmas, only 200 died, compared with 1,600 the week before. Services of thanksgiving were held in all of Stockholm's churches on April 30, 1771 for relief from the plague.

POLHEM, KRISTOFFER (1661–1751). Born to poor parents, he was 25 years old before he was able to develop his brilliant mechanical talents. He began by inventing pump engines for the copper mines in Falun. He became renowned for his repairs to the clock in Uppsala Cathedral. After traveling abroad, he returned to found a *laboratorium mechanicum* in Stockholm. He is credited with inventing the padlock, among many other things. He was engaged for canal-building by Karl XII (q.v.), who intended to create a canal from Gothenburg to Norrköping. The death of the king inhibited this project. Only Polhem's Gate, at Trollhättan, remains from a later canal project. At a late age, he managed to bring into being the Söder Sluice Gate (q.v.) in Stockholm.
See also SLUSSEN.

POLICE MUSEUM. Stockholm's Police Headquarters at Polhemsgatan 30 is one of the most interesting police museums in Europe. Unfortunately, it may only be visited by special arrangement. Collections include a history of police work, as well as a review of types of crime and criminal cases in the past and in modern times. (Telephone 08–769 76 09).

POPULATION. The population of Stockholm at the time of Gustav Vasa's (q.v.) entry into the city in 1523, is estimated to have been 2,000 to 3,000. In 1570 it was approximately 7,000; in 1635, approximately 16,000; in 1663, it was 40,000; in 1718, 45,000; in 1763, 73,000; and in 1840, 84,161. During 1995, it passed the 700,000 mark.

PORT OF STOCKHOLM. Apart from its importance as Sweden's second-largest trading port after Gothenburg, it is one of the major cruising ports in Europe. Millions of cruise passengers cross the Baltic

Sea, most of them headed to the island of Åland and the Finnish mainland. On arrival in Stockholm, a ship may dock at one of four centrally located quays: Nybrokajen, Skeppsbron, Stadsgårdshamnen, and Masthamnen. There also are two large harbors, Frihamnen (Free Port) (q.v.) and Värtan, about 15 minutes from the center of Stockholm. It was estimated that approximately 125 cruise ships, carrying a total of 70,000 passengers, visited Stockholm in 1994. Stockholm plans to build a special, centrally located terminal for cruise ships. Stockholm is often used as a so-called turn-around port: it is the departure and arrival point for Baltic Sea cruise ships, linking with air services at nearby Arlanda airport (q.v.).

POSTAL MUSEUM. Sweden's only postal history and philatelic museum, is situated at Lilla Nygatan 6. The building dates from the 17th century, and has been owned by the postal authorities since the 1700s. The building was altered from 1820 to 1825, and was given its present-day façade and columns. The work of the postal service from 1636 through the present day is depicted in a series of living scenes. Stamps and stamp production from 1855 onward, as well as envelopes, postmarks, and original artwork for stamp designs, are on display. The museum also has collections of Swedish and international rarities and a large library.

PRÄSTGATAN *(PRIEST STREET)*. Situated in *Gamla stan* (Old Town) (q.v.), it is the only truly medieval street in the Old Town, and thus in Stockholm. It is named after the priests who lived there during the 16th century. Yet the small part of Prästgatan to the north of *Storkyrkobrinken* (Great Church Hill) used to be known as *Helwitesgatan* (Hell Street). It twists and turns as it follows the contours of the old city wall. The priests from *Storkyrkan* (The Cathedral) (q.v.) lived on the left side (toward Stortorget) (q.v.) and those from the German Church (q.v.) lived on the right. It is said that the hangman's house used to be there. On the corner of Prästgatan and *Kåkbrinken* (Shack Hill), there is a runestone (q.v.). In front of the stone, stands an old cannon that protected the stone against damage from passing iron-clad wagon wheels. High up on some houses is a wooden beam, that was used together with a wheel and rope to heave up loads to the attics.

PRECIPITATION. The average annual precipitation in Stockholm is 538 millimeters. Precipitation is recorded approximately one day in three.

PRIPPORAMA *(BREWERY STREET)*. Located at Voltavägen 30, in Bromma. It is the museum of the well-known brewing company

Pripps. The emphasis is on the working environment and life associated with brewing through the ages.

PUPPET MUSEUM. Next to the Puppet Theater, on Brunnsgatan, is a museum full of puppets. There are about 4,000 exhibits, including one of the world's largest collections of puppets from Asia.

Q

QUEENS. See individual names.

R

RÅCKSTA. A western suburb. The number of communities of home-owner properties surrounded by gardens grew during the 1910s, '20s, and '30s in Råcksta. There also were English-styled terraced houses. See also SOLNA.

RÅDHUSET. See COURTHOUSE.

RADIO AND TELEVISION. Radio services from Stockholm commenced on January 1, 1925, by A.B. Radiotjänst. *SR (Sveriges radio)* (Swedish Radio) operates under government license as a corporation made up of a combination of organizations, including the press and industrial concerns. Broadcasting is controlled by the Radio Act, which is supervised by a broadcasting council. There are four radio stations, the latest having commenced in 1993. Since 1979, national radio, local Radio, and educational broadcasting have been reorganized into three independent companies, alongside television. Program One offers news bulletins and other information. Program Two carries mainly classical music. Program Three carries a light, non-stop program of sports and pop music aimed at the younger listeners. The new Program Four deals with more serious subjects and is intended for somewhat older listeners. Advertising on radio was first introduced in 1993.

Television came comparatively late to Sweden, starting in 1956. By January 1, 1965, the number of television licenses totaled 1,964,862. TV2 commenced in 1969, the year when color television arrived in Sweden. TV1 programs are mostly relayed from Stockholm. TV2 programs are mainly produced in other national regions. There are now three channels generally available together with various cable TV channels, which commenced in 1986. Sweden delayed the introduction of commercial TV, but has now offered it for a few years, since it was approved by Parliament in 1991. Swedish Radio's concert hall is named after the country's first great symphonist, Franz Berwald (1796–1868). The Radio Symphony Orchestra often gives concerts at Berwald Hall (q.v.), on Strandvägen 69. The concert hall has been blasted out of the rocky hillside and the granite interior is lined with birch. The walls can be moved to produce superb acoustics for chamber music and symphony performances.

RAILROADS. There are two railroad stations in Stockholm; Central Station (q.v.) and Syd (South) in Flemingsberg.

Sweden's first railroad, a private track, was opened in 1856. The year before, work had begun simultaneously on main-line tracks linking Stockholm-Gothenburg and Stockholm-Malmö. The leader of the project was inventor Nils Ericson (q.v.). He became known as "Father of the Swedish railroads".

The railroads had made a big impact on Swedish time. Trains had to run on a timetable, but by which time? Up until 1879, each town had its own local time. Stockholm's time differed from Gothenburg's by 24 minutes. On January 1, 1879, all the parts of the country adopted the same time, based on a meridian midway between those two main towns. The Swedish parliament was the first in the world to introduce standard time.

See also SUBURBS and TREDJE SPÅRET.

RÅLAMBSHOVSPARKEN. At the end of Norra Mälarstrand (q.v.). From here, there is a panoramic view over Riddarfjärden and Söder (qq.v.). Just past a marina, perched on a hill rising from the lakeside is a country house called Rålambshov, built in 1801. The park has an open-air theater and a play area, with sculptures created by Egon Möller-Nielsen. *Yxmannen* (The Axe man), was created by Eric Grate in 1967.

RÅSUNDA. See SUNDBYBERG and SOLNA.

RIDDARFJÄRDEN. The portion of Lake Mälaren (q.v.) containing Långholmen, the island closest to the city. A long-distance, mass swimming event takes place here each summer. The race finishes at the City Hall *(Stadshuset)*.

RIDDARHOLMEN (Knight's Island). An island west of *Gamla stan* (Old Town) (q.v.), initially called Kidaskär and, later, *Gråmunkeholmen* (Grey Friars Island) (q.v.). Magnus Ladulås (q.v.) granted the island to the Franciscans, who began building a church and monastery there in the 1280s. Klara Kloster (The Convent of St. Clare) also was built then (q.v.). On April 4, 1693, a blaze on Riddarholmen ravaged Wrangel Palace (q.v.). Another extensive fire raged on Riddarholmen on November 15, 1802. The large, private palaces on Riddarholmen were built by the generals of the Great Power era. Wrangel Palace, now houses the *Svea hovrätt* (Svea Civil and Criminal Appelate Court), which contains the Supreme Administrative Court. The Supreme Court has its offices in Bonde Palace.

RIDDARHOLM CHURCH. A brick church with a cast-iron spire on Riddarholmen, the island west of *Gamla stan* (Old Town) (q.v.). The spire is late-19th century. The original building was a Franciscan monastery. This is one of Stockholm's oldest churches, built between 1280 and 1300 with the support of Magnus Ladulås (q.v.) and others, in Gothic style. It is regarded as one of northern Europe's best preserved Franciscan churches. Magnus Ladulås was buried here in 1290. The church then consisted only of a central nave, a northern side nave and a sanctuary. The southern nave was added in the 15th century. Between 1569 and 1590, a tower was built on the western façade. In 1573, Johan III (q.v.) approved the erection of burial monuments over the graves of Magnus Ladulås and Karl III Knutsson (q.v.), who died in 1470. In 1593, bloody battles broke out in Riddarholm Church between the Swedes and Poles, because of religious antagonism.

From the beginning of the 17th century, it became the site for royal burials. The most recent was King Gustav V (q.v.), who was interred in 1950. Gustav II Adolf (q.v.) requested that he be given a burial chapel south of the sanctuary. He was buried there in 1634, and rests in a marble sarcophagus bearing the inscription "*Gustavus Adolphus Magnus.*"

The drawings for the altar arrangement were created by Tessin the elder (q.v.). In the lower-grave vaults lie other kings, including Gustav III (q.v.), but this vault is not open to the public. On the walls of the vault are carved panegyric inscriptions in Latin. Several of Gustav II Adolf's generals from the Thirty Year War also have mausoleums in Riddarholm Church. Between 1743 and 1783, the Caroline burial chapel was built opposite the Gustavian. The original drawings were executed by Nicodemus Tessin the elder, (q.v.) in 1671. Also Karl XII (q.v.) lies in a black marble sarcophagus. Further sarcophagi line the walls in the lower vault. The last sarcophagus is that of the Bernadottes, built between 1858 and 1860. There lies Karl XIV Johan, (q.v.) in a porphyr sarcophagus. He was buried in Riddarholm's Church in 1844. The last service held in the church was in 1807. Since then, it has been rebuilt several times. On July 29, 1835, a fire caused by lightning destroyed the tower of the church built under Johan III (q.v.). Repairs were made in new gothic style. The original cobblestone floor was replaced by grave slabs from different ages. The spire was replaced in cast iron, and it now forms a characteristic part of the Stockholm skyline. the interior of the church is adorned with the shields of the knights of the Order of the Seraphim. They are preserved from the year 1748. The church was last restored between 1914 and 1922. The original gravestones were replaced, the floor was partially lowered, and the remaining murals from the Middle Ages were renovated. There has been great controversy over one of the proposed new railroad tracks passing too close to this highly regarded church.

RIDDARHUSET (*HOUSE OF NOBILITY*). Architectural drawings for the Palace of Swedish Nobles were made by S. de la Vallée (q.v.). The foundations were laid in the north-west of *Gamla stan* (q.v.) in 1641. In 1657, the nobility began to use it for their meetings. The nobles were the most prestigious of the four estates in parliament. (See also RIKSDAG). The building was completed in 1675 in Dutch baroque style. It still stands as a reminder of that era of Swedish power. The color combinations are refined; with redbrick walls, grayish-white sandstone pillars, beams and window surrounds, a green copper roof, and gilded roof figures. Around the outer walls, just under the roof, is a frieze of Latin inscriptions. All that remains of the original interior fittings are the impressive allegorical ceiling paintings. Created between 1670 and 1675 they are called "Counsel of the Virtues".

In the nobles' banquet hall, there are more than 2,000 copper plates, that represent the various heraldic shields of the nobility. They include that of Sven Hedin, an explorer and the last man in Sweden to be knighted, in 1902.

After Karl XII (q.v.) was shot in Norway in 1718 Sweden was ruled from this building, during the period called the Age of Liberty (q.v.). The assassin of Gustav III, Anckarström (qq.v.), was flogged outside this building on April 19, 1792, just before his execution. Up until 1866, when the old form of parliament was dissolved, the nobility held their meetings here. The statue in front of Riddarhuset portrays Gustav Vasa (q.v.). It was created by Pierre-Hubert L'Archeveque and erected in 1774. On the north side of the garden is a statue of Axel Oxenstierna (q.v.).

RIKSBANKEN. See SWEDISH CENTRAL BANK.

RIKSDAG. The Swedish Constitution decrees that all public power proceeds from the people. The *Riksdag* is the elected and foremost representative of the people, and makes the decisions that concern the individual and the community. It also is in charge of the Central Bank. In 1435, a national meeting (*riksmöte*) was held in Arboga to discuss and decide upon affairs of the realm. Thus, the Arboga Assembly is sometimes called the first Swedish parliament. Requested by Engelbrekt (q.v.), the meeting can hardly be called representative of the people, by today's standards; for example, there is no indication that farmers were represented. It was not until Gustav Vasa's (q.v.) two national assemblies in 1527 and 1544 that a *Riksdag* representing the four estates—the nobility, the clergy, the burghers and the peasantry—evolved.

The term Riksdag came into use in the 1540s. Up until 1866, the word *Riksdag* referred only to those occasions when the four estates assembled. From 1660, the nobility held their assemblies in *Riddarhuset* (q.v.). The clergy had *Storkyrkan* (The Cathedral) as their assembly location, which they used for this purpose from the 1500s to 1834. The burghers assembled in *Stockholms rådhus* (Stockholm's Old Town Hall) from the 16th to the 18th century, when it was demolished to make room for *Börshuset* (The Stock Exchange) (q.v.), where their assemblies were held until 1834. The peasantry (agricultural class) met in Bonde Palace from 1765 to 1834. Earlier they had used *Vår frus gillestuga* (Our Lady's Assembly Rooms).

More permanent rules for the *Riksdag* were framed in the 17th century. The Caroline autocracy weakened the position of the *Riksdag*, which became an obedient pawn in the hands of the king. Nevertheless, the *Riksdag* maintained a dominant position in the 18th century. During the Age of Liberty (1718–1772) (q.v.), a system of parties, Hats and Caps (qq.v.) was established and parliamentarianism evolved toward the form of today. A 1742 uprising from Dalarna *(Daldansen)* (q.v.) demonstrated dissatisfaction with the Hat Party and the fact that the agricultural class was under-represented. The domination of the estates broke in 1772 with Gustav III's coup d'état. Power then gradually came under the king's control. In 1809, Sweden adopted a new constitution. An act of parliament in 1810 separated powers between the king and *Riksdag*. Among the changes that were made: In 1866, a bicameral system replaced the estates, to be abandoned for a single chamber in 1971. But the constitution remained in force until 1974. In the 1973 general election, the socialist and nonsocialist parties each won 175 seats. This required that several decisions were made by drawing lots. From 1976–77, the number of members dropped by one to 349. The last national government elections were held in 1994. Stockholm has 26 representatives in parliament, 14 of whom are women. The Social Democratic Party returned to power with 34.8 percent of the vote. They ousted the Conservatives

(Moderata Samlingspartiet), who received 32.2 percent. The Liberals *(Folkpartiet Liberalerna)* had 10.2 percent and the Communists *(Vänsterpartiet),* 8.4 percent. The Green Party received 5.8 percent, Center, Christian democrats, and New Democracy had 3.2 percent, 3.0 percent, and 1.3 percent, respectively. A few others received 1.1 percent of the vote.

The *Riksdag* convenes for a new session on the first Tuesday in October. Its work then continues until the beginning of the following June. *Riksdag* sessions used to open with a ceremony in which the king gives a brief address proclaiming the *Riksdag* open, but this tradition has been discontinued. It is significant that it is the speaker, not the monarch, who invites a party leader to form a government.

The *Riksdag* has its offices in a number of buildings. Most are on Helgeandsholmen in *Riksdagshuset* (Parliament Building) (q.v.).

RIKSDAGSHUSET *(PARLIAMENT BUILDING).* Situated on Helgeandsholmen. The massive building, in new baroque-classical style, consists of two parts: the western part, which formerly housed the Bank of Sweden, and the eastern part, which housed the young *Riksdag (q.v.).* The western part contains the main entrance, the assembly hall, the speaker's office, the secretariat of the chamber, the restaurant, and facilities for the media. The entrance to the public gallery is at the north end of the building. The gallery in the Plenary Chamber is open whenever parliament is in session. The Swedish parliament is not only a place for political debates; it is also something of an art museum. The eastern part contains rooms for permanent committees and for ministers, the parliamentary library and the publications section. It also contains the old first and second chambers. The Members' Building, where members of parliament have their offices and living quarters, and the Administrative Building are situated in *Gamla stan* (q.v.).

Previously, parliament assembled in *Riksens ständers hus* (Estates of the Realm Building) on Riddarsholm. It was the first fixed meeting place for the three plebeian parties. It continued to be used after the introduction of the two chamber parliament in 1867, even though it was too small and ill-designed for its functions. At the end of the 19th century, plans to build a new parliament building on Helgeandsholmen (q.v.) were drawn up.

The parliament building was finished in 1905, but didn't take on its present form until 1983, when the former Bank of Sweden building next door was incorporated and a new Plenary Chamber was built on top of the bank building. It was probably one of the largest and most exciting renovations of the 1980s.

Further information may be obtained from *Sveriges Riksdag,* 100

12 Stockholm. The former *Riksdag* building, a new Renaissance structure built between 1856 and 1866, is situated at Birger Jarls torg 5. It was used by the parliament until 1905, and is now a court building.

RINKEBY. In 1962, parts of Järvafältet (q.v.) were acquired from the state for residential development in the northern suburbs. As a result, Rinkeby came about at the end of the 60s and during the 70s.

RISSNE. The completion of building in the suburb of Rissne, in the mid–80s played an important part in easing the housing situation in Stockholm. Land there was taken over from the state in 1975, and digging commenced in the fall of 1980.

RÖRSTRAND. In 1726, the famous *AB Rörstrands porslinsfabriker* (Rörstrand's Porcelain Factories Ltd.) was established in Stockholm. The factory used clay from the nearby Uppland plains. The Rörstrandäs operation moved to Gothenburg 200 hundred years ago.

ROSENBAD. A building situated at Strömgatan 22–24. It was built in Jugend style between 1902 and 1904. It now houses the prime minister and some of his offices.

ROSENDAL GARDENS. Located beside Rosendal Palace (q.v.), this is a favorite place for Stockholmers. The Rosendal Gardens were run by the Garden Associations student school from 1861 to 1912. At one time, there were no less than 443 different types of fruit trees there. It is now run by a group of cultivators with an emphasis on anthroposophics.

ROSENDAL PALACE. A castle with finely preserved interiors that is situated on Djurgården. It was the summer residence of Karl XIV Johan and Queen Desirée (qq.v.). This castle was built in 1823–27 for Karl XIV Johan from plans by Fredrik Blom. The king wanted the castle to emphasize Djurgården as Stockholm's equivalent of the French Bois de Boulogne. The building has an elevated center section with lanterns and an Ionic portico. In the lantern room, there are paintings both in the dome and on the walls. It has a number of well-preserved interiors in the Karl-Johan (q.v.) style, or the Swedish equivalent of the Empire style. In 1817, Karl XI Johan approved construction of *Drottningens paviljong* (The Queen's Pavilion). The stables date from the 1820s. The castle is situated at Rosendalsvägen 41.

ROYAL ARMORY (*LIVRUSTKAMMAREN*). Situated at the royal palace, it is the oldest museum in Sweden, dating from 1628. On display are magnificent state coaches, suits of armor, hunting weapons, coronation costumes, masquerade costumes and much more. They are associated with royalty and greatness. It includes the equipment of the Vasa kings, Gustaf II Adolf's horse Streiff, his blood-stained shirt from the battle at Lützen, Karl X Gustav's magnificent wardrobe, and royal carriages. Recently, the exhibitions were enlarged to include a permanent display showing how the Swedish royal nursery has changed over time giving an historical insight into the rarely seen world of royal children.

ROYAL CHAPEL. Originally a baroque building, rococo decorations were added by architect Carl Hårleman in 1754. It is the church of the royal parish, although it is open to the public, including for services.

ROYAL DRAMATIC THEATER. Popularly known as *Dramaten*, it was built in Jugend style between 1904 and 1907. The official opening took place in 1908. Greta Garbo and Ingrid Bergman (qq.v.) began their careers on its stage. Ingmar Bergman became director in 1963.

ROYAL LIBRARY. See *KUNGLIGA BIBLIOTEKET.*

ROYAL MINT CABINET (*KUNGLIGA MYNTKABINETTET*) This is situated at *Historiska muséet* (The Museum of History) (q.v.). It exhibits the country's largest collection of coins, medals, currency notes, tokens etc. Of particular interest is *"the world's largest coin,"* a ten dollar copper-coin. The coin is from 1644 and weighs 19.7 kg. (about 43 pounds).

ROYAL PALACE. The most prominent building in the Old Town (q.v.). It is special among the royal palaces of the world, not so much for its size and beauty but because it is open to the public. Columns form a type of triumphal arch at the entrance. High up, in niches, are statues of men who were well-known at the time the palace was built. From the left, nearest the church, they are:
   Dahlberg, a fortifications officer and author. He was illustrator of "Svecia antiqva et hodierna" (Sweden Then and Now); *Linné*, a scientist who specialized in botany; *Stiernhielm*; a poet who wrote "Hercules," a well-known 1760s poem; *Tessin the younger*, (q.v.), the architect who, together with his father, designed the royal palace; *Adelcrantz*, (q.v.); the architect who continued work on the royal palace in the 18th century; *von Dalin*, a writer and historian; *Spegel*, an author, soldier, and bishop; *Aschberg*; a soldier.

With almost 600 rooms, the palace at one time was said to be the world's largest palace inhabited by a royal family. It is no longer the home of King Carl Gustav (q.v.) and Queen Silvia, who reside at Drottningholm Palace (q.v.). The nucleus of the old palace from the 13th century consisted of the defense towers known as *Tre Kronor* (The Three Crowns [q.v.]), which was built at the end of the 12th century. In 1419, when Stockholm was ravaged by fire, the palace was destroyed and many important documents were lost. The palace was again ravaged by fire in 1525, and the building and contents were badly damaged. Yet again, on November 25, 1642, the eastern part of the palace was ravaged by fire on November 25. In just two hours the old part was destroyed. During rebuilding, under the direction of Tessin the younger (q.v.), a fire destroyed several rooms of the palace on February 15, 1648, including those used by Queen Kristina (q.v.). The old Three Crowns castle burned down in 1697. With Tessin's son taking part in the reconstruction, the new palace was completed in 1754. The building program took more than 60 years from start to finish, and remains a remarkable tribute to the capabilities of one family of architects.

The first royal family to move into the palace was that of Gustav III (q.v.), then crown prince, together with his brother and sisters, father Adolf Fredrik and mother Lovisa Ulrika (qq.v.). In 1754, the fashionable court style was rococo. Decorating the castle was a task that involved the top eclectic artists of the day, including Carl Hårleman, Jean Eric Rehn and Louis Marseliez. Work on the palace provided them with the opportunity to create the type of rococo and Gustavian style for which Sweden is now famous. The elements of the style spread, first to the wealthy bourgeoisie, then out into the country. In other words, without the palace, Sweden would not look the way it does today.

See also BERNADOTTE APARTMENTS and THRONE ROOM.

ROYAL STABLES. The stables are situated on Helgeandsholmen, opposite the royal palace. They were erected in 1696; the architect was N. Tessin the younger. (q.v.). Previously, the royal stables had been on Norrmalm (q.v.), but they were moved in the 1670s. The stable was destroyed by fire; then rebuilt in 1696.

ROYAL SUITES. In the royal palace, exquisite suites and halls are open for public viewing. They include the Bernadotte Suite, with Lovisa Ulrika's audience chamber; the guest suite; the banquet rooms; the Karl XI Gallery; the White Sea House; and state bedroom.

ROYAL TENNIS STADIUM. See KUNGLIGA TENNIS HALLEN.

RUNESTONES. There is a runestone set in the walls of a house on the corner of Prästgatan and Kåkbrinken, in *Gamla stan* (the Old Town). The inscription reads, *"Torsten and Frögun had this stone raised in memory of their son."* It is the only runestone in the city. Most of the runestones in the Mälar Valley are on Selaön. One example tells of a Viking who ". . . . traveled in a manly way to England."

In the beginning of the summer of 1991, one runestone in Skansen (q.v.) was painted, in red, black, and white. The painting was similar to that of other known runestones, and was carried out under the supervision of *Riksantikvarieämbetet* (the Office of the King's Custodian). The intention was to demonstrate the historical coloring technique and to make the runestone more prominent.

RYDBERG HOTEL. Stockholm's first large hotel, the Rydberg Hotel, opened in 1857. It closed down on October 1, 1914.

RYDBOHOLM PALACE. Situated in Österåker, it was built in the 1500s. Its present appearance dates from the early 1700s. It houses a collection of portraits. According to tradition, Gustav Vasa (q.v.) was born at Rydboholm.

S

ST. ERIK. See ERIK IX.

ST. ERIKSBRON *(ST. ERIK'S BRIDGE)*. The bridge was officially opened on December 15, 1906. It carries St. Eriksgatan across the waters of Barnhusviken to link Kungsholmen to Vasastaden. St. Eriksgatan runs from Fridhelmsplan, in the center of Kungsholmen, northward to Norrtull (North City Gate).

ST. ERIKS KATOLSKA DOMKYRKA *(ST. ERIK'S CATHOLIC CHURCH)*. Located at Folkungagatan 46. The church was built between 1890 and 1892 in the Norman style, although it is generally free-formed. A parish home is located in *Pauliska huset* (Paul's House) in the grounds. It is a square building that may have been built for the trader Nicolaus Pauli in the 1680s.

ST. ERIK'S TRADE FAIR. The trade fair first opened in 1943.

ST. GERTRUDE'S CHURCH. See GERMAN CHURCH.

ST. GÖRAN'S CHURCH *(ST. GEORGE'S CHURCH)*. Consecrated in February 1910.

ST. NIKOLAI CHURCH. Initially called *Bykyrkan* (Town Church) and later St. Nikolai. It is now *Storkyrkan* (The Cathedral) (q.v.).

SALK. On September, 1993, the classic tennis arena, *SALK-hallen: Stockholms Allmänna Lawn-tennis Klubb Hall* (SALK Hall, Stockholm's Public Tennis Stadium) in Alvik burned to the ground. The stadium had been erected in 1937. It was rebuilt and ready for use in 1994. Swedish instructor Percy Rosberg coached Björn Borg and Stefan Edberg here in the early stages of their careers.

SALTSJÖBADEN. The high-class housing area of Saltsjöbaden was one of the first suburbs to be regarded as an "alternative residential district." Saltsjöbaden made use of the rail link with Stockholm, which was opened in 1893. Previously an independent municipality, it now is incorporated with Nacka.

This is suburban district of mainly villa-type properties. It is a popular bathing and sailing resort. Stockholm's observatory is situated here. Saltsjöbaden gave its name to an important agreement, reached in 1938 between LO (q.v.) and SAF (an employers' organisation). This agreement was a sort of "peace treaty" that regulated the relations between labor and management with regard to collective bargaining and industrial action. It was known as the Basic, or Saltsjöbaden, Agreement.

(SALTSJÖ) DUVNÄS. The high-class housing area of (Saltsjö) Duvnäs was one of the first suburbs to be regarded as an "alternative residential district." (Saltsjö) Duvnäs, made use of the rail link with Stockholm, which was opened in 1893. Previously an independent municipality, (Saltsjö) Duvnäs is now incorporated with Nacka.

SALTSJÖN. (SALT LAKE). Part of the Baltic Sea nearest to Stockholm. It is usually generally regarded as being the inner archipelago (q.v.).

SALUHALLEN *(THE MARKET HALL)*. Erected in Östermalmstorg, at Nybrogatan 29–33, between 1885 and 1889. The architect has attempted to catch the style of a southern European market hall. The building has rounded, bowed windows and towers. The corner building has a clock tower with lanterns and a slate roof. The large market hall is made of cast-iron with glass lanterns.

SÄTRA. In the manner of Vällingby and Farsta (qq.v.), Sätra opened a large town-center named Skärholmen, in 1968.

SCHERING ROSENHANE PALACE. A solid, square building on Norra Riddarholmen, that now houses several departments of Svea Hovrätt (the Swedish Lower Court of Appeal) (q.v.). Schering Rosenhane was a counselor, diplomat, and governor of Stockholm. He bought the site in 1648. The palace was designed by Nicodemus Tessin and Jean de la Vallée (q.v.) in French classical style. It is almost intact.

Nearby, up steep steps and set in the rock, is a plaque that proclaims the spot as the normal leveling point for Sweden. It was the starting point for the Swedish cartography system, so that all measurements stemmed from that point. The cartography department used to be housed in the Schering Rosenhane Palace. The present leveling point is in Varberg.

SCHOOLS. After decades of Socialist government, with emphasis on social equality, Sweden has a comprehensive school system. Stockholm is no exception, apart from the fact that most of the country's few private schools are in the capital.

Until recently, schooling did not begin before the age of 7, and even then for only a few hours per day. Entry depends on passing a maturity test.

Unlike in most countries, Swedish schools are uniform to the extreme in terms of quality. Even the personality of the principal has limited influence as he or she is very much controlled by a national curriculum and teachers' unions.

Swedes are generally against the concept of boarding school and the few that do exist are mainly for the children of temporary overseas visitors and a few children of Swedish parents working abroad. Even the latter would be likely to attend Swedish schools provided overseas, or take correspondence courses.

Sigtuna School has had a good reputation for many years, and probably is the nearest approach to the image of a British "public" (actually private) school.

For many years, Swedish royal children have attended local state schools. Prince Carl Philip recently attended college in the United States of America causing some debate in Sweden.

See also EDUCATION.

SERGEL, JOHAN TOBIAS (1740–1814). Sergel was one of Sweden's greatest sculptors. He lived and worked most of his adult life in Stockholm. On February 11, 1650, French philosopher, René Descartes, died. He had been summoned by Queen Kristina (q.v.) in 1649. One of the sculptures of him, executed by J. T. Sergel, was erected in Adolf Fredrik's Church (q.v.) in 1770. On January 28, 1808, Sergel's statue of Gustav III (q.v.) was unveiled on Skeppsbron (q.v.). Sergel's studio survived in the area of Norrmalm (q.v.) until the 1960s. Although it may have been expected to be preserved as part of Sweden's heritage, it was totally destroyed, along with so much else, as it conflicted with the plans for a new Stockholm.

SERGELS TORG *(SERGEL'S SQUARE)*. This constitutes the center of the city, the generally accepted name for that part of Norrmalm situated south of Kungsgatan (qq.v.). The focal point of Sergels torg is the much-debated glass sculpture that is part of a fountain. It is 37.5 meters tall and comprises 80,000 pieces of glass. It was erected in 1974. A lower level was built as a large and varied shopping mall, over time it became Stockholm's equivalent of London's famous Speaker's Corner before it deteriorated. It became a place where those dissatisfied with events or the political system, could expound their views. From that, developed the custom of arranging protest marches and other political events so that they started from Sergels torg and for this reason it became the center of Stockholm's radical reaction. But this has now ended.

On December 21, 1993, a new, computer-controlled, multi-colored illumination system went into operation in the glass sculptured pillar in Sergels torg. The system consists of 16 strong-beamed lights with color filters and reflecting plates. Earlier lighting had not been strong enough to sufficiently penetrate the layer of dirt caused by vehicle emissions, which dulled the pillars.

The chamber of commerce is pressing for a rebuilding of Sergels torg and Hötorg City. Specifically, the chamber wants to develop the square at street level and do away with existing split levels, in order to create a more attractive, safe and pleasant environment.

SIDEWALKS. On May 24, 1849, a royal decree concerning streets and public places introduced the provision of sidewalks.

SIGISMUND, KING (1566–1632). Sigismund was the son of Johan III (q.v.). He was chosen to be king of Poland in 1587. By inheritance, he was king of Sweden from 1592. His royal motto was "The king's heart in God's hand. Highness is a gift from God." Following the death of his father, Sigismund arrived in Stockholm on September 30, 1593, to take control of the country. He became King Sigismund III of Poland in 1587. He worked in vain to restore the Catholic faith but was prevented from doing so by strong opposition from his uncle, Duke Karl. The *Riksdag* (parliament) (q.v.) declared Sigismund to be deposed in 1599. Sigismund did not relinquish his claim to Swedish sovereignty and a war between Sweden and Poland continued until 1629. Sigismund remained king of Poland until his death.

SIGTUNA. A little town on the shores of Lake Mälaren (q.v.), it is in Stockholm County and has a population of around 32,OOO people. It is thought to be central Sweden's oldest town. It was probably founded by Olof Skötkonung in the beginning of the 11th century and was briefly the capital. It overtook Birka (q.v.) in importance. The first Swedish coins were minted here. It was a bishopric from around the year 1100 before it moved to Uppsala. In 1187, it was overrun by eastern Vikings, but did not lose its significance until after the reformation in the 16th century. In the 17th century, it was ravaged by many fires. Today, Sigtuna is an idyllic and thriving small town with many schools. Sigtuna school is one of the very few private schools in Sweden. St. Maria's church was built in the middle of the 13th century as an abbey for Dominican monks. Quite impressive ruins of St. Peter's and St. Olof's churches remain. Those of St. Lars and St. Nicholas are less splendid.

In the 13th century, Stockholm became a more important trading center. The court house (*Rådhuset*) was built in 1745, but the tower remains from an earlier 17th-century building that was destroyed by fire. A main tourist attraction is *Storgatan* (Main Street), which follows the same route as in the 11th century, but is about three meters higher. The street is lined with well-preserved wooden buildings from the 18th and 19th centuries. Many of the shops carry old sign-boards.

SKÅ. A childrens' village located in the parish of Skå in Ekerö district. It is home for the care of families with psychological problems. It was started as a home for Stockholm boys in 1947 by Gustav Johnsson, who became known as the legendary "Skå-Gustav". Later, after much experimentation and documentation, the home became well-known as trail-blazing center and the model for care giving.

SKANSEN OPEN-AIR MUSEUM. A popular tourist attraction situated on Djurgården. It is an open air-museum as well as a zoological garden; the first of its kind in the world. With some 2,000,000 visitors a year, it is Sweden's most popular tourist attraction. It is laid out on the sides of a 75–acre hill. It was founded by Artur Hazelius (q.v.) in 1891 in order to preserve Swedish traditional countryside buildings. Up until 1963, it was organized as a department of the Nordic Museum (q.v.) but is now independent. There are some 150 buildings from all parts of the country and from different epochs. There is a Lapp encampment and examples of mountain shielings. There are whole streets of country buildings, including an apothecary, a bakery, glass-blowing demonstrations, pottery-making, and gold and silver smiths. Skansen got its name from *"skans"* (earthwork defense), which previously existed in the 17th century. In 1910, Seglora Church was moved to Skansen. The wooden church is popular for weddings. It was built between 1729 and 1730 and was moved from the village of Seglora in the province of Västergötland in 1916. The tower and sacristy were built in 1780. During Craftsmen's Days, held in the spring and autumn and in August and December, visitors watch the making of old-fashioned handicrafts.

Traditional holiday celebrations such as Lucia Day on December 13th, the early morning Christmas Day service in Seglora Church, the bonfire on Walpurgis Night, May Day, and Midsummer Day gain an extra dimension when celebrated at Skansen. Skansen is the venue for the Swedish Flag Day, which Hazelius introduced in 1893. It is now known as Sweden's National Day.

On 29 May 1988, a cast-iron garden pavilion officially opened in Skansen with an orchestral concert. The pavilion was originally built in 1879 in the De Geerska garden at Västra Trädgårdsgatan. When the garden was reorganized in 1982, *Stadsmuséet* (the City Museum) requested it be saved and be erected at another site. It is now near Gubbhyllan and *Kägelbanan* (The Skittle Alley). In July, a Jazz and Blues Festival is held in Skansen, instead of the earlier one at Skeppsholmen. The traditional Christmas market is also held here.

In addition to the open-air museum, an animal park offers the opportunity to see Nordic animals, including species threatened with extinction such as the wolf, lynx, wolverine, and the European bison.

Skansen is the most well-attended cultural attraction in Stockholm. In 1993, 1.5 million visitors toured Skansen.

SKANSTULLSBRON *(FORTIFICATION TOLL BRIDGE)*. The bridge was erected between 1938 and 1947. It is 115 meters long and 17.4 meters wide. It features a strong curved span located above the railroad and *Hammarbyslussen* (Hammarby sluices). Skanstullbron was the largest entrance channel from the southern suburbs and very heavily used. A new high bridge was built in 1984 to relieve traffic over Skanstullbron.

SKÄRHOLMEN. See SÄTRA.

SKARPNÄCK. In the southern suburb of Skärpnack, the number of communities with property surrounded by gardens grew during the 1910s, '20s and '30s. English-styled terraced houses were also built during those years.

Fig. 1. The Royal Palace with Storkyrkan, Stockholm's cathedral, behind. *Courtesy of The Swedish Institute.*

Fig. 2. King Carl XVI Gustaf and Queen Silvia. *Photo by Hans Hammarskiöld, courtesy of The Swedish Institute.*

Fig. 3. Statue of Karl XII in Kungsträdgarden, with the famous elm trees behind.

Fig. 4. Riksdag Building with the city hall behind. *Photo by H. Fristedt, courtesy of The Swedish Institute.*

Fig. 5. City Hall (foreground) and the Old Town and Royal Palace (central island). *Courtesy of The Swedish Institute.*

Fig. 6. Slussen. City Hall is in the left background. *Courtesy of The Swedish Institute.*

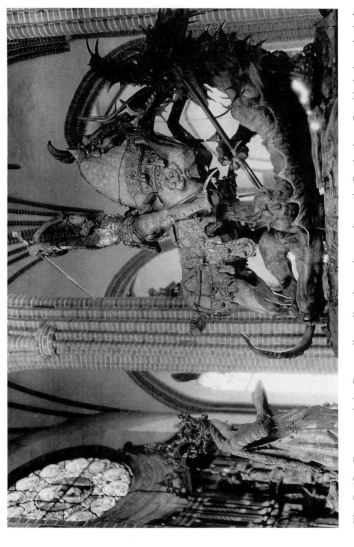

Fig. 7. "St. George and the Dragon," medieval wooden sculpture in Storkyrkan, Stockholm's cathedral. *Photo by The Swedish Tourist Traffic Association, courtesy of The Swedish Institute.*

Fig. 8. Göran Persson, social democrat, Prime Minister, 1996–. *Photo by Håkan Pettersson.*

Fig. 9. The Vasa Ship, raised from the waters of Stockholm and now on display in Vasa Museum.

Fig. 10. Author August Strindberg. *Courtesy of The Royal Library and The Swedish Institute.*

Fig. 11. Olof Palme, social democrat, prime minister assassinated in 1986. *Courtesy of The Swedish Institute.*

SKATTKAMMAREN *(TREASURE CHAMBER)*. A collection of national regalia housed in the royal palace. The oldest are two swords that belonged to Gustav Vasa (q.v.) and were made in southern Germany in 1541. Erik XIV's (q.v.) crown made in 1561, is outstanding.

SKEPPSBRON. Houses along the busy road of Skeppsbron are among the most obvious examples of the pomp of the 17th century Era of Great Power (q.v.). They were built by rich merchants, the Skeppsbro nobility, to show Europe that the Swedish capital was to be reckoned with. On January 24, 1808, J.T. Sergel's statue of Gustav III (qq.v.) was unveiled on Skeppsbron, followed by B.E. Fogelberg's statue of Karl XIV Johan (qq.v.) in 1854.

SKEPPSHOLMEN. Previously called Lustholmen, from 1640 forward, the island was Stockholm's naval station. This was Stockholm's most important harbor during the 18th century. In 1730, wooden jetties were replaced by a stone quay. Boat women (colorfully translated as "rowing-madames") were a feature of the times. Two women in each boat rowed passengers to nearby islands. The competition for passengers was tough. It is said that the beefy Stockholm ladies often fought with young, pretty competitors from outside the city.

Two buildings dominate the island. One is Skeppsholm's Church, built between 1824 and 1842. The other is the Kasern 1, barracks, with its high gable and pointed tower. The building is sometimes incorrectly called Johan III's (q.v.) summer house and was built between 1647 and 1650. From the beginning though, it was an admiralty building. North east of the church is *Tyghuset*, the present Museum of Far Eastern Antiquities (q.v.). It was built in 1699 by Nicodemus Tessin (q.v.). Other interesting buildings include Långa raden (Long row), which was originally built for Karl XII's (q.v.) bodyguard, and Exercishuset, which, until 1994, was the Modern Art Museum (q.v.). A new, grander museum is scheduled to open in 1998. At the quayside, the fully rigged vessel *af Chapman* (q.v.) lies tied up. The curiously un-Swedish name "af Chapman" is in memory of a great 18th-century shipbuilder whose forefathers came from Scotland. Shipyards were once the main source of employment on the island. Since 1948, the vessel is known as a popular Swedish Tourist Association Youth Hostel. Present-day Skeppsholm Bridge was completed in 1861.

On September 23, 1993, the two gilded crowns from Skeppsholm Bridge, which had on several occasions been wrenched from their places and thrown into the water, were replaced by newly cast bronze copies. The original crowns, built in 1861, are made of gilded cast iron.

SKEPPSHOLM CHURCH. Also known as Karl Johan's Church, it is an octagonal central building built between 1824 and 1842, and inspired by the Pantheon in Rome. The circular, central body of the church is separated from its lower-lying surroundings by Ionic columns. The original fittings have been retained. They include two groups of sculptures built between 1830 and 1832 and an altar piece built in 1840.

SKINNARVIKSBERGET *(SKINNARVIK HILL)*. Several sections of the original building survived the fire of 1759. *Gamle Lundagatan* (Old Grove Street) still has its wooden house structure on the north side. The southern side is edged with modern apartment buildings. *Yttersta Tvärgränd* (Outermost Crossing-Lane) is in the 18th century part of the town and consists mainly of a two-story stone house. Located at the foot of the hill and on its slopes are 17th century houses.

Skinnarviksberget is Stockholm's highest natural viewing point at 53 meters above sea level. It is marked by a triangular sign at the crest of the hill. It was here that Urban Målare painted the picture of the "mock sun", that hangs in *Storkyrkan* (The Cathedral)(q.v.).

SKOKLOSTER CASTLE. Sweden's most magnificent baroque castle was built by General Carl Gustaf Wrangel (q.v.) during the latter part of the 17th century in the Era of Great Power (q.v.). This was a brief period, little more than 50 years. The castle was never fully decorated. All the same, the treasures, most of which are fine loot and war trophies, are among the most valuable and interesting in the country.

Each July, there is a festival at Skokloster that lasts for five days. Included in the program are tilting and jousting tournaments.

SLAUGHTERHOUSE. In the fall of 1987, the Slaughterhouse Museum opened in the parish of Johanneshov; it is open to the public on a limited basis. A museum was founded in 1984, but it is only open for groups. In July 1988, the city's running of the Slaughterhouse enterprise was discontinued.

SLOTTSBACKEN. Stockholm had two large buildings for ball games and both were situated on Slottsbacken. *Stora bollhuset* (The large ball-building) was built in 1627 and became a theater in 1700. *Lilla bollhuset* (The little ball-building) dates from around 1650 and became the Finnish church in 1725. In 1773, Stockholm's governor took over Tessin's Palace on Slottsbacken, which was erected by N. Tessin the younger (q.v.) and was completed around 1703. The Obelisque (q.v.) is situated on Slottsbacken and was built in 1800.

SLUSSEN *(SLUICE GATES or LOCKS)*. The first sluice gates were built in 1637. All vessels entering Lake Mälaren (q.v.) had to be hauled up Söderströmmen (South Stream) by rope. Land rise increased their difficulties. Therefore, it was decided to build a lock, or sluice. Kristopher Polhem's (q.v.) program of extensive rebuilding of Slussen began in 1744 and was completed in 1753. At the time the rebuilding consisted of red and blue sluices.

The name Slussen also is generally used to refer to the road-traffic system above the actual sluice gates. An extensive reorganization of Slussen's road traffic was completed in 1850, under the direction of Nils Ericsson (q.v.). Slussen streets were rebuilt again in the 1930s, according to a clover-leaf system. It was completed in 1935. The plans already anticipated a possible changeover to a right-hand traffic system. Close to Slussen is *Katarinahissen* (Katarina Elevator) (q.v.). The nearby billboard advertising the tooth paste Stomatol is the oldest neon sign in Stockholm. The tooth paste tube was built in 1909. The tooth-brush and paste were added in the 1930s.

SNELL, JOHANN. Printed the first books in Stockholm, in 1483.

SNOILSKY, CARL (1841–1903). Count Snoilsky was a poet. In 1876, he became a member of the Swedish Academy (q.v.). He traveled widely and many of his poems were about southern Europe. However, he also wrote several poems about Stockholm, such as *Nya och gamla Stockholm* (New and Old Stockholm) in 1889. He also wrote *Stockholm i den svenska konsten.* (Stockholm in Swedish Art) and *Stockholmsnaturen i svensk dikt* (Stockholm's Nature in Swedish Poetry).

In 1890, Snoilsky returned to Sweden. An admirer, Oskar II (q.v.), arranged for him to be chief librarian at *Kungliga biblioteket* (The Royal Library) (q.v.).

SÖDERBERG, HJALMAR (1869–1941). The writer spent much of his life after 1917 in Copenhagen and is best remembered for his clear and ironic descriptions of disillusioned people in Stockholm at the turn of the century. His main address in Stockholm was at Östermalm. He is reputed by fellow authors to have been well-acquainted with many of Stockholm's restaurants and bars, establishments used extensively in his writing. His best-known novels are *Historietter* (Short Stories) (1898), and *Martin Bircks ungdom* (Martin Birck's Youth), (1901). He also wrote a successful play, *Doktor Glas* (1905), which was presented in London in the summer of 1995.

SÖDERMALM. "*Söder*" (the South Side) has, in some respects, its own identity. It is across a bridge to the south of the Old Town (q.v.).

The local residents have their own characteristics: streetwise, self-confident, and self-sufficient. The special Stockholm slang is mainly based on "Söder"and is known as *söderslang*. For example, a boy from Söder is a *Söderkis*. To some extent, there are similarities to London cockneys. But the once-working class area is now mildly upscale.

Södermalm's original name was *Åsön* (Ridge Island). It was donated to the town of Stockholm in the charter granted in 1436. In 1518, only seven households paid taxes to the town, and it was obviously quite sparsely populated. The area was mainly devoted to cabbage patches and grazing pastures. At *Klockviken* (Bell Creek), there were bell foundries, and at *Tegelviken* (Brick Creek) there were a couple of brickworks. Further away toward Saltsjön (q.v.) there were some whale-oil sheds.

In 1570, Södermalm, like Norrmalm, was incorporated with Stockholm. Around 1600, Södermalm was still mostly a haunt for all kinds of people with no fixed abode. Toll-gates separating Södermalm were built in 1622. The rebuilding took place in the 1640s. Södermalm was influenced by Klas Fleming's town plan. A Södermalmstorg was already referred to in the time of Gustav II Adolf (q.v.).

The islands two main routes originated from there, now known as Götgatan and Hornsgatan. Götgatan was the beginning of the road to Götaland, the southern province of Sweden. Hornsgatan led to the Horn brickworks in the western part of the city. When the city wall was dismantled, two large defense works were built in 1659 called Grindsskans and Danviksskans.

Most of the people of Södermalm worked for manufacturers and factories and on the shipping wharves created during the reign of Karl XI (q.v.). For a long time, Södermalm was a poor part of Stockholm and the people suffered from starvation and tuberculosis and impoverished living conditions.

The Lindhagen town plan (q.v.) during the later part of the 19th century brought great improvements to Södermalm. An important result was the creation of *Ringvägen* (Ring Street). Before the days of steam power and dynamite, the rocky hills could not be dealt with. Thus, the rocky ridge had shaped the fate of Södermalm. Although it was possible to improve conditions with modern methods, even today many of the old buildings remain. Small houses and shacks still dot Mariabergen and Katarinabergen's hilly roads as a reminder of days gone by.

On the crest of the hill at Hornsgatan, opposite Maria Magdalena Church (q.v.) where Evert Taube (q.v.) is buried, there are well-reputed art galleries. An area with more pubs than any other in Stockholm is near Götgatan. There also is a motley assortment of small, old shops.

The third largest-street on Söder, is another straight road running from Södermalmstorg, called Katarinavägen. It does not have any shops. It leads to Fjällgatan (q.v.), a main tourist attraction in the western part of Söder.

Not much remains of the original *Fjällgatan* (Fell Street). The buildings on Söder have long been associated with low, wooden shacks painted red and known as Söderkåkar (originally built by, and for, working-class people). These houses can be seen at Åsöberget, in the western part of Söder and are listed as buildings of rare cultural value. There is no typical Söder architectural style. Buildings range from great apartment blocks from the 1960s, to nearby beautiful 18th-century houses, mixed in with fin-de-siècle and modern creations.

The newest and most talked about buildings are in the Södra Station area, which has been likened to "walking into an architectural competition". The area is Sweden's most densely populated, with approximately 8,000 people living in an area the size of about 40 football fields. The most well-known of these buildings is the Bow, designed by the Spanish architect Ricardo Bofill. It is a semi-circular house located on *Medborgarplatsen* (Citizens' Square) (q.v.). Also in Medborgarplatsen are the newly built *Söderhallarna* (Söder Halls) with boutiques, cafés, restaurants, and delicatessens.

Eriksdalslund and Tantolunden have buildings of another nature. These are small colonies (workers' cottages) with flower-garden plots squeezed up against one another, presenting quite a contrast to life in the city. Some families live far out in the suburbs of Stockholm, then move into the cottages and the town in spring to live "in the country." The plots in Eriksdalslund are among the oldest in Stockholm and were first cultivated in 1906.

One of Stockholm's smallest and most visited parks is Ivar Lo's Park, located near Bastugatan. It is named after the author Ivar Lo Johansson (q.v.) and is a particular favorite with children. *Långholmen* (Long Island) (q.v.) is a much bigger park. In fact, it is an open space with several buildings of cultural and historical interest. Långholmen is linked over the water by *Västerbron* (West Bridge). Traffic moves in one direction to Hornstull on Söder and in the other direction to Kungsholmen (q.v.).

SÖDERMALMSTORG *(SÖDERMALM SQUARE)*. Close to Slussen (q.v.), this is a high traffic area and, consequently, not very attractive. However, the sloping square is dominated by 18th-century buildings with a pair of simple and genuine façades at numbers 6 and 8.

SÖDERPORT. The name of the old southern city gate. Söderport and Norraport (q.v.) were the only entrances to Stadsholmen (q.v.), the Old Town. There were inner and outer towers with a drawbridge.

SÖDERSTRÖM. The first sluice gates at Söderström, built in 1634.

SOFIA CHURCH. Located near Skånegatan. it has a central nave with a wide central tower surrounded by small towers. It was built between 1902 and 1906. The interior decorations were created between 1948 and 1951.

SOFIA av NASSAU, QUEEN (1836–1913). She married Oscar II (q.v.) and was particularly known for her religious and philanthropic work. In 1889, she founded the highly regarded private Sofia Hospital *(Sofiahemmet)* and nurses training college.

SOLHEM. One of the first suburbs to be regarded as an "alternative residential district." When the Västerås railroad line opened in 1876, it helped initiate the development of Solhem, in Spånga (q.v.). It is now incorporated into the city of Stockholm.

SOLNA. A result of the industrialization during the second half of the 19th century was the development of communities of workers in Solna. The opening of the Uppsala railroad line in 1866 became important for the growth of Solna's Hagalund. In the 1860s, Solna was still a farming district. But several suburbs sprang up that assumed the rank of municipalities; Hagalund in 1899, Nya Huvudsta in 1904, and Råsunda in 1911. In 1943, Solna was designated as a town.

In the new Solna, Råsunda, Hagalund and Nya Huvudsta formed a united municipality, while the Ulriksdal and Råksta housing communities remained isolated from them. Also separate was the royal palace of Haga (q.v.), Karlberg, and Ulriksdal (q.v.), with their large parks. The estates of Stora Frösunda and Huvudsta, and a number of state-owned districts which totaling 69 percent of the town's area—including areas for for hospitals, railroads, and the military,—were also separate. However, the buying of land, clearing out of older buildings—particularly Blåkulla and new construction mainly around Huvudsta and Bergshamra, resulted in the creation of a new unified whole.

Solna remains independent of Stockholm. Solna football stadium, originally opened in 1937, was reopened after reconstruction in 1985. It holds 40,000 spectators.

SOLVALLA. A well-known race track for trotting horses. It was opened in 1927.

SPÅNGA. Around the turn of the century, estates and areas of land in Spånga were purchased for future residential development and the creation of a suburb. In 1949, Spånga, with associated parts of Hässelby, came under city authority.

SPARE, KARL. Governor of Stockholm in 1773.

"SPÖKSLOTTET" *(GHOST PALACE)*. Located on Norrmalm (q.v.) and houses the Stockholm University (q.v.) art collection. The house lies behind a high, iron fence. From the exterior, it appears to be an undisturbed mansion in Dutch style, with two wings leading forward toward the road. The house was built in 1700 by a Dutchman, possibly Silesian, named Scheffler. In the latter half of the 1700s, it passed to the Knigge family. Knigge, the owner of a manufacturing estate, was known as a hard and cruel man, and it was during his time that the story of a haunted house came about. Apparently, Knigge disappeared mysteriously without trace, and was reported to have returned to haunt the house. In 1876, the property was bought by Lars Johan Hierta's (q.v.) widow. After the death of her three daughters, it passed to *Stockholms högskola* (Stockholm High School), later to become Stockholm University.

SPORT. Sweden is an active country and Stockholm is no exception. To a certain extent, the northern climate influences the type of sports enjoyed. Swedes have tended to favor individual sports, rather than team games, and sports such as running, jumping and swimming. Favorite sports involve snow and ice. But in more recent years, Sweden has excelled in tennis and golf has become more popular. A feature of Swedish sports is the well-structured associations and coaching programs, most often on a voluntary basis.

As the capital, Stockholm naturally attracts many sporting events and associations. The main ones are listed in APPENDIX NO. 4.

STADION *(THE STADIUM)*. On Valhallavägen and Lidingövägen. It was inaugurated on June 1, 1912. The Olympic Games were held here and opened on June 6. Swedish competitors reached their zenith that year. They won 24 gold medals, 24 silver, and 17 bronze. The arena is constructed in antique style and is surrounded by walls reminiscent of the Middle Ages. The space was enlarged to house the European games in 1958, when there were 27,000 spectators. Outside the stadium are several sculptures: *Staffetlöpare* (Relay Runner) and *Kulstotare* (Shot-Putter) by Carl Fagerberg; *Löpare vid målet* (The Runner at the Finish) by Carl Eldh (q.v.); and *Lek* (Play) by Bruno Liljefors (q.v.).

See also OLYMPIC GAMES.

STADSBIBLIOTEKET. On March 31, 1928, the large library building designed by the architect Gunnar Asplund (q.v.) and located on Svea-vägen was inaugurated. It is basically a cube with a cylinder on top. It is one of Stockholm's most famous and, many think, most beautiful buildings. It has elements of 1920s classicism. But above all, it can be seen as the predecessor of "functional" architecture. Light and airy, simplicity and consistency play important parts in the character of the building. Asplund was the greatest of Swedish functionalists.

In 1993, the total number of books loaned was 749,625. There were an estimated 345,000 visitors the same year.

On May 14, 1992, the placing of enamel plaques on buildings in the city under the "Literary Stockholm" project began. The plaques feature quotations from literature, together with Stockholm motifs. They were created by the city library in cooperation with the city museum.

STADSHOLMEN. An island, one of many in the region, where the city of Stockholm is believed to have had its earliest settlement.

STADSHUSET *(THE TOWN HALL,* also called *THE CITY HALL))*. Inaugurated on a midsummer's day in 1923, exactly 400 years after Gustav Vasa (q.v.) marched into town for his coronation. The archi-tect was Ragnar Östberg. Building began in 1911; it consists of 8 million bricks and 19 million pieces of gilded mosaic. It is one of the world's most costly town halls. It is located on Hantverkargatan, on the site of an old mill (See also ELDVKARN). It has become one of the most photographed buildings and known worldwide. The dark red-brick building is built in national romantic style, set not only in building materials from the Middle Ages but also in the style of the time. Many well-known Swedish artists contributed to the decora-tions.

Blå hallen (The Blue Hall) is the central feature in the western part of the building. It is a covered yard with a stairway leading up to the Golden Room. The Blue Hall is turned into the party room for the annual Nobel Prize winners' festivities. Actually, the hall is not blue, as originally planned. Instead, its red brickwork remained uncovered.

More ornate is the Golden Room. The banquet hall takes up most of the space on that floor and culminates in the Golden Room. The first room is called the Oval, in which hang the famous 17th-century tapestries from Tureholm Castle. Then comes the Prince's Gallery with the fresco "*Staden vid vattnet*" (The City by the Water) by Prins Eugen (q.v.). Passing through the small chamber known as *Rundeln*

(Circular Space) one comes to the room called *Tre kronor* (Three Crowns).

From there, one ends up in the Golden Room, with its walls of glittering mosaic created by Einar Forseth. On April 27, 1932, the statue of Engelbrekt (q.v.) was unveiled at the City Hall. Other statues by Carl Milles (q.v.) may be seen by the lakeside. Carl Eldh's statues of August Strindberg (q.v.) and the poet (Gustaf Fröding) are in the terraced garden.

From May to September, the tower *Tre kronor* (Three Crowns) is open from 10 a.m. to 3 p.m. It stands 106 meters above the waters of Lake Mälaren (q.v.) and its highest observation platform starts at 76 meters. There are 322 steps. The elevator only takes visitors halfway up. From there, a gently sloping, smooth surfaced brick pasageway winds upward. Finally, there are steep, old wooden ladders to complete the climb. The reward is a wide view over Stockholm and the waters. A magnificent view of the imposing outline of the City Hall, which seems to float on the waters of Lake Mälaren, is available from the quayside, near Riddarhustorget.

On May 6, 1995, "Open City Hall" was organized. This annual event gives some 20,000 Stockholmers an opportunity to meet the city's leading politicians.

STADSMUSEUM. See CITY MUSEUM OF STOCKHOLM.

STADSTEATERN. See STOCKHOLM CULTURAL CENTER.

STAGE COACHES. In March 1829, stage-coach traffic began between Stockholm and Uppsala. The departure point was originally at Gustav Adolf's Square (q.v.). Stage-coach mail, between Stockholm and Ystad, was introduced in 1831.

STAGNELIUS, ERIK JOHAN (1793–1823). Stagnelius is regarded as one of Sweden's outstanding poets. He was little known during his life-time. He was born on the island of Öland. After his studies, he took a post in a royal department in Stockholm, where he was a loner. His writings often were religious and he pondered the purpose of life. His best-known work is *Liljor i Saron* (The Lillies in Saron). He is buried in Maria Churchyard. In 1930, a street in *Fredhäll* was named after him.

STATISTICS. See USK.

STEAMBOATS. The first Swedish steamboats were tested across Riddarfjärden (q.v.) in 1810. Sweden's first steamship was built in Stock-

holm and started traffic on Lake Mälaren in 1818 (q.v.). The first
was called *Stockholms häxan* (the Stockholm Witch). Another famous
paddle steamer was *Amfitrite*. Steamboat service began to Åbo and
Ystad in 1822.

STENBOCK PALACE. One of the town's most beautiful houses. It now
is home to the country's highest court. Fredrik Stenbock and his wife
Katarina de la Gardie had this lavish Renaissance palace built in the
middle of the 17th century. The pair's coat of arms is placed over the
beautiful entrance.

STOCK EXCHANGE (*BÖRSEN*). The Stock Exchange building is on
Stortorget (Main Square) (q.v.). It was designed by architect E. Palmstedt (q.v.) and built in the 18th century during the early years of the
reign of Gustav III (q.v.), when it was completed in its present form.
Stockholm's exchange occupies the lower floor. It is open to the public every morning. It is generally regarded as one of the city's finest
buildings. The upper floors now house the Swedish Academy (q.v.)
and its Nobel Library (q.v.).

STOCKHOLM AIRPORT See STOCKHOLM-ARLANDA.

STOCKHOLM-ARLANDA. Stockholm-Arlanda Airport is Sweden's
main gateway to the rest of the world and an important focus for
communication among countries in northern Europe and around the
Baltic Sea. It is located just 42 kilometers north of Stockholm and 35
kilometers south of the city of Uppsala, in what is known as the Mälar
region. A vision for the community is to create a new, modern city
between Stockholm and Uppsala, located near the airport. The project
has started, but progress appears to be slow. The airport is easy to
reach by road. By 1998, the new Arlandabana (q.v.) express rail link
will connect the airport to the country's railroad network. This will
allow road, rail, and air to meet at the same point for the first time.
The 92-meter-long train is designed to travel at 160 kilometers per
hour and to complete the journey from Stockholm city to the airport
in 20 minutes. This project will be financed by a private consortium.
Early 1995 was the scheduled project starting date. Photographs published in March 1996 showed the tunnels to be well under way. The
summer of 1999 was then given as the target date for completion. The
route is designed in a bow-shape, linking with the existing north-
south main-line tracks.

The Swedish Government has also given permission for a Freeport
to be established on the edge of Stockholm-Arlanda Airport. Like all
of Sweden's 19 state-owned airports, Stockholm-Arlanda is owned

and administered by *Luftfartsverket (LFV).* (the Swedish Civil Aviation Administration) (CAA). No tax revenues are spent on Arlanda, but LFV puts several hundred million SEK (Swedish crowns) a year into the national treasury.

As the hub, Stockholm-Arlanda provides a valuable lifeline between all parts of Sweden and its capital city. Stockholm-Arlanda is within around an hour's flying time of anywhere in Sweden. The airport's operations can be compared to a community of around 50,000 people. It is already Europe's sixth-busiest airport in terms of aircraft movement, and expects to increase its ranking. In 1994, 13.3 million passengers used the airport and 230,000 takeoffs and landings occurred. Stockholm-Arlanda Airport is working hard to position itself as northern Europe's premier freight hub. In 1909, the first airplane flight over Swedish soil was made. On August 2, of the same year, the French aviator Leon Legagneux landed on Ladugårdsgärdet (q.v.). Nowadays, more than 40,000 people fly over Sweden every day. Stockholm's first airport was situated at Bromma (q.v.), but it was clear to the Swedish government towards the end of World War II, that a new, major airport was needed. The airport was built at Halmsjön, because it was considered the most suitable area both technically and for its potential for subsequent expansion. Construction work began in 1952 with restricted financial resources. The inaugural flight from Bromma to Halmsjö, with its single, concrete runway, took place on November 26, 1954. Immediate and severe criticism of the concrete runway followed. It became known as "the Hump" because of its shape and it was seldom used. A few years later, work resumed. The concrete runway was rebuilt and a second runway was added. The name *Halmsjö* (Straw Lake) was replaced and Arlanda was adopted in 1958 by parliament. The first regular flight to New York began on June 26, 1960 when a SAS DC–8 took off. On April 1, 1962, Stockholm-Arlanda Airport was officially opened by King Gustav VI Adolf (q.v.).

The aiport continued to grow. In 1976, Terminal 5 was opened. It is used by 35 scheduled airlines and about 10 charter companies for international flights. Terminal 4 was opened in 1983. The top domestic airline is *SAS* (Scandinavian Airlines System), which operates 220 flights a day from Terminal 4. Terminal 2, which became operational in 1990, is used exclusively by Transwede, Lufthansa, Finnair, and Lauda Air for their international and domestic flight partnership. Transwede has now discontinued its flights to England and is concentrating on domestic and freight flights.

A recent development is the opening of Sky City, a commercial center that includes shops, restaurants, and a hotel with conference and exhibition areas. The Sky City Hotel is the first in Northern Europe to be fully integrated with airport terminals. It was officially opened in November 1993. At the turn of the century, a third runway will open and the airport's capacity will increase from under 70 flights to around 105 flights per hour at peak periods. Detailed planning and more specified cost estimates were done in 1995. In December 1995, final estimates for Runway 3 were due. Work was scheduled to begin in January 1996. Construction is estimated to take four years. The Runway 3 project consists of four main parts. Based on a decision by the Swedish National Franchise Board for Environmental Protection, groundwater around the runway north of the SAS hangar is to be protected. A protective synthetic liner will be laid approximately 1 meter under the ground, covering 400,000 square meters.

A control tower will be built adjacent to the multistory car park (the largest in northern Europe, with spaces for 20,000 vehicles) at Terminal 5, and will be approximately 80 meters high. The new runway will require a new fire station, which will be located east of Runway 3.

Local public highways will be rerouted, including a two-tier interchange where aircraft are led over the motorway approach road on a viaduct. Sweden has hopes of hosting the Olympic Games in 2004. For a potential bid to be successful, it is essential that the nation be able to show that it is capable of transporting all the tens of thousands of visitors into and out of the country by air. The proposed improvements will obviously contribute that.

STOCKHOLM "BLOODBATH." A mass execution that took place in Stortorget (q.v.) on the November 8–9, 1520, after the Dane, King Kristian II (q.v.), forcefully laid claim to the Swedish throne and was crowned king of Sweden. There were 82 nationalist leaders who were accused of heresy and executed. The corpses were piled on carts and pushed to Södermalm (q.v.), where the bodies were buried. Accused of heresy against the Catholic Church, they were not allowed to be buried inside the city walls. Others were burned on a pile of bodies. Sten Sture's (q.v.) body was exhumed and slung onto the flames.

This event led to Gustav Vasa (q.v.) rallying a popular revolt and finally bringing an end to the Kalmar Union (q.v.).

STOCKHOLM CHAMBER OF COMMERCE. See CHAMBER OF COMMERCE.

STOCKHOLM CHARTER. The Swedish National Council issued the Stockholm Charter in 1434, called "Stockholm's Magna Carta."

STOCKHOLM CULTURAL CENTER (*KULTURHUSET*). A concrete and glass structure located at Sergels Torg 3. The building was built between 1968 and 1976 and consists of two parts. It was launched as a temporary seat of the one-chamber parliament, which moved there in 1971. They met in the so-called Theater Building, where Klara Theater and the Theater Café are located. When parliament returned to Helgeandsholmen after renovations were completed, *Stadsteatern* (Stockholm Town Theater) moved to the Cultural Center; it has five stages. The other part is mainly used for exhibition purposes. The Center has cultural activities and exhibitions on several floors. On the ground floor is the reading room, a kind of activity center where one may listen to music or lectures, read or play chess. The building is representative of the architectural style that typified the rapid renovation of the city center during the 1960s and 1970s. The Cultural Center serves as a living cultural center with limited-period exhibitions of paintings, sculpture, architecture, crafts, design, photography, video, etc.

In April 1991, an international conference on city planning was held in *Kulturhuset* (Cultural Center) to present suggestions for improving Stockholm.

This is the second-most visited cultural institution in Stockholm, after Skansen (q.v.). In 1993, the center attracted 1.25 million visitors. However, in 1985 it reached a high of 3 million visitors.

STOCKHOLM ENSKILDA BANK. One of Sweden's oldest banks and the country's first modern commercial bank. It was founded by A.O. Wallenberg (q.v.) in 1856. It became Enskilda Bank and the Skandinaviska Enskilda Bank. The Swedish word *enskilda* means "private."

STOCKHOLM'S EXHIBITION. The grandest of them all, a World Fair was held at Djurgården (q.v.) in 1897, the year of the 25th anniversary of the reign of Oskar II (q.v.).

Another large exhibition of industrial arts and crafts was held at Ladugårdsgärdet (q.v.) on Djurgården in 1930. It was visited by more than 4 million people. It presented functionalism (q.v.), for which the architect Asplund (q.v.) was largely responsible. It is regarded as a milestone in Sweden's development.

STOCKHOLM FESTIVAL. The annual *Festspel* (Festival) of music, dance, and theater, began in 1953. It is held in June and includes well-known foreign artists. Concerts are held in historical environments and opera performances are held at Drottningholm Theater (q.v.).

STOCKHOLM INFORMATION SERVICE. The Stockholm Information Service's main task is to supply information about Stockholm and to market the city for tourists and other visitors. The service is the regional tourist organization in Stockholm County. It also runs the tourist bureaus in Stockholm. In order to increase the number of congresses in Stockholm, the institution Congress Stockholm was formed. Its task is to market Stockholm as a conference and congress city. It is located at Sweden House (q.v.).

STOCKHOLM MARKETING LTD. (SML) A company serving the entire business community. It markets Stockholm to companies abroad as a center for international congresses and events. It negotiates the distribution of industrial land and supplies commercial properties.

Another important aspect of SML's work is to monitor the job market and relevant educational issues, as well as coordinate contacts between research, development, and the commercial sector.

STOCKHOLMS LOKALTRAFIK (SL), (STOCKHOLM'S LOCAL TRAFFIC COMPANY). A distance of 160 kilometers between the bus stops in the extreme north of the region served by SL and those in the south.

From the bus stops in the east, to the commuter rail station in the west, is just over 80 kilometers.

Although the county of Stockholm occupies only 1.6 per cent of the total area in Sweden, it is a much more densely populated region than the rest of the country. About a fifth of Sweden's population live in the county of Stockholm.

The Stockholm County Council owns SL, which is responsible for providing overland transportation within the county. SL's services include commuter trains, subways, streetcars, and buses. SL claims that its 110 kilometers of subway track makes it one of the longest in the world. Currently, SL accounts for more than 40 percent of all local and regional trips made over a 24–hour period, most of which are by rail. During peak traffic, the share of trips into central Stockholm reaches more than 70 per cent. Yet, in spite of this, during an ordinary weekday, more than 600,000 trips are made by automobile to and from the inner city.

STOCKHOLM'S PALACE. See ROYAL PALACE.

STOCKHOLMS POSTEN. On October 29, 1778, the newspaper *Stockholms Posten* began publishing. During the time of author J. H. Kellgren's leadership (1788–1795) it was Sweden's most illustrious cultural medium.

STOCKHOLM STADSMUSEUM. See *STADSMUSEUM*. (The City Museum of Stockholm.)

STOCKHOLM UNIVERSITY. The university offers undergraduate and postgraduate education and research in four faculties: humanities, law, social sciences and natural sciences. Undergraduate education is offered as study programs and separate courses. General study programs are directed toward a wide range of professions. The university has about 32,000 undergraduates and about 2,000 postgraduate students.

The university was given its name in 1960, when the College of Stockholm *(Stockholms högskola)* became a state university. 1970 saw the beginning of the exodus from the center to Frescati, just north of Stockholm, where the university administration, most of the departments, and the university library are found. The departments of physics, earth sciences and geography are still located in the city center. There also are other departments spread out over the city.

In the early 1980s, the university area became a modern campus and an inspiring and pleasant environment for study, research, and work, thanks to the creation of *Allhuset.* Housed in *Allhuset* are the university bookshop, restaurants, a post office, the student union premises, a travel agency, the university library (one of the most modern in Europe), and the gymnasium. The atmosphere is enhanced by *Allhuset's* closeness to nature and excellent recreational facilities.

The academic year starts at the end of August and continues through the beginning of June.

STOCKHOLM WATER PRIZE. Since 1991, in conjunction with the Water Festival (q.v.), the Stockholm Water Prize has been presented to people who make outstanding contributions toward the work of water preservation. The prize has gained international recognition and its prestige continues to grow. Winners include David W. Schindler (Canada), 1991; Poul Harremoes (Denmark); 1992, Dr. Chitale (India), 1993; and Dr. Takeshi Kubo (Japan), 1994; In 1995, the prize was awarded to Water Aid, a small British aid organization that specializes in providing pure water to more than 3 million people in Africa and Asia. In 1996, the prize was awarded to Dr. Jörg Imberger, professor of environmental engineering and director of the centre for water research at the University of Western Australia.

See also WATER FESTIVAL.

STOCKHOLMS-TIDNINGEN (THE STOCKHOLM NEWS). A daily newspaper in Stockholm published from 1889–1966, was founded by Anders Jeurling (1851–1906) as a popular paper for a low price, mainly for distribution in the rural areas. In 1931, it joined with *Stockholms dagblad* (q.v.). Originally politically independent, the paper adopted a liberal stance and supported *folkpartiet* (the People's Party,

Liberal) until 1956, when the owner, Torsten Kreuger, sold it to LO (q.v.). *Stockholms-Tidningen* was the main voice of the Social Democrats from 1958 to 1966. During 1981–1984, a Social Democratic daily paper with the same name was published. This was specially published for Stockholm and Stockholm County.

STOCKHOLMS DAGBLAD (STOCKHOLM DAILY). Founded in 1824 as a conservative daily, it was combined with Stockholms-Tidningen (q.v.) in 1931. The paper was a leading cultural medium, especially at the turn of the century.

STOCKSUND. A suburb developed partly because of the Rimbo railroad line from Stockholm Östra (East).

STORÄNGEN. A high-class housing area and one of the first suburbs to be regarded as an "alternative residential district." Storängen made use of the rail link with Stockholm, which opened in 1893. Originally an independent municipality, it is now incorporated with Nacka.

STORA DALDANSEN. In 1743, after the war in Russia, the men who marched on Stockholm from Dalarna were defeated by troops stationed in the capital. This was known as *"Stora daldansen"* (The great Dalecarlian Dance).

STOR FRÖSUNDA. See SOLNA.

STORKYRKAN (THE GREAT CHURCH or THE CATHEDRAL). Located on *Slottsbacken* (Castle Hill), it is the church for royal weddings and coronations. It is dedicated to the patron saint of seafarers, St. Nikolai (St. Nicholas).

Building of the first church began in the 1250s and was completed in 1264. In the north wall of the current building, one can still see a few preserved parts of an original wall, presumably from the 13th century. The church is reputed to have been founded by Birger Jarl (q.v.). It was initially called *Bykyrkan*, (town church), and later St. Nikolai. In 1306, the church was consecrated. During the start of the 14th century, the church was enlarged. Probably, there was a wood-covered basilica in the western half of the current central nave. In the middle of the 14th century, a sanctuary dedicated to "Our Lady", was added south of the two most easterly vault units. The vault paintings of the sanctuary are preserved. For several hundred years, it was the only parish church in Stockholm. On December 31, 1489, in commemoration of the Battle of Brunkeberg (q.v.) and the victory over the Danes, a statue of St. *Göran* (George) and the dragon, was carved in wood, gilded by Bernt Notke and unveiled in *Storkyrkan*. It was commissioned by King Sten Sture (q.v.). A copy is mounted in Öster-långgatan. An optical phenomenon was seen in the sky on April 20, 1535. A so-called *"mock sun"* or parhelion caused considerable agitation and unease. It was later reproduced in a picture that was preserved in *Storkyrkan*. It is the oldest picture of Stockholm. A copy of it is in the City Museum of Stockholm, where it is much easier to view.

The current church is the diocesan church. It has a beautiful interior, done in late-gothic style with high rib vaulting from the 15th century, gilded royal boxes, and a pulpit. The altar is made of black ebony, yet it is named the Silver Altar. The church consists of five naves. The exterior has a baroque style that originated in a restoration in the 18th century. Outside the church stands a statue of Olaus Petri (q.v.) He is buried underneath the pulpit in the church.

There are 250 steps leading up to a platform in the tower. From there look for a fine view over the Old Town.

STORTORGET. The main square in *Gamla stan* (the Old Town). It was the center of the Middle Ages town. Executions were carried out here. And it was here that Stockholm's Blood Bath (q.v.) took place. In the middle of the square, is a well surmounted by a sculpture in the shape of a mountain with faces and masks, reminiscent of the Middle Ages. They were created by Masreliez, a theater artist to Gustav III (q.v.). This well was a meeting place for residents and visitors that satisfied daily needs and was aesthetically pleasing. Architect Erik Palmstedt (q.v.), who designed the well in front of Börshuset (Stock Exchange Building) (q.v.), was also responsible for the one in Stortorget. The old pillory gave its name to *Kåkbrinken* (q.v.), a narrow passageway opening off the square. Above the pillory was a statue, *Kopparmatte*, with a man holding a whipping birch in his hand. The statue is now in *Rådhuset* (The Court House) (q.v.). The pillory, which had been removed for some time, was replaced in Stortorget in 1602. In the wall of a corner house on Skomakargatan (Cobbler Street), a cannon ball is embedded. It is said that it was intended for King Christian of Denmark, known in Sweden as Christian the Tyrant, but this is most probably a myth. The well came into use in the 1700s. When it dried up in the 1850s, it was moved to Brunkebergstorget. It was returned to its original place in Stortorget in 1953.

On the north side of Stortorget, with its gable facing the square, was the medieval town hall, which contained a large council chamber on the first floor. That building was demolished in the 18th century. There are some well-known buildings around the main square; for example, Grillska huset (q.v.) at number 3 which is now owned by the City Mission. The house was built in the 1640s by a German merchant and was later owned by a family named Grill. The interior of the house has been renovated. In a bakery on the ground floor, old wooden roof beams were revealed. The entrance doorway at number 20, was built in the 1650s. With its prone soldiers, it is typical of the work carried out by stone-mason Johan Wendelstam. On many of the houses, the iron wall supports are visible and often finished off in various decorative forms. Different periods have different shapes and these often help to date a particular building. In 1915, the traditional Christmas Market reopened here, after being closed for eight years.

STRANDVÄGEN *(SHORE STREET)*. The street was still not completely finished in time for the exhibition in 1897 on Djurgården (q.v.). In spite of vehicular and pedestrian traffic, riding tracks and tree plantations, it gave a rather sorry impression. The idea of having a grand esplanade alongside Nybroviken was proposed in the 1850s. Twenty years later, the idea became once again topical, this time because of royal initiative. It would take 15 years to prepare and then build the 742-meter-long stretch between Nybrohamnen and *Djurgårdsbron* (Djurgårds Bridge) (q.v.). The first houses built on Strandvägen were numbers 23 to 27, built between 1881 and 1883. The final property was the impressive Jugend-style palace at number 7, built between 1907 and 1911.

On March 2, 1994, the building at Strandvägen 47 was extensively damaged by fire that raged for several days. Damage has been estimated at 50 million SEK.

STRÄNG, GUNNAR (1906–1992). A Social Democrat politician, was born December 12, 1906. He was a colorful personality and became finance minister in 1955. His economic policies aimed to facilitate the current policy of *jämnlikhet* (equality) to the greatest extent possible. He was a forceful speaker and his clear, uncomplicated presentation of the national budget on TV and radio were models of good political pedagogy.

STREETCAR MUSEUM. At Tegelviksgatan 22, one may see how transportation in Stockholm developed from the early 19th century until the present day. The future of Stockholm's public transportation system also is on display. There are horse-drawn streetcars, trolley buses, electric streetcars, a railcar from 1896, and a Leyland bus from 1928. Visitors may drive a streetcar simulator. The museum is located at the SL (Greater Stockholm Transport) bus depot, known as *"Söderhallen,"* at Danvikstull. (*NOTE*: Not to be confused with "Söderhallarna" at Medborgarplatsen.) In April 1989, the Streetcar museum at the Odenplan subway station was closed and moved to more spacious accommodations at Tegelviksgatan, on Södermalm. The new site also provides more room to exhibit some older vehicles that had previously been kept in storage.

STREETCARS. Stockholm's new streetcar company started horse-drawn traffic in the north of the city in 1877. In 1901, electrification of the southern tramway track was carried out. Most streetcars were replaced by buses in the 1950s and 1960s, but two Stockholm suburbs retained theirs. The environment debate revived interest in streetcars as a means of public transport. Tourists and locals regularly ride the streetcars to Skansen outdoor museum and the Wasa Man-of War (qq.v.). On June 2, 1991, a streetcar route between Normalmstorg and Oakhill on Djurgården opened. The streetcars are operated by volunteers of the Swedish Streetcar Society.

Stockholm's streetcars were featured on a set of postage stamps, issued May 12, 1995.

STREET CLEANING. The first street-cleaning department started in 1859.

STREET LAMPS. On December 19, 1853, the first gas street lamps were used. Electric street lighting in Stockholm started in 1883.

STRINDBERG, AUGUST (1849–1912). Born in Stockholm, where his parents worked at the Old Palace Bakery. His early literary work in 1872, *Mäster Olof,* was based on the life of Olaus Petri (q.v.). In 1879, Strindberg's *The Red Room* was published. Strindberg moved his residence a number of times in Stockholm—25 in all. He lived his first and last years in Vasastan. He lived at Norrtullsgatan 14 (North Toll Street) on three different occasions when he was young. The home was then a farm with grazing cows, apple trees, and greenhouses. It was there that he met Siri von Essen, the unhappy wife of a guard officer. August and Siri were married from 1877 to 1891. In 1893, he married Frida Uhl; it lasted until 1895. He was married to Harriet Bosse from 1901 to 1904. Between 1907 and 1912, Strindberg lived in *Blå tornet* ("Blue Tower") at Drottninggatan 85. The apartment in Blå tornet is the only place where Strindberg lived that has been preserved for posterity in its original style. One of his homes currently is a wing of the townhouse Jakobsberg, which stood in Hornstull. It is now in Skansen (q.v.) and is used as a staff residence. On January 22, 1912, August Strindberg was celebrated with a torchlight procession. On May 14, he died in his home at Blå tornet. Stockholmers lined the route of his funeral procession. He is buried in Norra Churchyard.

He is generally regarded as Sweden's most versatile and talented writer. Some of his most renowned works, in chronological order, are:—1872, *Mäster Olof* (Master Olof); 1879, *Röda rummet* (The Red Room); 1884–1886, *Giftas* (Getting Married); 1886–1887 and 1909, *Tjänstekvinnans son* (The Son of a Servant); 1887, *Hemsoborna* (The People of Hemsö); 1887, *Fadren* (The Father); 1888, *Fro*‑ *ken Julie* (Lady Julie); 1898–1904, *Till Damaskus* (To Damascus);‑ 1899, *Gustav Vasa;* 1902, *Ett drömspel* (A Dream Play).

For the second successive year, a Strindberg in Stockholm Festival was held, from September 2 through September 10, 1995. The theme that year was "In Defense of Freedom of Speech."

STRINDBERG'S MUSEUM. Located at the last known residence of Sweden's most famous writer at Drottninggatan 85. The floor on which Strindberg lived became a museum in 1973. The building is in the Jugend style and is commonly known as *Blå tornet* (the Blue Tower). His library is kept here. There are basic exhibitions about Strindberg's life, times, and writings. Concerts, talks, discussions, and theater peformances are held here. There is also a video about Strindberg's literature.

STRÖMMEN *(THE STREAM)*. This is the fast-flowing stretch of water that joins Lake Mälaren (q.v.) and the Baltic Sea.

On July 18–19, 1992, a northern Europe steamboat meeting was held with a cortege on Strömmen and an exhibition for the public at Vasa Museum. Some 30 Swedish and Danish vessels assembled. In the summer of 1995, a 20-kilogram salmon was caught in Strömmen. This is only slightly less than the record. It is thought to be one of the two-year-old young salmon "planted" a few years earlier.

In February 1995, two amateur divers discovered a wreck between 3 and 4 meters below the surface between Skeppsholmen and Kastellholmen. It is a historical marine treasure, in the form of a Russian galley from the end of the 17th century or beginning of the 18th century. No other such wrecks are known but there may well be others among the many wrecks lying in the area.

STRÖMPARTERREN. A terrace at Norrbro, facing Strömmen. It is the entrance to the Medieval Museum (q.v.) of Stockholm. It has recently been given a face-lift and is now a pleasant lakeside park. Carl Milles' (q.v.) statue *"Solsångaren"* (The Sun Singer) is situated here. It is a good place from which to watch the few remaining circular fishing nets being lowered into the water. On April 23, 1992, a newly built hoop-net boat was added to the three existing ones. They are a popular tourist feature of Stockholm. The purpose of the new boat is to provide small fish for the *Östersjöakvariet* (Baltic Sea Aquarium) on the islands of *Fjäderholm*(q.v.).

STURE, NILS SVANTESSON (1543–1567). Nils Sture was suspected of treason by Erik XIV (q.v.), and forced in 1566 to make an ignominious parade through Stockholm. He and Svante Stensson Sture, son of Sten Svantesson Sture (the younger) (q.v.), were killed in the so-called Sture Murder in Uppsala.

STURE, STEN GUSTAFSSON (the elder) (1440–1503). Sten Sture the elder was regent from 1470 to 1497. In 1471, On October 10, 1471 Sten Sture led the Swedes to victory over Kristian I and the Danes at the Battle of Brunkeberg (q.v.). In March 1497, The National Council withdrew its support of Sten Sture, who appealed to a National Assembly. On October 16, 1501, Sten Sture the elder laid siege to the palace, which was defended by King Han's consort, Queen Kristina (q.v.). On November 12 of the same year, he was proclaimed regent, for the second time.

STURE, STEN SVANTESSON (the younger) (1493–1520). On July 23, 1512, Sten Sture the younger was chosen as regent in Stockholm with the support of the city's burghers. In 1518, negotiations began between representatives of Kristian II (q.v.) and Sten Sture the younger at Kaknäs, on northern Djurgården (q.v.). Sten Sture was buried in the Black Friars Monastery (q.v.).

STUREHOV. An estate located in Botkyrka. The main building is in the Gustavian style and was built in 1781 according to the design of architect C. F. Adelcrantz (q.v.). Many of the few remaining Marieberg-tiled (fayence) stoves are found here.

STUREPLAN. In the 1930s, '40s, and '50s, Stureplan was probably the most popular meeting place in town. A prime rendezvous was under *"Svampen"* (the Mushroom), which was a concrete shelter, built in 1937. A replica was put in its place in May 1990 as part of the improvements to Stureplan when a copy of *Svampen* was unveiled. The rain shelter, from 1937 forward was a popular rendezvous place, but it was dismantled in 1988. Stureplan was given a breath of fresh air, with its shopping arcade and more human scale dimensions. It is now able to compete with its former, popular image.

SUBURBS. Up until the 20th century, residential construction was not a communal concern. But high rents and environmental conditions—

where one spoke of "the back-yards of the stone city as breeding grounds for tuberculosis," spawned demands for action by the community. In addition there was a steady increase in population. The population rose from 168,775 in 1880, to 300,624 in 1900, and 342,929 in 1910. To deal with the housing shortage, the city authority had to buy its own land. Therefore, around the turn of the century, estates and areas of land were acquired. Several communities were incorporated into the city. Negotiations to include Solna (q.v.) were unsuccessful.

The number of communities with home-owner properties surrounded by gardens grew during the 1910s, '20s and '30s. There also were terraced houses, in the English style. The continued population increase necessitated a more intensive use of land. In 1930, inhabitants numbered 502,219, in 1940 there were 590,503 people and in 1950 the figure was 744,143. Consequently, in addition to continued building of single-family homes, the number of apartment blocks increased rapidly. Building continued until World War II. During the war, construction focused on large apartment blocks, which characterized post-war home-building as well.

Some private homes continued to be built, mainly as terrace houses. From the beginning, these suburbs were nothing more than dormitory towns. Their small commercial centers proved sufficient for the daily needs of the inhabitants, but they did not satisfy their demands for a wider choice of goods within a reasonable distance. Thus, larger centers offering a better range of services were planned, but placed on hold until the end of the war. Larger town centers followed with more comprehensive and varied commercial, social, and cultural services. In 1954, the Vällingby (q.v.) trading center was inaugurated. This became a model showpiece.

By 1965, Stockholm had 793,714 people. The housing boom required more communities be incorporated into the city.

By 1962, parts of Järvafältet (q.v.) were acquired from the state. This allowed continued residential development in the northern suburbs. However, Stockholm's development seems to have been severely limited by lack of land.

But a new chapter had begun in the town's building history: Greater Stockholm. A plan for the Stockholm region was adopted in 1957 by the regional planning association and has been followed in certain respects in subsequent years. The region that the plan encompasses is considerably larger in area than the standard suburban community. An important consideration in solving Stockholm's housing problem at the end of the 19th century and beginning of the 20th: suburban communities. At the time they were springing up close to the city. Rapid industrialization in the 1870s, along with housing shortages, resulted in the use of suburbs partly because it became fashionable to move to the surrounding communities, "alternative residential areas," and to well-planned, rural housing estates.

Another result of industrialization during the second half of the 19th century was the increase in worker communities of workers. Better-class housing areas developed as "alternative residential districts." Access to communal transportation was a condition for suburb development. They made use of new rail links with Stockholm, and streetcar routes were extended. But the alternative residential areas have now become of less importance.

In 1971, the concept of *"stad"* (town) was replaced by *"kommun"* (municipality). The development of a Greater Stockholm depended on the expansion of its transportation systems, in particular the subway and commuter rail routes. *AB Stockholms Lokaltrafik* (Stockholm's Local Traffic Company [q.v.]), or *SL*, took over Stockholm's streetcars in 1967, and now operates a commuter service through Märsta, Kunsängen, Södertälje, and Nynäshamn. In principle, feeder buses cover the remainder of the county of Stockholm.

SUBWAY. Entrances to subway trains are marked with a blue letter T on a white background. T is for Tunnelbana.

In 1945, serious work began south of Slussen on the first subway. On October 1, 1950 the stretch between Slussen-Johanneshov-Hökarängen was inaugurated. In 1952, work on the line between Kungsgatan, (now Hötorget) Lindhagensgatan, and Vällingby, which had started in 1945, was completed. On November 24, 1957, Hötorget-Slussen was opened, linking the northern and southern systems. In 1965, a second *T-bana* (subway), which combined the southeastern parts with Östermalm, was completed. The first part, the stretch between Fruängen, Örnsberg and T-central (central station) had been inaugurated the year before. On September 2, 1967, Östermalmstorg-Ropsten was officially opened. In March of the same year, Sätra-Skärholmen began service. The third *T-bana* branch began operating in 1975. It was the Järva line ending at Hjulsta. In January of the same year, connections with Norsborg opened. In 1977, the Järva line was extended to Akalla and Kungsträdgården. In 1978, Östermalm's line was lengthened to Mörby. In 1985, the *T-bana* from Västra Skogen was opened, and later extended toward Rinkeby.

On October 26, 1987, an experiment with television advertising started in the central subway station.

On August 15, 1994, the king officially opened Skarpnäck subway station, the 100th in Stockholm.

SUNDBYBERG. As a result of industrialization, during the second half of the 19th century, workers' communities sprang up in the suburb of

Sundbyberg. Sundbyberg was built on plots that at one time comprised the Sundbyberg estate. Access to communal transportation was a condition for suburb development. Sundbyberg evolved when the Västerås railroad line opened in 1876.

The introduction of the streetcar route from Stockholm through Haga, Råsunda, to the edge of Sundbyberg from 1886, to 1910, plus the railroad, helped build Sundbyberg, which became a town in 1927. The streetcar route was extended into the town in 1928. Until 1949, it was only a small town. That year, however, the municipalities of Duvberg, Ursvik, and Alby were incorporated. A clearance and extended building program during the '60s and '70s for the districts of Örby and Hallonbergen, increased Sundbyberg's role in the housing residential development of Stockholm.

SVARTBRÖDRAKLOSTRET *(DOMINICAN FRIARY).* A street in the Old Town (q.v.) called Svartmangatan leads from Stortorget to the friary. This friary was built by Magnus Eriksson (q.v.) for the Dominican Order (q.v.) of monks in 1336.

SVEA LOWER COURT OF APPEAL *(SVEA HOVRÄTTHUS).* Established in May 1614, it is located in Wrangel Palace (q.v.), which now houses the *Svea hovrätt* (Svea Civil and Criminal Appelate Court) and the Supreme Administrative Court. The Supreme Court has its offices in the Bonde palace.

SVEAVÄGEN. In the 17th century, Jean de la Vallée (q.v.) suggested constructing a wide boulevard for parades, stretching northward from the Three Crowns Castle (q.v.). Gustav III (q.v.) took up the same idea: A broad avenue should be built to lead from the palace out to Haga. The project was taken up again in the 1920s, when Sveavägen was extended to Kungsgatan (q.v.). In 1945, the authorities decided that Sveavägen should terminate at *Sergels torg* (Sergel's Square), at Hamngatan and Klarabergsgatan. The old idea of a long street for parades from the palace collapsed quite definitely.

SVEDMYRA. During and after the war, mostly large apartment blocks were constructed. The suburb of Svedmyra is an example of this. It played an important part in easing the Stockholm housing shortage.

SVENSKA DAGBLADET. This conservative daily paper was founded in 1884 in Stockholm. It was the leading newspaper of the political right. Since 1897, it has become more liberal. It is a quality newspaper with a circulation of 203,500 as of 1993, and is read by 15 percent of households in the Stockholm region.

SVERIGEHUSET. See SWEDEN HOUSE.

SWEDEN HOUSE. The Swedish Institute (q.v.) is housed here. It is a main source of information about Sweden and things Swedish. It has a library and a bookshop devoted to Swedish topics. On sale in the bookshop are inexpensive fact sheets covering a host of aspects of Swedish life. These fact sheets are constantly being updated. Visitors also may inquire about Stockholm at the institute and make reservations for accommodations and various tours and events. The Tourist Information Office also is located here.

The building is situated at Hamngatan 27, which is next to Kungsträdgården and opposite the large NK store.

See also STOCKHOLM INFORMATION SERVICE.

SWEDEN'S NATIONAL SPORTS MUSEUM. On October 15, 1992, Prince Bertil officially opened Sweden's National Sports Museum next to the Globe Stadium in Stockholm. It covers the highlights of Swedish sporting events and personalities from the early 19th century.

As well as the numerous permanent exhibits there are occasional exhibitions. The museum also offers hands-on activities to test your own physical fitness.

SWEDISH ACADEMY. The stock exchange building, drawn by architect E. Palmstedt (q.v.), was completed in its present form in 1778. It now also houses the Swedish Academy and its Nobel Library (q.v.). The Swedish Academy, founded in 1786, was one of King Gustav III's (q.v.) creations and was modeled on the French Academy. Its 18 members, commonly known as "the eighteen," meet on the top floor of the stock exchange building. The academy selects the winner of the Nobel Prize (q.v.) for literature and various other award winners, including the annual Bellman prize.

SWEDISH ACADEMY OF SCIENCE. See ACADEMY OF SCIENCE.

SWEDISH CENTRAL BANK, *(SVERIGES RIKSBANK). Riksdagshuset* (the Parliament Building) (q.v.) and the Swedish Central Bank building dominate Helgeandsholmen (q.v.). Both buildings were erected between 1894 and 1905 according to plans by Aron Johansson. The buildings were renovated about 20 years ago, during which time parliament met in *Kulturhuset* (q.v.) on Sergels torg. The old Bank has been incorporated with the parliament building and includes a restaurant. The huge doors above Riksgatan remain as a link between the two buildings. The Swedish Central Bank has moved to new premises in Brunkebergstorg.

The Swedish Central Bank was founded in 1668 and claims to be the oldest central bank in the world. It originally was given the name *Riksens Ständers Bank* (Bank of the Estates of the Realm). The bank always has been administered by the Swedish parliament.

The working capital of the Bank of the Estates of the Realm came from deposits received and the profits made. In 1668, the government ordained that the crown's current holdings should be deposited with the bank, with a view to increasing the bank's working capital. In the same year, the administration of the royal mint was transferred to the bank.

From the day the bank began operations, the crown was an active borrower, and the wartime requirements of the crown sometimes placed the Bank in a precarious situation. In 1701, the so-called "transfer notes" were introduced. They were intended to be used as a means of payment in general circulation. In 1745, the Government decreed that the bank's transfer notes were legal tender for all payments. Two years later, the bank established a special note-printing office within the bank building and, in 1755, it started its own paper mill in Tumba.

During the 1830s, several private banks sprouted up and they also issued bank notes. They were allowed to use funds deposited with the Bank of Estates of the Realm as cover for their note issue: the Bank of the Estates of the Realm thus became "The bank of the banks." In 1855, a single unit—the *riksdaler riksmynt* (National currency riksdaler)—was adopted as the Swedish currency.

In the middle of the 19th century, the idea of a Swedish central bank took shape, and in 1867 the bank received its present name, *Sveriges riksbank*. During the second half of the 19th century, the Riksbank established a network of branches throughout the country.

In 1873, Denmark and Sweden formed the Scandinavian monetary union, with a currency based on gold called the *krona* (crown). Norway joined the union in 1875.

In 1897, the Riksbank became the sole note-issuing bank in Sweden, and by the turn of the century the process of organizing the Riksbank as a central bank was completed.

Between 1668 and 1680 the bank rented premises in the Oxenstierna Palace (q.v.) in Stockholm. In 1680, it moved to new building built for the purpose, and then in 1906 moved to a building at Helgeandsholmen (q.v.).

Incidentally, Stockholm's beloved Carl Michael Bellman (q.v.) worked at Riksbanken beginning at age 17, from 1757, to 1763. This is proudly recorded in a little booklet by Torgny Lindgren, published by Riksbanken in 1989, entitled *Några handlingar om Bellman i Riksbanken* (Some Notes on Bellman in the National Bank). Apparently, he made a good start but was eventually dismissed.

In 1976, the Riksbank moved to its present location at Brunkebergstorg. In the fall of 1992, there was a period of instability for the European currency and speculation against the Swedish krona. The resulting crisis ended in mid-November, when *Riksbanken* stopped defending the "hard" krona by separating it from the European currency unit (ECU), so it could float freely against other currencies. This resulted in a sharp decline in the value of the krona.

SWEDISH INSTITUTE (SVENSKA INSTITUTET). The Swedish Institute began modestly as a combination of private and state interests to promote information about Sweden internationally. In 1945, it was housed in three rooms of the Thule building on Sveavägen. It subsequently moved to Kungsgatan. As the enterprise grew, there was talk about the possibility of moving to a larger building. In 1961, the present site was considered, but it was already occupied. After much debate, permission was finally granted.

Architect Sven Markelius was hired and he made ambitious proposals. In 1969, the Foreign Office suggested that the institute should become a state foundation; soon after the state took over financial responsibility. It originally was intended to cover Sweden House (q.v.) in white marble. But while plans were in progress, the finance minister, Gunnar Sträng (q.v.) announced heavy cuts in government building projects. Instead of marble, concrete was used. But to add texture to the surface, stone was left exposed and the concrete was patterned.

See also SWEDEN HOUSE.

SWEDISH MUSEUM OF ARCHITECTURE. Opposite the Museum of Modern Art and at the top of the hill of Skeppsholmen, the museum archives thousands of photographs as well as half a million drawings and sketches of buildings from the 19th and 20th centuries.

SWEDISH MUSEUM OF NATURAL HISTORY. Housed in a large, imposing building on Roslagsvägen, near the university, at Frescativägen 40, it was inaugurated in 1916. Displays include animals, fossils and minerals from all over the world, and even a few pieces of gravel from the moon. In the exhibition halls there are 150,000 articles on display. There are 11 million objects for scientific research. The basement is an exhibition of the polar regions.

SWEDISH ROYAL ACADEMY OF SCIENCES (*KUNGLIGA VETENSKAPSAKADEMIEN*). The *KVA* was founded in 1739 and promotes the sciences, in particular natural science and mathematics. The academy publishes scientific papers, and allocates financial support and payment to researchers. It is instrumental in awarding the annual Nobel (q.v.) prizes for physics and chemistry. It is also active with the *KVA* library and scientific institutions such as the Bergiansk Foundation. The *KVA* supervises the Natural History Museum, the National Ethnographic Museum, and others. It also publishes a copyright almanac.

SYNAGOGUE (SYNAGOGAN). Located on Wahrendorfsgatan 3, it serves the 5,000–strong membership of the Jewish community. It was built between 1861 and 1870, in an oriental style. The interior was renovated in 1932. This richly decorated building—with rosette windows, palm reliefs, and Hebraic lettering in gold—is remarkable for its clear lines. The interior has many colors, from various types of wood. See also JEWISH MUSEUM.

T

TÄBY. A well-known race track for trotting horses is located here. It was opened in 1960.

TÄNDSTICKSPALATSET *(MATCH-STICK PALACE)*. Located at Västra Trädgårdsgatan 15, it was built in 1928. The well in the gardens has sculptures by Carl Milles. (q.v.)

TAUBE, EVERT (1890–1976). An author, ballad singer, composer and painter, this popular troubadour is associated with the restaurant *Den Gyldene Freden* (The Golden Peace) (q.v.), where he had a reserved table and a name plate on his chair. Outside the restaurant, near *Järntotget* (Iron Square), is a statue of him waiting for a taxi. He sang *"Stockholmsmelodi"* (Stockholm's Melody) on stage at Skansen every summer. Currently, there is a terrace named in his honor on Riddarholmen. On March 12, 1990, on the 100th anniversary of the birth of Evert Taube, a plaster copy of a statue to be erected on Lake Mälaren quayside at Riddarholmen (q.v.) was unveiled. The bronze statue was unveiled in August.

He is buried in the Maria churchyard not far from his studio at Södermalmstorg.

TAUBE, SVEN BERTIL. Born in 1934, the son of Evert Taube. He was an actor at Dramatem and also a ballad singer. Through recordings in

English, he has popularized many of his father's works, and also those of Bellman and Nils Ferlin (qq.v.).

TECHNICAL COLLEGE. See *TEKNISKAHÖGSKOLAN*.

TECHNOLOGY MUSEUM. Located at Museivägen 7, Norra Djurgården. This is the central museum of Sweden's technical history. Its aim is to exhibit development in industry and engineering knowledge. On the lower floor in the machine hall that includes the oldest surviving steam engine in the country, constructed in 1832 by the Englishman Samuel Owen. In the basement is a reconstruction of rock management during various epochs. On the central floor, electronics, physics, and mechanics—together with a collection of technical antiques of the 18th century, from *Kongliga Modellkammaren* (The Royal Model Chamber)—are displayed. On the upper floor a model railroad and a section dealing with forestry and the manufacture of paper pulp.

On July 14, 1988, a 35 meter-high windmill of Danish manufacture was built outside the Technical Museum in association with an exhibition called *Vindenskraft* (Windpower).

See also TELEMUSEUM.

TEKNISKAHÖGSKOLAN. On December 11, 1798, the Technical High School was instituted. The new building, on Valhallavägen, was completed in 1922.

TELEMUSEUM. A museum at Museivägen, it is a subsidiary department of *Tekniska muséet* (Technology Museum) (q.v.), and has a special section dealing with the history of teletechnics, the development of ancient optical telegraphy, and present-day computer techniques and satellite activities.

TELEPHONES. The first public telephone network came into service in 1881. A telephone station built on Malmskillnadsgatan (q.v.) in 1887 claimed to be the world's largest. On January 15, 1924, an automatic telephone system began. Outside *Storkyrkan* (The Cathedral)(q.v.) stands a 1900–style telephone kiosk. This was the only model available in Stockholm until 1934.

TELEVISION. See RADIO AND TELEVISION.

TENSTA. In 1962, parts of Järvafältet (q.v.) were acquired from the state. This allowed a gradual residential development in the northern suburbs. At the end of the '60s, and during the '70s, this resulted in the creation of Tensta.

TESSIN, NICODEMUS the elder (1615–1681). Retained as an architect by the Crown. He was the city architect in 1661. During the latter part of the 17th century, he created some of Sweden's most impressive buildings. In 1652, the house of Axel Oxenstierna was built at Stor-kyrkobrinken 54, probably according to plans drawn by Nicodemus Tessin the elder. He is best-known for his building of Drottningholm Palace (q.v.) on Lovön in Lake Mälaren (q.v.).

TESSIN, NICODEMUS, the elder (1654–1728). During the rebuilding of the palace under the direction of Tessin the younger (q.v.), on February 15, 1648, a fire destroyed several rooms including those used by Queen Kristina (q.v.). Tessin's drawings for the rebuilding of Three Crowns Palace which was destroyed by fire, were approved in 1697. The younger Tessin worked at directing the reconstruction. The palace was not completed when the royal family took up residence there in 1754. Tessin's Palace on Slottsbacken was built by N. Tessin the younger, and completed around 1703.

TESSIN'S PALACE. A baroque-style building located at Slottsbacken 4. It is where palace designer Nicodemus Tessin the younger lived. It was built between 1694 and 1700. The fittings are baroque, the entrance is lavishly sculptured sandstone, and the gardens are in the Roman style. After passing through the hands of several owners, it became the property of Stockholm city. It is now the residence of the Stockholm county governor (equivalent of a lord lieutenant)

THEATER. Stockholm is a theater town. Despite the fact that there are more than a hundred theaters, they are often sold out, and tickets have to be booked months in advance. At Norrmalmstorg (q.v.), there is a booth for selling last-minute tickets. A popular venue for musicals was the China Theater, located in Berzeli Park next to Berns Restaurant (q.v.). When it was a cinema, Greta Garbo (q.v.) was its first star on the big screen, appearing in *Anna Karenina* in 1928. More recently, popular musicals have been staged at the China. Statistics show it was the most popular theater in town when the number of visitors attending its 213 performances in the 1992–93 season was 236,714. Cirkus functioned not only as a theater, but also as a revue and dance hall, circus, and TV studio. It opened in 1891 and has become well-known recently through television. It was re-inaugurated after a thorough renovation in 1990. It is an unusual building standing alongside the entrance to Skansen on Djurgården (qq.v.).

Confidencen is one of Sweden's oldest theaters, it was inaugurated in 1753. It stands near Ulriksdal Palace (q.v.). Beautifully staged performances are presented through the summer. Ballet, opera, and concerts are regular features. *Dansens hus* (The House of Dance) is at Norra Bantorget and the stage of Stockholm's Dance Theater is in *Folkets hus* (The People's Building [q.v.]). All types of dance are performed there. *Dramaten, Kungliga Dramatiska Teatern* (The Royal Dramatic Theater) is Sweden's national theater. It is located on Nybroplan. It was started by Gustav III (q.v.) in 1788, but the building is from the turn of the century (1901 to 1908). It is in the Jugend style. Some of the sculpting decorations were made by Carl Milles (q.v.). Carl Larsson (q.v.) painted some of the decorative works. Performances take place on several stages and cover a wide range of theater from classic to experimental.

There also is the Drottningholm Palace Theater (q.v.), while *Folkan* is a classic revue theater. Hasse Wallman has recently taken over as director, following such popular Swedish names as Karl Gerhard and Kar de Mumma. *Folkoperan* (The People's Opera) is at Horngatan 72. Its aim is to perform opera in an unconventional manner. *The Tales of Hoffmann, The Magic Flute,* and *Die Fleidermaus* have been successsfully performed there. *Intiman* is located at Odengatan 81. It is one of the traditional revue theaters. Its presentations are as intimate, as the name implies, and sometimes include stand-up comics.

Konserthuset is at Hötorget (q.v.). This is the concert hall where Stockholm's Philharmonic Orchestra performs usually a few times each week. A variety of Swedish and foreign artists appear.

Maxim, on Karlaplan, is one of Stockholm's revue theaters in Östermalm. It is renowned for its farces. Operan (q.v.) is located on Gustav Adolf's Square. Opera and ballet are performed at this Swedish national opera in the autumn, winter, and spring. *Oriontheater* (Orion Theater) is at Katarina Bangata 77. This is on Söder (q.v.) and is described as a "theater with a difference." It is a former workshop and has been successful at home and abroad.

Oscar's has been the classic opera and musical theater in Stockholm since the turn of the century. It is at Kungsgatan 63. In the spring of 1993, *The Phantom of the Opera* was staged for the 800th time there, in Swedish. The premiere was on October 27, 1989. *Parkteatern* (The Park Theater) is well attended in the summertime in Stockholm. Two shows are presented each year in the city's inner parks and in the outlying areas. The first, *Stadsteatern* (The Town Theater) is at Kulturhuset (q.v.) in Sergels Torg. It has five stages. The large performances, usually classics, are presented on the main stage. *Södra teatern* (South Theater) at Mosebacke Square, is reserved for visting companies, both Swedish and foreign. It has three stages: The main stage is ornate, the Kägelbanan (Skittle Alley) stage is at floor level and the Café Theater indeed looks like a café. *Vasan* is on Vasagatan. A great number of farces and comedy successes have run here, under the direction of Per Gerhard.

THEN SWÄNSKA ARGUS. In December 1732, a newspaper, *Then Swänska Argus* (The Swedish Argus), appeared in the capital and caused a considerable sensation for years. It was published by Olof Dalin (q.v.).

THIEL ART GALLERY *(THIELSKA GALLERIET).* Started in 1904, the gallery was taken over by the state on January 7, 1925. It is situated at Sjötullsbacken 6, on Djurgården (q.v.). At the end of the last century, banker Ernest Thiel could no longer store all his paintings in his Strandvägen apartment, so he had a house built on Djurgården. His guests included such people as Verner von Heidenstam, Ellen Key, Bruno Liljefors (q.v.), Carl Larsson (q.v.), Hugo Alvén, and Hjalmar Söderberg (q.v.). When Thiel went bankrupt, the Swedish government bought the gallery in 1924 and opened it to the public. The original environment is well-preserved and comprises a unique collection of art, including 12 by Edvard Munch from the turn of the century.

THREE CROWNS PALACE *(TRE KRONOR SLOTT).* In the 1540s, the highest tower of Gustav V's castle was embellished with the new national symbol of three crowns. Thirty Hungarian gold coins were smelted down to gild the crowns. On May 7, 1697, the Tre Kronor Palace was destroyed by fire. The royal family resided for the next 57 years in the Wrangel Palace (q.v.) on Riddarsholmen (q.v.). It is now called *Kungshuset* (The King's House) (q.v.).

THRONE ROOM. Located at the royal palace, it was inaugurated in 1755. On view in the Hall of State is Queen Kristina's (q.v.) throne stool, fashioned in silver for her coronation in 1650.

TJOCK-SARA *(FAT SARAH).* The name by which Sara Simonsdotter was best known. She not only ran a popular brothel in Stockholm but was a central figure in the underworld of organized crime. She was Stockholm's gangster queen of the 1600s.

She is featured in Åke Erikkson's book *Från Olaus Petri* (q.v.) *till Tjock-Sara* (From Olof Petri to Fat Sara). The book is a compilation of stories taken from the minutes of Stockholm courts. These minutes were discovered in the beginning of the 20th century and cover the period 1474 to around 1660. It provides vivid insight into some aspects of the life of those times.

TOBAKSMUSÉET *(THE TOBACCO MUSEUM)*. Located at Gubbhyllan in Skansen. In the 1960s, the original museum moved from Hasselbacken, where the building since the 1820s had housed a popular tea gardens complete with a veranda where punch was served. This museum focuses mainly on the history of tobacco in Sweden from the early 17th century onward. The exhibits which take up four floors, include a series of tins of moist snuff, pipes, cigar racks and cutters, cigarette boxes and packets, posters and advertising, lighters, and other accessories. On some Sundays, extinct brands such as Puck, Bridge, and Broadway Blend are produced in the museum factory and sold in the museum shop.

TOREKÄLLSBERGET MUSEUM. In Södertälje and reminiscent of Stockholm's Skansen, it is an open-air museum of cultural history, with buildings from old Södertälje and the country around. There are house and workshop interiors decorated and equipped with furniture, tools, appliances etc, of the era. There are farms and crofts with the livestock of the period. A school, a town quarter, a bakery, a potter's studio and homes are included in the exhibition.

TOURISM. An important industry for Stockholm, which offers attractions similar to other capital cities, plus a natural beauty.

Although few visitors to Sweden travel to the more northerly, isolated regions of this long country, most do visit this delightfully situated capital. Published 1992 data of destinations preferred by Swedish and foreign travelers, based on the number of nights spent in commercial accommodations, showed Stockholm as No. 1 with 4.2 million Gothenburg and Bohuslän 2.98 million and Dalarna 2.7 million. were the three most popular.

The rate of exchange is favorable for overseas visitors, and has bolstered the tourist industry in recent years.

TOURIST INFORMATION. Information and guidance may be obtained from the Tourist Information Office at *Sverigehuset* (Sweden House) (q.v.).

TOWN PLAN (17TH CENTURY). The 17th century was an expansive, disruptive period in the history of Stockholm. The population increased and many parts of the city were altered. Existing areas were enlarged and more land was purchased by the city authority. A completely new plan was drawn up for the suburbs (q.v.). During the

1630s and 1640s, these plans resulted in the construction of most of the streets and residential blocks. These alterations were made outside the central section of the Middle Ages *Gamla stan* (the Old Town) (q.v.).

The execution of this plan can be followed relatively closely in the archives, and much has been written about it. However, what is missing is an investigation of the motivation behind the planning and the construction of the town plan. The approved town plan has, unfortunately, not been preserved. It is presumed that the plan was drafted with the help of the town planning theory of the time and most likely on the assumption that the city would be encircled by defenses of some kind.

The Stockholm town plan carries marked indications of developments in other countries. It seems quite likely that a master plan could have been prepared in the time of Gustavus Adolphus (q.v.). Toward the end of the reign of Gustav Adolphus, economic resources and manpower were concentrated on military campaigns and so domestic reforms were put on hold.

TOWN PLANNING. At the end of the 1800s, interest in townscape design increased internationally and Stockholm followed these trends. The English garden city idea was influential. Instead of baroque grid plans, town plans with historic, romantic features were in fashion. Architect P. O. Hallman became the spokesman for these ideas during the first decades of the 20th century. He was employed by the Stockholm Building Committee for nearly 30 years. During this period, interest increased in greater government responsibility for city planning.

As early as 1907, Sweden adopted a city planning act. The ideal of nature and the English influence led to the construction of a number of single-family homes as permanent dwellings outside towns. Previously, this area had been limited to the rich. But housing shortages and lack of suitable building land in big cities such as Stockholm led to the growth of suburbs, many of them with single-family home districts. These were often influenced by a traditional, rural style. The government supported an "own-your-own-home program," which began in 1904 and rapidly accelerated the building of villas. The movement backed the ideal of town living combined with the advantages of the countryside. After 1910, there was a gradual change from individually designed homes to projects of single-family home districts with houses of standardized design. This was the beginning of the large-scale suburbs, that arose in the 1950s.

The Stockholm Exhibition (q.v.) of 1930, with its accent on functionalism, proved to be an architectural and societal turning point in

Sweden. It was associated with great optimism for societal changes. In 1932, the Social Democrats came to power, a position they would hold for 44 years. Many master plans for Stockholm were drawn up in the 1930s, prepared in part by traffic considerations. The new trend considered environmental issues and led to land-use separation concerning residential and industrial areas. This was a strict policy that remained until the 1970s.

World War II brought economic paralysis to Sweden in spite of neutrality. But there was recovery by the mid–1940s. The rational and schematic view of planning and building of the 1930s gave way to a more humanistic and artistic approach. The new ideals led to more varied design and grouping of buildings. At the same time, building was carried out on a larger scale, with bigger units being constructed. Influences came from English garden cities. Separation of pedestrian and traffic areas became the rule for most residential areas.

Årsta Center is an example of such neighborhood planning. The center is situated close to the residential area and consists of shops, a post office, film theater, library, music hall, and other facilities. There are many examples of good residential areas from the 1940s, with rich architecture and beautifully shaped outdoor spaces.

In 1947, a new building law was enacted that implied that planning responsibility rested with municipal authorities. They could decide when, where, and how building was to be done. The boom period of the 1950s enabled the continued growth of the welfare state with models of physical and social planning being developed. Well-organized urban areas were created, and criticized toward the end of the 1960s as gloomy and lacking character. City planning based on the American model gained acceptance, and increasing automobile travel contributed to the building of enormous (by Swedish standards) new shopping centers and parking facilities on the outskirts of the city. Human-scale architecture, with roots in tradition, gave way to the "international style," with concrete as the predominant material. This was the result of influences, mainly from the United States, but also of standardization and rationalization in construction. Consequently, criticism of giant buildings could already be heard in the 1950s. There are, however, many residential areas with simple and modest designs from the 1950s.

In Stockholm, the varied topography and vast area of water suggested a unique scheme for future expansion. The scheme may be described as a "finger plan," with subway lines running out through the fingers. Vällingby (q.v.) was the first satellite town in the Stockholm region, largely completed by 1955. The aim was to create an independent town instead of a dormitory suburb with residents working nearby. However, it proved to be unpopular. From then on, the suburbs were planned primarily for housing with shopping centers. Farsta (q.v.) is an example of this. Stockholm's new satellite towns attracted much international interest.

During the 1960s, five-year programs were imposed on municipalities. The demand for housing was stimulated by the generally thriving economy, but housing shortages were still widespread. By the end of the decade, criticism of the 1950s urban areas increased. Therefore, the government introduced the so-called "million program," calling for a million dwellings to be built over a 10-year period by means of advantagous loans, measures to make it easier for municipalities to buy land, and the promotion of large-scale building. Entire districts were built at once. Increasing vehicular traffic was not questioned, so roads were extended. Shopping centers grew bigger. Sweden attained the highest housing standards in the world but the external environment was dreary. Much of the criticism focused on the suburbs, such as Skärholmen.

Meanwhile city centers were demolished to make way for new, modern ones, and Stockholm center was one of them. In 1966, Stockholm proposed a plan under which the city was to be developed as an international commercial center. The population expected to double by the millenium. The regional plan came under strong criticism. The redevelopment of the center of Stockholm, the poor impression of the new suburb of Skärholmen, the new formless urban areas and the lack of public hearings led to lively newspaper debate. This debate inspired a shift in Swedish town planning.

In the beginning of the 1970s, the housing shortage came to an abrupt end, and in many municipalities there were empty apartments. The intense debate at the end of the 1960s led to new interest in environmental matters. Especially toward the end of the 1970s, preservation of old buildings came to the fore in planning and building. Renewal of old residential blocks in town centers was stimulated by improved state loans to building owners. By the end of the 1970s, the demand for apartments increased again, especially in the metropolitan areas. Some new housing blocks were built, the best of which were more carefully designed—including environmentally speaking—than their 1960s counterparts. The first large-scale area designed in the Stockholm region with these new ideas in mind was Kista (q.v.).

Housing standards are high today. There are virtually no slum areas. Nowadays, nearly all large-scale development has been called into question, particularly the buildings of the "million program." Large-scale planning has, to a great extent, been replaced by district planning. Service apartments were constructed as of the 1930s; nowadays, blocks of them are built, especially for elderly people, replacing traditional homes. It allows the aged to live independently as long as possible in their own apartments with a fully equipped kitchen, bathroom, balcony, and pantry. The blocks include service facilities such as reception area, restaurant, rooms for therapy, laundry and recreation facilities.

Urban renewal programs have been drawn up for many cities. The reconstruction of the parliamnent building (q.v.) in Stockholm was one such large-scale renewal project. Södra station (q.v.) is an example of a new area with post-modern features within the framework of an old grid plan in central Stockholm.

See also TOWN PLAN (17th CENTURY), ARCHITECTURE and BUILDINGS.

TOY MUSEUM. Situated on Mariatorget, it opened in 1980. It has one of the largest collections of toys in Europe, more than 10,000 on four floors. There are special model railroads in different scales.

TRADE. After Gothenburg, Stockholm is Sweden's foremost port. It has approximately 15 kilometers of quayside and processes about 6 million tons of imports and exports a year. The most important areas are the freeport (q.v.) and oil ports at Loudden and Värtan; the section in Värtan that handles traffic with Finland; and the new Masthamnen and train ferry position along Skeppsbron and Stadsgården. The port in Stockholm represents a gateway eastward and to the continent. The main cargoes handled at the port consist of imports. Stockholm is Sweden's leading industrial location. Its major products are produced by the metal and machine industries, the paper and graphics industries, and the food and chemical-technical industries. Among the big industrial companies are Electrolux and Ericsson.

The country's largest wholesale company is in Stockholm, which accounts for 20 percent of Sweden's retail trade. Banking and finance also are concentrated in Stockholm. In addition, many of the larger industries are situated in municipalities close to the city and numerous companies conduct business in rural areas, but have their headquarters in Stockholm.

From the Middle Ages until the end of the Age of Liberty (q.v.) in 1765, it was forbidden for Baltic coast towns to trade with any town other than Stockholm. Stockholm was called the nation's storehouse, as goods were stored in large warehouses for distribution in and out of the country.

TRADE FAIR. See ST. ERIK'S TRADE FAIR.

TRANEBERG BRIDGE. Inaugurated on August 31, 1934. At the time, it was the longest bridge of its kind in the world. It carries the road and subway out to the western suburbs, including Drottningholm, Bromma, Hässelby, and Järvafältet (qq.v.).

TREASURY. Situated at the royal palace, Sweden's regalia may be seen here. It includes Gustav Vasa's (q.v.) two swords of state. Other treasures include the crowns of kings and princes, scepters, and orbs.

TREDJE SPÅRET *(THIRD TRACK)*. Still in the planning stages, along with the re-organization of Stockholm's roadways. This third railroad track would run south. Delays in decisions regarding the third track have caused concern that it may not come into fruition. Much of the delay concerns whether or not Riddarholm Church, Riddarhuset, and Riksarkivet (qq.v.) would be put at risk, along with Hessenstein Palace and Hebbe's House. King Carl VI Adolf (q.v.) was said to have joined the protest in his capacity as owner of the contents of Riddarholm Church, where several members of royalty lie buried.

The government decided in May 1995 to postpone development of the third track because it would compromise the environment of Riddarholmen. A committee is being organized to solve the problem of traffic between Södermalm and Tegelbacken. There are three alternatives:

(i) A railroad tunnel between Stockholm *Södra* (South) and Central Station leading northward.

(ii) A third track on the outer edge of Riddarholmen that would be more environmentally friendly.

(iii) A third track or tunnel for motor traffic under Riddarfjärden.

The committee's work was expected to be completed ready by September 1996. The government does not intend to spend any more money on any of these three alternatives.

TULLGARN PALACE. Located in Vagnhärad, not far from Södertälje. It is the castle which Gustav V (q.v.) and Queen Viktoria used in the summer. It became a royal out-of-town residence in 1722. Of particular interest is the well-preserved apartment of Duke Frederik Adolf, and Queen Viktoria's breakfast room in the south German Renaissance style. There is a nature reserve close by.

TUNNELBANAN. See SUBWAY.

TYSKA KYRKAN. See GERMAN CHURCH.

TYRESÖ PALACE. Built in the 1630s for State Chancellor Gabriel Oxenstierna. In 1930, it was bequeathed to *Nordiska muséet* (the Nordic Museum) (q.v.).

U

UGGLEVIKSKÄLLAN. An old well situated in Lilljansskogen (q.v.)

ULRIKA ELEONORA, the elder. (1656–1693). A Danish princess. In 1680, she married Karl XI (q.v.) and was crowned queen in *Storkyrkan* (The Cathedral)(q.v.).

ULRIKA ELEONORA, the younger. (1688–1741). The daughter of Ulrika Eleonora the elder and Karl XI (q.v.). In 1715, she married Fredrik of Hessen. She succeeded Karl XII (q.v.) and reigned as queen from 1718 until 1720. Her royal motto was "In God my Hope." Fredrik I of Hessen (q.v.) was king between 1720 and 1751.

ULRIKA ELEONORA'S CHURCH. Located on Hantverkargatan, on Kungsholmen (q.v.), it is also known as Kungsholm's Church. It was built between 1672 and 1689 according to plans drawn by Mathias Spieler, who worked for Jean de la Vallée and Nicodemus Tessin (qq.v.). In the baroque style, the church was vaulted in 1756. The architecture of the church appears to be influenced by Jean de la Vallée's work on Katarina Church (q.v.). Kungsholm Church was consecrated after 15 years of construction. Among the church fittings, the lavishly sculptured baptismal font barrier is particularly noticeable. It was built in 1707. The church tower was not completed until 1810. The church was restored in 1951.

ULRIKSDAL. See SOLNA.

ULRIKSDAL PALACE. Located in Solna, north of the city center, it is also referred to as Ulriksdal Castle. It dates from the 17th century, the era when Sweden was a major regional power. It was last used by Gustav VI Adolf (q.v.) and Queen Louise. It contains many fine antiques and furniture designed by Malmsten. The royal palace was originally built for Jakob de la Gardie (q.v.). At the castle is the coronation carriage (1650) of Queen Kristina (q.v.), with its rich embroideries, as well as an orangery from the turn of the 18th century, with trees and plants from the Mediterranean and sculptures from Sweden (1700–1900). The park has walks through unique natural and cultural surroundings. Belonging to Ulriksdal is *Confidencen*, which was fitted out as a palace theater in the 1700s. It is Sweden's oldest theater.

On June 18, 1988, the rebuilt orangery at Ulriksdal Palace was opened as a museum for older Swedish sculpture. Since May 1991, some of the rooms from the time of Karl XV (q.v.) at Ulriksdal Palace have been on display. They were recreated in cooperation with the

National Museum. On March 16, 1993, authorities approved the suggestion that guidelines be drawn up for the protection of Ulriksdal, by the Haga, Brunnsviken, Djurgården, Solna, and Stockholm municipalities.

See also *EKOPARKEN.*

UNIVERSITY. See STOCKHOLM UNIVERSITY.

URSVIK. See SUNDBYBERG.

USK: STOCKHOLM OFFICE OF RESEARCH AND STATISTICS. The city's institution for statistics, prognoses, and statistical surveys. USK produces figures on practically everything about the city. A large amount of data on Greater Stockholm, as well as Stockholm and its sub-areas, are published in the *Statistical Yearbook of Stockholm.*

USK also investigates and conducts surveys in everything from simple syntheses to advanced analyses. Basic data for the surveys often are obtained from USK's department for interviews and inquiries.

USK is proud of the *NORDSTAT database*, which contains comparable statistics on major Nordic cities and regions. The statistics are updated annually and cover 16 major areas: four in Denmark, four in Finland, Reykjavik in Iceland, four in Norway and Gothenburg, Malmö, and Stockholm, in Sweden.

Among their less important data: Swedes are Europe's most avid icecream eaters, at 14 liters per person, per year; Swedes eat 17 kilograms of bananas per person, per year, which is more than other Europeans; and Swedes drink 177 liters of coffee per person, per year, second only to the Finns in world consumption.

V

VALDEMAR BIRGERSSON. Son of Birger Jarl (q.v.), he became king in 1250. He was defeated by his brother Magnus in 1275, and was forced to relinquish the throne. He died in prison in 1302.

VÄLLINGBY. During and after World War II, mostly large apartment blocks were constructed. The suburb of Vällingby is an example of this style of living. In 1954, the large trading center of Vällingby (q.v.) was inaugurated. It became a model showpiece.

See also TOWN PLANNING.

VÅRBERG. In 1961, the suburb of Vårberg was incorporated into the city.

VASA. A 17th-century battleship. See also WASA.

VASA BRIDGE (*VASABRON*). Vasa Bridge was completed in 1878. It crosses Norrströmmen (q.v.) from Mälarstrand on Norrmalm to Riddarhuset (q.v.) in the Old Town (q.v.).

VASA, GUSTAV (1496–1560). Gustav Eriksson Vasa was the son of Privy Councilor Erik Johansson Vasa. In 1521, he led an assembly of country folk in *Dalecarlia* (Dalarna) in a revolt against King Kristian II (q.v.). He besieged the city, which was controlled by Danish troops. With help from Lübeck, Stockholm was taken and capitulated to Gustav Vasa. The following day, he issued a letter of safe-conduct for Stockholm. Gustav, who had become regent in 1521, was chosen as monarch on June 6, 1523. On July 23, Gustav Vasa made his procession into Stockholm. His first royal motto was "All power comes from God". He later added "Glory to the one who fears the Lord. If God is for us, who then can be against us?" Later, in 1523, Gustav Vasa ordered that burghers from every town in the land should immediately take up residence in Stockholm.

In 1526, a royal bookbinding workshop was appointed in Stockholm by order of Gustav Vasa. It was the only one until 1611. In April 1535, German burghers in Stockholm were instructed to leave the city. In the fall of the same year, Gustav Vasa ordered burghers from other towns to move to Stockholm. In 1552, after fire had destroyed a large part of the town, Gustav Vasa prohibited the erection of wooden buildings in the city within the bridges.

Gustav Vasa was a powerful leader, a wise economist, and the distinguished founder of the independent Swedish state.

At the time of his death, Sweden was a well-run, secure, independent nation. On June 23, 1774, a statue of Gustav Vasa, sculpted by H. L'Archeveque, was erected outside *Riddarhuset* (the House of Nobility) (q.v.).

VASA THEATER. Opened in 1886. It is located at Vasagatan 19–21.

VASASTADEN. A part of the city that is popularly known as Vasastan. The area contains the largest part of Stockholm north of the city. It was built in the 1880s. At the time, using wood for building was definitely out of date in Stockholm. Vasastan's stone buildings and its distance from the water gave rise to the name "The Stone Desert". Vasastan was long regarded as a suburb of Stockholm; or, more accurately, since it was only partly constructed, a collection of suburbs. The foremost example is Siberia, which lies between Odengatan and Vanadislunden and was at the turn of the century the most densely populated part of town. At the time it was surrounded by meadows, cattle, and barns. The boundaries of Vasastan's built-up area have now spread out and the rural remnants have been erased. Around Odenplan, in the heart of Vasastan, are shops, local restaurants, and several theaters. The central church is Gustav Vasa's Church (q.v.). It is in the new baroque style, designed by Agi Lindegren. It was consecrated in 1906.

A popular shopping street is the part of Odengatan directly opposite Vasaparken. There are small antique shops, and clothing stores. A special calm surrounds nearby Vasaparken, despite many varied sporting activities. The park is a popular place for sunbathing. In the winter, the playing areas are cleared and hosed for iceskating. At St. Eriksplan, in the area of Vasastan known as Birkastan, lies the beginning of one of Stockholm's most charming streets: Rörstrandsgatan. It features a number of small shops and restaurants.

During the Middle Ages, there was a village called Rörstrand (q.v.), an area mostly known for its porcelain and faience factory. It lasted for 200 years in Stockholm, from 1726 to 1926, when the factory was demolished and manufacturing moved to Gothenburg. *Norra Bantorget* (North Railroad Square) nudges the city. It is the part of town that is really Norrmalm, a name seldom used nowadays. Norra Bantorget is on the boundary between Vasastan and the city. Before the railroads were built and the central station was inaugurated in 1871, the square was beside a railroad station. Today, Norra Bantorget is mostly known as a hub for Sweden's Labor Movement. The *"Loborgen"* (Trade union "Fort") and *Folkets hus* (The People's Building) (q.v.) are located here. In the early days of Norra Bantorget in the 17th century, there was an orphanage for the town's poor children where *Folkets hus* is today. The area is now known as *Barnhuset* (the Orphanage). Nearby is a place called *Rosenkammaren* (Rose Chamber), but the name gives lie to what it was used for: *Rosenkammaren* used to be a torture chamber. A street running out of Norra Bantorget was called *Tunnelgatan* (Tunnel Street) for a hundred years, until May 1, 1986. The name was changed to Olof Palme's Gata (q.v.), in memory of the *Statsminister* (prime minister) who was assassinated on February 28, 1986 on the corner of Sveavägen and Tunnelgatan. Today, people still lay red roses on the murder spot. Sveavägen is the broad, busy road that runs from *Sergels torg* in the City to the edge of Vasastan. It ends at the Wenner-Gren Center (q.v.). This is an international research center that has, in part, been financed by the financier Axel Wenner-Gren. Among other things, he founded Electrolux in 1919, and maintained ownership until 1956. *"The Wenner-Gren Skyscraper"* was designed by Sune Lindström and Alf Bydén, and built in 1960. *Observatorielund* (Observatory Meadow) is a park that can easily be missed. It still retains some of its academic character, even though the majority of the university establishments moved to Frescati, northeast of the city in the 1960s. The prestigious *Handelshögskolan* (Business School), the "old" Stockholm University, and *Juridicum* (the Law School) encircle Observatorielunden. From the top of the hill, Carl Hårleman's observatory (q.v.), which dates from 1735, can be seen. The house and its tower were used until the beginning of the 1930s for astronomical research. Nowadays, it is a museum.

The City Library and Strindberg's home in Norrtullsgatan are also both in Vasastan (qq.v.).

VASASTAN. See VASASTADEN.

VÄSTERBRON *(WEST BRIDGE)*. Officially opened in 1935. It is the largest in Stockholm—it is 610 meters long and 29 meters high. It is also Sweden's largest arched bridge. Bridges are important for Stockholm, *"the city on the water."* A fine view of the arches of this bridge may be obtained from the quay near Riddarhustorget. Nowadays, it attracts bungy jumpers. A light plane flew between the spans during a recent Stockholm Water Festival (q.v.).

VÄSTERLÅNGGATAN. In the 14th century, this stone-paved street wound its way outside the old city wall, lined with shops and stalls.

VÄSTERTORP. During and after World War II, mostly large apartment blocks were constructed. The suburb of Västertorp exemplifies this style of living.

VÄSTRA BLACKEBERG. During and after World War II, mostly large apartment blocks were constructed. The suburb of Västra Blackeberg exemplifies this style of living.

VAXHOLM FORT MUSEUM. Vaxholm, in the archipelago, is an hour by boat from the city center. The citadel, or fort, is the town's best-known building. The first fort was built in 1548. Like many forts it was out of date before it was completed—the ribbed cannonball was capable of breaking apart the building's walls. It was closed as a fort in 1863 and now serves as a museum of historical artillery equipment. It also has exhibits about how the archipelago was defended betwen 1500 and 1900.

VEGA. The explorer A. E. Nordenskiöld (q.v.) returned to Stockholm in 1880 aboard the steamship *Vega*, having completed a voyage of the North East Passage.

VIEWS. The best overlooks in Stockholm include Åsöberget, Fjällgatan, Fåfäng, Kaknästornet, Katarinahissen, Mariaberget, Stadshuset Tower, and Västerbron (qq.v.).

VIRABRUK. See WIRA BRUK.

VIKTORIA, PRINCESS (1977–). As the first-born child of King Carl XVI Gustav (q.v.) and Queen Silvia, she is the current heir to the throne. An amendment to the Act of Succession, in 1978 allows the first-born child of the monarch to succeed to the throne, irrespective of gender.

W

WALDERMARSUDDE. See EUGENE, PRINCE.

WALLENBERG. A leading Swedish family, members of which were leaders of the Stockholm Enskilda (Private) Bank.
    WALLENBERG, JACOB (1746–1778). A priest and traveller in the East Indies.
    WALLENBERG, ANDRE OSCAR (1816–86). Nephew to Jacob, who founded Stockholm Enskilda (Private) Bank (q.v.). He was a member of the middle-class and a member of parliament.
    WALLENBERG, KNUT (1853–1938). The son of Andre Oscar and director of the bank from 1886 to 1911. He was a member of parliament from 1907 to 1919, and foreign minister from 1914 to 1917.
    The Wallenberg Foundation was established in 1917, by Knut Wallenberg, who was one of Sweden's richest men. Twenty million SEK were donated for scientific research and education.
    WALLENBERG, MARCUS (1864–1943). Half-brother to Knut. He was active in reorganizing many industrial enterprises during World War I.
    WALLENBERG, JACOB. (1892–1980) He was the son of Marcus and became director of the bank from 1927 through 1946. He was responsible for many important negotiations during World War II.
    WALLENBERG, MARCUS JUNIOR (1899–1982). Brother of Jacob and director of the bank from 1946 to 1958. He was involved in founding the Scandinavian Airline System. He has given considerable

financial support to Swedish tennis, and was a member of the Swedish Davis Cup team in 1925.

WALLENBERG, RAOUL (1912–1947). Nephew of Marcus. As legation secretary in Budapest during World War II, he was instrumental in saving the lives of many Jews. But he was transported by the Russians and it is presumed that he died in a Russian prison. In the Smoltov report, a camp physician's letter indicates that he probably died on July 17, 1947.

WALLENBERG, MARCUS (1924–1971). Son of Marcus Junior. He was director of the bank as of 1958.

WALLIN, JOHAN OLOV (1779–1839). A poet and priest. He wrote 140 original hymns. For many years he was *pastor primarius* in the church in Stockholm. His speech at the opening of the new churchyard in Stockholm is reported to exemplify his oratorial strength. He became archbishop in 1837, and a member of the Swedish Academy (q.v.) in 1810. He virtually created the 1819 hymn book.

WALLIN'S SCHOOL. Stockholm's oldest girls' school, began in 1831.

WASA. A 50-meter-long warship launched in 1628, armed with 64 bronze cannons. It sank on its maiden voyage in Stockholm harbor and lay in 110 feet of water. The wreck was discovered in 1956. The vessel was raised and docked in 1961, more than three centuries after it had sunk. The work of lifting and preserving the ship took six years. More than 24,000 artifacts from the ship were discovered by divers, who sifted through no less than 40,000 cubic yards of mud to find the ship's equipment and the belongings of its crew. Eighteen skeletons were found intact, as were articles of clothing worn by seamen of the early 17th century. There was even a flask of rum, that remained drinkable. *Wasa* was on view for the public at its original dock, but later was moved to Wasa Museum (q.v.).

WASA MUSEUM *(WASA WHARF)*. The raised and restored wreck of the 17th century battleship *Wasa* (q.v.) may be seen here. This is one of Stockholm's biggest tourist attractions. It is said to be the only remaining 17th-century ship in the world. It is the second-oldest, identified ship, after Britain's *Mary Rose*. The ship may be viewed from six different levels, at a distance and close up. A scale model, 7 meters long, represents the *Wasa* before she sank. The other exhibitions on the ship include an extraordinary variety of possessions— 400-year-old eating and drinking utensils, weapons, cannon balls, tankards, coins, and many other items. The new exhibition, *Det Seglande Skeppet* (The Sailing Ship) included *Wasa's* salvaged sail.

The museum is on Djurgården, near Skansen (q.v.). An estimated 793,000 people visited the museum in 1993.

WÄSTERBERG, PER (1933–) An author who lived in Östermalm (q.v.) and later moved to Klara district. He was editor of the newspaper *Dagens Nyheter* (Daily News) (q.v.). He has written numerous books, mostly set in Stockholm. Per Wästberg now lives near *Johannes' Church* (q.v.).

WATER FESTIVAL. The festival has become one of the world's biggest folk festivals, with the number of visitors topping 350,000. The Police have expressed pleasant surprise over the fact that proceedings have run so smoothly, with little disorderly conduct. Because Stockholm is "The City on the Water," the main theme is the protection of water and the environment. Since 1991, Stockholm Water Prize (q.v.), of $150,000 has been presented to people who have made outstanding contributions to the work of water preservation.

The events include a parade of steamboats, a midnight run, musical performances, parachute-jumping, and the world's largest crayfish party in Gustav Adolf's Square (q.v.). The first year 75,000 crayfish were consumed at this party.

The program includes a festival of music, various cultural activities, a huge children's party, sporting events—including a dragon-boat race, a circus, and a festival of international foods. All plates, cutlery, mugs, and napkins are recyclable. At Gustav Adolf's Square (q.v.), plants are placed in beds of compost from the previous year's materials. There is also a spectacular firework display, which several overseas countries are joining, so that an unofficial, international competition is developing.

Sweden made a goal of reducing by 50 percent between 1985 and 1995 water borne emissions of nitrogen from human activities. Efforts have focused on emissions occurring along Sweden's western and southern coasts, as far north as the Stockholm archipelago (q.v.). Steps to limit emissions into the Baltic Sea have received priority. To improve the water in the Baltic Sea, a purification plant is currently being built in Estonia, with the help of funds from the Stockholm Water Festival and other sources.

WATER QUALITY. Improved remarkably during the early 1970s. It became possible to bathe almost anywhere in Stockholm. Bacteria content in water tests are well within required limits. This was not the case just 30 years ago, when 20 percent of the water was shown to be unfit for swimming.

By August 1995, Stockholm was said to enjoy the world's best fawcet water.

Raw material from Lake Mälaren, efficient purification efforts and a thorough replacement of pipes have resulted in good test results for some time; 700 tests are conducted each year on the water. Unfortunately, other parts of the country still struggle with water quality. Four thousand people became ill in 1994 due to water contamination.

WATER-SERVICE. The city's first water-service system began operating in Skanstull on July 1, 1861. Now, *Stockholms Vatten AB* (Stockholm Water Ltd.) is a private company that has been responsible for its own budget for the last five years.

WENNER-GREN CENTER. The Wenner-Gren Foundation (WGS) was initiated with a donation by Axel Wenner-Gren (1881–1961), a successful financier, and his wife Marguerite in 1958. The foundation's Wenner-Gren Center for Scientific Research (WGC) was established in 1962. It was officially inaugurated by King Gustaf VI Adolf (q.v.). In 1986, the Axel Wenner-Gren Foundation for International Scientific Exchange (AWG) was founded.

WGC built and owns the WGC's a building complex in the northern part of Stockholm, where various scientific organizations gather. The complex has a 70-meter-high, 24 story building called the Pylon; the Tetragon which is an office building; and a semi-circular building called the Helicon that has 150 apartments for visiting scientists who are working for more extended periods in Stockholm. It also has hotel rooms for short visits. WSG sold the Pylon and the Tetragon. The additional capital enabled the foundations to support other activities in the area. The Helicon continues under the management of WGS as a center for foreign scientists in Stockholm. Guests may stay for up to two years at moderate costs. The main purpose of WGS is to facilitate the exchange of scientists between Sweden and other countries through fellowships to post-doctorates, travel grants, invitations to lecturers, etc.

WEST BRIDGE. See VÄSTERBRON.

WINE AND DISTILLERY MUSEUM (*VIN- OCH SPRITHISTORISKA MUSÉET*). Located at Dalagatan 100, it depicts the history of wine and distilling in Sweden and internationally since the Middle Ages. Exhibitions concentrate on the history of production, but also cover grape-growing and winemaking, as well as drinking customs. Recreated interiors include a wine seller's shop and a potato spirit distillery. There is also a bouquet cupboard stocked with the aromas of various spices used in the wine manufacturing process. The museum is the only one of its kind in Sweden.

WIRA BRUK *(WIRA SMITHY)*. *Vira bruk* (alternative spelling) was one of Sweden's first armor workshops. It is located at Vira, in Roslagen. A sword smithy was established here in 1635 by settlers from Germany. In the 17th and 18th centuries, Vira bruk made Sweden's best rapiers. Vira bruk was restored during the 1970s.

WORLD POLICE AND FIRE GAMES. Stockholm was chosen to host the games in 1999. It is a major sporting event with about 10,000 competitors, and will bolster Stockholm's tourism industry. The games, which are open to all police officers and firefighters, represent an important and prestigious event for the host city. Many of the competitors will be accompanied by families and friends. It is estimated that between 200 and 300 milion SEK will be spent by the visitors. The games include sports and some spectacular police and firefighting activities.

WRANGEL, KARL GUSTAV (1613–1676). One of the most celebrated fighting heroes of the mid-17th century. He took advantage of his popularity and position to concentrate on building fine palaces, the most renowned of which is Skokloster (q.v.). He also was able to fill these buildings with war trophies and loot from his various victories. Only marginally less impressive, perhaps, was Wrangel Palace, built on Riddarholmen (qq.v.) as a private residence. It was on par with the highly renowned *Makalös* (Peerless) Palace of Jakob de la Gardie (q.v.), with its strange, excessive style.

WRANGEL PALACE, LOWER COURT OF APPEAL *(SVEA HOVRÄTTS HUS)*. Located on Birger Jarls torg, the building originally belonged to the noble Sparre family. It was altered between 1652 and 1670 for Karl Gustav Wrangel (q.v.). The architect was Tessin the elder (q.v.). Wrangel had received the plot of land on Riddarholmen from a grateful Queen Kristina (q.v.) in 1648 after his victory over the Germans. On April 4, 1693, a blaze on Riddarholmen (q.v.) ravaged Wrangel Palace. A fire destroyed the *Tre kronor* (Three Crowns) Palace (q.v.) May 7, 1697. The royal family resided for the next 57 years in the Wrangel Palace on Riddarholmen. It is now called *Kungshuset* (The Kings House) (q.v.).

Y

YOUTH HOSTELS. Central Stockholm has four so-called touring club hostels. In addition to *af Chapman* and Långholmen (qq.v.), there are the Skeppsholmen and Zinken hostels.

Skeppsholmen has more than 150 beds and is located beside af Chapman, where breakfast is available. There also is limited accommodations for disabled visitors. Parking facilities are extremely limited. Zinken has 250 beds. Prior booking is advised for all hostels.

There also are hundreds of hotels in Stockholm. The prices range greatly. *Hotellcentrallen* is Stockholm's official accommodation agency, and is run by the Stockholm Information Service (q.v.). It is at Central Station (tel: 08-24 08 80).

There also are nine hostels in Stockholm County and 10 in the archipelago (q.v.).

See also CAMPING.

Z

ZOOLOGICAL GARDENS. See SKANSEN.

ZORN, ANDERS. In 1887, the artist Anders Zorn received the first-class medal at the World Exhibition in Paris at age 27 for the oil painting *"Une Premiere,"* which showed a well-fed cook and a skinny working-class boy taking a first dip of the spring, in a lake. The painting was done on Dalarö and on sailboat outings around the archipelago. It was the first time that Zorn had captured the effect of cold, clean water against warm, female skin. The motif later made him famous. He died in 1920. See also GOLDEN PEACE.

Appendix 1:
Mayors of Stockholm *(Borgmästare)*

The original title was *"borgmästare,"* translated as "mayor." It is no longer used in modern-day Swedish. In an international context, the title is used, sometimes by *Kommunfullmäktiges ordförande* (The Chairman of the Council) and sometimes by *Finansborgarrådet* (The Chairman of the Finance Committee). Nowadays, it is the latter, who is Mats Hulth, Stockholm's "Mayor" for international representation.

In a few of the earlier records, there appears to be vagueness about precise dates. The result is a contradiction between the order the office was held and the chronological order. In these cases, the date is followed by a question mark. The dates that follow are for the first time a mayor took office.

1.	Before 1289	Gödeke van Memel.
2.	1282	Tideman Fris the elder.
3.	1297	Henrik van Heden.
4.	1291	Tideman Fris the younger.
5.	1336	Tyrgils
6.	1337	Henrik Borchardson Kvit (Albus)
7.	1340	Frövin van Endrichusen.
8.	1353	Johan Berkhof.
9.	1353	Johan Litle Krämare.
10.	Before 1370	Nils Helsing.
11.	Before 1370	Folquin Brakel.
12.	1367	Albert Grotte.
13.	1367	Alf Greveroden.
14.	1370	Peter Hjemborgason.
15.	1376?	Everhard Kantsten.
16.	1371	Tideman van der Wesen.
17.	1375	Bertold Brun.
18.	1376	Nils Stratta.
19.	1376	Lambrecht Westfal.
20.	1376	Johan Geslind.

21.	1376	Johan Myntare.
22.	1385	Johan Nagel.
23.	1389	Wilkin Stenkinge.
24.	Before 1396	Gotscalk Warmeskerk.
25.	1396	Johannes Westfal.
26.	1400	Olof Hofman.
27.	1415	Johan Dæne.
28.	1415	Evert Greveroden.
29.	1418	Johannes Petri.
30.	1405	Herman Svarte.
31.	1405	Marquad van Deventer.
32.	1420?	Tideman Svarte.
33.	1420?	Jöns Petterson.
34.	1417	Engelke (van der) Lörenberg.
35.	1417	Henrik Westfal.
36.	1422?	Alf van der Mysten.
37.	1420	Ficke van der Oldenstadt.
38.	1426	Johan Gustafsson.
39.	1426	Klaus (van der) Lörenberg.
40.	Before 1420?	Johan Mynta.
41.	1420	Kristoffer van Dunsen.
42.	1430	Werner Gesth.
43.	1430	Wilhelm Nagel.
44.	1430	Johannes (Hans) Bismark.
45.	Circa 1436	Broder Jönsson Diekn.
46.	1437	Olof Svarte.
47.	1437	Johannes (Hans) Hoppener.
48.	1439	Henrik van Husen.
49.	1442	Peter van (der) Water.
50.	1444	Lambert Westfal.
51.	1444	Gerhard (Gerd) Sodde.
52.	1448	Jurgen Meideborgh.
53.	1451	Mårten Lindblom (Lindormsson?).
54.	1457	Mårten Nilsson.
55.	1458	Ludvig Westman.
56.	1458	Johannes (Hans) Smed.
57.	1458	Klaus Wijse.
58.	1459	Deterd Krake.
59.	1464	Björn Helsing.
60.	1464	Henning Pinnow.
61.	1465	Nils Pedersson.
62.	1471	Magnus Eriksson.
63.	1475	Bengt Smålänning.
64.	1472	Johan Svensson.

65.	1478	Jöns Magnusson.
66.	1480	Jakob Nilsson.
67.	1487	Peter Jönsson.
68.	1490	Erik Jensson.
69.	1491	Philpus Jensson.
70.	1495	Erik Johansson (Jonsson).
71.	1498	Anders Svensson Bjur.
72.	1500	Nils Jönsson Skrifvare.
73.	1500	Olof Mickelsson.
74.	1503	Rawald Jonsson.
75.	1505	Peder Slatte.
76.	1507	Jöns Gudmundsson.
77.	1513	Jöns Jonsson (Johansson).
78.	1515	Lars Nilsson.
79.	1517	Anders Henriksson.
80.	1518	Anders Olsson.
81.	1520	Gorius (Gregorius) Holst.
82.	1520	Hans Larsson.
83.	1521	Klaus Boye.
84.	1521	Per Månsson.
85.	1524	Lars Larsson (Larensson).
86.	1524	Ivar Ivarsson.
87.	1525	Anders Simonsson.
88.	1526	Nils Larsson (Larensson).
89.	1526	Johannes (Hans) Skeel.
90.	1528	Herman Fossert.
91.	Before 1534?	Björn Björnsson.
92.	1533	Olof Svart.
93.	1534	Lambrecht Mattson.
94.	1534	Nils Jönsson (Utter).
95.	1537	Olof Mårtensson.
96.	1540	Peder Nilsson.
97.	1541	Sven Skute (Skutta).
98.	1543	Peder Andersson.
99.	1553	Mickel Bengtsson.
100.	1553	Josef Arfvidsson.
101.	1559	Olof Eriksson.
102.	156	Matts Persson Skulte.
103.	1562	Henrik Olofsson.
104.	1564	Gunnar Olsson.
105.	1568	Hans Gammal.
106.	1572	Nils Hansson Brask.
107.	1575	Lars Eriksson.
108.	1575	Olof Gregersson.

109.	1590	Henrik Simonsson.
110.	1590	Gynte Olofsson.
111.	1599?	Mårten Olofsson.
112.	1598	Nils Eriksson.
113.	1600	Herman Andersson.
114.	1608	Olof Pedersson Humbla.
115.	1608	Olof Nilsson.
116.	1616?	Jakob Eriksson.
117.	1614	Erik Ingemundsson.
118.	1617	Olof Andersson.
119.	1621	Olaus Bureus.
120.	1624	Hans Nilsson (Benick).
121.	1630	Hans Henriksson.
122.	1630	Erik Eriksson Tranevardius. Titled Geete.
123.	1633	Jöns Henriksson.
124.	1636	Mattias Trost.
125.	1636	Jakob Grundell.
126.	1637	Peter Gavelius.
127.	1645	Börje Pedersson Roman.
128.	1645	Johan Westerman. Titled Lilljecrantz.
129.	1648	Nils Nilsson (Silenius).
130.	1652	Hans Hansson.
131.	1652	Erik Holm.
132.	1653	Peter Claesson Prytz.
133.	1660	Johan Claesson Prytz.
134.	1664	Wilhelm Leuhusen.
135.	1663	Anders Henriksson Boij.
136.	1665	Arfwed Gustafsson.
137.	1666	Peter Trotzig. Titled Trotzenfelt.
138.	1667	Hans Oloffson Törne.
139.	1668	Anders Jönsson (Utterclo).
140.	1668	Olof Thegner. Baron Thegner.
141.	1671	Anders Gerner. Titled Gerner.
142.	1671	Johan de la Vallée.
143.	1674	Petter Kyronius.
144.	1681	Daniel Caméen. Titled Caméen.
145.	1683	Michael Törne.
146.	1683	Olaus Austrell.
147.	1692	Mårten Bunge.
148.	1694	Olof Hansson Törne. Titled Törnflycht.
149.	1694	Gustaf Holmström.
150.	1696	Christopher Thesmar.
151.	1699	Nils Hansson Thörne.
152.	1705	Anders Hyltéen. Titled von Hyltéen.

153.	1705	Anders Strömberg.
154.	1708	Axel Pedersen Aulævill.
155.	1709	Mårten Nyman.
156.	1715	Olof (von) Brehmer.
157.	1716	Samuel Hadelin.
158.	1717	Göran Adelcrantz.
159.	1719	Jacob Bunge.
160.	1726	Johan Boström.
161.	1728	Joachim Neresius. Titled von Nerès.
162.	1729	Johan Salan.
163.	1731	Johan Leijel.
164.	1731	Peter Aulævill.
165.	1739	Joel (von) Brehmer.
166.	1745	Elias Torpadius.
167.	1745	Magnus Bröms.
168.	1747	Thomas Plomgren.
169.	1747	Johan Bengtsson Schening.
170.	1755	Anders Giöding.
171.	1755	Georg Soth.
172.	1758	Gustaf Kierman.
173.	1758	Jonas Robeck.
174.	1758	Pehr Falck.
175.	1761	Gustaf Johan Rath.
176.	1764	Carl Fredrik Sebaldt.
177.	1766	Engelbert Gother.
178.	1775	Johan Ekerman.
179.	1777	Olof L. Forsberg.
180.	1782	Johan in de Betou.
181.	1783	Carl Fredrik Ekerman.
182.	1789	Johan Dreijer.
183.	1789	Carl Abraham Schrickell.
184.	1789	Anders Bengtsson Lijdberg.
185.	1792	Carl Ulner.
186.	1793	Anders Wallin.
187.	1798	Carl Anton Beve.
188.	1798	Carl Ernst Oldenburg.
189.	1801	Edvard John Sondell.
190.	1802	Anders Norelius.
191.	1808	Per Eric Hallquist.
192.	1813	Johan Peter Sandsberg.
193.	1813	Christian Lovén.
194.	1820	Carl Fredrik Landberg.
195.	1826	Lars Ludvig Weser.
196.	1828	Jonas Ullberg.

197.	1831	Nils Sandblad.
198.	1845	Gustaf Holm.
199.	1845	Johan Anders Björck.
200.	1847	Johan Fredrik Eklund.
201.	1860	Johan Fredrik Gråå.
202.	1868	Lars August Weser.
203.	1884	Arvid Erik Ulrich.
204.	1890	Frans Gustaf Krook.
205.	1903	Carl Albert Lindhagen.

From 1904, the position of *Stadsfullmäktiges ordförande* (chairman of the city council) replaced *Borgmästare* (mayor). The chairman is referred to as "mayor" in more solemn contexts.

206.	1904	Sixten Gabriel von Freisen.
207.	1915	Johan Östberg.
208.	1919	Gustav Gerhard Magnusson.
209.	1920	Allan Cederborg.
210.	1927	Knut Axel Tengdahl.
211.	1935	Johan-Olov Johansson.
212.	1938	Fredrik Ström.
213.	1942	Carl Albert Anderson.
214.	1968	Eva Remens.
215.	1970	Ewald Johannesson.
216.	1976	Albert Aronson.
217.	1976	Rutger Palme.
218.	1982	Anne Marie Sundbom.
219.	1985	Lennart Lööf.
220.	1991	Margareta Schwartz.
221.	1994	Ingemar Ingevik.

Appendix 2: Buildings

Following is a list of buildings with construction dates that are of historical or architectural interest.

The design of burgesses' houses was regulated by the general urban code. During the Middle Ages, two *Magister aedificorum*, were the city's representatives responsible for building regulations. They were not generally professional builders but rather prominent burgesses and councillors.

Very little is known about the earlier secular buildings except that they were probably constructed mainly of wood. However, brickyards were established near Stockholm in the late 13th century, mainly to supply material for the castle, churches, friaries, and convents. Wooden buildings on Stadsholmen were repeatedly banned because of fear of fire. In 1582, the city had 429 stone and 164 timber or partial wood buildings. Many wooden or part wood buildings were later replaced by brick buildings. Wood finally disappeared in the 17th century.

Surveys by the city museum of Stockholm have uncovered a number of medieval vaults and masonry piled several stories high and concealed beneath façades. Building techniques are then identified as each layer is stripped away.

circa 1200	*Bromma Church tower.*
1200–1500s	*Storkyrkan* (The Cathedral) St. Nikolai, Old Town.
1280–1400s	*Riddarholm' Church.* Spire built 1838.
1400–1900s	*Kungsträdgården.* Present layout of the park from 1953.
1530	*"Birger Jarl's Tower"*, Riddarholmen.
1500s	*Kronobageriet* (Royal Bakery). Sibyllegsatan 2. Extended 1600–1700s. Rebuilt as the Music Museum 1975–78.
circa 1600	*Residence.* Klevgränd 1C.
1641–1674	*Riddarhuset* (House of the Nobility), Old Town.
1642	*Lantmäterihuset* (Land-surveying Building), Lantmäteribacken.
1653	*Axel Oxenstierna's Palace,* Storkyrkobrinken.

1656–1672	*Hedvig Eleanora Church*, Sibyllegatan. New tower 1868.
1656–1690	*Katarina Church*, Högbergsgatan 13.
1662–1686	*Drottningholm Palace*, Lövön.
1664–1685	*Södra Stadshuset* (Södra's Town Hall), Södermalms torg. Rebuilt 1942 as the City Museum of Stockholm.
1675–1683	*Maria Church*. West tower from 1430.
1690–1700s	*Royal Palace*, Old Town.
1694–1700	*Tessin's Palace*, Slottsbacken, Old Town.
1699–1700	*The long row*, Skeppsholmen. Barrack buildings. Designed by N. Tessin the younger.
1699–1700s	*Museum of Eastern Antiquities*, Skeppsholmen.
1720	*Wooden building*. Mäster Mikaels gata.
1740	*Svindersvik*, Nacka. Summer residence.
1763	*China Palace*, Drottningholm.
1764–1791	*Drottningholm Theater*. Lovön.
1773–1778	*Börsen (Stock Exchange)*, Stortorget, Old Town.
1780–1797	*Haga Park*, Solna.
1783–1794	*Arvfursten Palace*, Gustaf Adolf's torg 1. Currently the Swedish Foreign Office.
1787–1789	*The King's Pavilion*, Haga Park.
1790–1791	*Listonhill*, Djurgården
1700–1800s	*Djurgårdstaden*, Breda gatan, Långa gatan.
1816–1837	*Garnisonssjukhuset* (Garrison Hospital), Hantverkargatan 45.
1818	*Borgen* (the castle), Ladugårdsgärdet. Reconstructed in 1981 after a fire in 1977.
1823–1927	*Rosendal's Castle*, Djurgården.
1824–1942	*Skeppsholm Church*, Skeppsholmen.
1846–1866	*National Museum*, Södra Blasieholmshamnen.
1852	*Södra Theater*, Mosebacketorg.
1855–1856	*Ludvigsberg*, Torkel Knutssonsgatan 2. Mechanical workshop.
1855–1871	*Konradsberg*, Rålambshovs Hospital, Gjörwellsgatan 16.
1861–1870	*The Synagogue*, Wahrendorffsgatan.
1862–1863	*Berns Salonger (Bern's Saloons)*, Näckströmsgatan 8, Berzeli Park. Extended with offices, hotel and veranda 1988.
1865–1878	*Royal Library*, Humlegården.
1867	*Lyran*, Ålgrytevägen 90, Bredäng. Summer villa, now a café.
1883–1890	*Johannes Church*, Kammakargatan 1.
1885	*Maria Elevator*, Söder Mälarstrand 21.

1880s	*Brunkeberg Tunnel,* Tunnelgatan.
1885–1889	*Östermalm Market Hall,* Nybrogatan.
1887	*Old National Archives,* Arkivgatan 3.
1888–1891	*Södra Latin School,* Skaraborgsgatan.
1889–1891	*Norra Reals School,* Roslagsgatan 1.
1889–1907	*Nordic Museum,* Djurgården.
1880–1890	*Strandvägen.*
1891–1898	*Operan.* Extended 1973.
1893–1898	*Hallwyllska Palace,* Hamngatan 4.
1894–1906	*Parliament Building and National Bank,* Helgeandsholmen.
1898–1904	*Central Post Office,* Vasagatan 28–34.
1901–1908	*Dramatic Theater,* Nybroplan.
1902–1905	*Central Baths,* Drottninggatan 88
1904	*Thielska Gallery.* Djurgården.
1909–1914	*Engelbrekt's Church,* Uggelvikksgatan.
1909–1915	*Rådhuset (court house).*
1910–1912	*Stadion (stadium),* Lidingövägen.
1911–1923	*Stadshuset (City Hall),* Hantverkargatan 1.
1912–1915	*NK's Store,* Hamngatan.
1914–1925	*Liljevalch Art Gallery,* Djurgårdsvägen 60.
1920–1924	*Wine and Spirits Center,* Norrastationsgatan 55–57. Architect, E. G. Asplund (q.v.).
1920	*Skandia Film Theater,* Drottninggatan 82. Architect, E. G. Asplund.
1922–1936	*Kanslihuset (the chancery),* Mynttorget
1923–1926	*Konserthuset (The concert house),*Hötorget
1924–1928	*Stadsbiblioteket (city library).* Sveavägen 73. Architect was E. G. Asplund.
1926–1928.	*Tändstickspalatset (Match-stick Palace),* Västra Trädgårdsgatan. 15.
1930	*Gärdet.* Residential area.
1935	*Slussen (the sluice gates).*
1931–1935	*Västerbron (West Bridge.*
1934–1935	*Maritime History Museum,* Ladugårdsgärdet.
1934–1936	*Kungsklippan (King's Cliff),* Kungsholmsgatan 2–13. Residential area.
1935–1940	*Heliga korsets kapell (Holy Cross Chapel),* Skogskyrkogåden. Architect E. G. Asplund (q.v.).
1936	*Katarinahissen (Katarina Elevator),* Stadsgården 2–12.

1937–1944	*Södersjukhuset (Southern Hospital)*, Ringvägen 52.
1943–1953	*Årsta Center.*
1945–1946	*Chancery Annexe.* Riddarhustorget 7–9.
1952–1956	*Vällingby Center.*
1955	*Skattehust (Tax Building)*, Götgatan 76.
1955–1959	*PUB*, Drottninggatan 63. Department store.
1955–1966	*Hötorgcity (Haymarket City)*, Office buildings and shops.
1956–1961	*Radiohuset (Radio House)*, Oxenstiernsgatan 2.
1957	*Vattenfalls office building*, Jämtlandgatan 99.
1959	*St. Thomas' Church*, Vällingby Center.
1960	*Farsta Church*, Lingvägen 145–149.
1960–1961	*Farsta Center.*
1964–1967	*Kaknäs Tower*, Ladugårdsgärdet.
1964–1971	*Tensta.* Residential area.
1965–1971	*Garnisonen (the garrison)*, Karlavägen 100.
1967–1970	*Filmhuset (film house)*, Borgvägen 1–5.
1968–1976	*Kulturhuset (culture house)* and *Riksbanken (national bank)*, Sergels torg, Brunkebergstorg.
1969–1975	*Subway stations Tekniska Högskolan and Stadion.*
1972–1977	*Kista.* Residential area.
1973–1977	*Gallerian*, Regeringsgatan 7–13.
1973–1975	*Galleria*, Sparbankshus, Hamngatan 31.
1974	*Subway station Kungsträdgården.*
1977–1978	*Peoples' Museum*, Djurgårdsbrunnsvägen.
1980s	*Subway stations Huvudsta, Vreten, Duvbo, Rissne, Sundbybergs centrum and Bergshamra.*
1980–1983	*Tomteboda Post Terminal*, Terminalvägen 14, Solna.
1981–1983	*University Library*, Stockholm University, Frescati.
1982–1983	*Sports Arena.* Stockholm University, Frescati.
1983–1987	*Skarpnäck Town.*
1985–1989	*County Council Building* and *Hotel Scandic*. Guldgränd 8, Hornsgatan.
1985–1987	*SAS Head Office*, Frösundavik, Solna.
1986–1989	*City Terminal*, Klarabergsviadukten.
1986–	*Södra Station.* Residential area.
1986–1990	*Vasa Museum*, Djurgården.
1987–1989	*Globen*, Johanneshov. Sports Arena.
1987–1990	*Ekerö.* Residential area.
1990	*Stureplan.* Reconstruction.
1990s	*Office buildings*, Medborgarplatsen.

Appendix 3: Museums

The following is a list of some museums in Stockholm.

Aquaria-Water Museum.
Bergian Botanical Gardens.
Block-Maker's House.
Butterfly House, Hagaparken.
City Museum of Stockholm.
Cosmonova.
Dalarö Customs Museum.
Drottningholm Palace Theater and Museum of Theater.
Gustav III Museum of Antiquities.
Gustavberg Center of Ceramics and the Porcelain Museum.
Hallwylska muséet (Hallwyl Museum).
History Museum.
History of Marine Technology Museum.
Jewish Museum.
Liljevalch's Art Gallery.
Mediterranean Museum.
Medieval Museum of Stockholm.
Millesgården (Milles Museum).
Museum of Biology.
Museum of Dance.
Museum of Far Eastern Antiquities.
Museum of Modern Art.
Museum of National Antiquities.
Museum of Music.
National Swedish Museum of Fine Arts.
National Swedish Museum of Science and Technology.
Nordic Museum.
Palace Museum.
People's Ethnographic Museum.
Police Museum.
Postal Museum.
Puppet Museum.
Rosendal Castle.

Royal Chapel.
Royal Armory.
Royal Palace (including seven museums).
Royal Suites open to the public.
Skansen Open-Air Museum.
Stockholm Cultural Center (Kulturhuset).
Streetcar Museum.
Strindberg Museum.
Swedish Museum of Architecture.
Swedish Museum of Natural History.
Thiel Art Gallery.
Throne Room.
Tobaksmuséet (The Tobacco Museum).
Torekällsberget Museum.
Toy Museum.
Treasury.
Tullgarn Castle.
Ulriksdal Castle.
Vaxholm Fort Museum.
Wasa Museum.
Wine and Distillery Museum.
Wira bruk (Wira Smithy).

For more information on each museum listed, see the dictionary entry under individual names.

Appendix 4: Sporting Events and the Most Important Sports Associations

Associations

AIK (Officially belongs to Solna). Football. In June 1995, The women's football world championships were held in Sweden, with the Finals played at Råsunda stadium in Solna, on June 18, 1995.
AIK. (as above) Ice Hockey.
Ängby KBK. Table Tennis.
Brommagymnasterna. Gymnastics.
Djurgårdens IF (DIF). Football.
Djurgårdens IF. (DIF). Ice Hockey.
Essinge IK. Bandy.
Hammarby IF. Athletics.
Hammarby IF. Bandy.
Hammarby IF (HIF). Football.
Hässelby IF. Athletics.
Hellas. Athletics.
Hellas. Swimming.
KFUM. (YMCA) Gymnastics.
Neptun. Swimming.
Polisens IF. (Police) Hand-ball.
Polisens IF. (Police) Swimming.
SALK. Tennis.
Solflickorna. (Ladies) Gymnastics.
Spårvägen. Athletics.
Spårvägens IF. Table Tennis.
Stockholm Capital. Basketball.

Athletic Events

Finnkampen. International event between Sweden and Finland, held annually and rotates between host countries.
Stockholm Marathon.

DN-Galan (Dagens Nyheter Gala).
Stockholmsloppet (half marathon)
DN-Games (indoors).
Tjejmilen. (women's mile).
Midnattsloppet (midnight race).

Cycling

Tjejtrampet. (women's event).

Football

Stockholm Soccer Cup. Fireball Cup. (youth tournament)

Golf

Scandinavian. Enterprise Open (held every other year).

Handball

Ekens Cup (youth tournament).

Tennis

Stockholm Open. Originally held at Kungliga Tennishallen (q.v.). The
event moved to Globen (q.v.) in 1989. Since 1995, the Stockholm
Open has been held at *Kungliga Tennishallen* (Royal Tennis Stadium).

Triatholon

Stockholmstriaden.

Stockholm's Sports Association was founded in 1898. It publishes annually addresses of administration and personnel. To get a copy, write
Stockholms Idrottsförbund, Svetsarvägen 4, 171 41 SOLNA.

Sports associations in the address calendar include: archery, athletics, badminton, bandy, baseball, basketball, billiards, bob and rodel, boule, bowling, boxing, budo, canoeing, canoe-sailing, casting, curling, cycling, dancing, disabled sports, diving, fencing, flying sports, football, frisbee, golf, gymnastics, handball, icedance, indoor bandy, icehockey, icesailing, judo, land hockey, miniature golf, motorcar racing, motorboat racing, orienteering, riding, rowing, rugby, sailing, shooting, skiing, skishooting, skating, soft ball, squash, swimming, tabletennis, tennis, tug-of-war, varpa, volleyball, walking, waterskiing, weightlifting, wrestling.

See also ANNUAL EVENTS.

Appendix 5: Authors Connected with Stockholm

The following is a list of authors associated with Stockholm by residence and/or their writings from the 1330s to the 1990s.

ADOLPHSON, OLLE (1934–)
AHLBERG, HARRY (1920–)
ALMQVIST, CARL JONAS LOVE (1793–1866) (q.v.)
ANCKER, BO (1924–)
ANDERSSON, DAN (1888–1920)
ARENDORFF, VICTOR (1878–1958)
ARNÉR, SIVAR (1909–)
ARVIDSSON, INGRID (1919–)
ASKLUND, ERIK (1908–1980)
ASPENSTRÖM, WERNER (1918–)
ASPLUND, KARL (1890–1978)
AXELSSON, CARL-ANTON (1933–)
BEIJER, HARALD (1896–1955)
BELLMAN, CARL-MICHAEL (1740–1795) (q.v.)
BERGER, HENNING (1872–1924)
BERGMAN, BO (1869–1967)
BERGMAN, HJALMAR (1883–1931)
BJÖRKLUND, INGEBORG (1897–1974)
BLANCHE, AUGUST (1811–1868) (q.v.)
BLOMBERG, HARRY (1893–1950)
BORN, HEIDI von (1936–)
BOTWID, HANS (1901–1989)
BRANNER, PER-AXEL (1899–1975)
BROWALLIUS, IRJA (1901–1968)
BRUNNER, ERNST (1950–)
CARLSSON, STIG (1920–1971)
CEDERBORGH, FREDRIK (1784–1835)
CLAESSON, STIG (1928)
DAGERMAN, STIG (1923–1954)
DAHL, TORA (1886–1982)

DAHLGREN, CARL FREDRIK (1791–1844)
DAHLSTIERNA, GUNNO (1661–1709)
EKELÖF, GUNNAR (1907–1968)
ENGSTRÖM, ALBERT (1869–1948) (q.v.)
ENGSTRÖM, CLAS (1927–)
ERIKS, GUSTAF RUNE (1918–)
ERIKSKRÖNIKAN (1330) (q.v.)
ESPMARK, KJELL (1930)
FAGERBERG, SVEN (1918–)
FALLSTRÖM, DANIEL (1858–1937)
FERLIN, NILS (1898–1961) (q.v.)
FLYGARE-CARLÉN, EMILIE (1807–1892)
FOERSTER, SVANTE (1931–1980)
FOGELSTRÖM, PER ANDERS (1917–) (q.v.)
FOLCKE, NILS-MAGNUS (1891–1977)
FORSSELL, LARS (1928–)
FRIBERG, GÖSTA (1936–)
FRIDEGÅRD, JAN (1897–1968)
GELOTTE, ANN-MADELEINE (1940–)
GRANDIEN, BO (1932–)
GREIDER, GÖRAN (1959)
GRUNDSTRÖM, HELMER (1904–1986)
GUILLOU, JAN (1944–)
GULLBERG, HJALMAR (1898–1961)
GUSTAF-JANSON, GÖSTA (1902–)
HAGSTRÖM, EMIL (1907–1970)
HAMMENHÖG, WALDEMAR (1902–1972)
HANSSON, OLA (1860–1925)
HEDBERG, OLLE (1899–1974)
HEDBERG, TOR (1862–1931)
HEIDENSTAM, VERNER von (1859–1940) (q.v.)
HELLSTRÖM, GUSTAF (1882–1953)
HENRIKSON, ALF (1905–)
HOLMBERG, ÅKE (1907–)
ISAKSSON, ULLA (1916–)
JERSILD, PC (1935–)
JOHNSON, EYVIND (1900–1976)
JONSSON, THORSTEN (1910–1950)
KARLFELDT, ERIK AXEL (1864–1931)
KEY, ELLEN (1849–1926) (q.v.)
KJELLGREN, JOSEF (1907–1948)
KOCH, MARTIN (1882–1940)
KRUSENSTJERNA, AGNES von (1894–1940)
KULLMAN, HARRY (1919–1982)

LAGERKRANTZ, OLOF (1911–)
LAGERLÖF, SELMA (1858–1940) (q.v.)
LENNGREN, ANNA MARIA (1754–1817) (q.v.)
LEOPOLD, CARL GUSTAF (1862–1906)
LEVERTIN, OSCAR (1862–1906)
LIDNER, BENGT (1757–1793)
LINDER, GURLI (1865–1947)
LINDGREN, ASTRID (1907–) (q.v.)
LINDGREN, BARBRO (1937–)
LINDORM, ERIK (1889–1941)
LJUNGDAHL, ARNOLD (1901–1968)
LO-JOHANSSON, IVAR (1901–1990) (q.v.)
LÖWENHJELM, HARRIET (1887–1918)
LUCIDOR, LASSE (1638–1674) (q.v.)
LUGN, KRISTINA (1948–)
LUNDEGÅRD, ERIK (1900–1982)
LUNDELL, ULF (1949–)
LYSHOLM, GUSTAF ADOLF (1909–1989)
LYTTKENS, ALICE (1897–)
MALM, EINAR (1900–1988)
MALMSTEN, BODIL (1944–)
MÅRTENSON, JAN (1933–)
MARTIN, BENGT (1933–)
MOBERG, VILHELM (1898–1973) (q.v.)
NICANDER, KARL AUGUST (1799–1839)
NILSON, RUBEN (1893–1971)
NILSSON PIRATEN, FRITIOF (1895–1972)
NORDSTRÖM, LUDVIG (1882–1942)
NORÉN, LARS (1944–)
NORLANDER, EMIL (1865–1935)
ODD, ORVAR (1811–1869)
OLJELUND, IVAN (1892–1978)
OLSSON, JAN-OLOF (1920–1974)
ÖSTERGREN, KLAS (1955–)
PALMAER, HENRIK BERNHARD (1801–1854)
POHL, PETER (1940–)
RÅDSTRÖM, PÄR (1925–1963)
REENSTIERNA, MÄRTA HELENA (1753–1841)
RÖNBLOM, H.K. (1901–1965)
ROSENGREN, BERNT (1937–)
RUNDQUIST, PER ERIK (1912–1986)
RUNIUS, JOHAN (1679–1713)
SANDEL, MARIA (1870–1927)
SEHLSTEDT, ELIAS (1808–1874)

SELANDER, STEN (1891–1957)
SETTERLIND, BO (1923–1991)
SIWERTZ, SIGFRID (1882–1970)
SJÖDIN, STIG (1917–)
SJÖMAN, VILGOT (1924–)
SJÖWALL, MAJ (1935–)
SNOILSKY, CARL (1841–1903) (q.v.)
SÖDERBERG, HJALMAR (1869–1941) (q.v.)
STAGNELIUS, ERIK JOHAN (1793–1823) (q.v.)
STIERNSTEDT, MARIKA (1875–1954)
STRINDBERG, AUGUST (1849–1912) (q.v.)
SUNDSTRÖM, GUN-BRITT (1945–)
SVEDLID, OLOV (1932–)
TAUBE, EVERT (1890–1976) (q.v.)
TIDHOLM, THOMAS (1943–)
TRENTER, STIEG (1914–1967)
TRENTER, ULLA (1936–)
VÄRNLUND, RUDOLF (1900–1945)
VENNBERG, KARL (1910–)
VITALIS (1794–1828) pseudonym of Erik Sjöberg.
VREESWIJK, CORNELIUS (1937–1987)
WÄGNER, ELIN (1882–1949)
WAHLÖÖ, PER (1926–1975)
WÄSTBERG, PER (1933–) (q.v.)
WIDDING, LARS (1920–)
WIVALLIUS, LARS (1605–1669)
WOLGERS, BEPPE (1928–1986)
ZETTERHOLM, TORE (1915–)
ZETTERSTRÖM, ERIK (1904–)

See dictionary entries for the more widely known authors:
ALMQVIST, BELLMAN, BLANCHE, BREMER, ERIKSKRÖNI-
KAN, FOGELSTRÖM, JOHANSSON (LUCIDOR), KEY, LAGERLÖF,
LINDGREN, LO-JOHANSSON, SÖDERBERG, STAGNELIUS, WÄS-
TBERG and STRINDBERG.

Appendix 6: Art Museums and Art Galleries

Art museums and art galleries found in Stockholm are:

Museums	*Address*
Kulturhuset (q.v.)	Sergels Torg 3
Liljevalchs (q.v.)	Djurgårdsvägen 60
Millesgården (q.v.)	Carl Milles väg 2, Lidingö
Moderna Muséet (q.v.)	Birger Jarlsgatan 57
Olle Olsson huset	Hagalundsgatan 50, Solna
Thielska Galleriet (q.v.)	Sjötullsbacken 6–8, Djurgården
Prins Eugens Waldemarsudde (q.v.)	Prins Eugens väg 6, Djurgården

Galleries	*Address*
Adlercreutz-Björkholmen	Norra Hamnvägen 20c
Ahlner	Österlånggatan 22
Andréhn-Schiptjenko	Stureparken 1
Argo	Sturegatan 12
Aronowitsch	Sturegatan 24
Axlund	Stortorget 5
Bergman	Nybrogatan 48
Blanche	Sturegatan 26
Lars Bohman	Karlavägen 16
Bobrino	Narvavägen 34
Andreas Brändström	Nybrogatan 25
Cupido	Svartmangatan 27
Doktor Glas	Kungsträdgården 4
Embla	Hornsgatan 42
Engström	Karlaplan 9a
Krister Fahl	Grevgatan 36
Färg och Form	Sturegatan 36
Grafiska Sällskapet	Rödbodtorget 2
Gröna Paletten	Odengatan 52
Galleri H, Lars Hagman	Hornsgatan 42–44
Christina Höglund	Jungfrugatan 6
Konstakademien	Fredsgatan 12

Konstförmedlarna	Bellmansgatan 11
Konstnärshuset	Smålandsgatan 7
Konstruktiv Tendens	Nybrogatan 69
Lilla Bleue	Sturegatan 42
Lucidor	Hornsgatan 36
Charlotte Lund	Riddargatan 17
Max	Grev Turegatan 25
Nordenhake	Fredsgatan 12
Överkikaren	Hornsgatan 2
Svenska Bilder	Karlavägen 69
Tre	Nybrogatan 25
Ann Westin	Styrmansgatan 52

Appendix 7: Miscellaneous Statistics

The following statistics have been supplied by Stockholm city's *Utredn-ings-och Statistik-kontoret (USK)* (Stockholm Office of Research and Statistics) and are extracts from the 1995 edition of the Statistical Year-book of Stockholm. They have been up-dated from USK's *Stockholm '96 Sifferguide* (Data Guide).

The city was mentioned for the first time in 1252.

The oldest buildings in the city are:
Stockholm Cathedral *(Storkyrkan)* and the Riddarholm Church, built around the end of the 13th century.

The highest buildings are:
Kaknäs Tower, 155 meters (508 feet).
Klara Church, 108 meters (354 feet).
City Hall, 106 meters (348 feet).

1 January 1996.

	Stockholm	Greater Stockholm
Land area, square kilometers	187	3,458
thereof parks and green open spaces.	63	
Population density inhabitants/sq. km	3,803	454
Number of municipalities.	1	22
Number of parishes.	28	101

Population in January 1, each year.

	Stockholm	Greater Stockholm
1971	744,911	1,349,173
1981	647,214	1,386,980
1991	674,452	1,491,726
1994	692,954	1,532,803
1996	711,119	1,570,320
2000 (estimate)	720,303	1,607,276

The Stockholm density of population is 3,803 inhabitants per square kilometer (approximately 9,700 per square mile). The average for the country is 21 inhabitants per square kilometer (approximately 52 per square mile).

Aliens 1, January 1996.
72,520

Population changes in 1995.

	Stockholm	Greater Stockholm
Births	9,095	20,679
Deaths	8,595	14,354
Immigrants	43,787	45,314
non-Swedish	6,455	12,550
Emigrants	36,863	35,354
Immigration surplus	6,924	9,960
Change in number of inhabitants	7,492	16,411
Marriages	3,993	7,959
Divorces	2,036	4,672

Housing January 1, 1996

	Stockholm	Greater Stockholm
Stock of dwellings.	396,300	772,300

Construction in 1995

	Stockholm	Greater Stockholm
Housing started	755	2,543
Housing completed	796	2,956
Housing reconstructed	6,801	
Housing demolished	6	

Weather in 1995

			Normal
Mean temp.	(Jan.–March)	C0	− 2
		F32	
	(June–Aug.)	C + 18	+ 16
		F64	
Max. temp.	(June)	C + 30	
		F86	
Min. temp.	(Feb.)	C − 15	
		F5	
Water temp.	(June–Aug.)	C + 18	
		F64	

Sunny hours per month	(Jan.–March)	71	82
	(June–Aug.)	292	258
Precipitation per	(Jan.–March)	47	31
month mm.	(June–Aug.)	52	61

Transportation

Private automobiles in use (Jan 1, 1996)	220,967
Passenger automobiles per 100 inhabitants	31
Air travel, millions of departing and arriving passengers (1995).	14.1

Trade and shipping.

Exports from Stockholm millions SEK (1993)	15,311
Imports to Stockholm millions SEK (1993)	18,168
Ships entered and departed (1993)	13,585
Registered 1000 tons	122,172

Labour market in 1995 (Persons 16–64 years)

		Whole country
Employed in all	347,100	3,987,800
Employed women in *percent* of all women.	75.9	70.9
Unemployed in *percent* of labor force		
Men	7.1	8.4
Women	6.0	6.9

In 1993, there were 66,823 government employees in Stockholm, almost exactly divided between men and women. This figure has dropped from 90,279 in 1975.

Mean income in 1993; for all employees age 20–64
176,000 SEK

Purchasing power of the Swedish krona.
100 kronor in 1938 was worth 5 kronor in 1994.
From January 1, 1984 to January 1, 1994, 100 kronor dropped in worth to 56 kronor.

Bankruptcies.
In 1994, the number of company bankruptcies was 3,241, virtually double the 1990 figure of 1588.

Taxes 1996

Total local tax	30.00 per 100 SEK.
Stockholm municipal	18.41 per 100 SEK.
county	10.84 per 100 SEK.
church	0.75 per 100 SEK.

NOTE: The average local income tax in Sweden, is about 31 percent.

The use of local tax in 1993

Education and culture	28 percent
The elderly and handicapped	27 percent
General social care	17 percent
Child care	15 percent
Leisure and sport	4 percent
Administration of social districts	4 percent
Traffic and street maintenance	2 percent
Central administration, energy etc.	2 percent

Education

Students at comprehensive schools age 7–15 in 1995	59,222
At upper secondary schools age 15–18	21,467
Number of languages taught in the native tongue in 1995–96	92
Students at communal adult schools, 1994–95	20,712
Registered at universities and colleges in 1992	49,154
Social welfare	
Persons on social assistance in 1995	67,742
Value of aid, SEK in thousands in 1995	1,178,666

Marriages and live births

In 1993, there were 3,771 marriages, the lowest figure since 1984.

Of 9,724 live births, 5,012 were born to married mothers and 4,712 babies (48,5 percent) to unwed mothers.

Health and medical service
(The County of Stockholm)

Beds in general hospitals in 1994	8,902
Number of physicians in 1996	c. 6,500
Number of dentists in 1996	c. 2,000
Number of dentists per 1,000 inhabitants	1.2
Number of nurses in 1996	c.15,100
Number of nurses per 1,000 inhabitants	8.7

Average life expectancy in 1993.
Men   74.1 years   Women   80.5 years.

Culture.

Theaters	54
Film theaters	88
Museums	57
Churches	63
Public libraries	41
Daily newspapers	7

Stockholm Finance in 1995.

Imposition (excluding church rate)	18.01%
Revenue total, millions SEK	33,683
taxes	15,349
Expenditures total, millions SEK	34,995
salaries	7,734
Assets, millions SEK	70,240
fixed assets	62,917
Liabilities	24,445
long-term liabilities	17,226
City of Stockholm employees	55,800

Municipal Council Election 1994.

	Votes percent	Seats
Social Democratic Party	33.0	37
Conservative Party	28.7	29
Communist Party	9.2	11
Liberal Party	7.9	9
The Green Party	7.8	8
Center Party	5.4	5
Stockholm Party	3.4	2
Christian Democratic Party	2.1	—
Others	1.5	
—		
New Democracy	1.0	—
	100	101

Number of votes   456,899
Polling percent   81.2
8 percent of the electoral roll consisted of immigrants.

Selected Bibliography

The Swedish characters å, ä, and ö are treated alphabetically as a, a, and o.

The vast majority of the books listed in this bibliography are in English. Those in Swedish often contain a summary in English, especially in the case of academic works. Only a small number of books in other languages are included. Each year, the Royal Library in Stockholm publishes *Suecana Extranea*, which lists books on Sweden and Swedish literature in foreign languages.

Further help may be obtained from the annual outline of Stockholm's literature, which appears in *Sankt Eriks årsbok.* (St. Erik's Yearbook), published by Samfundet St. Erik.

Attention is drawn to *Monografier: utgivna av Stockholms Kommunalförvaltning*. (Monographs: published by the local government of Stockholm). Stockholm: Stockholmia förlag, 1941– (118 monographs to 1955; many have English summaries). An English translation of their titles in order of publication appears as the last section of this bibliography.

Reference is made in various entries to the book *Forska själv!, En bok om arkiven i Sockholm* (Research By Yourself!, A Book About Archives In Stockholm). Editor Leif Gidlöf. Stockholm: Stockholms stad, 1990. Further details on the monographs referred to above can be found on pages 234–236.

The Swedish Institute is located in Stockholm. It commissions and distributes up-to-date publications on a variety of aspects of cultural and political life in Sweden. The address is: Swedish Institute, Box 7434, S–10391, Stockholm, Sweden.

I. General Works and Collections

1. Bibliography, Library Science

Grönberg, Lennart. *The Library of the Swedish Parliament 1851–1980.* Uppsala: Self-published, 1981.

Guide to Libraries in the Stockholm Region: A Selection. Stockholm: International Federation of Library Associations (IFLA), 1990. English text with foreword in English and Swedish.

Krigsarkivet [The Royal Military Archives]. Translated by Gordon Elliott. Stockholm: Krigsarkivet, 1984.

Quality Issues in the Library and Information Services: proceedings of a conference organized by NORDINFO and the British Library (Research and Development Department). Esbo: Nordinfo, 1994.

Riksarkivet, The Diplomatic Collection in the Swedish National Archives. Sören Tommos. Stockholm: LiberFörlag/Allmänna förlag, 1980.

Royal Library. Stockholm: Kungliga biblioteket, 1984.

Swedish Bibliography of Urban History: a selection of books and articles published up to 1992. Stockholm: Stads- och kommunhistoriska institutet, 1994.

2. Biography

Aaseng, Nathan. *The Disease Fighters: The Nobel Prize in Medicine.* Minneapolis: Lerner Publications, 1987.

———. *The Inventors: Nobel Prizes in Chemistry, Physics and Medicine.* Minneapolis: Lerner, 1988.

———. *The Peace Seekers: The Nobel Peace Prize.* Minneapolis: Lerner Publications, 1987.

Bergengren, Erik. *Alfred Nobel.* Edinburgh: Nelson and Sons, 1962.

Carlsson, Clas Göran. *Silvia: Bilder ur en drottnings liv (Silvia: Pictures of a Queen).* Höganäs, Sweden: Wiken, 1986.

Charles, Alexandra. *Alexandra on the Rocks.* Stockholm: Askelin and Hägglund, 1986.

Engfors, Christina. *E. G. Asplund: Architect, Friend and Colleague.* Translation by Roger Tanner. Stockholm: Arkitektur, 1990.

Enlightenment Science in the Romantic Era: The Chemistry of Berzelius and its Cultural Setting. Edited by Evan M. Melhado and Tore Frängsmyr. Uppsala Studies in History of Science, 10. Cambridge: Cambridge University Press, 1992.

Fant, Kenne. *Alfred Nobel: a Biography.* Translated by Marianne Ruuth. New York: Arcade, 1993.

Gray, Tony. *Champions of Peace: The Story of Alfred Nobel, the Peace Prize and the Laureates.* London: Paddington Press, 1976.

Hellberg, Thomas. *Alfred Nobel.* Sölvesborg, Sweden: Lagerblad, 1986.

Lives of the Laureates: Ten Nobel Economists. Edited by William Brett and Roger W. Spencer). Cambridge: MIT Press, 1990.

Mosey, Chris. *Cruel Awakening: Sweden and the Killing of Olof Palme.* New York: St. Martin's Press, 1991.

Nobel Prize Winners: an H. W. Wilson Biographical Dictionary. Edited by Tyler Wasson. New York: H.W. Wilson, 1987.

222 • SELECTED BIBLIOGRAPHY

Nobel Prize Winners: Literature. Edited by Frank N. Magill. Pasadena, CA: Salem Press, 1987.
Nobel Prize Winners: Physiology or Medicine. Edited by Frank N. Magill. 3d vol. Pasadena, CA: Salem Press, 1991.
Nobel, the Man and His Prizes. New York: Elsevier Publishing Co., 1972.
Oleinkoff, Nils. *The Family of Alfred Nobel.* Värmdö, Sweden: Oleinikoff, 1982.
Olof Palme: un missatger per la pau. (a Messenger for Peace). Badalona: Ajuntament de Badalona, 1987.
Opfell, Olga S. *The Lady Laureates: Women Who Have Won the Nobel Prize.* 2d ed. Metuchen, NJ: Scarecrow Press, 1986.
Skarke, Lars. *Björn Borg: Winner Loses All.* London: Blake, 1993.
Sohlman, Ragnar. *The Legacy of Alfred Nobel.* London: The Bodley Head, 1983.
Ståhle, Nils K. *Alfred Nobel and the Nobel Prizes.* Stockholm: The Swedish Institute, 1989.
Sundfeldt, Jan. *af Chapman: a Full-Rigger That Became a Hostel.* Translated by Jeremy Franks. Stockholm: Swedish Touring Club, 1988.
Who's Who of Nobel Prize Winners, 1901–1990. Edited by Bernard S. Schlessinger and June H. Schlessinger. Phoenix: Oryx Press, 1986.
Zubkov, Georgij Ivanovic, *Olof Palme.* Translated by Gulhamid Sobrattee. Moscow: Novosti, 1990.

3. Maps

Landell, Nils-Erik. *Stockholmskartor* (Maps of Stockholm). Stockholm: Rabén and Sjögren, 1992.
Parkering i Stockholm. (Parking in Stockholm.) Stockholm: Stadsbyggnadskontoret, 1988.
Stockholm stad: turistkarta. (tourist map.) Stockholm: Stadsbyggnadskontoret, 1988.
Stockholmskartan: Bus, Train and Subway Lines in Inner and Outer City Stockholm: SL, 1988.
Stockholm vatten. The Stockholm Sewer System Master Plan, 1983. Stockholm: Stockholm vatten, 1990.

4. Guide Books

Åkqvist, Rune. *Stockholm Day and Night: A Guidebook About Things to See, Where to Eat, Amuse Yourself and Go Shopping.* Stockholm: Bonnier, 1962.
Ancker, Bo. *21 promenader i Stockholm. Del 1. Inner staden* (21 Walks in Stockholm. Part 1. Inner city). Stockholm: Rabén and Sjögren, 1977.
———. *21 promenader i Stockholm. Del 2. Utkanter: i de närmaste omgivningarna* (21 walks in Stockholm. Part 2. The Outskirts: in the Nearest Surroundings). Stockholm: Rabén and Sjögren, 1979.
———. *21 promenader i Stockholm. Del 3. Vatten vägar: på och utmed våra vatten vägar* (21 Walks in Stockholm. Part 3. Ways by the Water: On and Along Our Waterways. Stockholm: Rabén and Sjögren, 1981.
The Atlas Guide to Stockholm. Issued by the Stockholm Tourist Traffic Association. Stockholm: Tiden, 1989.
Att se och göra i Stockholms stad och län (What to See and Do in and Around Stockholm). Stockholm: Stockholm Information Service, 1987.
Berg, Elly. *Stockholm Town Trails.* Stockholm: Akademilitteratur, 1979.

————. *Stockholm Town Trails: From The Old Town to the New City: Four Guided Tours.* Stockholm: Akademilitteratur, 1979.

Brynolf, Lars. *Cyckelguide Stockholm. Norra delen med Uppsala och Östhammar* (Stockholm's Cycle Guide. The Northern Part: Uppsala and Östhammar). Stockholm: Esselte, 1984.

————. *Cyckelguide Stockholm. Södra delen med Strängnäs och Nyköping* (Stockholm's Cycle Guide. Southern Part: Strängnäs and Nyköping). Stockholm: Esselte, 1984.

De la Gardie, Chris. *Stockholmsguide* (Stockholm Guide). Stockholm: Bonnier, 1973.

Fimmerstad, Lars. *Fimmer's Guide to Stockholm.* Translated by Mikael Karlström. Stockholm: Bonniers, 1987.

Kindborg, Ulf. *The Stockholm Guide.* Stockholm: Kindborg / Wilander, 1974.

Korotynska, Magdalena. *Close to Stockholm: The Whole City in a Hand-Painted Panorama; A Guide to 160 Buildings That Are Worth a Visit.* Stockholm: Byggförlaget, 1993.

Maze, Edward. *NK Pocket Guide to Stockholm.* Stockholm: nordiska kompaniet, 1960.

New Stockholm Guide. Solna: Pogo Press, 1975.

Stockholmsguide. Stockholm: Swedish Architects' Association (SRA), 1966.

87 Stockholm Restaurants. Malmö: Liber, 1981.

Stockholms skildringar. Stockholm: W and W, 1980.

What to See and Do In and Around Stockholm: Sights, Excursions, Maps, Restaurants: the Complete Stockholm Guide. Stockholm: Stockholm Information Office, 1987. *Stockholm City Hall.*

5. Research Institutions, Libraries

Bernhard, Carl Gustaf. *The Royal Swedish Academy of Sciences 1739–1989.* Translated by Roger Tanner. Stockholm: Swedish Academy of Sciences, 1989.

Biörnstad, Arne. *Skansen, Stockholm, Sweden.* Stockholm: Skansen, 1991.

Crawford, Elisabet. *The Beginnings of the Nobel Institution: The Science Prizes.* New Rochelle, NY: Cambridge University Press, 1984.

Espmark, Kjell. *The Nobel Prize in Literature: A Study of the Criteria behind the Choices.* Boston: G.K. Hall, 1991.

Fogelmarck, Stig. *Skattkamaren: rikets regalier och dyrbarheter; Stockholms slott.* (Swedish National Regalia and Royal Treasures, Stockholm's Palace.) Stockholm: Skattkammaren, Husgerådskammaren, 1987.

Gyllensten, Lars. *The Nobel Prize in Literature.* Stockholm: Swedish Academy, 1987.

Klevard, Åsa. *Karolinska Institute: Research and Training Today-Better Health Tomorrow.* Stockholm: Karolinska institutet, 1991.

Livrustkammaren—Sveriges äldsta museum. Edited by Lena Nordström. Stockholm: Livrustkammaren, 1985.

The Nobel Century: A Chronicle of Genius. Introduction by Asa Briggs. London: Chapman, 1991.

Nobel Prize Conversations with Sir John Eccles, Roger Sperry, Ilya Prigogine, Brian Josephson. Commentary by Norman Cousins. San Francisco: Saybrook, 1985.

Nordiska museet; A Guide to Nordiska museet, Stockholm. Translated by Skans Victoria Airey. Stockholm: Museet, 1986.

Skagegård, Lars-Åke. *The Remarkable Story of Alfred Nobel and the Nobel Prize.* Translated by George Varcoe. Uppsala: Konsultförlag., 1994.

Skansen, Stockholm: A Short Guide for Visitors. Stockholm: Skansen, 1984.

Skansen, Stockholm, Sweden: kort vägledning över friluftsmuseet och de zoologiska anläggningarna. (Short Guide to the Open-Air Museum and the Zoological Grounds). Stockholm: Skansen, 1986.

Ståhle, Nils K. *Alfred Nobel and the Nobel Prizes.* Stockholm: Nobel Foundation, Swedish Institute, 1993.

Stohlman, Ragnar. *The Legacy of Alfred Nobel: The Story Behind the Nobel Prizes.* Translated by Elspeth Harley Schubert. London: Bodley Head, 1983.

Sweden. Utredningen om tekniska förutsättningar för utökade sändningar av radio och television till allmänheten (Technical Scope for Additional Broadcasting: Extracts from Swedish Government Official Report 1994:34). Stockholm: Ministry of Culture (Kulturdepartement), 1994.

Swedish Institute. Stockholm: Swedish Institute, 1968.

Wilhelm, Peter. *The Nobel Prize: Stockholm 1983.* London: Springwood Books, 1983.

6. Newspapers and Periodicals

The main daily newspapers appearing in Stockholm each morning are *Dagens Nyheter* and *Svenska Dagbladet.* Evening newspapers are *Aftonbladet* and *Expressen.*

Stockholm periodicals in English are: *Stockholm City, Stockholm This Week, Stockholm Information Service, Globen City* magazine, *Stockholm's Kommun, Stockholm Business Magazine: the magazine for business people visiting Stockholm.*

II. History

1. General History of Stockholm

Åberg, Alf. *The Swedish Foreign Service 1791–1991.* Translated by David Cante. Stockholm: Swedish Ministry for Foreign Affairs, 1992.

Almqvist, Bertil. *The Vasa Saga: (The Story of a Ship).* Stockholm: Bonnier, 1994.

Bergman, Bengt. *Stockholm genom tiderna* (Stockholm Through the Ages). Stockholm: Thule, 1937.

Boström, Jan. *Š var det* (As it was). Stockholm: Dagens Nyheter, 1933.

Frölén, Dan. *Bland storborgare och småfolk i det gamla Stockholm* (Amongst Rich Citizens and Ordinary Folk). Stockholm: Fröléen, 1935.

German Church of St. Gertrud. Stockholm: The German Church, 1962.

Hallman, Mila. *Målare och urmakare, flickor och lösdrivare* (Painters and Clock-Makers, Girls and Vagabonds). Stockholm: 1907.

Hansson, H. *Stockholms stadsmurar* (The City Walls of Stockholm). Stockholm: 1976.

Historia kring Stockholm. (History of Stockholm). Vols. 1–3, Stockholm: 1965–67.

Högberg, Staffan. *Stockholms historia. 1. Den medeltida köpstaden. Hans nådes stad. Stormaktens huvudstad. Borgarnas stad* (Stockholm's History. 2. The Medieval Trading Town. His Grace's Town. The Capital in the Era of Great Power. The Burghers' Town). Stockholm: Bonnier fakta, 1981.

————. *Stockholms historia. 2. Småstaden. Fabriksstaden. Storstaden* (Stockholm's History. 2. Small Town. Industrial Town. Metropolis). Stockholm: Bonnier fakta, 1981.

Järbe, Bengt. *Arbetsliv i Stockholm. Hantverkare och dagakarlar* (Working Life in Stockholm: Craftsmen and Day-laborers). Stockholm: Tiden, 1976.

————. *Arbetsliv i Stockholm. Mästare och gesäller.* (Working Life in Stockholm: Masters and Apprentices). Stockholm: Tiden, 1980.

————. *Förändringarnas torg* (The Square of Change). Stockholm: Tiden, 1989.

————. *Sagornas och sägnernas Stockholm* (Stockholm in Sagas and Tales). Stockholm: Tiden, 1978.

Lager, Birgitta. *Stockholms befolkning på Johan IIIs tid* (Stockholm's Population in the Time of Johan III). Stockholm: Stockholms stad, 1962.

Lang, Signe. *The House of Nobles in Stockholm: History.* Stockholm: Riddarhuset, 1965.

Lindorm. Per-Erik. *Stockholm genom sju sekler* (Stockholm Through Seven Centuries). Stockholm: Sohlman, 1951.

Matovic, Margareta R. *Bastardy and its Comparative History: Studies in the History of Illegitimacy and Marital Nonconformism in Britain, France, Germany, Sweden, North America, Jamaica and Japan, 336–345. Illigitemacy and Marriage in Stockholm.* Edited by Peter Laslett. Cambridge: 1980.

Matz, Erling. *Vasa.* Translation by The Swedish Trade Council, Clare James. Stockholm: The Vasa Museum), 1990.

Odelberg, Maj. *Lägret, Krubban och Ädelmän större.* (Three Large Housing Blocks Near the History Museum). Stockholm: Statens historiska muséet, 1951.

————. *A Key to the Doors of History.* Stockholm: Statens historiska museum, 1983.

Royal Armoury: the Assembling of Royal Relics, Costumes, Arms, Armour, Uniforms and Coaches: From About 1500 to the Present. Stockholm: Livrustkammaren, 1979.

Sankt Eriks Årsbok (St. Eric's Yearbook). A History of Stockholm. Stockholm: Samfundet St. Erik, 1903 onward.

Stockholmsbilder från fem århundrader, 1523–1923 (Pictures of Stockholm from Five Centuries). Stockholm: 1923.

Stockholms stads privilegiebref 1423–1700. (The Stockholm City Charter). Uppsala: 1900–1913.

Studier och handlingar rörande Stockholms historia. (Studies and Documents on the History of Stockholm.) 1938.

Svärdström, Svante. *The Royal Armoury: A Guide to Historical Momentoes from Five Centuries.* Stockholm: Livrustkammaren, 1966.

Tallerud, Berndt. *Fakta om Stockholm under 800 år* (Facts about Stockholm During 800 years). Solna: Almqvist & Wiksell, 1989.

Westermark, Nils. *En studie i Djurgårdens äldre historia* (A study of Djurgård's Early History). Stockholm: Self-published, 1970.

William-Olsson, Tage. *The Royal Palace of Stockholm and Its Surroundings: Past, Present and Future.* Stockholm: Byggmästaren, 1959.

2. Pre-History. The Viking Period and The Middle Ages

Ahnlund, Nils. *Stockholms historia före Gustav Vasa* (Stockholm's History Before Gustav Vasa). Stockholm: Stockholms stad, 1953.

Beskow, Hans. *Myten om Stockholms grundläggning* (The Myth about the Founding of Stockholm). Stockholm: Atlantis, 1984.
Bolin, Gunnar. *Stockholms uppkomst* (Stockholm's Origin). Uppsala: Appelbergs, 1933.
Dahlbäck, Göran. *I medeltidens Stockholm* (In Medieval Stockholm). Stockholm: Stockholms monografer utgivna av Stockholms stad, 1988.
Historia kring Stockholm före 1520 (The History of Stockholm before 1520). Stockholm: Wahlström & Widstrand, 1965.
Nordberg, Tord O:son. *The Black Friar Monastery Cellars: A Relic from the Middle Ages in the "Town Between the Bridges."* A Short Guide for Visitors. Stockholm: Stadsmuseet, 1961.
Schück, Henrik. *Stockholm vid 1400-talets slut* (Stockholm at the End of the 15th Century). Stockholm: Geber, 1951.
Stockholms stads ämbetsbok 1419–1544 (The Stockholm City Book of Offices), Stockholm: 1927
Stockholms stads jordbok 1420–98 (The Stockholm City Land Register). Stockholm: 1876–1914.
Stockholms stads skattebok 1460–1525 (The Stockholm City Tax Register), Vols. 1–3. Stockholm: 1889–1935.
Stockholms stads tänkeböcker (The Stockholm City Minutes Book), 1474–1520. 5 vols. 1917–1933; 1524–29. 2 vols. 1929–40; 1544–91. 8 vols. 1936–48; 1592–1625. 14 vols. 1939–79, Stockholm: Lund.

3. The Vasa Period

Adama-Ray, Edward. *Stockholm: A Masque.* Stockholm: 1923.
Från Olaus Petri till Tjock-Sara (From Olof Petri to Fat Sarah). Stockholm: Carlsson, 1988.
Historia kring Stockholm. Vasatid och Stormaktstid (The History of Stockholm. The Time of Vasa to the Era of Great Power). Stockholm: Wahlström & Widstrand, 1966.
Stockholms stads tänkeböcker (The Stockholm City Minutes Book), 1474–1520. 5 vols. 1917–1933; 1524–29. 2 vols. 1929–40; 1544–91. 8 vols. 1936–48; 1592–1625. 14 vols. 1939–79. Stockholm: Lund.

4. The Era of Great Power

Åkerman, Susanna. *Queen Christina of Sweden and Her Circle: the Transformation of a Seventeenth-Century Philosophical Libertine.* Brill's Studies in Intellectual History. New York: E.J. Brill, 1991.
Historia kring Stockholm. Vasatid och Stormaktstid (The History of Stockholm. The Time of Vasa to the Era of Great Power). Stockholm: Wahlström & Widstrand, 1966.
Ohlsson, Martin Arvid. *Stormaktstidens privatpalats i Stockholm* (Stockholm's Private Palaces During the Era of Great Power). Stockholm: Forum, 1951.
Roberts, Michael. *Gustavus Adolphus.* London: Longman, 1992.
Tydén-Jordan. *Queen Christina's Coronation Coach.* Stockholm: Livrustkammaren, 1989.

5. The Age of Liberty

Historia kring Stockholm. Från frihetstiden till sekelskiftet (The History of Stockholm. From the Age of Liberty until the end of the Century). Stockholm: Wahlström & Widstrand, 1967.

6. The Gustavian Period

Historia kring Stockholm. Från frihetstiden till sekelskiftet (The History of Stockholm. From the Age of Liberty Until the End of the Century). Stockholm: Wahlström & Widstrand, 1967.

Söderberg, Johan. *A Stagnating Metropolis: The Economy and Demography of Stockholm, 1750–1850*. Cambridge Studies in Population, Economy and Society in Past Time. Cambridge: University Press, 1991.

7. 19th and 20th Centuries

Bergström, Birgitta. *Från sekelskiftet till tjugotal* (From the Turn of the Century to the Twenties). Stockholm: Carlsson, 1985.

Järbe, Bengt. *Frederika Bremers Stockholm*. Stockholm: Tiden, 1974.

———. *Med Frederika Bremer och flyttkärra i 1800–talets Stockholm*. (With Frederika Bremer and a Removal Cart in 19th Century Stockholm). Stockholm: Billbergs bokhandel, 1971.

Larsson, Janerik. *Turning Point: The Book on the October 4th, 1983, Protest March in Stockholm*. Translated by John-Henri Holmberg. Stockholm: Timbro, 1984.

III. Geography

Åkerhielm, Helge. *Stockholm i berättelse och bilder* (Stockholm in Story and Pictures). Stockholm: Hökerberg, 1953.

Alm, Henrik. *Djurgården*. Stockholm: Norstedt, 1948.

———. *Djurgårdsstaden, en trehundraårig idyll* (The Town of Djurgården, A 300–Year Idyl). Stockholm: Antiquarius, 1964.

Alm, Henrik. *Klara i förvandling.* (Changing Klara). Stockholm: Natur och kultur, 1965.

———. *The Old Town of Stockholm.* Translated by John E. Carbines. Stockholm: Norstedt, 1947.

Ancker, Bo. *I radions kvarter.* (In Radio's Buildings) Stockholm: Sveriges radio, 1981.

———. *In the Summer City Stockholm.* Stockholm: Geber, 1967.

———. *Mormors portar.* (Grandma's Doorways). Stockholm: Rabén and Sjögren, 1977.

———. *Stockholm 1940.* Stockholm: Bok och bild, 1972.

Anderson, Burnett. *Stockholm, Capital and Crossroads.* Stockholm: The Swedish Institute, 1953.

Andersson, Gunder. *3 x Stockholm.* Stockholm: Carlsson, 1990.

Andersson, Karin. *Karlberg Castle.* Translated by William M. Pardon. Stockholm: Fortifikationsförvaltningen, 1992.

Andersson, Torbjörn. *Stockholm.* Malmö: Bild och media, 1987.

———. *Stockholm: lite grand från ovan-en bok med flygbilder* (Stockholm: A Little from on High. A book with Aerial Pictures). Malmö: Bild and Mediaproduktion, 1987.

Andrén, Erik. *Skogaholm Manor.* Stockholm: Skansen, 1976.

Arfvidsson, Sverker. *Gamla stan* (Old Town). Stockholm: Byggförlaget, 1984.

———. *Gamla stan: uppför gränder, nerför brinkar.* Stockholm: Byggförlaget, 1984.

Asker, Bertil. *Stockholms parker innerstaden* (Stockholm's Inner City Parks). Stockholm: Liber förlag, 1986.

Asklund, Erik. *Ensamma lyktor* (Lonely Streetlights). Stockholm: Kooperativ förbund, 1947.

———. *En kille från Hornstull* (A Guy from Hornstull). Stockholm: Rabén and Sjögren, 1968.

———. *Se min stad* (See My City). Stockholm: Rabén and Sjögren, 1953.

———. *Stad i Norden* (City in the North). Stockholm: Bonnier, 1941.

———. *Staden mellan broarna* (The City between the Bridges). Stockholm: Nord. rotografyr, 1965.

———. *Stockholm—The City on the Water.* Stockholm: Norstedt, 1968.

———. *Stockholm—The City on the Water.* Adapted into English by Paul Britten Austin. Stockholm: Norstedt, 1968.

———. *Under Stockholms broar* (Under Stockholm's Bridges). Stockholm: Nord. rotografyr, 1964.

Aurén, Sven. *Livet i Stockholm* (The life in Stockholm). Stockholm: Natur och kultur, 1942.

———. *Stockholmspromenad* (Stockholm's Walk). Stockholm: Bonniers, 1938.

Barton, H. Arnold. *Canton vid Drottningholm* (Canton at Drottningholm). Spånga: Arena, 1985.

Berg, Micke. *Stockholm Blues.* Translation by Carolina Johansson. Stockholm: Journal, 1994.

Bergengren, Kurt. *När skönheten kom till City* (When Beauty Came to City). Stockholm: Aldus, 1976.

Bergkvist , Sven O. *I Klarabohemernas värld* (In the World of Klara's Bohemians). Stockholm: Carlsson, 1993.

Bergman, Bo. *Stockholm dygnet runt* (Stockholm Night & Day). Uppsala: Lindblad, 1961.

———. *Längs drakens rygg* (Along the Dragon's Back). Stockholm: Carlsson, 1985.

———. *Stockholm—en vykorts dröm* (Stockholm—A Picture-Postcard's Dream). Stockholm: Komm. för Stockholms forskning, 1987.

———. *Stockholm.* Malmö: Allhems landskaps böcker, 1967.

Beyron, Ulla. *Stockholm i gasljus* (Stockholm by Gaslight). Stockholm: Norstedt, 1962.

Billinghurst, Kevin. *Discover Stockholm.* Stockholm: Svenska turistförening, 1993.

Biörnstad, Arne. *Djurgårdsbron* (Djurgård Bridge). Stockholm: Forum, 1977.

Blomberg, Anton. *Stockholmsliv i Anton Blombergs bilder* (The Life of Stockholm in Anton Blomberg's Pictures). Stockholm: Natur och kultur, 1981.

Blomé, Gunni. *Gå och cyckla kring Stockholm* (Walk and Cycle around Stockholm). Stockholm: Dagens Nyheter, 1980.

———. *Utflyktsmål bortom Stockholms tullar* (Destinations for Trips Outside the City Gates). Stockholm: Marieberg, 1980.

————. *Ditt Stockholm—Stockholm For You*. Stockholm: Marieberg, 1983.

Brunius, August. *Det nya Stockholm* (The New Stockholm). Stockholm: Bonnier, 1926.

Claesson, Stig. *Nya Stockholmsbilder* (New Pictures of Stockholm). Stockholm: Wahlström & Widstrand, 1987.

————. *Sommarstockholm* (Stockholm in Summer). Hudiksvall: Winberg, 1989.

————. *Stockholmsbilder* (Pictures of Stockholm). Stockholm: Askild & Kärnekul, 1975.

Colbing, Sören. *Stockholms skärgård* (The Stockholm Archipelago). Translated by Rolli Fölsch. Trångsund, Sweden: Läsförlaget, 1993.

Corall Bryn, Gerd. *Vandringar i Gamla stan* (Strolls in the Old Town). Stockholm: Prisma, 1979.

Coutourier, Catherin. *Stockholm vår hembygd* (Stockholm, our Hometown). Stockholm: Stockholm läns hembygdsförbund, 1990.

Cronström, Monica. *Inom tullarna* (Within the City Gates). Stockholm: Forum, 1988.

Dahlström, Marie. *Djurgårdsstaden och dess grannskap* (The Town of Djurgård and its Neighborhood). Stockholm: AWE/Geber, 1979.

Discover Stockholm. English edition: Kevin Bilinghurst. Stockholm: Stockholm Information Service, 1993.

————. *Trafik, broar, tunnelbanor, gator* (Traffic, Bridges, Subways and Streets). Stockholm: LiberFörlag, 1985.

Ek, Gustaf Fredrik. *Stockholms gatuskyltar berättar (Stockholm's Streetlights Tell Their Story)*. Stockholm: Geber, 1933.

Ekenberg, Arne. *Strolls in the Old Town and Its Streets and Alleys*. Stockholm: Self-published, 1970.

Eklund, Hans. *Djurgårdsnöjen* (Djurgård's Pleasure). Stockholm: Natur och kultur, 1974.

————. *Stockholmtavlor* (Stockholm's Pictures). Stockholm: Natur och kultur, 1975.

Englund, Kay G. *Mina Djurgårdsminnan från ungdomstiden* (My Memories of Djurgård from the Days of My Youth). Stockholm: Stockholm, Geber, 1934.

Eriksson, Åke. *Brommaliv* (Life in Bromma). Stockholm: Norstedt, 1977.

Etzler, Gunner (Editor). *Levande stad* (The Living City). Stockholm: Rabén and Sjögren, 1959.

Feininger, Andreas. *Stockholm 1933–1939*. Text by Gösta Flemming. Translated by Carolina Johansson. Stockholm: Stockholms stadsmuseum, 1991.

Fogelström, Per Anders. *Ett berg vid vattnet* (A Hill by the Water). Stockholm: Bonnier, 1969.

————. *En bok om Söder* (A Book about Söder). Stockholm: Bonnier, 1953.

————. *En bok om Stockholm* (A Book about Stockholm). Stockholm: Bonnier, 1978.

————. *En bok om Kungsholmen* (A Book about Kungsholmen). Stockholm: Bonnier, 1965.

————. *Kring Strömmen* (Around Strömmen). Stockholm: Bonnier, 1980.

————. *Ladugårdslandet som blev Östermalm* (Ladugårdslandet which Became Östermalm). Stockholm: Bonniers, 1964.

————. *Stad i bild* (A City in Pictures). Stockholm: Bonnier, 1970.

————. *Stockholm*. Translated by Paul Britten Austin. Stockholm: Bonnier, 1979.

————. *Söder om tullen* (South of the City Gates). Stockholm: Bonnier, 1969, 1980.

————. *Tanto*. Malmö: Sockerbolaget, 1978.

————. *Utsikt över stan* (View over the City). Stockholm: Stockholm, Bonnier, 1974.

Forsberg, Arne. *Från min port i Nicolai* (From My Front Door in Nicolai). Stockholm: Proprius, 1974.

————. *Stad mellan strömmar* (The City Between the Waters). Stockholm: Norstedt, 1971.

Forsstrand, Carl. *Från Slottsbacken till Ladugårdslandet* (From Slottsbacken to Ladugårdlandet). Stockholm: Geber, 1921.

————. *Malmgårdar och sommarnöjen i gamla Stockholm* (Town Houses and Summer Residences in Old Stockholm). Stockholm: Gebers, 1919.

————. *Skeppsbroadelen* (The Skeppsbro Area). Stockholm: Geber, 1916.

————. *Storborgare och stadsmajorer* (Rich Citizens and High-Ranking Officers). Stockholm: Gebers, 1918.

Friman, Helena. *Elva Stockholmsvandringar* (Eleven Strolls in Stockholm). Stockholm: Prisma, 1987, 1989.

Glase, Béatrice. *Gamla stan med Slottet och Riddarholmen* (The Old Town With the Royal Palace and Riddarholmen). Stockholm: Trevi, 1977, 1978, 1988, 1993 .

————. *Gamla stan* (The Old Town). Stockholm: Trevi, 1988.

————. *The Old Town: A Guide to Gamla Stan. The Royal Palace and Riddarholmen.* Translated by D. Simon Harper and Roger G. Tanner. Stockholm: Trevi, 1978.

Gould, Dennis E. *Let's Visit Sweden.* London: Burke, 1984.

Grundström, Torbjörn. *Stockholm panorama.* Stockholm: T. Grundström, 1991.

Gullers, Karl Werner. *Gamla stan* (The Old Town). Stockholm: Norstedt, 1953.

Gullers, Karl Werner. *The Old Town of Stockholm.* Stockholm: Norstedt, 1953.

————. *Stockholm bakom fasaden* (Stockholm behind the Façade). Stockholm: Koop. förbund, 1949.

————. *Stockholm.* Stockholm: Gullers, 1979; 1991.

Gullers, Peter. *Den överkörda gatan* (The Run-Over Street). Stockholm: Prisma, 1972.

————. *Stockholm Photographs: Peter Gullers and Others.* Translated by Jeremy Franks. Stockholm: Gullers Pictorial, 1988.

Häggqvist, Arne. *Stockholm à la carte.* 1962.

Hall, Bo G. *Mälarhöjden med omnejd* (Mälarhöjden and Surroundings). Stockholm: Stockhoms stad, 1988.

Hammenhög, Waldemar. *I en svensk sovstad* (In a Swedish Dormitory Town). Stockholm: Wahlström & Widstrand, 1954.

Hasselblad, Björn. *Djurgårdsvandringar på norra och södra* (Strolls in North and South Djurgård). Stockholm: Kungl. Djurgården, 1990.

————. *Stockholmsgator* (Stockholm's Streets). Stockholm: AWE/Geber, 1975.

————. *Stockholmskvarter* (Stockholm's Blocks of Houses). Stockholm: AWE/Geber, 1979.

Heimer, Oscar. *Bilder från Stockholms malmar 1894–1912* (Pictures from Stockholm's Districts 1894–1912). Stockholm: Sveriges radio, 1972.

————. *Bilder från Södermalm 1895–1912* (Pictures from Södermalm 1895–1912). Stockholm: Sveriges radio, 1979.

Hellbom, Thorleif. *Ett stilla gathörn* (A Quiet Street-Corner). Stockholm: Carlsson, 1992.

————. *Författarnas Stockholm.* (Authors' Stockholm). Stockholm: Norstedt, 1991.

Henrikson, Alf. *Fotograf Elmblad* (The Photographer Elmblad). Stockholm: Geber, 1968.

Henrikson, Carl-Henrik. *Alla dessa promenader i Stockholmstrakten* (All These Walks in the Stockholm Area). Bromma: Ordalaget, 1992.

Hentzel, Roland. *Mälardrottningens underliga öden* (The Mysterious Fate of Mälardrottningen). Stockholm: Natur och Kultur, 1939.

Herrmanns, Ralph. *The Royal Palace of Stockholm.* Stockholm: Bonnier, 1978.

Hirdman, Yvonne. *Magfrågan* (A Question of the Stomach). Stockholm: Rabén and Sjögren, 1983.

Hodell, Björn. *Wärdshus förbi* (Inns of the Past). Stockholm: Joker, 1945.

Holmbäck, Bure (Editor). *Huvudstadens hästar* (The Capital's Horses). Stockholm: Höjering, 1990.

Holmberg, Gunnar. *Södermalm.* Stockholm: Norstedt, 1981.

Holmin, Lorrie. *Stockholm, I Love You!* Stockholm: Författares bokmaskin, 1984.

Horn, Paridon von. *Staden sjunger* (The Town Sings). Stockholm: Prisma, 1975.

———. *Städernas stad* (The City of Cities). Stockholm: Prisma, 1976.

Horn, Vivi. *Roslagstull.* Stockholm: Wahlström & Widstrand, 1958.

Hurd, John. *Inside Stockholm.* Stockholm: Askild & Kärnekull, 1970.

Imber Liljeberg, Evert. *Från Slussen till Hornstull* (From Slussen to Hornstull). Stockholm: Läseleket, 1989.

Jacob Westerlund, K. *Järvabanan* (The Järva Line). Stockholm: Stockholm Trafiken, 1977.

Janson, Mats. *The Summer Farmstead From Älvdalen.* Stockholm: Skansen, 1976.

Jarl, Per. *Stockholm in Your Pocket.* Stockholm: Barrikaden, 1982.

Johansson, Ann-Helé. *Barnens Stockholm* (Children's Stockholm). Stockholm: 1994.

Johansson, Gotthard. *Ur svenska hjärtans djup* (From the Depth of Sweden's Heart). Stockholm: Wahlström & Widstrand, 1953, 1987.

K'ang, Yu-wei. *K'ang Yu-weis svenska resa 1904* (K'ang Yu-weis' Swedish Journey, 1904). Stockholm: Almqvist & Wiksell, 1970

Knutsson, Johan. *Flanör i Stockholm* (A Saunterer in Stockholm). Stockholm: Norstedt, 1977.

Kumlien, Bertil. *Segla i hamn* (Sail into Harbor). Stockholm: AWE/Geber, 1979.

Lager-Kromnow, Birgitta. *Att vara stockholmare på 1560 talet.* (Being a Stockholmer in the 1560s). Stockholm: Stockholms stad, 1992.

Landell, Nils-Erik. *Den gröna staden* (The Green Town). Stockholm: Albe, 1979.

———. *Den vita staden* (The White Town). Stockholm: Albe, 1980.

———. *Stockholms gröna hjärta* (Stockholm's Green Heart). Stockholm: Interpublish, 1983.

———. *Stockholms solitärer* (Stockholm's Loners). Stockholm: Interpublish, 1986.

———. *Den växande staden* (The Growing City). Stockholm: Rabén and Sjögren, 1992.

Landquist, John. *Livet i Katarina* (Life in Katarina). Stockholm: Natur och kultur, 1965.

Langenfelt, Gösta. *Staden vid de ljusa vattnen* (The City With the Shining Waters). Stockholm: Kooperativa förbundet, 1953. Lind, Manne. *Norra Smedjegatan.* (North Smedjegatan). Stockholm: Norstedt, 1970.

Lindberg, Birgit. *Malmgårdarna i Stockholm* (The Mansions of Stockholm). Stockholm: LiberFörlag, 1985.

Lindblad, Eric. *Djurgårdsår* (Djurgård Years). Stockholm: Wahlström & Widstrand, 1956.

Lindgren, Rune. *Gamla stan förr och nu* (The Old Town Past and Present). Stockholm: Rabén and Sjögren, 1992.

Lindhagen, Anna. *Idyller och utsikter* (Idyls and Views). Stockholm: Rekolid, 1990.

———. *Stockholms enskilda bank 1856–1956.* Stockholm: Åhlén & Åke, 1956.

Lindroth, Hasse. *Stockholm nyligen* (Recent Stockholm). Stockholm: Alfabeta, 1990.

Lindskog, Carin. *Clas på hörnet* (Clas on the Corner). Stockholm: 1932.

Linnell, Stig. *Stockholms spökhus och andra ruskiga ställen* (Stockholm's Haunted House and Other Gruesome Places). Stockholm: Prisma, 1993.

Lundin, Claes. *Gamla Stockholm* (Old Stockholm). Stockholm: Bonnier, 1983.

———. *Nya Stockholm* (New Stockholm). Stockholm: Bonnier, 1969.

Lundquist, Jan. *Stockholm.* Stockholm: Stadskollegietsreklamkommitté, 1975.

———. *Mariaberget.* Stockholm: Geber, 1965.

Making Friends with Stockholm. Distributed by AB Stockholms spårvägar. (Stockholm's Streetcar Company). Stockholm: Stockholm Streetcars, 1961.

Malmström, Axel. *Stockholm.* Stockholm: Gidlund, 1963; 1966; 1979.

Megarry, Andrew. *Stockholm: Photography by Andrew Megarry.* Toronto: Vision works, 1987.

Meissner, Hjalmar. *Gamla glada Stockholm* (Happy Old Stockholm). Stockholm: 1939.

Mellin, Gustaf Henrik. *Stockholm and its Environs: Comprehending the History and Curiosities of the Capital, and a Description of Everything Remarkable in Its Neighborhood.* Translated by George Stephens. Stockholm: Rylander, 1841.

Mitt Stockholm (My Stockholm). Södertälje: Fingraf, 1959, 1993.

Möller, Anna. *Stockholm: The Capital of Sweden.* Stockholm: 1924.

Murmästareämbetet i Stockholm (The Mason's Guild in Stockholm). Stockholm: 1935.

Näsström, Gustaf. *Kungliga Riddarholmen* (Royal Riddarholmen). Stockholm: Norstedt, 1973.

Neuhaus, Heinrich. *Panorama över Stockholm på 1870–talet* (Panorama of Stockholm in the 1870s). Stockholm: Generalstabe, 1954.

Norbelie, Harald. *Gata upp och gata ner* (Street Up and Street Down). Stockholm: Rabén and Sjögren, 1991.

———. *Mera gata upp och gata ner* (More Streets Up and Street Down). Stockholm: Rabén and Sjögren, 1993.

Nordberg, Tord. *Stockholm i tolv vandringar* (Stockholm in Twelve Walks). Stockholm: 1946.

Norden, Åsa. *Stockholm.* Stockholm: LiberFörlag, 1986.

———. *Sällsamheter i Stockholm* (Strangenesses in Stockholm). Stockholm: Rabén and Sjögren, 1990.

Nordensvan, Georg. *Vandring i det glada Stockholm* (Strolling in Happy Stockholm). Stockholm: Nornan, 1962.

Nordström, Alf. *Vad skall jag se i Stockholm* (What Shall I See in Stockholm). Stockholm: Svensk turistföreningen, 1958.

Nordström, Ludvig. *Bolsieviken Stockholm* (The Bolshevik Stockholm). Stockholm: Bonnier, 1936.

Ohlsson, Bengt. *Ohlssons Stockholm.* Stockholm: Norstedt, 1993.

Olsson, Jan-Olof. *Stockholm.* Stockholm: Stadskollegietsreklamkommitté, 1963.

Paulsson, T. *Den glömda staden* (The Forgotten City). Stockholm, 1959.

Petersens, Lennart. *Från Klara till City* (From Klara to the City). Stockholm: LiberFörlag, 1985.

————. *Hötorgcity förr och nu* (Hötorgcity Past and Present). Stockholm: Bibliotekens, 1964.

————. *Klara.* Stockholm: Norstedt, 1957. Rådström, Pär. *Det Klara som försvinner* (The Disappearing Klara). Stockholm: Bok-Konsum, 1955.

Reinius, Gunnar. *Bilder från gamla Stockholm* (Pictures of Old Stockholm). Stockholm: Prisma, 1981.

————. *Livet i ett svunnet Stockholm* (Life in a Vanished Stockholm). Stockholm: Bonnier, 1963.

————. *Stockholm då och nu* (Stockholm Then and Now). Stockholm: Bonnier, 1965.

————. *Ett svunnet Stockholm* (A Vanished Stockholm). Stockholm: Bonnier, 1963.

Ring, Herman A. *Stockholm, dess gator, torg, allmänna platser och monumentala byggnader i våra dagar* (Stockholm: Its Streets, Squares, Public Places, and Monumental Buildings of Our Time). Stockholm: Geber, 1897.

Roeck Hansen, Donald. *Gamla stan* (The Old Town). Stockholm: Utbildningsförlag, 1989.

————. *Upptäck naturen i Stockholm tillsammans med barnen* (Discover Nature in Stockholm, Together with the Children). Stockholm: Rabén and Sjögren, 1987.

Rosengren, Bernt. *Söders Manhattan* (Söder's Manhattan). Stockholm: HSB (Hyresgästernas sparkasse-och byggnadsförening), 1981.

Rubenson, Mauritz. *Vid Mälaren och Nevan* (By Mälaren and Nevan). Stockholm: Bonnier, 1869.

Rudbeck, Ture Gusta. *Stockholm.* Stockholm: Redivivia, 1975.

Rüster, Reijo. *Stockholm, öarnas stad* (Stockholm, City of islands). Stockholm: Tjernquist, 1982.

————. *Stockholm, City of Islands.* Translated by Keith Bradfield. Stockholm: Tjernquist, 1983.

Rydberg, Olle. *Från Årsta till Farsta* (From Årsta to Farsta). Stockholm: Natur och kultur, 1979.

————. *Se på Söder* (Look at Söder). Stockholm: Natur och kultur, 1984.

————. *Söder om Söder* (South of Söder). Stockholm: Natur och kultur, 1977.

Rydelius, Ellen. *Stockholm på 8 dagar* (Stockholm in 8 Days). Stockholm: Bonnier, 1930.

Sadolin, Ebbe. *På vandring i Stockholm* (Wandering in Stockholm). Stockholm: Almqvist & Wiksell, 1954.

————. *Vandringar i Stockholm* (Strolls in Stockholm). Stockholm, Almqvist & Wiksell, 1953.

Sax, Ulrika. *Den vita staden* (The White Town). Stockholm: Komm. för St., 1989.

Schubert, Elspeth Harley. *Brief Encounter with Stockholm.* In collaboration with Georg K:son Kjellberg. Stockholm: Norstedt, 1959.

Selling, Gösta. *Hur Gamla stan överlevde* (How the Old Town Survived). Stockholm: 1973.

————. *När Stockholm blev storstad* (When Stockholm became a Metropolis). Stockholm: 1955.

————. *Si Ulla dansar* (Look, Ulla is Dancing). Stockholm: Wahlström & Widstrand, 1945, 1987.

————. *Stockholm i närbild* (Stockholm in Close-up). Stockholm: Wahlström & Widstrand 1943, 1987.

Sernander, Rutger. *Stockholms natur* (Stockholm's Nature). Uppsala: Almqvist & Wiksell, 1926.

Setterwall, Åke. *The China Pavilion at Drottningholm.* Translated by Louise Setterwall and Paul Britten Austin. Malmö: Allhem, 1974.

Siöcrona, Vera. *Granne med Kungen* (Neighbor to the King). Stockholm: Natur och kultur, 1945.

————. *Mitt Gamla stan.* (My Old Town). Stockholm: Natur och kultur, 1966.

Sjöberg, Göran & Hentzel, Roland. *Söder.* Stockholm, 1967.

Sjöman, Margit. *Vandringar med ungar* (Strolls With Young People). Stockholm: SÖ förlag, 1969.

Snellman, Gemma. *Stockholmsbilder förr och nu* (Stockholm Pictures Past and Present). Stockholm: Rabén and Sjögren, 1974.

Söderberg, Elow. *Haga lustpark* (Haga Pleasure Grounds). Stockholm: Plus, 1980.

Söderberg, Rolf. *Stockholmsspegel* (Mirror of Stockholm). Stockholm: LiberFörlag, 1984.

————. *Stockholmsgryning* (Dawn of Stockholm). Stockholm: LiberFörlag, 1986.

Sommar, Carl-Olov. *Stockholmspromenad med Strindberg* (A Walk in Stockholm with Strindberg). Stockholm: Sälls. bokv.

————. *Strandvägen.* Stockholm: Bonnier, 1987.

Stadsvandringar (City Strolls). Stockholm: Stockholm stadsmuseum, 1976.

Stenström, Matts. *Staden inom broarna* (The City Within the Bridges). Stockholm: Hjalmar Lund, 1918.

Stockholm 1251–1952. Stockholm: 1951.

Stockholm. (Guides of the Swedish Tourists' Club). Stockholm: Wahlström / Widstrand, 1896.

Stockholm. Guildford: Clour Library Books, 1986.

Stockholm. Stockholm: Appelgren, 1981.

Stockholm: a Capital in Europe. Edited by Peter Gullers, Marianne Rydkvist. Stockholm: Gullers, 1993.

Stockholm och dess nejder (Stockholm and Its Neighborhood). Stockholm: Rediviva, 1970.

Stockholm och dess omgivningar (Stockholm and Its Surroundings). Stockholm: Wahlström & Widstrand, 1923.

Stockholm—the Convention City. Stockholm: Stockholms turisttrafikförbund, 1969.

Stockholm: The High Tech Center of Scandinavia. Stockholm: Stockholm Information Service, 1986.

Stockholm This Week. Stockholm: Stockholm Information Service, 1986–.

Stockholmsfotografer vol. 5: Kasper Salin. Introduction by Lars Johannesson and Lars Westberg. Stockholm: Stadsmuseum, 1985.

Stockholms offentliga toaletter (Stockholm's official Toilets). Stockholm: Stockholms gatukontor, 1991.

Stockholms stadsmuseum. Småskrifter. (The Stockholm City Museum: Papers). Volumes 1–6, 1963–66.

Storm, Ingvar. *Lusthus i Stockholm* (Summerhouses in Stockholm). Stockholm: Askild & Kärnekul, 1981.

Strindberg, August. *Gamla Stockholm* (Old Stockholm). Stockholm: Bonnier, 1922, Strindlund, Martin. *Några anteckningar om Gamla stan* (Some Notes About Old Stockholm). Stockholm: Solaett, 1990.

Ström, Sven. *Stockholm.* (English edition). Stockholm: Generalstaben, 1972.

————. *Stockholm.* Translated and revised by Mac Lindahl. Stockholm: Generastab. 1973.

Sundfeldt, Jan. *Stockholms vildmarker* (Stockholm's Wildernesses). Stockholm: Prisma, 1986.

Swahn, Waldemar. *Haga.* Stockholm: Norstedt, 1922.

Svedfelt, Torsten. *Ur Stockholmslivet* (From the Life of Stockholm). Stockholm: Wahlström & Widstrand, 1949.

Thorén, Lill. *Det hände vid Johannes* (It Happened at Johannes). Stockholm: Forum, 1993.

Tikkanen, Henrik. *Kär i Stockholm* (In Love with Stockholm). Stockholm: Wahlström & Widstrand, 1955.

Tjerneld, Staffan. *En bok om Djurgården* (A Book About Djurgården). Stockholm: Bonnier, 1968.

———. *Gröna Lund och andra Djurgårdsnöjen* (Gröna Lund and Other Djurgård Pleasures). Stockholm: Norstedt, 1978.

———. *Hundra år på Östermalm* (A Hundred Years on Östermalm). Stockholm: Höjering, 1984.

———. *Stockholmsliv i vår tid* (Stockholm Life in Our Times). Stockholm: Norstedt, 1972.

———. *Stockholmsliv. Bd. 1. Norr om strömmen* (Stockholm Life. Vol. 1. North of Strömmen). Stockholm: Norstedt, 1950, 1988.

———. *Stockholmsliv. Bd. 2, Söder om strömmen* (Stockholm Life. Vol. 2. South of Strömmen). Stockholm: Norstedt, 1988.

Tollstorp, Jacob P. *Stockholm och dess omgifning* (Stockholm and Its Surroundings). Stockholm: Rediviva, 1975.

Tongue, Michael. *The Stockholm Time Walk.* Stockholm: Discovery Books, 1995.

Trenter, Stieg. *Huset vid Skanstull* (The House at Skanstull). Stockholm: Rabén and Sjögren, 1960.

Unge, Ingemar. *Paradiset under Globen* (The Paradise Under the Globe). Stockholm: Höjering, 1992.

Ward, Frank. *Äta ute i Stockholm* (Eat Out in Stockholm). Stockholm: Prisma, 1973.

———. *The Pick of Stockholm.* Stockholm: Norstedt, 1983.

Wästberg, Per. *Ett hörntorn vid Riddargatan och andra Stockholmsskildringar* (A Corner Tower at Riddargatan and Other Descriptions of Stockholm). Stockholm: Wahlström & Widstrand, 1980.

———. *Innan gaslågan slocknade* (Before the Gaslight Went Out). Stockholm: Billberg, 1963.

———. *Östermalm.* Stockholm: Wahlström & Widstrand, 1962.

———. *Kungsträdgården.* Stockholm: Bonnier, 1986.

———. *Stockholm i minnet och nuet* (Stockholm in the Memory and the Present Day). Stockholm: Höjering, 1987.

Wickman, Mats. *The Stockholm City Hall.* Translated by Paul Britten-Austin. Stockholm: Sellin and Partner, 1993.

Wigardt, Björn. *Södermalm.* Stockholm: Kvadraten, 1978.

Wigardt, Gaby. *Stockholmsrond* (Round Stockholm). Stockholm: LiberFörlag, 1977.

Wikström, Jeppe. *Harmony of the Stockholm Skerries.* Stockholm: Dagens Nyheter. 1994.

Winter, Kris. *Happy Days in Stockholm: An Informal Guide to Amusements in the Capital of Sweden.* Stockholm: Lindqvist, 1950.

Wrangel, Frederick U. *Stockholmiana. Samling 1–4* (Collection 1–4). Stockholm: Norstedt, 1912.

Zweigbergk, Eva von. *Litet Stockholmsalbum* (The Little Album of Stockholm). Stockholm: Bonnier, 1962.

———. *Se på stan i Stockholm* (Look at Stockholm Town). Stockholm: Bonnier, 1961.

———. *Stockholmspromenader* (Stockholm's Walks). Stockholm: Wahlström & Widstrand, 1956.
———. *Upptäcksfärd i Stockholm* (Journey of Discovery in Stockholm). Stockholm: Almqvist & Wiksell, 1957.

IV. Education

Bedoire, Fredric. *Stockholm University: A History.* Translated by Allan Tapsell. Stockholm: Stockholm University, 1987.
Hagelin, Ove. *The Art of Writing and Drawing, a selection of one hundred books from the Ekström collection in the National Library for Psychology and Education, Stockholm: a descriptive and annotated catalogue of 16th through 18th century rare and important books on Calligraphy, Perspective, Architecture, Drawing, Anatomy, Colors and Related Arts.* Stockholm: The National Library for Psychology and Education, 1987.
Jones, Lawrence E. *Visiting Students in Stockholm: Encountering and Adjusting to Swedish Culture.* Stockholm: The Rectorate, University Division of International Affairs, University Office of the Foreign Student Advisor, Federation of Student Unions in Stockholm, 1992.
Karolinska Institute: A Presentation. Edited by Bengt Pernow. Stockholm: Karolinska institutet, 1980.
Lindberg, Leif. *Konstfack, the Academy of Arts, Crafts and Design.* Text by Håkon Östlundh. Stockholm: Konstfack, 1986.
Lundén, Thomas. *On Stockholm.* Stockholm: International Graduate School, 1982.
Mårtenson, Dick. *Educational Development in an Established Medical School: Implementing Change at the Karolinska Institute.* Translated by Ann B. Weissman. Lund: Studentlitteratur; Bromley, Kent: Chartwell-Bratt, 1985.
Olsson, Nils-Olof. *Stockholm's Day-care Centers 1974–1984.* Translated by Keith Bradfield. Stockholm: Stockholm Real Estate Office, 1985.
Stockholms universitet. Stockholm: University of Stockholm, 1979.

V. Ethnography, Anthropology

Manker, Ernst. *Guide to the Exhibits in Nordiska museet and at Skansen Open-Air Museum.* Stockholm: Nordiska museet, 1956.
Rehnberg, Mats. *The Mora Farm.* Stockholm: Skansen, 1976.
Scheffere, Charlotte. *Roman Cineray Urns in Stockholm Collections.* Stockholm: Medelhavsmuseet, 1987.
Schoultz, Gösta von. *The Iron-Master's Farm.* Stockholm: Skansen, 1976.
Strömberg, Elisabeth. *The Bollnäs House, the Delsbo Farm.* Stockholm: Skansen, 1976.

VI. Economics

Almquist, J. *Stockholms stads brandförsäkringskontor 1746–1921.* (The Stockholm Fire Insurance Office).

Artle, Roland. *The Structure of the Stockholm Economy: Towards a Framework for Projecting Metropolitan Community Development.* Ithaca, New York: Cornell Univesity Press, 1959.

Bass, Britt and Holmqvist, Lasse. *Gadelius 1880–1990: en familj och ett företag* [Gadelius 1880–1990: a Family and a Business Enterpris). Stockholm: Gadelius, 1990.

Beckers 125 år (Beckers 125 year). Stockholm: Beckers, 1990.

87 Stockholm restaurants. Malmö: Liber, 1981.

Hansson, Björn A. *The Stockholm School and the Development of Dynamic Method.* London: Croom Helm, 1982.

Industriens utredningsinstitut. Measurement and Economic Theory. (The Industrial Institute for Economic and Social Research). Stockholm: The Industrial Institute, 1979.

Jägergren, Bengt. *The Story of the Göta Canal Steamship Company: A Summary.* Translation by Anthony Skeat. Gothenburg: B. Jägergren, 1994.

Lanesjö, Bo. *Development of Stockholm.* Stockholm: City of Stockholm, 1989.

Larsson, Janerik. *Turning Point: The Book on the October 4, 1983 Protest March in Stockholm.* Stockholm: Timbro, 1984.

Liljeblom, Eva. *Stock Price Reactions to Financial Decisions: Some Results on Data for the Stockholm Stock Exchange.* Ekonomi och samhälle; (Economy and the Community), 43. Helsingfors: Svenska Handelshögskola, 1989.

Lundén, Thomas. *Land Use decisions in a Time-Space Framework: Some Stockholm Examples.* Stockholm: University of Stockholm, Cultural Geographic Institute, 1980.

Malkamäki, Markku. *Institutional Arrangements and Efficiency on the Swedish Stock Market.* Vaasa, Finland: Vaasan korkeakoulu, 1989.

New Perspectives in North-South Dialogue: Essays in Honour of Olof Palme. Edited by Kofi Buenor Hadjor. London: Tauris, 1988.

Postal Museum. Post Office Information Department. Stockholm: Postverket, 1980.

Ratzka, Adolf Dieter. *Sixty Years of Municipal Leasehold in Stockholm: An Econo-metric and Cost-Revenue Analysis.* Ann Arbor, MI: University Microfilm, 1982.

Stockholm: A Short Guide Dedicated to the Delegates of the 4th Congress of the International Chamber of Commerce, By the Stockholm Chamber of Commerce. Stockholm, Tullberg, 1927.

Stockholm restaurants. Solna, Sweden: Quatre Critiques, 1986.

Sverges riksbank, the Swedish Central Bank. Stockholm: Information Secretariat, Sveriges riksbank, 1994.

The *Sveriges Riksbank Act (1988:1385).* Stockholm: Sveriges riksbank, 1944.

Sweden in a Boundless Stock Market: Essays Given at the 125th Anniversary of the Stockholm Stock Exchange on August 18–19, 1988. Publication Stock Exchange; 3. Stockholm: Stock Exchange, 1988.

Telecommunications Museum, Stockholm. Stockholm: Telemuseum, 1982.

Zahka, William J. *The Nobel Prize Economics Lectures: A Cross-Section of Current Thinking.* Aldershot: Avebury, 1992.

VII. Politics, Social Sciences and Law

Anderstig, Christer. *An Expanded Model of Housing Choice Applied to Stockholm.* Umeå, Sweden: Centrum för regionalvetenskaplig forskning, 1986.

238 • SELECTED BIBLIOGRAPHY

Anton, Thomas J. *Governing Greater Stockholm: A Study of Policy Development and System Changes.* Berkeley: University of California Press for the Institute of Governmental Studies, 1975.

Blom, Tarras. *Old-Fashioned Residences in the Heart of Stockholm.* Stockholm: A. Johnson and Co., 1985.

Brzeski, W. Jan. *Rental Apartment Trade-Ups in Resale-Home Transactions: A Market Response to Lock-In Problems in Stockholm During the Mid–1980s.* Stockholm: Tekniska högskolan, 1988.

Calmfors, Hans. *Urban Government for Greater Stockholm.* New York: Frederick A. Praeger, 1968.

Centrum för invandringsforskning: CEIFO: (Center for Research in International Migration and Ethnic Relations at Stockholm University: A Presentation). Stockholm: Centrum för invandringsforskning, 1992.

City of Stockholm: Local Self-Government. Stockholm: City of Stockholm, 1990.

Democracy and Human Rights. Stockholm: Department for International Development Cooperation, Ministry for Foreign Affairs, 1993.

Dufwa, Arne. *Snöröjning, renhållning, återvinning* (Snow clearance, Street cleaning and Recycling). Stockholm: LiberFörlag, 1989.

En sammanfattning av miljöplan för Stockholm. (*An Abstract of Environmental Stockholm*). Stockholm: Miljö och hälsoskyddsförvaltning, 1991.

Forselius, Tilda Maria; Högberg, Lena and Öberg, Lisa, *Stockholmskan* (Stockholm Swedish). Stockholm: Stadsmuseum, 1991.

Freeman, Ruth. *Death of a Statesman: the Solution to the Murder of Olof Palme.* London: Hale, 1989.

Gurr, Ted Robert. *The Politics of Crime and Conflict: A Comparative History of Four Cities [London, Stockholm, Sydney, Calcutta].* Stockholm: The Politics of Crime and Conflict pp. 215–320. Beverley Hills, CS: Sage, 1977.

Gustafson, Uno. *The Censuses in Stockholm 1860–1910: Some Preliminary Findings.* Stockholm: 1973.

Hall, Thomas. *"i nationell skala-": studier kring cityplaneringen i Stockholm* (On a National Scale), Studies on the Redevelopment of Stockholm's City Center).

———. *Stockholms förutsättningar och uppkomst: en studie i medeltida urbanism* (The Preconditions for Stockholm's Birth: A Study in Medieval Urbanization). Stockholm: 1973.

Hemdahl, Reuel G. *Cologne and Stockholm: Urban Planning and Land-use Controls.* Metuchen, NJ: Scarecrow, 1971.

Housing in Stockholm: Information from the Stockholm City Housing and Real Estate Office. Stockholm: Mark-och lokaliseringsbolaget (Land and Localisation Company, 1986. Stockholm: City Housing and Real Estate Office, 1987.

Information on the Physical Planning in Stockholm. Vols. *1–5.* Stockholm: Stockholms stadsplanekontor, 1970.

Janson, Carl-Gunnar. *"Working-Class Segregation in Stockholm and Some Other Swedish Cities".* Stockholm: Sociologiska institutet. University, 1987.

Järbe, Bengt. *Polisen i Stockholm förr och nu* (The Police in Stockholm, Past and Present). Stockholm: Tiden, 1975.

Kista, Husby, Akalla: A Digest for Planners, Politicians and Critics. Stockholm: Information Stockholm, 1983.

Krehbiel, Carl C. *Confidence and Security-Building Measures in Europe.* Westport, CT: Praeger, 1989.

Lanesjö, Bo. *The Development of Stockholm.* Stockholm: Stadskansliet (City Administrative Office), 1987.

Lindström, Eric. *The Swedish Parliamentary System: How Responsibilities Are Divided and Decisions Are Made*. 2d. ed. Stockholm: Swedish Institute, 1983.
Local Government in Stockholm. Stockholm: Stockholm Information Service, 1983.
Monografier: utgivna av Stockholms Kommunal-förvaltning(Monographs: Published by the Local Government of Stockholm). Stockholm: Stockholmia förlag, 1941–.
Olof Palme Memorial Lecture on Disarmament and Development: Riverside Church, January 21, 1987. Edited by Cora Weiss. New York: Riverside Church Disarmament Program, 1987.
On Social Assistance in the Nordic Capitals. Torben Fridberg. Copenhagen: Socialforskninsinstitutet, Nordisk Ministerråd, 1993.
Parental Leave—A Question of Equality. Stockholm: Personnel and Organization Administration, City of Stockholm, 1989.
Park, Heon-Joo. *Housing Land in Government Intervention: With Special Reference to Land Readjustment in Seoul, Korea and Municipal Site-Leasehold in Stockholm, Sweden*. Stockholm: Stockholm University, 1991.
Pass, David. *Vällingby and Farsta—From Idea to Reality: The New Community Development Process in Stockholm*. Cambridge: 1973.
Pilevsky, Philip. *Captive Continent: The Stockholm Syndrome in European-Soviet Relations*. New York: Praeger, 1989.
Regional Planning in the County of Stockholm. Stockholm: Regional Planning Office, Stockholm County Council, 1983.
Riksdag: A History of the Swedish Parliament. Edited by Michael F. Metcalf. Stockholm: Swedish Riksdag, Bank of Sweden Tercentenary Foundation, 1987.
Ringen—the Stockholm Ring Road: Implementation Plan. Translated by Graham Ainsscough. Stockholm: Stockholmsleder AB, 1992.
Rudberg, Eva. *Några bostadsområden i Stockholm 1920–1985: Arkitektmuseets sommarutställning 1985* (Some Housing Areas in Stockholm 1920–1985: Summer Exhibition of the Museum of Architecture). Translated by David Sheppard. Stockholm: Arkitekturmuseum, 1985.
Scarlat, Alexander Segal. *The Development of Shopping Centres in the Stockholm Area*. Stockholm: 1962.
Scarlat, Sacha Segal. *Key to Stockholm*. Stockholm: Christofer, *1960*.
Selling, Gösta. *Esplanadsystemet och Albert Lindhagen* (The System of Esplanades and Albert Lindhagen). Stockholm: Stockholms kommunalförvaltning, 1970.
Shiels, Barbara. *Winners: Women and the Nobel Prize*. Minneapolis: Dillon, 1985.
Söder '67: Outline Planning Programme for the Southern Part of the Central City called Södermalm. Stockholm: 1968.
Söderberg, Johan. *Stockholm: Growth Problem 1760–1850 in a Comparative European Perspective*. Stockholm: Department of Economic History, Stockholm University, 1982. *Mortality Patterns in 18th and 19th Century Stockholm in a European Perspective*, 1984. No. 3 *Realm Wage Trends in Urban Europe, 1730–1850. Stockholm in a comparative pespective*. No. 4 *Stagnating Metropolis: Economy and Demography in Stockholm, 1750–1850*. 1984. Stockholm: Department of Economic History, Stockholm University, 1986.
Söderberg, Johan; Johnsson, Ulf and Persson Christer. *A Stagnating Metropolis: The Economy and Demography of Stockholm, 1750–1850*. Cambridge: Cambrige University Press, 1991.
Stadshistorisk revy (Review of Municipal History). Stockholm: 1922–.
Stockholm City Housing and Real Estate Office. Stockholm: Fastighetskontoret, 1987.

Stockholm. Miljö-och hälsoskyddsförvaltningen. (The Environment and Public Health Administration in Stockholm). Translated by David Knight and Co. Stockholm: Environment and Public Health Administration, 1990.

Stockholms internationella fredforskningsinstitut. [Stockholm International Peace Research Institute: the facts, figures and people.) Prepared by Richard Nyström. Solna, Sweden: SIPRI, 1991.

Stockholms län. Landstinget. (The Stockholm County Council). Translated by Peter Bilby. Stockholm: The Information Department, County Council, 1990.

Stockholms län. Landstinget. (the Stockholm County Council: A Presentation). Stockholm: Information Department, The County Council, 1992.

Summary of the Stockholm Environment Plan. Stockholm: Environment and Public Health Administration, 1990.

Surviving Together: the Olof Palme Lecture on Common Security 1988. Edited by Radmila Nakarada and Jan Öberg. Lund University Peace Research Institute, LUPRI. Aldershot: Dartmouth, 1989.

Svensson, Gudrun. *Women's Houses: A Booklet Based on Experiences From a Seminar on the Theme "Women's Rights and Women's Houses, Organized in Stockholm 1990.* Stockholm: National Federation of Social Democratic Women in Sweden, 1991.

Swant, Frank Terrell. *Stockholm's Housing and Urban Planning Policies: A Study of Systematic Change.* Ann Arbor, MI: University of Michigan, 1989.

Sweden: The Supreme Administrative Court (Basic documents series, 14). Brussels: IIAS, 1986.

Sweden: Riksdagen, Sveriges riksdag. Stockholm: Riksdagen, 1984.

Swedish Riksdag in an International Perspective: Report from the Stockholm Symposium, April 25–27 1988. Edited by Nils Stjernquist. Stockholm: Bank of Sweden Tercentenary Foundation, 1989.

Sweden: Utrikesdepartement. (Sweden's Foreign Service.) Stockholm: Ministry of Foreign Affairs, 1993.

Sweden = Sverige. Vällingby: Strömberg, 1944.

Talk Straight about Crime: A Manifesto for the Prevention of Crime. Stockholm: Stockholm Police Force and Tiofoto, Swedish National Police Board, 1992.

Wikström, Jeppe. *Harmony of the Stockholm Skerries.* Stockholm: Dagens Nyheter, 1994.

William-Olsson, W. *Stockholm, Structure and Development.* Uppsala: 1960.

Women, Work and Health: Stress and Opportunities. Edited by Marianne Frankenhaeuser, Ulf Lundberg and Margaret Chesney. New York: Plenum, 1991.

VIII. Society, Religion

Bergquist, Lars. *Saint Birgitta.* Translation by Roger Tanner, from the author's Swedish original ms. Stockholm: Swedish Institute [Svenska institutet], 1991.

Birgitta. *Life and Selected Revelations.* Edited with a preface by Marguerite Tjader Harris; translation and notes by Albert Ryle Kezel; introduction by Tore Nyborg. New York: Paulist Press, 1990.

Jones, C. H. *A Record of the Work of the English Church at Stockholm and Some Other British Activities in Sweden during the Second World War.* Stockholm: G. Lindström, 1945.

Saint Birgitta, Her Order and Her Words. Translated by Tryggve Lundén. Vadstena: Birgittasystrarna, 1990.
Saint Birgitta's Church in the Parish of Västerled, Stockholm. Translated by Harry Arvidson. Bromms: Västerleds Parish, 1963.
Westlund, Per-Olof. *"The Great Church," Storkyrkan (St. Nicolas'), A Guide for Visitors.* Translated by Edward Adams-Ray. Stockholm: Storkyrkan, 1934.

IX. Culture

1. Language, Linguistics

Jansson, Sven B.F. *Runes in Sweden.* Tralation by Peter Foote. Stockholm: Royal Academy of Letters, History and Antiquities, 1987.
Pred, Allan. *Lost Words and Lost Worlds: Modernity and the Language of Everyday Life in Late Nineteenth-Century Stockholm.* Cambridge: Cambridge University Press, 1990.

2. History of Literature

Bellquist, John Eric. *Strindberg as a Modern Poet: a Critical and Comparative Study.* University of California Publications in Modern Philology. Berkeley: University of California Press, 1986.
Dürrenmatt, Friedrich. *Play Strindberg: The Dance of Death Choreographed.* Translated by James Kirkup. New York: Grove Press, 1979.
File on Strindberg. Compiled by Michael Meyer. London: Methuen, 1986.
Fisher, Carla. *August Strindberg: Hemsöborna.* Studies in Swedish Literature, Vol. 14. Hull: Dept. of Scandinavian Studies, University of Hull, 1982.
Gavel Adams, Ann-Charlotte. *The Generic Ambiguity of August Strindberg's "Inferno": Occult Novel and Autobiography.* Ann Arbor, MI: University of Michigan, 1990.
Geddes, Tom. *Söderberg: Doktor Glas.* Studies in Swedish Literature; Vol. 3. Hull: University of Hull, 1980.
Hurwitz, Johanna. *Astrid Lindgren: Storyteller to the World.* New York: Viking Kestrel, 1989.
Hutt, Inger Margareta. *Time in Hjalmar Söderberg's Novels: A Narratological Study of the Function and Treatment of Time.* Ann Arbor, MI: University Microfilms International, 1983.
Inglis, William Heard. *Strindberg and Williams: A Study in Affinities.* Ann Arbor, MI: University Microfilms International, 1976.
Jaspers, Karl. *Karl Jaspers' Strindberg and Van Gogh: An Attempt at a Pathographic Analysis With Reference to Parallel Cases in Swedenborg and Höderlin.* Translated by Oskar Grunow and David Woloshin. Tucson: Arizona University Press, 1977.
Johnson, Walter. *August Strindberg.* Twayne's World Authors Series. Boston: Twayne, 1976.
Kieft, Robert Henry. *The Correspondent Self: A Reading of August Strindberg.* Ann Arbor, MI: University Microfilms International, 1979, 1981.
Lagerkrantz, Olof. *August Strindberg.* Translated by Anselm Hollo. New York: Farrar, Strauss, Giroux, 1984.

Lindgren, Astrid. *Pippi Longstocking.* Oxford: Oxford University Press, 1977.
Lundell, Torborg. *Lars Ahlin.* Twayne's World Authors Series. New York: Twayne, 1977.
Meyer, Michael. *Strindberg, A Biography.* New York: Random House, 1985.
Reinhardt, Nancy Simonds. *Visual Meaning in Strindberg's Theater.* Ann Arbor, MI: University Microfilms International, 1991.
Robinson, Michael. *Strindberg and Autobiography: Writing and Reading a Life.* Norvik Press, Series A; Vol. 1. Norwich: Norvik Press, 1986.
Söderberg, Hjalmar and Butt Wolggang. *Martin Birck's ungdom.* (The Youth of Martin Birck). Studies in Swedish Literature. Hull: University of Hull, 1979.
———. Lofmark, Carl. *Hjalmar Söderberg: Historietter.* Studies in Swedish Literature. Hull: University of Hull, 1977.
Scott-Chandler, Mary Patricia. *The Dance of Death in the Works of Strindberg, Ensor and Mann: A Study in the Grotesque.* Ann Arbor, MI: University Microfilms International, 1981.
Sprinchorn, Evert. *Strindberg as Dramatist.* New Haven: Yale University Press, 1981.
Steene, Birgitta. *August Strindberg: An Introduction to His Major Works.* Carbondale: Southern Illinois University Press, 1973.
Steffensen, Erik. *Strindberg's metode.*(Strindberg's method). Valby: Borgen, 1993.
Strindberg, August. *Eight Best Plays.* Translated by Edwin Björkman and N. Erichsen. London: 1979.
———. *Strindberg's Letters.* Selected, edited and translated by Michael Robinson. 2d vol. Chicago: University of Chicago, 1992.
Strindberg and Genre. Edited by Michael Robinson. Norwich, CT: Norvik Press, 1991.
Strindberg and History. Edited by Birgitta Steene. Stockholm: Almqvist and Wiksell International, 1992.
Strindberg on Stage: Report from the Symposium in Stockholm, May 18–22, 1981. Edited by Donald K. Weaver. Stockholm: Sv. teaterunionen- Sv. ITI, Strinbergssällskap, 1981.
Strindberg's Dramaturgy. Edited by Göran Stockenström. The Nordic Series, 16. Minneapolis: University of Minnesota Press, 1988.
Structures of Influence: A Comparative Approach to August Strindberg. Edited by Marilyn Johns Blackwell. University of North Carolina Studies in the Germanic Language and Literatures. Chapel Hill: University of North Carolina Press, 1981.
Törnqvist, Egil. *Strindbergian Drama: Themes and Structure.* Stockholm: Almqvist and Wiksell International, 1982.
———. *Strindberg's Miss Julie: A Play and Its Transpositions.* Vol. 5. Norwich CT: Norvik Press, 1988.
Vogler, Stephen Henry. *Expressionistic Theatricialism Signal in the Damascus Trilogy by August Strindberg.* Ann Arbor, MI: University Microfilms International, 1981.
Ward, John. *The Social and Religious Plays of Strindberg.* London: Athlone, 1980.

3. Fiction with Stockholm Motifs

Anna Maria Lenngren. 1754–1817. Translated by Philip K. Nelson. Stockholm: Imprimé, 1984.

Bellman, Carl Michael. *Fredman's Epistles and Songs.* Translated by Paul Britten Austin. Stockholm: Proprius, 1990.
Havard, Jonathan. *The Stockholm Syndrome.* Leicester, England: Charnwood, 1987.
Ozick, Cynthia. *The Messiah of Stockholm: A Novel.* New York: Knopf, 1987.
Sinclair, Clive. *Augustus Rex: A Novel.* London: André Deutsch, 1992.

4. Fine Arts

Andersson, Henrik O. *Stockholm: Architecture and Landscape.* Stockholm: Prisma, 1988.
Art Goes Underground: Art in the Stockholm Subway. Edited by Göran Söderström. Translated by Laurie Thompson. Solna: Lettura, 1988.
Arvidson, Gunnar. *Inside the Royal Palace.* Translation Write Right. Stockholm: Gullers, 1991.
Aurora 4: Kulturhuset Stockholm 15.11.1991–12.1.1992 Helsinki: Nordiskt konst-centrum, 1991.
Björkman, Helena. *Stockholm Globe Arena: a Document on its Conception and Creation.* Translated by Jeremy Franks. Stockholm:
Bjurström, Per. *Nationalmuseum: 1792–1992.* Stockholm: Nationalmuseum, 1992.
Brummer, Hans Henrik. *The Muse Gallery of Gustavus III.* Stockholm: Almqvist / Wiksell, 1972.
Constant, Caroline. *The Woodland Cemetery: Toward a Spiritual Landscape. Erik Gunnar Asplund and Sigued Lewerentz 1915–61.* Stockholm: Byggförlag, 1944.
Copenhagen Papers in the History of Art. Institute of Art History. No. 4 Les pays du Nord et l'Europe: art et architecture au XVI siècle. pp 143–162. *Christian II in Stockholm in 1520.* University of Copenhagen, 1975.
Cornell, Elias. *Stockholm Town Hall.* Stockholm: Byggförlaget, 1992.
Dittman, Reidar. *Eros and Psyche: Strindberg and Munch in the 1890s.* Studies in the Fine Arts. The Avant-garde. Ann Arbor, MI: University of Michigan Research Press, 1982.
Edgren, J. Sören. *Catalogue of the Nordenskiöld Collection of Japanese Books in the Royal Library.* Stockholm: Kungliga biblioteket, 1980.
Efraimsson, Ralf. *The Flower Year at Waldemarsudde.* Stockholm: Lantbruksförbundets Ekonomi AB, 1982.
Ericson, Deborah. *In the Stockholm Art World.* Stockholm: Department of Anthropology, University of Stockholm, 1988.
Glase, Gösta. *Storkyrkan: The Stockholm Cathedral.* Stockholm: Storkyrkoförsamling, 1981.
Guide to the Eldh Studio Museum. Edited by Brita Eldh. Stockholm: Carl Eldhs ateljémuseum, 1981.
Guide to the Museum of National Antiquities. Stockholm: Statens historiska museum, 1963.
Hasselrot, Titti. *Villa Bonnier.* Stockholm: Riksdagen, 1990.
Karling, Sten. *The Stockholm University Collection of Paintings: Catalogue.* Translated by Patrick Smith. Stockholm: University of Stockholm, 1978.
Lamm, Carl, Johan. *Glass from Iran in the National Museum, Stockholm.* Stockholm: Almqvist and Wiksell, 1935.
Landström, Björn. *The Royal Warship Vasa: a Book on the Building and Embellishment, the Rigging and Armaments of the Vasa, the Swedish Warship that Sank on*

her Maiden Voyage in Stockholm Harbour in 1628. Translated by Jeremy Franks. Stockholm: Interpublishing, 1988.

Larsson, Carl. *A Family.* New York: G.P. Putman's Sons, 1979.

———. *Carl Larsson: The Autobiography of Sweden's Most Beloved Artist.* Translated by Ann B. Weissmann. Iowa City: Penfield Press, 1992.

———. *On The Sunny Side.* Translated by Allan Lake Rice. Silver Spring, MD: Nordic Heritage Services, 1984.

———. *The World of Carl Larsson.* Translated by Allan Lake Rice. La Jolla, CA: The Green Tiger Press, 1982.

Leander, Touati, Ann-Marie. *Gustav III's Museum of Antiquities.* Stockholm: Nationalmuseum, 1993.

Lidén, Elisabeth. *Between Water and Heaven: Carl Milles Search for American Commissions.* Stockholm: Almqvist & Wiksell International, 1986.

Lindell, Lage. *Lage Lindell: Stilen är människan själv* (Lage Lindell: the Style is Man Himself). Stockholm: Moderna museet, 1993.

Lindgren, Gustaf. *Prins Eugen's Waldermarsudde, Stockholm, Sweden: a Guide.* Stockholm: 1966.

Lindwall, Bo. *Art in the Riksdag building.* Translated by Roger and Kerstin Tanner. Stockholm: Swedish Riksdag, 1990.

Milles, Carl. *Carl Milles: Episodes from My Life.* Edited by Karl Axel Arvidsson. Lidingö, Sweden: Millesgården, 1991.

Millesgården. Lidingö, Sweden. Millesgården, 1980.

Nordström, Lena. *White Arm of the Royal Armoury.* Stockholm: Royal Armoury Foundation, 1984.

O'Reilly, Willem Thomas. *Ingmar Bergman's Theatre Direction, 1952–1974.* Ann Arbor, MI: University Microfilms International, 1981.

Pictures from Drottningholm. Translated by Roger G. Tanner. Edited by Göran Alm. Original title: *Bilder från Drottningholm.* Stockholm: Royal Collections, 1985, 1990.

Söderlund, Göran. *Prince Eugen's Waldemarsudde, A Guide.* Translated by Angela Adegren. Stockholm: Waldemarsudde, 1992.

———. *Millesgården.* Lidingö, Sweden: 1987.

Soop, Hans. *The Power & the Glory: The Sculptures of the Warship Wasa.* Stockholm: Almqvist & Wiksell International, 1986.

Stockholm: A Picture Album. München-Pullach: L.Simon, 1958.

Stockholm bygger: om 1980–talets byggnande i Stockholm. Edited by Cecilia Björk. Stockholm: Liber Förlag, 1986.

Stockholms arkitektur: en guide (Stockholm's architecture: a Guide). Translated by William M. Pardon. Stockholm: Stockholms arkitektförening. 1990.

Stockholms stadshus (Stockholm City Hall). Solna, Sweden: Esseletegrako, 1982.

Stockholm Water Festival. Edited by Katarina Reinius and Mats Wickman. Translated by Sheila Smith. Stockholm: Sellin and Partner, 1992, 1993.

Triumph of Simplicity: 350 Years of Swedish Silver: an Exhibition from Nationalmuseum. Translation by Patrick Hort. Stockholm: Nationalmuseum, 1988.

Tomaszewska, Anna. *The Verdures of the Hallwyl Palace: A Study.* Stockholm, 1991.

The Vasa Museum: Information From the National Board of Public Building. Stockholm: Byggnadsstyrelsen (KSB), 1990.

Wirgin, Jan. *Ming Porcelain in the Collection of the Museum of Far Eastern Antiquities: Hongwu to Chengua.* Excerpt from Bulletin 63 of The Museum of Far Eastern Antiquities. Stockholm: Museum of Far Eastern Antiquities, 1991.

Wrede, Stuart. *The Architecture of Erik Gunnar Asplund.* Cambridge: MIT Press, 1980.
Zorn, Anders. *Anders Zorn: Master of Light and Color.* Espoo: Gallen-Kallelan Museo, 1992.

5. Music

Edgington, Harry. *ABBA.* London: Methuen Paperbacks, 1978.
Gustavian Opera: An Interdisciplinary Reader in Swedish Opera, Dance and Theater 1771–1809. Stockholm: Royal Swedish Academy of Music, 1991.
The Royal Swedish Academy of Music. Edited by Hans Åstrand and Gunnar Larsson. Stockholm: Akad., 1983.
Rydberg, Enar. *The Opera by Stockholm's Stream.* Translated by Jon Kimber. Stockholm: Informationsförlag, 1993.
Stockholm: A Musical Capital. Stockholm: Musikrevy, 1978.
Tobler, John. *ABBA Gold: The Complete Story.* Edited by Dick Wallis. Iver Heath: Century 22, 1993.

6. Theater

Bergman, Ingmar. *Project for the Theater.* Edited and introduced by Frederick J. Marker. New York: Ungar, 1983.
Drottningholm Theatre Museum. Edited by Barbro Stribolt. Stockholm: Drottningholm Theater Museum, 1984.
Gustav III and the Swedish Stage: Opera, Theater and other Foibles. Lewiston, New York: E. Mellen Press, 1993.
Marker, Lisa-Lone. *Ingmar Bergman: Four Decades in the Theater.* Cambridge: Cambridge University Press, 1982.
Niet alleen Strindberg: Zweden op de planken (Not only Strindberg: Sweden on Stage.) Published for the Holland Festival 1985. Netherlands: s.n., 1985.
Strindberg, August. *Strindberg: IVAM Center Julio Gonzalez 16 February–2 May 1993.* Translated by Kjersti Board. Valencia: IVAM, 1993.
Swedish Plays in English Translation from Strindberg to the Present. 3d. ed. Stockholm: ITI, 1985.
Waal, Carla. *Strindberg's Muse and Interpreter.* Carbondale: Southern Illinois University Press, 1990.
Wikander, Matthew H. *Princes to Act, Royal Audience and Royal Performance, 1578–1792.* 264–313. Baltimore: Johns Hopkins University Press, 1933.
Zorn, Anders. *Självporträtt: möten med Anders Zorn* (Self-Portraits: Meetings With Anders Zorn). Translated by Kendal von Sydow. Mora: Zornsamlingar, 1994.

7. Film

Affron, Charles. *Star Acting: Gish, Garbo, Davis.* New York: Dutton, 1977.
Bergman, Ingmar. *Images: My Life in Film.* Translated by Marianne Ruuth. New York: Arcade, 1994.
———. *Ingmar Bergman and Society.* London, Tantivity Press. South Brunswick, NJ: Barnes, in collaboration with The Swedish Film Institute and The Swedish Institute, Stockholm, 1978.

————. *Magic Lantern: an Autobiography.* Translated by Joan Tate. New York: Viking, 1988.

————. *Sjöman, Vilgot, L136; Diary with Ingmar Bergman.* Translated by Alan Blair.

Bergman, Ingrid. *Ingrid Bergman, My Story.* London: Michael Joseph, 1980.

Calhoun, Alice Ann. *Suspended Projections: Religious Roles and Adaptable Myths in John Hawke's Novels, Francis Bacon's Paintings and Ingmar Bergman's Films.* Ann Arbor, MI: University Microfilms, 1979.

Conway, Michael. *The Complete Films of Greta Garbo.* Introductory essay by Parker Tyler. Introduction by Jerry Vermilye. Secaucus, NJ: Citadel Press, 1991.

Cowie, Peter. *Ingmar Bergman: a Critical Biography.* New York: Limelight, 1992.

Daum, Ingvar. *Walking with Garbo: Conversations and Recollections.* Edited and annotated by Vance Muse. New York: Harper Collins Publishing, 1991.

Film and Dreams: An Approach to Bergman. Edited and introduced by Vlada Petric. South Salem, NY: Redgrave, 1981.

Gado, Frank. *The Passion of Ingmar Bergman.* Durham, NC: University Press, 1986.

Garbo, Greta. *Garbo on Garbo.* London: Bloomsbury, 1991.

Gibson, Arthur. *The Right of Redemption in Films of Ingmar Bergman: The Rite, The Virgin Spring, Hour of the Wolf, Shame, Passion of Anna, The Touch, Cries and Whispers.* Lewiston, NY: E. Mellen Press, 1993.

Greta Garbo; Portraits 1920–1951. Introduction by Klaus-Jürgen Sembach. New York: Rizzoli, 1986.

Gronowicz, Antoni. *Garbo: (Her Story).* Publisher's postscript by Richard Schickel. Harmondsworth, England: Penguin Books, 1991.

Haining, Peter. *The Legend of Garbo.* London: W.H. Allen, 1990.

Ingmar Bergman at 70; A Tribute. Svenska filminstitutet (The Swedish Film Institute), 1988.

Ingrid Bergman. Introduction by Shridan Morley. Legends. London: Pavilion, 1985.

Johns, Marilyn Elizabeth. *Strinberg's Influence on Bergman's Det sjunde inseglet, Smultronstället and Persona.* Ann Arbor MI: University Microfilms, 1977.

Kawin, Bruce. *Mindscreen.* Princeton, NJ: Princeton University Press, 1978.

Koskinen, Maaret. *Ingmar Bergman.* Stockholm: Swedish Institute, 1993.

Leamer, Laurence. *As Time Goes By: A Life of Ingrid Bergman.* London: Hamilton, 1986.

Livingstone, Paisley Nathan. *Ingmar Bergman and the Rituals of Art.* Ithaca, Cornell University Press, 1982.

————. *The Snakeskin: Ingmar Bergman and the Rituals of Art.* Ithaca: Cornell University Press, 1982.

Long, Robert Emmet. *Ingmar Bergman: Film and Stage.* New York: Harry N. Abrams, 1994.

Mosley, Philip. *Ingmar Bergman: The Cinema as Mistress.* London: Marion Boyars, 1981.

Payne, Robert. *The Great Garbo.* London: W. H. Allen, 1976.

Pepper, Terence. *The Man Who Shot Garbo: The Hollywood Photographs of Clarence Sinclair Bull.* New York: Simon and Schuster, 1989.

Sands, Frederick. *The Divine Garbo.* New York: Grosset and Dunlap, 1979.

Taylor, John Russell. *Ingrid Bergman.* London: Hamilton, 1983.

Vickers, Hugo. *Loving Garbo: the Story of Greta Garbo.* New York: Random House, 1994.

Walker, Alexander. *Garbo: a Portrait.* London: Weidenfeld and Nicolson, 1980, 1990.

Wimberley, Amos Darryl. *Bergman and the Existentialists: A Study in Subjectivity.* Ann Arbor, MI: University Microfilms, 1979.

8. Archeology

Ambrosiani, Björn. *Birka on the Island of Björkö* (Cultural Monuments in Sweden). Stockholm: Central Board of National Antiquities, 1988.

Birka: Untersuchungen und Studien. Kungliga Vitterhets-, historie- och antikvitsakademien Katalog–1955 *(The Burial Customs: A Study of the Graves on Björkö).* Stockholm: Almqvist & Wiksell International, 1980.

Excavations at Helgö. Stockholm: Kungliga Vitterhets historie-och antikvitetsakademien, 1961. 12. Wilhelm Holmqvist: (The Helgö Scholar. Building groups 1, 4 and 5: Structures and Finds). 1994.

Holmquist Olausson, Lena. *Aspects on Birka: Investigation and Surveys 1976–1989.* Stockholm: Archaeological Research Laboratory, 1993.

Holmqvist, Wilhelm. *Swedish Vikings on Helgö och Birka.* Stockholm: Swedish Booksellers Assoc., 1979.

Investigations in the Black Earth. Stockholm: Birka Project, 1992.

9. Sport and Games

Audette, Larry. *Björn Borg.* New York: Quick Fox, 1979.

Cox, Mark and Gould, Dennis. *The Swedish Way to Tennis Success.* London: Arthur Barker, 1990.

X. Industry

Byggnadsarbetarnas historia på Helgeandsholmen, 1890–1906 (The Story of Construction Workers on Helgeandsholmen, 1890–1906). Stockholm: Svensk byggnad, 1983.

Hesselmann, G. *Historik över byggnads yrket i Stockholm 1250–1950* (The History of the Building Trade in Stockholm). Stockholm: 1952.

———. *Från skråhantverk till byggnadsindustri. Om husbyggen i Stockholm 1840–1940* (From Crafts to the Building Industry: Housebuilding in Stockholm). Stockholm: 1945.

Interiors in Stockholm, Göteborg, Malmö Stockholm: SIR, 1968.

Johansson, Ingemar. *Stor-Stockholm bebyggelsehistoria* (Greater Stockholm's Building History). Stockholm: Gidlund, 1987.

Josephson, R. *Stadsbyggnadskonst i Stockholm intill år 1800.* (Town Construction in Stockholm up to 1800).

———. *Borgarhus i gamla Stockholm. 1. Byggnadshistoria* (Burgesses' Houses in Old Stockholm). Stockholm: 1916.

Wallenberg, Olga. *Grand Hotel, Stockholm.* Stockholm: Atlantis, 1988.

Walton, Ann Thorson. *Ferdinand Boberg—Architect: The Complete Work.* Cambridge, MA: MIT Press, 1994.

XI. Communications

Bartlett, N. R. *Stockholm Public Transport.* Chelmsford, England: Westbury Marketing, 1986.
Berglund, Helge. *Greater Stockholm.* Stockholm: Stockholms lokaltraffik, 1972.
Borgenstam, Curt. *Why Wasa Capsized.* Stockholm: Wasa Rediviva, 1985.
Landström, Björn. *The Royal Warship Vasa: a Book on the Building and Embellishment.* Stockholm: Interpublishing, 1988.
Lindberg, Axel. *Båt nummer X: Helgeandsholmen, Stockholm: dokumentation av rekonstruktion av båt nr. X.* Stockholm: Medeltidsmuseet, 1989.
Matz, Erling. *Vasa.* Stockholm: Museet, 1990.
Port of Stockholm. Stockholm: Hamnkontoret, 1957.
Ringen—The Stockholm Ring Road.: Implementation plan. Translated by Graham Ainscough. Stockholm: Stockholmsleder AB, 1992.
Soop, Hans. *The Power and the Glory: The Sculptures of the Warship Wasa.* Stockholm: Kungliga Vitterhets-historie och antikvitetsakademien, 1986.
Stockholm. Stockholm: Mälaren Tourist Traffic, 1921.
Stockholm Underground '75: a Technical Description. Stockholm: Stockholms läns landsting, 1976.
Traffic Route Plan for Stockholm: English Summary of the Comprehensive Traffic Plan Submitted to the Master Planning Commission of Stockholm, February 20th, 1960. Stockholm. Stockholms stad, 1960.
Vasa Monument: Information from the National Board of Building and Planning. Stockholm: Byggnadsstyrelsen, 1990.
Vinberg, Sal. *The Port of Stockholm.* Stockholm: Self-published, 1935.

XII. Science

Brzezinski, Richard. *The Army of Gustavus Adolphus.* London: Osprey, 1991.
Gyldenstolpe, Nils. *Types of Birds in the Royal Natural History Museum in Stockholm.* Stockholm: Vetenskapsakademien, 1926.
Manne Siegbahn Institute of Physics, Stockholm, Sweden. Stockholm. Stockholm: Manne Siegbahn Institute, 1991.
Pipping, Gunnar. *The Chamber of Physics: Instruments in the History of Sciences Collections of The Royal Swedish Academy of Sciences, Stockholm.* Stockholm: Almqvist & Wiksell, 1977.

XIII. Technology

Andersson, H. and Bedoire, F. *Stockholms byggnader* (The Buildings of Stockholm). Stockholm, 1977.
Arkitektur (Architecture). Stockholm: 1901–.
Bedoire, F. and Stavenow-Hidemark, J. *Arkivguide för byggnadsforskare.* (An Archive Guide for Architectural Reseachers). Stockholm: Berg, Micke. *Stockholm Blues.* Translated by Carolina Johansson. Stockholm: Journal, 1994.
Bohm, Håkan. *Combatting Subsidence in The Old Town of Stockholm.* Stockholm: Swedish Council for Building Research, 1981.

A Book about the Folksam Building and How We Built It: a Story in Pictures. Stockholm: Folksam, 1960.

Constant, Caroline. *The Woodland Cemetry: Toward a Spiritual Landscape.* Stockholm: Byggförlaget, 1994.

Cronström, Anders. *Vattenförsörjning och avlopp* (Water Supply and Drainage). Stockholm: LiberFörlag, 1986.

Hallström, Björn Henrik. *Russian Architectural Drawings in the National Museum.* Stockholm: Nationalmuseum, 1963.

KTH in Search of Excellence. Translated by Bernard Vowles. Stockholm: Royal Institute of Technology, 1986.

Kommitten Miljö '82, Acidification Today and Tomorrow; A Swedish Study Prepared for the 1982 Stockholm Conference on the Acidification of the Environment. Stockholm: Swedish Ministry of Agriculture, 1982.

Mobility and Transport for Elderly and Disabled Persons. Proceedings of a conference held at Stockholmsmässan, Älvsjö, Sweden, 21–24 May 1989 organized by the Swedish Board of Transport in cooperation with the Department of Traffic Planning and Engineering, Lund Institute of Technology. Philadephia, Pa: Gordon and Breach, 1991.

Rudberg, Eva. *Sven Markelius, Architect.* Translated by Roger Tanner. Stockholm: Arkitektur, 1989.

Some Notes on The Graphic Institute, The Institute of Advertising, The Institute of Journalism. Stockholm: Grafiska institutet, 1961.

Stockholm vatten. The Stockholm Sewer System Master Plan, 1983. Stockholm: Stockholm vatten, 1990.

Swedish Grace: Modern Classicism in Stockholm. London: International Architect, 1982.

Waters of Stockholm: a publication about the Aquatic Environment in and around Stockholm Water Ltd. (Stockholm vatten AB) and how we are working to improve it. Stockholm: Stockholm Water, 1992.

William-Olsson, William. *Stockholm, Structure and Development.* Uppsala: 1960.

XIV. Medicine

Cernerud, Lars. *Growth and Social Conditions: Height and Weight of Stockholm's Schoolchildren in a Public Health Context.* Gothenburg: Nordiska hälsovårdshögskolan, 1991.

Evolving Environmental Perceptions: From Stockholm to Nairobi. Edited by Mostafa Kamal Tolba. London: Butterworths, 1988.

Rudestam, Kjell Erik. *Stockholm and Los Angeles: A Cross-cultural Communication of Suicidal Intent.* Ann Arbor, MI: University of Michigan, 1989.

Stockholm County Medical Information System. Berlin: Springer Verlag, 1978.

XV. Swedish Fiction Translated to English

Fiction, Poetry and Drama by Authors with Stockholm Connections

Almqvist, Carl Jonas Love. *The Queen's Diadem.* Translated by Yvonne L. Sandstroem. London: Skoob, 1992.

————. *Why not!: a Picture out of Life.* Translated by Lori Ann Ingalsbe. Seattle: Mermaid Press, 1994.

Bellman, Carl Michael. *Fredman's Epistles and Songs.* Translated by Paul Britten Austin. Stockholm: Proprius, 1990.

Bergman, Ingmar. *A Film Trilogy.* Translated by Paul Britten Austin. London: Marion Boyars, 1989.

————. *Best Intentions.* Translated by Joan Tate. London: Harvill, 1993.

————. *Face to Face.* Translated by Alan Blair. London, Marion Boyars, 1976.

————. *Fanny and Alexander.* Translated by Alan Blair. New York: Penguin, 1989.

————. *Four Screenplays of Ingmar Bergman.* Translated by Lars Malmstrom and David Kushner. New York: Simon and Schuster, 1989.

————. *Four Stories.* Translated by Alan Blair. London: 1977.

————. *From the Life of the Marionettes.* Translated by Alan Blair. New York: Pantheon, 1980.

————. *Marriage Scenarios.* Translated by Alan Blair. New York: Pantheon, 1988.

————. *Marriage Scenarios.* Translated by Alan Blair. London: Aurum, 1989.

————. *Serpent's Eggs: A Film by Ingmar Bergman.* Translated by Alan Blair. New York: Bantam Books, 1978.

————. *Seventh Seal.* Translated by Lars Malmström. London: Lorrimer, 1984.

Ekland, Britt. *Sweet Life.* Translated by Joan Tate. London: 1994.

Larsson, Carl. *The Farm.* Original text: *Spadarvet.* Amsterdam: V.O.C., 1980.

Nobel Reader: Short Fiction, Poetry and Prose by Nobel Laureates in Literature. Edited by Jonathan Eisen and Stuart Troy. New York: C. N. Potter, 1987.

Sjöwall, Maj. *The Laughing Policeman.* Translated by Alan Blair. Original title *Den skrattande polisen.* New York: Vintage Books, 1992.

————. *The Man on the Balcony.* Translated by Alan Blair. London: Victor Gollancz, 1990.

Söderberg, Hjalmar. *Short Stories.* Selected and translated by Carl Lofmark. Norwich, CT: Norvik Press, 1987.

Strindberg, August. *Apologia and Two Folk Plays.* Translated and introduced by Walter Johnson. Seattle: University of Washington Press, 1981.

————. *By the Open Sea.* Translated by Mary Sandbach. Athens, GA: The University of Georgia, 1985.

————. *The Chamber Plays.* Translated by Eivor Martinus. Bath: Absolute Press, 1991

————. *Dance of Death, Parts I and II.* Translated by Arvid Paulson. New York: Norton, 1976.

————. *The Father.* Translated by Michael Meyer. Chicago: Ivan R. Dee, 1992.

————. *The Father: A Tragedy in Three Acts; and A Dream Play.* Translated by Valborg Anderson. Arlington Heights, IL: H. Davidson, 1985.

————. *The Father, Miss Julie and The Ghost Sonata.* Translated by Michael Meyer. London: Eyre Methuen, 1976.

————. *Five Plays.* Translated and introduced by Harry G. Carlson. Berkeley: University of California, 1983.

————. *The Great Highway.* Translated by Ivor Martinus. Bath: Absolute Press, 1990.

————. *In Midsummer Days and Other Tales.* Translated by Ellie Schleussner. Plainview, NY: Books for Libraries Press, 1976.

————. *Inferno and From an Occult Diary.* Translated with an Introduction by Mary Sandbach. Harmondsworth, Middlesex: Penguin, 1979.

———. *Miss Julie.* Translated by Edwin Björkman. New York: Dover Publications, 1992.

———. *Miss Julie.* Introduction by Helen Cooper. Translation by Helen Cooper. London: Methuen Drama, 1992.

———. *Motherly Love; Pariah; The First Warning.* Translated by Eivor Martinus. Oxford: Amber Lane Press, 1987.

———. *Plays.* Translated with an Introduction by Michael Meyer. London: Methuen, 1991.

———. *Plays.* Translated with an Introduction by Michael Meyer. London: Methuen, 1982.

———. *Plays From the Cynical Life.* Translated by Walter Johnson.

———. *Plays of Confession and Therapy.* Translated by Walter Johnson. Seattle: University Press of Washington, 1979.

———. *Roofing Ceremony; and The Silver Lake.* Translated by David Mel Paul and Margareta Paul. Lincoln: University of Nebraska Press, 1987.

———. *Selected Plays.* Translated and introduced by Evert Sprinchorn. Minneapolis: University of Minnesota Press, 1986.

———. *Sleepwalking Nights on Wide-awake Days* and *Biographical.* Translation by Arvid Paulson. New York: Law-Arts Publications, 1978.

———. *Strindberg's The Father and Ibsen's Hedda Gabler.* Adapted by John Osborne. London: Faber and Faber, 1989.

———. *Thunder in the Air.* Translated by Eivor Martinus. Bath: Absolute Press, 1989.

Wallenberg, Jacob. *My Son on the Galley.* Translated by Peter Graves. London: Norvik, 1994.

XVI. Children's Books

Lagerlöf, Selma. *The Changeling.* Translated by Susana Stevens. New York: Knopf, 1992.

Lindgren, Astrid. *Cherry Time at Bullerby.* Translated by Florence Lamborn. London: Mammoth, 1991

———. *Children on Troublemaker Street.* New York: Aladdin Books, 1991.

———. *Children of Noisy Village.* Translated by Florence Lamborn. New York: Viking Penguin, 1988.

———. *Christmas in the Stable.* London: Hodder and Stoughton, 1990.

———. *The Day Adam Got Mad.* Translated by Barbara Lucas. Stockholm: Rabén & Sjögren, 1991.

———. *Dragon With Red Eyes.* Translated by Patricia Crampton. London: Methuen, 1986.

———. *Emil's Little Sister.* Translated by David Scott. London: Hodder and Stoughton, 1985.

———. *Emil's Pranks.* New York: Viking Kestrel, 1988.

———. *Emil's Sticky Problem.* Translated by David and Judy Scott. London: Hodder and Stoughton, 1986.

———. *Ghost of Skinny Jack.* New York: Viking Kestrel.

———. *Happy Days at Bullerby.* Translated by Florence Lamborn. London: Mammoth, 1991.

————. *I Don't Want to Go to Bed.* Translated by Barbara Lucas. Stockholm: Rabén & Sjögren, 1988.

————. *I Want a Brother or Sister.* Translated by Eric Bibb. Stockholm: Rabén & Sjögren, 1988.

————. *I Want to Go to School Too.* Translated by Barbara Lucas. Stockholm: Rabén & Sjögren, 1987.

————. *Karlson Flies Again.* Translated by Patricia Crampton. London: Mammoth, 1992.

————. *Karlson on the Roof.* Translated by Patricia Crampton. London: Mammoth, 1992.

————. *Lotta.* Translated by Gerry Bothmer. Harmondsworth: Puffin, 1979.

————. *Lotta's Christmas Surprise.* London: Methuen, 1979.

————. *Lotta Leaves Home.* Translated by Gerry Bothmer. London: Mammoth, 1991.

————. *Lotta on Troublemaker Street.* Translated by Gerry Bothmer. New York: Aladdin Books, 1991.

————. *Lotta's Bike.* Stockholm: Rabén & Sjögren, 1989.

————. *Lotta's Easter Surprise.* Translated by Barbara Lucas. New York: Rabén & Sjögren, 1991.

————. *Lotta's Christmas Surprise.* Stockholm: Rabén & Sjögren, 1990.

————. *Mardie.* Translated by Patricia Crampton. London: Methuen, 1979.

————. *Mardie to the Rescue.* Translated by Patricia Crampton. London: Mammoth, 1993.

————. *Mardie's Adventures.* Translated by Patricia Crampton. London: Mammoth 1993.

————. *Mio, My Son.* Translated by Marianne Turner. New York: Viking Penguin, 1988.

————. *Mischievous Martens.* Translated by Gerry Bothmer. London: Mammoth, 1991.

————. *My Nightingale is Singing.* Translated by Patricia Crampton. New York, NY: Viking Kestrel, 1986.

————. *Of Course Polly Can Do Almost Everything.* Chicago: Follett, 1978.

————. *Pippi Goes Aboard.* Translated by Marianne Turner. Oxford: Oxford University Press, 1979.

————. *Pippi Goes on Board.* Translated by Florence Lamborn. New York: Viking-Press, 1988.

————. *Pippi Longstocking.* Translated by Edna Hurup. Harmondsworth: Puffin Books, 1976.

————. *Pippi Longstocking.* Translated by Florence Lamborn. Santa Barbara, CA: Cornerstone Books, 1989.

————. *Pippi on the Run.* New York: The Trumpet Club, 1990.

————. *Rasmus and the Vagabond.* Translated by Gerry Bothmer. New York: Viking Penguin, 1987.

————. *Ronia the Robber's Daughter.* Translated by Patricia Crampton. New York: Viking Penguin, 1985.

————. *Runaway Sleigh Ride.* New York: The Viking Press, 1984.

————. *Six Bullerby Children.* Translated by Evelyn Ramsden. London: Mammoth, 1991.

————. *Springtime in Bullerby.*

————. *That's My baby.* London: Methuen, 1979.

Sjögren, 1991.
———. *Tomten and the Fox*. Edinnburgh: Floris Books, 1992.
———. *World's Best Karlson*. Translated by Patricia Crampton. London: Methuen Children's Books, 1980.
Roeck Hansen, Donald and Berg, Elly. *Gamla stan. Två stadsvandringar.* (The Old Town. Two city strolls). Stockholm: Bildningsförlaget, 1989.
Sörensen, Margareta. *Stockholm, Stockholm- staden som växer på vattnet.* (Stockholm, Stockholm—The City Which Grows on the Water). Stockholm: Rabén & Sjögren, 1993.

XVII. Monographs

The following is an English translation of the series titles, in numerical order of publication. *Monografier: utgivna av Stockholms Kommunal-förvaltning.* (Monographs: published by the local government of Stockholm). Stockholm: Stockholmia förlag, 1941– (Many have English summaries).

1. 1941 Stockholm's future development.
2. 1943 The magistrates bench and the burghers in Stockholm, 1719–1815.
3. 1943 Stockholm's artisan class, 1720–1772.
4. 1945 Studies dealing with Stockholm's history under Gustav Vasa.
5. 1945 A study of Gustavian architecture and the art of city building.
6. 1946 Studies dealing with Stockholm's police department in the 18th century.
7. 1947 Education and school results of children from various social groups in Stockholm.
8. 1950 Stockholm burghers during the time of the Stures, with special reference to its political situation.
9. 1950 Decorative stonemasons' art in the earlier Vasa style.
10. 1950 The police system in Stockholm, 1776–1850.
11. 1951 Stockholm's diocesan annals from the reformation up to the formation of Stockholm's diocese.
12. 1951 Contentment in the southern suburbs. A social investigation in Hägersten and Hökmosse, 1945–1950.
13. 1953 Population development and urbanisation in Sweden, 1911–1950.
14. 1953 Stockholm's Finance Commission, 1814–1816. The Stock Exchange, bridges and port buildings management committee 1515–1846.
15. 1953 Stockholm's history before Gustav Vasa.
16. 1954 19th century Stockholm's homes. A study of the workers' home planning in rented apartment buildings.
17. 1955 Musical life in Stockholm, 1890–1910.
18. 1976 Stockholm's city walls
19. 1957 Stockholm högskola (University) before 1950.
20. 1957 C.F. Adell, architect.
21. 1958 Self-government and royal power politics within Stockholm city's adminstration, 1668–1697.

22. 1958   Stockholm's development during the last hundred years.
      I   Stockholm's population development after 1850.
   1970 II   Stockholm in the Swedish economy, 1850–1914.
   1980 IV   The changing city. Stockholm's City Council, 1862–1900.
   1967 IV   On the march toward democracy. From a means test to a general franchise, 1900–1920.
   1977 IV   My life in the City Hall. (Part 1. From an oligarchy to a democratic system). (Part 2. In the service of this proud city).
   1970 V   1. The esplanade system and Albert Lindhagen city planning in Stockholm, 1857–1887.
   1977 V   3. Planning for Stockholm, 1923–1958.
23. 1959   The forgotten city. Swedish town planning during the beginning of the 20th century with special emphasis on Stockholm.
24. 1960   The poor in the land. A study of long-term support in Stockholm.
25. 1963   The dreamer from Norrlandsgatan. A study of Henning Berger's life.
26. 1964   222 Stockholm boys. A social psychiatric investigation of school-age boys.
27. 1964   Phonologic studies of quantity in Swedish. Based on material from Stockholm speakers. (In English).
28. 1966   The history of Spånga village.
29. 1967   Village meetings and council administration in Stockholm, up to 1864.
30. 1968   The choice between home and career. A sociological analysis of a choices faced by married nurses.
31. 1970   Emigration from Stockholm to North America.
32. 1971   Cholera epidemic in Stockholm, 1834.
33. 1972   217 Stockholm families. Psycho-dynamic treatment of interview material.
34. 1973   Adopted children and their families.
35. 1975   The Old Town in Stockholm. A cultural, historic description, house-by-house.
36. 1975   Kungsholmen up until the beginning of the 20th century.
37. 1976   Industrialism's big town. Studies concerning Stockholm's social, economic, and demographic structure, 1860–1910.
38. 1976   How are the boys of the 50s getting on in Stockholm?. A follow-up of 222 ordinary schoolboys and 100 boys who attended the special Skå-school, founded by Gustav Jonson.
39. 1978   Stockholm University, 1878–1978.
40. 1979   The unemployed and the 1930 crisis.
41. 1980   Workers on strike. Stockholm, 1850–1909.
42. 1981   Drottningholm Palace Theater in the times of Lovisa Ulrika and Gustav III.
43. 1981   Children of alcoholic fathers.
44. 1981   Journeyman printers and bookbinders in Stockholm, 1850–1914.
45. 1982   Stockholm's 19th century theaters.
46. 1983   Einar Forseth. A book about an artist and his work.
47. 1982   Stockholm *nation* (college) in Uppsala, 1649–1800.

48. 1982   Helgeandsholmen. 1,000 years in Stockholm's *ström* (stream).
49. 1984   J. H. Carlberg, Stockholm's city architect, 1727–1773.
50. 1982–1984   Stockholm's street names, 1982–1984.
51. 1984   *Makalös* (Peerless). General Count Jakob de la Gardie's palace in Stockholm.
52. 1983   Care of homeless alcoholics. An evaluation of care at Skarpnäcksgården.
53. 1983   Stockholm in the Baltic seaway. Stockholm's Baltic trade area during the late Middle Ages and the time of Gustav Vasa.
54. 1987   Visions and reality. A study of Stockholm's 17th century city plan. I and II.
55. 1987   Summer pleasures in the archipelago. Summer buildings in Stockholm's inner area, 1860–1915.
56. 1984   The poor and beggars in Stockholm city and county during the 18th century.
57. 1984   Stockholm's marriages. Building families and chosing partners.
58. 1985   Hjorthagen.
59. 1984   Stockholm harbour, 1909–39. Commerce and politics in co-operation.
60. 1984–1985   Stockholm mirror. A cultural, historic chronicle in sketches and watercolors from a treasure trove of pictures in the hiding places of Stockholm's museums.
61.   A hundred years with the metal-workers' union. Part I 1984, 1881–1928. Part II 1986, 1928–1984.
62.   Stockholm's technical history.
    1986 I   Traffic, bridges, subways, and streets.
    1986 II   Stockholm's parks. Inner city.
    1986 III   Water supplies and drainage.
    1986 IV   Snow clearing, street-cleaning, and recycling.
    1986 V   Light, power, and warmth. Energy supply in Stockholm.
63. 1985   We are the future. Ten young people.
64. 1985   A meat factory with tradition. A description of daily life in Stockholm in the 1950s.
65. 1985   A world underground. Color and pictures in the subway.
66. 1985   Norrmalm renewed, 1951–1981.
67. 1985   From Klara to the City. Stockholm's inner city under change.
68. 1986   Theater eyes. The audience meets the presenters.
69. 1987   The Academy of Fine Arts 250th anniversary.
70. 1986   Stockholm builds. About Stockholm's buildings in the 1980s.
71. 1989   Burghers houses and shacks. Stadsholmen Company's repairs and restorations in Stockholm, 1936–1986.
72. 1988   Mälarhöjden and district.
73. 1986   Drottninghuset. 300 years.
74. 1987   "Deeds of trouble and despair." Unmarried mothers suffering because of pregnancies and childbirth. Stockholm's conditions, 1887–1901.
75. 1986   Stockholm's dawn. A photographic wandering in Karl XV's Stockholm.
76. 1990   Buildings and communities during the Iron Age.
77. 1991   Organ building in Stockholm, from Baroque to Romantic.

78. 1993   Sympathy's secret power. Stockholm's homosexuals, 1860–1960.
79. 1988   Plaster cats and barrel organs. Italians in Stockholm, 1896–1930.
80. 1987   Stockholm's three defenses. From a Viking blockading stronghold to a Middle Ages' castle.
81. 1987   The Middle Stockholm Ages.
82. 1987   Stockholm: A postcard dream. A photographic portrait from the 1930s and 1940s.
83. 1988   Hässelby Palace. From manor house to Nordic cultural center.
84. 1988   Burghers and bureaucrats. The change in the city administration.
85. 1988   Stockholm's dockers before the breakthrough of the trade union movement.
86. 1989   The white town. Hammarhöjden during 50 years.
87. 1989   Sign of the times. The formation of a Stockholm workers' library and the creation of a community, 1892–1927.
88. 1990   The real earthenware stove. Factory-made tiled stoves, 1892–1927.
89. 1990   Selling light and liberty. About the spirit of the time, the workers' movement and the social awareness of ecology in Stockholm, 1938–1969.
90. 1989   Georg A. Nilsson, architect.
91. 1990   Criminals. Prison life on Långholmen, 1850–1918.
92. 1990   Långholmen, the green island.
93. 1998   Ragnar Östberg and Stockholm's City Hall.
94. 1991   Bachelors' hotel. The Söderhem association, private philanthropy and public social care, 1900–1986.
95. 1993   Gröndal and Aspudden. A model community outside the city's hub-bub.
96. 1989   Skerries and fishing shacks. Nature, the countryside and food resources. I 1989. II 1990.
97. 1989   Bonde Palace. A memoriam at the 200th anniversary of the High Court of Justice.
98. 1991   Carl Christoffer Gjörwell, 1766–1837.
99. 1994   Kungsholmen east of Fridhelmsplan.
100. 1990   Research by yourself. A book about archives in Stockholm.
101. 1990   The theater at the center. A book about *Stockholms stadsteater* (Stockholm City Theater).
102. 1990   Between Torneå and Amsterdam. An investigation into Stockholm's role as an intermediary for products in regional and international trade.
103. 1991   Loads and supporting power. Burghers and civil servants in Stockholm, 1644–1672.
104. 1991   From poor housing to dream homes. Stockholm's cooperative housing association, 1916–1991.
105. 1991   In the shadow of the palace. Stockholm and the crown, 1599–1620.
106. 1992   Strolling players' theater in 17th century Stockholm.
107. 1995   Lovisa Bellman née Grönlund. A book about Carl Michael Bellman's wife.

108. 1992 Pioneer years and the pioneer spirit. The experimental school epoch in Stockholm, 1945–1946
109. 1991 Market women. Selling, from baskets and sheds in Stockholm, 1819–1946.
110. 1992 To be a Stockholmer in the 1560s.
111. 1992 Cottage and sacred edifices in the capital. Revivalist building.
112. 1993 Tobacco twisters in Stockholm.
113. The dream of a new heart: the City.
114. 1995 The time of change. About the people's movement in the southern suburbs around the end of the 20th century.
115. Brännkyrka village history.
116. 1993 Årsta. Pictures from a Stockholm suburb.
117. 1994 Pictures of Stockholm.
118. 1994 Human values and power. About the civilizing process in Stockholm, 1600–1850.

About the Author

Dennis E. Gould (B.A., Honours, University College, London) graduated in Scandinavian Languages.

He was born in London, England, in 1926. He trained as a teacher at St. Luke's College, Exeter. He taught in secondary schools and was head of the Mathematics Department at the Sir William Nottidge School, Whitstable, Kent, until 1971.

When visiting Sweden for the second time in 1950, he met his wife-to-be, Inga-Lisa. They were married in Uppsala in 1954. They have a son and three daughters. Two of the daughters live in Sweden. Three of the four grandchildren live in Sweden.

In 1968, he spent a six-month sabbatical in Sweden to study the new comprehensive school system and reported back to the Kent Education Committee. He also taught at Skövde Technical School.

In 1971, the family emigrated to Sweden when he obtained a post at the Anglo-American School in Stockholm, of which he became principal. In 1978, he was awarded the MBE (Member, Order of the British Empire) medal by Queen Elizabeth for services to international education in Stockholm.

In 1978, he took up a post at the Teacher Training College in Francistown, Botswana, in Southern Africa.

He has written several travel books, the first of which was *Let's Visit Sweden.* His most recent book was *The Swedish Way to Tennis Success,* which was co-authored with the British tennis player Mark Cox, who won the Stockholm Open event in 1976.

He visits Sweden two or three times a year, and usually spends summer vacations there.